GLOBAL GENDER CONSTITUTIONALISM AND WOMEN'S CITIZENSHIP

Have constitutions around the world – so far, mostly men's creations – helped women and sexual minorities affirm their equal citizenship status or rather acted as stumbling blocks? By drawing examples of jurisdictions from all continents and engaging with a wide set of themes (including employment and marital status discrimination, abortion and reproductive rights, motherhood rights, political gender quotas, multicultural accommodations, violence against women, same-sex marriage, gender identity, and the distribution of care and domestic work), this book takes us through a journey from the inception of constitutionalism to the present day and from an exclusionary gender constitutionalism (which denied women equal citizenship) to an inclusive gender constitutionalism (which affirmed their equality measured against male standards that privileged the public realm), to a more recent, and still tentative, form of transformative gender constitutionalism that asserts the political relevance of the private domain and foregrounds the need to disestablish gender roles within it, and which has been facilitated by a participatory turn demanding that women join in constitution-making and that constitutionalism facilitates women's access to decision-making.

RUTH RUBIO-MARÍN is Professor of Constitutional Law at the University of Sevilla, a part-time professor at the School of Transnational Governance of the European University Institute, Florence, and Director of the UNIA UNESCO Chair in Human Rights and Interculturalism. She has taught in many other prestigious academic institutions including New York University, Columbia Law School, and Princeton University. Her research, focused on comparative constitutionalism, law and gender, immigration and citizenship, as well as transitional justice, represents an attempt to understand how public law creates categories of inclusion and exclusion around different axes including gender, citizenship, nationality, and ethnicity.

CAMBRIDGE STUDIES IN CONSTITUTIONAL LAW

The aim of this series is to produce leading monographs in constitutional law. All areas of constitutional law and public law fall within the ambit of the series, including human rights and civil liberties law, administrative law, as well as constitutional theory and the history of constitutional law. A wide variety of scholarly approaches is encouraged, with the governing criterion being simply that the work is of interest to an international audience. Thus, works concerned with only one jurisdiction will be included in the series as appropriate, while, at the same time, the series will include works which are explicitly comparative or theoretical – or both. The series editors likewise welcome proposals that work at the intersection of constitutional and international law, or that seek to bridge the gaps between civil law systems, the US, and the common law jurisdictions of the Commonwealth.

Books in the series

Non-Statutory Executive Powers and Judicial Review Jason Grant Allen

The Law as a Conversation among Equals Roberto Gargarella

Micronations and the Search for Sovereignty Harry Hobbs and George Williams

Fundamental Rights and the Legal Obligations of Business David Bilchitz

Courting Constitutionalism: The Politics of Public Law and Judicial Review in Pakistan Moeen Cheema

Ruling by Cheating: Governance in Illiberal Democracy András Sajó

Local Meanings of Proportionality Afroditi Marketou

Property Rights and Social Justice: Progressive Property in Action Rachael Walsh

Carl Schmitt's Early Legal-Theoretical Writings: Statute and Judgment and the Value of the State and the Significance of the Individual Lars Vinx and Samuel Garrett Zeitlin

Remedies for Human Rights Violations: A Two-Track Approach to Supranational and National Law Kent Roach

Europe's Second Constitution: Crisis, Courts and Community Markus W. Gehring

A.V. Dicey and the Common Law Constitutional Tradition: A Legal Turn of Mind Mark D. Walters

Administrative Competence: Reimagining Administrative Law Elizabeth Fisher and Sidney A. Shapiro

Legal Sabotage: Ernst Fraenkel in Hitler's Germany Douglas Morris

Proportionality in Action: Comparative and Empirical Perspectives on the Judicial Practice Edited by Mordechai Kremnitzer, Tayla Steiner and Andrej Lang

Constitutional Dialogue: Democracy, Rights, Institutions Edited by Geoffrey Sigalet, Grégoire Webber and Rosalind Dixon

The Veiled Sceptre: Reserve Powers of Heads of State in Westminster Systems Anne Twomey

Vigilance and Restraint in the Common Law of Judicial Review Dean Knight

The Alchemists: Questioning Our Faith in Courts as Democracy-Builders Tom Gerald Daly

Australia's Constitution after Whitlam Brendan Lim

Building the Constitution: The Practice of Constitutional Interpretation in Post-Apartheid South Africa James Fowkes

Dimensions of Dignity: The Theory and Practice of Modern Constitutional Law Jacob Weinrib

Reason of State: Law, Prerogative, Empire Thomas Poole

Bills of Rights in the Common Law Robert Leckey

The Guardian of the Constitution: Hans Kelsen and Carl Schmitt on the Limits of Constitutional Law Translated by Lars Vinx, with an introduction and notes by Lars Vinx

Parliamentary Bills of Rights: The Experiences of New Zealand and the United Kingdom Janet L. Hiebert and James B. Kelly

Lawyering for the Rule of Law: Government Lawyers and the Rise of Judicial Power in Israel Yoav Dotan

Balancing Constitutional Rights: The Origins and Meanings of Postwar Legal Discourse Jacco Bomhoff

Judges on Trial: The Independence and Accountability of the English Judiciary Shimon Shetreet and Sophie Turenne

Proportionality and Constitutional Culture Moshe Cohen-Eliya and Iddo Porat

The Politics of Principle: The First South African Constitutional Court, 1995–2005 Theunis Roux

The New Commonwealth Model of Constitutionalism: Theory and Practice Stephen Gardbaum

Searching for the State in British Legal Thought: Competing Conceptions of the Public Sphere Janet McLean

Judging Social Rights Jeff King

Proportionality: Constitutional Rights and their Limitations Aharon Barak

Parliamentary Sovereignty: Contemporary Debates Jeffrey Goldsworthy

GLOBAL GENDER CONSTITUTIONALISM AND WOMEN'S CITIZENSHIP

A Struggle for Transformative Inclusion

RUTH RUBIO-MARIN
Universidad de Sevilla

CAMBRIDGE
UNIVERSITY PRESS

CAMBRIDGE
UNIVERSITY PRESS

University Printing House, Cambridge CB2 8BS, United Kingdom

One Liberty Plaza, 20th Floor, New York, NY 10006, USA

477 Williamstown Road, Port Melbourne, VIC 3207, Australia

314–321, 3rd Floor, Plot 3, Splendor Forum, Jasola District Centre, New Delhi – 110025, India

103 Penang Road, #05–06/07, Visioncrest Commercial, Singapore 238467

Cambridge University Press is part of the University of Cambridge.

It furthers the University's mission by disseminating knowledge in the pursuit of education, learning, and research at the highest international levels of excellence.

www.cambridge.org
Information on this title: www.cambridge.org/9781107177024
DOI: 10.1017/9781316819241

First published 2022

A catalogue record for this publication is available from the British Library.

Library of Congress Cataloging-in-Publication Data
Names: Rubio-Marín, Ruth, author.
Title: Global gender constitutionalism and women's citizenship: a struggle for transformative inclusion / Ruth Rubio-Marin, Universidad de Sevilla.
Description: Cambridge, United Kingdom; New York, NY: Cambridge University Press, 2022. | Series: Cambridge studies in constitutional law | Includes bibliographical references and index.
Identifiers: LCCN 2022010618 (print) | LCCN 2022010619 (ebook) | ISBN 9781107177024 (hardback) | ISBN 9781316630303 (paperback) | ISBN 9781316819241 (epub)
Subjects: LCSH: Women's rights. | Constitutional law–Social aspects. | Law and globalization.
Classification: LCC K3243 .R83 2022 (print) | LCC K3243 (ebook) |
DDC 342.08/78–dc23/eng/20220430
LC record available at https://lccn.loc.gov/2022010618
LC ebook record available at https://lccn.loc.gov/2022010619

ISBN 978-1-107-17702-4 Hardback

I dedicate this book to Javier Pérez Royo and Reva Siegel for their lifelong teachings, inspiration, and support; to the many women constitution-makers around the world, silenced for centuries in official accounts of the history of constitutionalism; and to the younger generations of scholars, who should not feel that their passion for feminist engagements with constitutional law is marginal to the discipline.

CONTENTS

FOREWORD

The scholarly chasm between feminism and constitutionalism confronts constitutionalists who are also feminists. Ruth and I met over articulations of this chasm. On sharing, our relief was palpable. Given our own distinctive backgrounds (Spain and Canada), we set out to expand existing scholarship about gender analysis of constitutional law by remediating its virtual absence in comparative constitutionalism. Our strategy included an international conference in 2000 that led to the publication of a coedited book in 2005. The contributors to the book relied on our feminist constitutional agenda for their country-specific gender analyses of constitutional jurisprudence. Our theme of gender analysis of comparative constitutionalism reappeared with the publication in 2012 of *Feminist Constitutionalism*, a book that I coedited and to which Ruth contributed a chapter.

The widespread uptake of these works by feminist constitutionalists amazed me, but their comparative constitutional counterparts did not follow suit. Three Canadian colleagues provided a domestic exception in 2019. They invited Ruth and me to theorize feminist constitutionalism for a handbook on the Canadian constitution. We did not limit our theory to Canadian constitutionalism. Instead, we conceptualized constitutional legitimacy writ large, framing it as dependent on taking women (in their multiple identities including indigenous, immigrant, refugee, and trans women) seriously. Normatively, we argued, taking women seriously means advancing women's equality rights. Assuming a sizable readership of domestic and other constitutionalists for this fifty-chapter handbook, did the inclusion of our chapter theorizing feminist constitutionalism have the potential to challenge them?

I'd like to think it did. But I have doubts. Feminists have advocated women's equality as a constitutional right domestically and internationally for decades, if not centuries. Repetitive advocacy, while admirable, suggests the objective is, if not ephemeral or imaginary, unmet. For their part, what do constitutionalists say? Jumping the chasm, they report that women have equality; women do not need equality; women are the second (or subordinate) sex; or women are the dominant sex. Or, returning to their own side of the chasm, they either excuse equality's ineffectiveness because it is the most difficult right, the most elusive right, and the least precisely defined right; or, if equality rights are violated, they recite the refrain that no rights are absolute to justify the violation. Therefore, while Ruth and I framed feminist constitutionalism in a normative theory that is true to feminists, it may not resonate with or even reach constitutionalists.

In this new sole-authored book, Ruth has redefined the chasm challenge by moving away from the prevailing reactive narratives to a creative, globally detailed counternarrative. The book develops a creation story, a her-story of comparative constitutionalism that begins with the insight that constitutionalism everywhere was gendered from its inception. It may partially or even fully remain as such. Her objective is to advance possibilities for women's betterment. Ruth draws on her phenomenal knowledge of many jurisdictions globally to illustrate specific possibilities for changes that are responsive to women's needs, interests, issues, and rights. She also identifies changes (or failures to change) that hinder women's lives and adeptly deploys comparison to point out the direction that their remediation might take.

Ruth's original and distinctive theory advances feminist constitutionalism's agenda and women's equality rights by developing two new concepts: gender constitutionalism and periodization. Gender constitutionalism deposes constitutionalism's most sacred artifact – the distinction between what falls under constitutionalism's mandate and what does not, which is to say, the domain of constitutional law. Constitutionalists revere this distinction as the gender-neutral public/private divide; feminists critique it as gendered separate spheres. Ruth bridges it by rendering visible its gender performativity. More specifically, she genders the public/private divide by upending constitutionalism's pretension of recognizing only the public side of the public/private divide. Inviting constitutionalists to explain what features constitutions (the public) use and how they use them to shape – facilitate and hinder – women's marital and family lives (the private) frames the relations between constitutions and women as gender relations. The public sphere no longer consists of constitutions unmodified. In sum, constitutions are gender constitutions that rely on the public/private divide to entrench a foundational gender order that contemporary constitutionalism seeks to disestablish.

In other words, gender constitutionalism need not be static; it can be performative, an attribute Ruth sculpts as periodization. Performative periodization realizes the capacity of gender constitutions to change. However, their changes are based not on the temporal stages through which constitutionalism might pass but rather on the forms it might take. Ruth conceptualizes four forms that give shape to periodization, starting with exclusionary gender constitutionalism, that manifested from the birth of written constitutionalism until post–World War II. Based on the role that constitutional law played or plays in women's citizenship claims, the others are inclusive gender constitutionalism, participatory gender constitutionalism, and transformative gender constitutionalism. Each merits its own chapter rich with details that apply its features to multiple gender constitutions around the world over extended time periods. Reading these chapters is to be treasured for their insights into the myriad ways gender constitutions facilitate or hinder women's equal citizenship claims.

I highlight some of the valuable insights I found in these chapters. First, its optimism: even before the chapters begin, the table of contents signals the potential for optimism through its conceptual overview of the evocative concepts of exclusionary, inclusive, participatory, and transformative periodization. Second, its realism: the themes of motherhood and abortion, caring, and violence are threaded throughout (Ruth prefers "woven" as a tapestry). Third, its relevance: the very apposite analysis of substantive equality that should prevail. Fourth, its diversity plus: the recognition of identities – multicultural, trans, etc. – pivotal to understanding and essaying resolutions of contemporary controversies. Fifth, its breadth: how generously, comprehensively, and knowledgeably Ruth shared her phenomenal understanding of the ways in which a very broad range of countries address, or not, key constitutional concerns that women contest. Sixth and never least, its goal: proffering resolutions where none seem available to advance women's plights.

Ruth's thesis is that gender transformative constitutionalism offers a new emancipatory vision, the disestablishment of patriarchal constitutionalism's foundational gender order. This vision offers a counternarrative to all forms of human exploitation; it is radical and normatively compelling for feminists and constitutionalists alike. Both would make changes to achieve it, including reevaluating how they frame gender and the private sphere, respectively. If realized, however, they might bring some closure to the immeasurable space, the chasm, that separates them. Ruth has argued brilliantly and compellingly about the importance of trying.

Bev Baines
August 15, 2021

ACKNOWLEDGMENTS

Inevitably, a work that has taken years to produce can only be the result of a collective effort. My family has provided the emotional support system that has always kept me going. Throughout the years, the research assistance of Elena Brodeala, Stefano Osella, Lucrecia Rubio-Grundell, Alba Ruibal, Maria José Schmidt Kessen, and Fulvia Staiano has been of essence. Generous readers of the manuscript have provided precious feedback and reassured me in my interpretation of the various legal orders I address. They include Cristóbal Alvear, Beverley Baines, Stéphanie Hennette-Vauchez, Rory O'Connell, Cara Röhner, and Elettra Stradella. Luigi Celentano has been nothing less than an angel fallen from the sky, assisting me with language edition and the checking of sources. At Cambridge University Press, Finola O'Sullivan, executive publisher in law, deserves a big thank you for not losing trust in this project despite its many delays, as does Marianne Nield, who has supported it upon Finola's retirement. To all of you, my most sincere gratitude.

TABLE OF CASES

A.

Argentina

National Supreme Court of Justice

Australia

High Court

Austria

Constitutional Court

B.

Belgium

Constitutional Court

Bolivia

Plurinational Constitutional Court

Botswana

Supreme Court

Brazil

Federal Supreme Court

C.

Canada

Supreme Court

Ontario

Superior Court of Justice

Chile

Constitutional Court

Colombia

Constitutional Court

Costa Rica

Constitutional Chamber of the Supreme Court

Supreme Electoral Tribunal

Croatia

Constitutional Court

E.

El Salvador

Constitutional Court

European Union

European Court of Justice

European Court of Human Rights

F.

France

Constitutional Court

Cour de cassation (Cassation Court)

Civil Chamber

Council of State

G.

Germany

Federal Constitutional Court

Constitutional Court of Thuringia

Brandenburg Constitutional Court

H.

Hungary

Constitutional Court

I.

India

Supreme Court

Delhi

High Court

Bombay

High Court

Punjab-Haryana

High Court

Indonesia

Constitutional Court

Inter-American Court of Human Rights

Ireland

Supreme Court

Israel

Supreme Court/High Court of Justice

Jerusalem District Court

Italy

Supreme Court

Constitutional Court

J.

Japan

Supreme Court

M.

Malaysia

Constitutional Court

Mexico

National Supreme Court of Justice

Electoral Court of the Judiciary of the Federation

N.

Nepal

Supreme Court

Netherlands

Central Council of Appeal

P.

Pakistan

Supreme Court

Lahore

High Court

Peru

Constitutional Court

Philippines

Supreme Court

Poland

Constitutional Tribunal

Portugal

Constitutional Court

S.

Slovakia

Constitutional Court

Slovenia

Constitutional Court

South Africa

Constitutional Court

Johannesburg

Equality Court

South Korea

Constitutional Court

Spain

Constitutional Court

Switzerland

Federal Supreme Court

T.

Taiwan

Constitutional Court

Turkey

Constitutional Court

U.

United Nations

Human Rights Committee

United Kingdom of Great Britain and Northern Ireland

Employment Tribunal

House of Lords

Supreme Court

High Court of Justice, Queen's Bench Division (Northern Ireland)

United States

Supreme Court

California

Supreme Court

Connecticut

Supreme Court

Hawaii

Supreme Court

Iowa

Supreme Court

Massachusetts

Supreme Judicial Court

Minnesota

Supreme Court

Introduction

The When, Why, What, and How of the Book and How the Personal Becomes Political

I.1 The When and Why of This Book

To some extent, this book owes its existence to the COVID-19 pandemic. It had been a few years since the contract to write it had been signed, and every year, with truly commendable patience, the publisher asked me the much-dreaded question: is it almost ready? The truth was that, as much as I wanted to, it had been extremely difficult for me to write a book, instead of articles or other pieces in shorter or collaborative formats. Writing a book requires constant dedication, committed and uninterrupted working time slots, and a degree of isolation that I have simply found difficult to combine with the rest of my academic obligations (classes, exam grading, thesis supervision, mentoring, conferences, preparation, direction, or coordination of research projects, reviews, travels abroad, etc.) and with the obligations of my role as first, a de facto, and then, a de jure single mother of two (food provision, calendar organization, homework, playdates, sports, doctors, housekeeping, holidays, etc.), despite the fact that I have always enjoyed a set of privileges (middle class, fairly white skin, and Spanish-European origin). Put together, this set of traits have no doubt allowed me to delegate part of that care work on other women who were economically more vulnerable – often, though not always, of immigrant origin. Without their assistance, not just this book but combining motherhood and an academic career would have simply been impossible. Add to this the more or less common, yet often painful, vicissitudes of life (moving between countries several times, sentimental turmoil, periods of illnesses, or loss of loved ones), and the bare truth is that, for a long time, I came to think that the time would never come for this book to see the light of day.

For this reason, when the COVID-19 pandemic broke into our lives and I saw how, suddenly, conferences, trips, and commitments of various kinds fell off the agenda and socialization routines were necessarily reduced, I glimpsed a unique occasion to, once again, pick up the book project from where I had left it off the last time I had managed to put aside sustained time to work on it (my university cannot really afford paid sabbaticals). This time I faced the endeavor with the renewed hope to see it through. And I have. As I write these words, I am fully aware that, for many of my colleagues – and not only for those whose health has been seriously compromised – the pandemic has not represented a window of opportunity in any sense of the word. I am thinking of colleagues with dependent children, whose schools were unable to continue teaching online, who have had to cope without the respite that school hours entail, and who, far from enjoying a context of peace and tranquility, have been confined to more or less narrow spaces (my house in Seville is large, bright, and has a lovely terrace). Moreover, to their roles as academics and caregivers, they have had to add that of schoolteachers while also losing any possibility of outsourcing some of the care work to the paid employment sector. Certainly, they too are still privileged compared to women who, without the possibility of teleworking or the relative economic security of academic work, have had to expose their lives daily, assisting in essential tasks of care and provision of basic goods – tasks that are often little recognized and poorly paid; those who have completely lost their sources of employment or income – precarious jobs, work in the informal economy or in the care sector, in homes and countries that became impenetrable overnight; not to mention those who have not had a place to confine themselves and their families, or those who have lived confinement not as a forceful retreat but as a source of permanent anguish by sharing an intimate space with violent family members or loved ones whose most basic needs they could simply not provide for.[1]

If I look back today, I realize that, throughout this time, several things helped me keep afloat the hope that this book would come to fruition, despite it living for the longest time only in my mind. First, the conviction that the book was needed and that the time was ripe for it. When

[1] For an overview of the impact of COVID-19 on women, see UN Women, *From Insight to Action: Gender Equality in the Wake of Covid-19* (United States: United Nations, 2020), https://www.unwomen.org/-/media/headquarters/attachments/sections/library/publications/2020/gender-equality-in-the-wake-of-covid-19-en.pdf?la=en&vs=5142.

nearly two decades ago, Bev Baines and I organized in Seville what must have been the first international workshop on gender and comparative constitutionalism ever – a workshop from which our edited volume, *The Gender of Constitutional Jurisprudence*, emerged in 2005,[2] we were not fully aware of the extent to which we were opening what has since become a vibrant research agenda. Of course, we were not starting from scratch, not even then. As Helen Irving recalls, "The modern understanding that constitutions are not neutral with respect to sex or gender" took root in the last decades of the twentieth century, but "it was poorly recognized," and, with some few exceptions, "the history was little known outside feminist historians' circles, and the insights it generated were neglected in the broader literature on constitution-making" and constitutionalism.[3] Also, a burgeoning literature appeared, which began to apply a gender lens to a range of constitutions or at least attempted to describe the more or less limited role of women in their crafting. This practice has only grown ever since.[4] Yet our interest was sparked by the intersection between comparative constitutional law and feminist legal theory, and we felt the need to call on the academic community to

[2] Beverley Baines and Ruth Rubio-Marín, *The Gender of Constitutional Jurisprudence* (Cambridge: Cambridge University Press, 2005). This was, I believe, the first book-length treatment of gender issues in comparative constitutional law. In its introduction, we set out a synoptic vision of the agenda to reflect on the interaction between constitutionalism and gender equality.

[3] Helen Irving, ed., introduction to *Constitutions and Gender* (Cheltenham, UK: Edward Edgar, 2017), 2. She rightly cites Akhil Reed Amar, "Women and the Constitution," *Harvard Journal of Law and Public Policy* 18, no. 2 (1995): 465–74 as one relevant exception.

[4] See, for some examples, Lynn Smith and Eleanor Wachtel, *A Feminist Guide to the Canadian Constitution* (Ottawa, ON: Canadian Advisory Council on the Status of Women, 1992); Sandra Liebenberg, ed., *The Constitution of South Africa from a Gender Perspective* (Cape Town: Community Law Centre, University of the Western Cape, 1995); Helen Irving, ed., *A Woman's Constitution?: Gender and History in the Australian Commonwealth* (Sydney: Hale & Iremonger, 1996); Asunción Ventura Franch, *Las mujeres y la Constitución Española de 1978* (Madrid: Instituto de la Mujer, 1999); Helen Irving, *To Constitute a Nation: A Cultural History of Australia's Constitution* (Cambridge: Cambridge University Press, 1999); Alexandra Dobrowolsky, *The Politics of Pragmatism: Women, Representation, and Constitutionalism in Canada* (Don Mills, ON: Oxford University Press, 2000); Miria Matembe, *Gender, Politics and Constitution Making in Uganda* (Kampala: Fountain Publishers, 2002); Sibyl A. Schwarzenbach and Patricia Smith, eds., *Women and the United States Constitution: History, Interpretation, and Practice* (New York: Columbia University Press, 2003); Blanca Rodríguez Ruiz, *Género y constitución: mujeres y varones en el orden constitucional español* (Lisbon: Juruá Editora, 2017); Marilisa D'Amico, *Una parità ambigua: costituzione e diritti delle donne* (Milan: Raffaello Cortina Editore, 2020).

critically engage in the analysis of central concepts of the discipline and some of the assumptions underlying mainstream constitutional theories; to identify emerging trends, but also remaining textual and doctrinal differences; to analyze opportunity structures; and, ultimately, to craft academic alliances and repositories of inspiration to advance in our shared endeavor: an analysis of how constitutional law could be turned into a tool of transformation in the struggle for women's justice. If the transnational women's movement, articulated around groundbreaking international conferences had – starting in the 1970s but especially since the mid-1990s – been able organize itself to set feminist agendas in the field of human rights, offering a horizon of possibilities of a shared struggle for gender justice beyond national borders, wasn't it also reasonable to delve into how constitutions – those norms that sit in the apex of national legal orders but also in that space of confluence and exchange between national, regional, and international normative standards – were shaping the contours of emancipatory possibilities? Why not look abroad and not just above to gain a better grasp of the strengths and shortcomings of existing design and doctrinal alternatives, and their evolutions in time, drawing from the rich source of different national constitutional cultures? After all, didn't constitutionalism offer that meeting point between the vocationally universal and the contingent, historic, and culturally specific that would allow us to better understand the true dimensions of the challenge of building political communities able to overcome patriarchy-infused foundational gender legal orders?

Since then, it has been a true joy to watch this subfield of comparative constitutional law grow over the last two decades, going well beyond the focus on rights jurisprudence. Even if we limit ourselves to the literature published in English, this significant body of work began to foreground questions of constitutional design – see, for instance, Helen Irving's *Gender and the Constitution: Equity and Agency in Comparative Constitutional Design*[5] – and also to expand, through collaborative

[5] Helen Irving, *Gender and the Constitution: Equity and Agency in Comparative Constitutional Design* (Cambridge: Cambridge University Press, 2008). In her book, Irving adopts a three-dimensional approach: a textual, structural, and applied perspective, looking at what the words of the constitution say and mean, how the sections of the constitution are structured, and how the constitution's provisions work in practice, analyzing the relationship between gender equity and agency and constitutional opportunities structures. Other important work had preceded her in exploring key questions of institutional and procedural design in gender-responsive ways. See, for all, Kathleen Sullivan, "Constitutionalizing Women's Equality," *California Law Review* 90 (2002): 735;

efforts, the range of constitutional themes and constitutional country experiences beyond those that had so far dominated the agenda (often countries in the Global North as well as English-speaking jurisdictions). Among these contributions, we could mention Susan Williams's edited collection *Constituting Equality: Gender Equality and Comparative Constitutional Law*;[6] Beverley Baines, Daphne Barak-Erez, and Tsvi Kahana's *Feminist Constitutionalism: Global Perspectives*;[7] Kim Rubenstein and Katharine G. Young's *The Public Law of Gender: From the Local to the Global*;[8] and Helen Irving's *Constitutions and Gender*, the first handbook specifically devoted to the subject.[9] At the same time, we have also seen the proliferation of books comparatively analyzing the experiences of women in constitution-making – for instance, the pioneer *Women Making Constitutions: New Politics and Comparative Perspectives*, edited by Alexandra Dobrowolsky and Vivien Hart[10] – and a research agenda that has continued to expand with – I sincerely hope – our recent *Women as Constitution-Makers: Case Studies From the New Democratic Era*,[11] where Helen Irving and I made the purposeful attempt to capture recent efforts by women to influence the constitutions in their countries, with a particular emphasis on relatively underexplored experiences from Muslim countries. Interestingly, the flourishing of this academic literature – which must, of course, be enriched by the vast academic literature in languages other than English – has been accompanied by the growth of a set of feminist guides and toolkits that, nourished by academic findings, have increasingly been applied across

Paula Monopoli, "Gender and Constitutional Design," *Yale Law Journal* 115 (2006): 2643; Judith Resnik, "Categorical Federalism: Jurisdiction, Gender and the Globe," *Yale Law Journal* 11 (2002): 619.

6 Susan Williams, *Constituting Equality: Gender Equality and Comparative Constitutional Law* (Cambridge: Cambridge University Press, 2009). The volume represents a comparative, design-oriented approach to gender equality in constitutional law with a global and interdisciplinary perspective that considers culture, politics, and theory along with law.

7 Beverley Baines, Daphne Barak-Erez, and Tsvi Kahana, eds., *Feminist Constitutionalism: Global Perspectives* (Cambridge: Cambridge University Press, 2012).

8 Kim Rubenstein and Katharine G. Young, eds., *The Public Law of Gender: From the Local to the Global* (Cambridge: Cambridge University Press, 2016). This book draws meaningful connections between administrative, constitutional, and international public law in trying to account for a more wholesome description of the gender bias in public law.

9 Helen Irving, ed., *Constitutions and Gender* (Cheltenham, UK: Edward Elgar, 2017).

10 Alexandra Dobrowolsky and Vivien Hart, eds., *Women Making Constitutions: New Politics and Comparative Perspectives* (Basingstoke: Palgrave Macmillan, 2004).

11 Ruth Rubio-Marín and Helen Irving, eds., *Women as Constitution-Makers: Case Studies from the New Democratic Era* (Cambridge: Cambridge University Press, 2019).

the world by both national and international actors, who have joined in the task of "engendering" constitution-making processes and constitutional texts as a crucial element in the strengthening of the legitimacy of contemporary constitutional systems.[12] It is also worth mentioning the surveys, engines, online forums, and databases that have also appeared and now facilitate research and new quantitative approaches.[13]

With all this groundwork, I felt that the time was ripe to attempt a global analysis of constitutionalism through a gendered lens in the hope that it might provide a feminist perspective of constitutionalism both as a discipline and as it has evolved over time – a (her)story that, despite women's different positionalities (albeit duly recognizing them), "we" could collectively own; a story that could bring to the surface recurrent tensions and dilemmas but also recover agendas and forms of contribution thus far neglected, challenging dominant conceptions in the field and allowing us to identify, whether in textual expressions or doctrinal constructions, key milestones and landmarks. I was also hoping that

[12] As Irving remarks (*Constitutions and Gender*, 4), these feminist guidelines for constitution-making and for "incorporating gender equality in constitutions under construction and for 'assessing' its recognition in existing constitutions" began to appear in the context of women's increased role in new constitution-making in the 1980s and 1990s. See, for instance, Gwen Brodsky and Shelagh Day, *Canadian Charter Equality Rights for Women: One Step Forward or Two Steps Back?* (Ottawa, ON: Canadian Advisory Council on the Status of Women, 1989); Lynne Smith and Eleanor Wachtel, *A Feminist Guide to the Canadian Constitution* (Ottawa, ON: Canadian Advisory Council on the Status of Women, 1992). These guidelines have multiplied since the United Nations and the United Nations Development Program have embraced gender equality principles in their "Guidance Notes" on constitution-making. See Christina Murray and Cindy Wittke, "International institutions, constitution-making and gender," in Irving, *Constitutions and Gender*, 107–32. On the creation of a "Constitution Assessment for Women's Equality" toolkit by International IDEA and its Constitution-Building Program, see Melanie Allen, "A Practitioner's Account: The Constitution Assessment for Women's Equality," in Irving, *Constitutions and Gender*, 195–220. In 2016, an "ABC for a Gender Sensitive Constitution" was drafted under the auspices of Euromed Feminist Initiative IFE–EFI, cofounded by the Swedish Government and the European Union.

[13] For a comparative survey of constitutional gender equality rights and provisions that recognize women, see Kristin Van der Leest et al., "Engendering Constitutions: Gender Equality Provisions in Selected Constitutions – A Comparative Study Accompanied with Case Studies in Bosnia and Herzegovina, Kosovo, Montenegro and Serbia" (United Nations Development Fund for Women, 2007). UN Women has created a "Global Gender Equality Constitutional Database" with a repository of gender equality-related provisions in 195 constitutions from around the world (https://constitutions.unwomen.org/en), and *Constitute* (https://www.constituteproject.org/?lang=en) is a comparative database of the world's constitutions, allowing to systematically compare constitutions across a broad set of topics, including "gender" and "women."

these very milestones and landmarks would help expand the scope of what is considered canonical in the discipline while challenging some of the disciplinary and jurisdictional hegemonies that have, until now, characterized both constitutional and comparative constitutional law. Perhaps, as a result, I could try to periodize and typify the forms and stages of constitutionalism in ways that would relate to the central question of how effectively constitutional law has responded to women's evolving and diverse citizenship claims and gendered citizenship understandings, giving women's agencies and voices a predominant role throughout the process. Doing so, I thought, required connecting the study of the configuration of gender in constitutional law with the exclusion of women from the very origins of the state construct, as other authors, like Catharine MacKinnon and Carole Pateman, had already done.[14] This would allow me to reclaim the intrinsic and systemic dimension of women's distinct and subordinate constitutional membership status as a starting point (the established gender order) from which to then address the ways in which the tools of constitutional law have acted both as mechanisms of resistance (especially in old constitutionalism) and subversion (especially in new constitutionalism) of the original gender order in a progressive, though by no means linear, fully shared, and contradiction-free process of "gender-order disestablishment."

This book is the outcome of this endeavor. Building on the proliferation of "micro" qualitative studies (focused on single national jurisdictions and duly allowing us to appreciate nuances, contexts, and cultural traits) and, more recently, quantitative studies (which, for the first time, offer us the possibility to observe wider and textual patterns – even though they are, nonetheless, sometimes lacking in context and hence difficult to interpret), my aim is to offer a diachronic "meso" level of analysis that would allow us to transcend the particular and to think through more regionally, but also more systemically, the concept of a "gender order," as opposed to separate but narrow themes, or, at least, allow us to connect the various particulars as pieces of a puzzle that, when put together, would provide a more general account. In this sense, this book aspires to be read and interpreted as a collective endeavor, even though, as it could not be otherwise, I take individual responsibility for the mistakes it may contain, or worse, for wrongs it may do.

[14] See Catharine A. MacKinnon, *Toward a Feminist Theory of the State* (Cambridge, MA: Harvard University Press, 1989); Carole Pateman, *The Sexual Contract* (Stanford: Stanford University Press, 1989).

Another of the driving forces behind this book's felt need is my commitment to a new generation of academics and the lingering traces of my intimate collection of small "academic traumas." To this day, I still vividly remember the reaction of one of the great professors and academic authorities in the first department that hired me, just after finishing my doctoral thesis in 1997 (a thesis that had focused on the constitutional status of migrants in various jurisdictions), when I informed him that my new research agenda would turn to gender and constitutional law. A liberal man at heart, "Of course, why not?" was his reaction, but only, if he could kindly suggest, as long as I did this "on the side," which is to say, as long as I did not make it the central object of my intellectual inquiry – or, in other words, as long as I was able to prove my credentials as a "true constitutional scholar" by sufficiently writing about the important constitutional matters (perhaps the principle of proportionality?). And, although I have indeed written about issues other than gender and constitutional law (while never really abandoning the underlying passion of uncovering the possibilities and limits of public law to subvert group domination), I must have failed to sufficiently prove my "mainstream constitutional scholar credentials." Otherwise, how could anyone explain this more recent experience? In this case, the remarks came from another well-established professor, chosen to preside the exam board for the open competition that the Spanish academic system foresees as the only method through which to consolidate the status of full professor. Commenting on my scientific work, an equally liberal and decent man (and just like the former, white, hetero, cis, and abled), this professor acknowledged that my work was no doubt of high quality and its international scope truly impressive but, drawing an analogy to the Argentine soccer player Leo Messi, whom he literally considered "the total soccer player" (in the sense, as he explained, that Messi handled *all* and not just *some* of the skills of soccer like no other), did I not feel the need to become more of a "total constitutionalist"? A remark, in short, that only makes sense if one interprets that the gender-focused, or more broadly speaking, the gender critical theoretical analysis of constitutional law does not require a "total" or at least comprehensive and sophisticated mastery of the history, key concepts, and central scholarly debates in constitutional law because it is something sectorial, confined, and, surely, of a minor order.

I'm aware that I'm not alone. In her foreword to *Feminist Constitutionalism*, Catharine MacKinnon accurately writes that "in the legal academy, feminist analysis is not yet considered an expertise; it remains regarded as autobiographical and ideological: that stuff about women, the statement about the speaker rather than the spoken-about, a narrow solipsistic fixation rather than an approach to comprehending reality that increases accuracy by identifying a bias in prior approaches that makes them incapable of meeting even their own standards. Instead, it has become at best an academic niche to be occupied, if minimally; a little square of turf to be tilled by perhaps one person per faculty, likely a visitor; an eddy at the edge of the mainstream; a brand to be cultivated and competed over; a private faith like a religion, internally sustaining but unbecoming and unscholarly and stigmatic to expose or acknowledge, far less explicitly to pursue as the backbone or compass of an intellectual agenda."[15] She wrote this statement only ten years ago, and I am acutely aware that this type of pressure has not disappeared. In fact, I often encounter scholars in the beginning of their academic careers who confess to me that they are confronted with the dilemma of "passion versus career": dedicating themselves to what they are really passionate about (such as, for instance, the study of critical race, gender, and queer theory) compared to what is required of them to demonstrate their credentials of competence if they want to obtain a position and advance within this discipline that, like all disciplines, bears the traces of the historically privileged, who have so far defined its confines, central concepts, and priorities, undoubtedly in an exercise of epistemic supremacy.

In this context, this book, I hope, can be a modest contribution to the evidence of resilience and joins the existing scholarly work written in gender and comparative constitutional law with the intention of offering counternarratives. It celebrates the existence of this body of work from which I have learned immensely, as well as some other (still modest) signs of hope, including the fact that a serious publisher, like Cambridge University Press, has, in the English-speaking world, become a de facto "hub" of much (though certainly not all) of the significant work on feminist constitutionalism over the years. It also celebrates the fact that an international society of public law of recent creation and as vibrant as ICON·S has embraced the rule of parity in all its governance structure and makes a conscious effort to take into account various axes of diversity and existing patterns of discrimination when defining the contents

[15] Catharine A. MacKinnon, foreword to *Feminist Constitutionalism: Global Perspectives*, eds. Beverley Baines, Daphne Barak-Erez, and Tsvi Kahana (Cambridge: Cambridge University Press, 2012), xii.

and modus operandi of its increasingly successful yearly conferences; and the fact that more and more articles on gender and other critical approaches to public law have appeared in recent years in several international journals on constitutional law and constitutionalism – of which the *International Journal of Constitutional Law* deserves a special mention, since its editorial team recently took the bold step of explicitly inviting submissions by women and minorities.[16] More importantly, this book tries to convey the message to a new generation of young and passionate scholars that they are not alone and that, to the extent we can (we must all pay our bills and it is easy to preach from the comfortable position of a tenured professor, which, however, I was not at the time I decided NOT to follow the advice I was given), we should all follow our passions (why choose to be an academic otherwise?) and reject the trap that passion-driven research cannot be analytically sophisticated or lead to serious scholarship. The possibility of a counternarrative is real, however imperfectly I might have achieved it here, and I hope it may invite the further proliferation of agendas and additional counterhistories, which, by focusing the gaze on other axes of exclusion that have marked the way in which constitutionalism has evolved and been narrated as a discipline, may help us to jointly build an account of the discipline that is closer to that ever-evasive goal that we call "scientific truth."

For those tempted to follow this path, perhaps the only modest piece of advice I can offer is that it might be of essence to feel part of a community, a community of academics that in fact exists, even if it is often not there in a tangible and face-to-face way in many of our daily lives; even if we do not necessarily see it, when we attend our ordinary faculty meetings. It is with and through that community that I have found one is able to advance in the construction of disciplinary counternarratives, a task that, more than ever, seems critical as we watch the proliferation of organized movements seeking to delegitimize the scientific and academic entity of various strands of critical theory in academia in many countries. The sense of community, as I say, is key. At least for me, this has been the case. And, as I said before, in my eyes, this book certainly represents a collective achievement. The book synthesizes two decades of my own research, but anyone who knows me will know that

16 See Michaela Hailbronner, Marcela Prieto Rudolphy, and Gráinne de Búrca, "Gender in Academic Publishing," *International Journal of Constitutional Law* 17, no. 4 (2019): 1025–44.

something that has characterized my academic career – in this, too, against the (male-defined) current that applauds great soloists more than great orchestras – has been my absolute conviction that academic collaborative work is essential in general and, when it comes to comparative law, absolutely indispensable if one is to engage in a serious effort to become aware, first, and try to minimally overcome, next, one's own bias.

I feel an enormous trepidation at publishing this book. I am deeply aware that the account I offer will inevitably reflect the epistemic limits and biases conditioned by my individual position and my particular vision of the world and of the field as a European woman, white (most of the times, a white-European; other times, though, as sometimes in the United States, a brown-Hispanic), heterosexual, fully abled, middle-aged, upper-middle class, head of household, and mother of two healthy children, raised and educated between Spain, Italy, Canada, and the United States, predominantly in Anglo-speaking academic elite circles. Daring, as I do in this book, to talk about "the world" and about "women," will probably make me subject to the well-known and often rightful accusations of falling into essentialism, false universalism, and Western/Global North–centrism. In my defense, I will only say that one of reasons that it took me such a long time to write this book is that I would have never even dared to do so without first engaging in various collective projects at the intersection between feminist theory, comparative constitutionalism, and women's citizenship. Many of these collaborative projects have in fact found expression in – in my view – the unjustly (when rigorously elaborated) vilified category of edited volumes.[17] If, in the pages to come, you see me often referring to this work, it is not to

[17] In particular, besides the authors involved in the two abovementioned volumes, I am indebted to the various coeditors and authors who have contributed to the production of *Gender Parity and Multicultural Feminism: Towards a New Synthesis* (coedited with Will Kymlicka) (Oxford: Oxford University Press, 2018); *Transforming Gender Citizenship: The Irresistible Rise of Gender Quotas in Europe* (coedited with Eleonore Lépinard) (Cambridge: Cambridge University Press, 2018) and *The Battle for Female Suffrage in Europe: Voting to Become Citizens* (coedited with Blanca Rodriguez Ruiz) (Leiden: Brill, 2012). Currently, there is work in progress for three additional edited volumes and one special issue. The first two of these new edited volumes are already under contract and should see the light of day more or less around the same time as this volume is published – namely, *The Cambridge Companion on Law and Gender* (coedited with Stéphanie Hennette-Vauchez) (Cambridge: Cambridge University Press, forthcoming) and *Gender, Sexuality and Constitutionalism in Asia* (coedited with Wen-Chen Chang, Kelly Loper, Mara Malagodi) (Oxford: Hart Publishing, forthcoming). Two additional projects, one on gender and constitutionalism in Eastern Europe (in collaboration with Barbara Havelková, Matthias Möschel, and Anna Śledzińska-Simon) and one on gender

indulge in self-reference. After all, beyond trying to offer a theoretical framework, a common grid of analysis, and a synthesis of the lessons learned, in many of these volumes, my contribution (commonly shared with other coeditors) has been limited to the role of the insistent editor providing, on average, three rounds of comments to patient authors. If I refer to this work, then, it is mainly because it is work that I have studied over the years. This is exactly what I mean to say. Over the years, I have not only read the authors whom I have collaborated with but I have also studied their work and the literature they have led me to discover in an attempt to truly understand their accounts of legal events in foreign jurisdictions. This is why, above all, my expression of gratitude goes to all those authors whose voices I have tried to integrate, as a symphonic choir, in this book.

To a certain extent, I see my work as that of a carpet weaver. "Three years of work of three women!," said the young man at the Grand Bazaar in Istanbul when he sold me the beautiful carpet you see in the cover of this book. Its back reveals little woven knots, each of them contributing in a tiny way to the formation of the pattern that emerges as the final result. My book was conceived, in a similar way, as a carpet: The threads and knots are the contributions by each and every one of the persons who, across time and across the globe, have fought to have a constitutional law that would help women consolidate their full and equal citizenship status. They also represent the voices of all those academics whom I have learned from throughout the years in this growing field, including the many I have had the opportunity to work closely with on shared projects. In that sense, too, this book really aims to be a story of women's voices. This is also why I would like the reader to receive the rich compilation of notes it provides, with references to legal materials and academic sources, as the rich treasure it has been for me.[18]

I.2 The What and How of This Book

This book is an attempt to explain, in broad terms and in an almost fairy-tale fashion, the ways in which written constitutionalism, as a historically

and constitutionalism in Latin America (in collaboration with Paola Bergallo, Francisca Pou Giménez, and Verónica Undurraga) are also ongoing.

[18] Nevertheless, I am of course aware that, while not exclusively so, the cited literature is mostly in English. I am preparing a Spanish edition of the book in which I plan to make much more extensive reference to non-English, especially Spanish, sources.

formed branch of positive law (which sets out to define the structures of power and processes of decision-making, including through rights-based limits within states), has facilitated or hindered women's equal citizenship in the various national communities it structures, throughout history and around the world. While placing due emphasis on Western constitutionalism, especially the United States and continental Europe – not only because of my own limited knowledge but also because of its leading role in the early history and philosophical foundations of written modern constitutionalism – the book tries to look at every region in the world and in fact recognizes that some of the more exciting developments in terms of gender-responsive constitutionalism are to be found in countries that have consolidated their democratic credentials in more recent times. These developments are often the result of constitutional moments epitomized by the creation or deep reform of a constitutional text, often under the aegis of evolved human rights standards and an emerging form of participatory constitutionalism, which we can call "new constitutionalism." In fact, as we speak, this form of participatory constitutionalism is offering Chile the opportunity to showcase the first experience of a fully "gender-parity" constituent assembly in world history.[19]

In providing an account of how constitutionalism has shaped women's equal citizenship claims, the book takes into account not only women's exclusion, first, and gradual access, then, to the rights first conquered by men and to government structures initially designed and inhabited by men but also raises the question of whether and how the forms of participation traditionally assigned to women – neither in the state nor in the marketplace, but rather in the household and in the family, concerning the physical and symbolic reproduction of the human

[19] Moreover, the constituent assembly includes the most diverse sectors of Chile's population (such as the youth, indigenous peoples, sexually diverse people, and at least one differently abled person) and people from various socioeconomic and professional backgrounds. Many of them ran as independent candidates, challenging the hegemony of political parties and indirect forms of constitution-making that had defined the constitutional setup of the country so far and are now pushing for a wide array of claims, such as a right to water, a healthy environment, a strong list of social rights, a life free of gender-based violence, participatory, decentralized, and democratic mechanisms, and the recognition of indigenous forms of self-determination. For some of the profiles, see Héctor Basoalto et al., "¿Quiénes son, qué piensan, qué hacen?: Radiografía a los 27 constituyentes de la Lista del Pueblo," *Clinic*, May 14, 2021, https://www.theclinic.cl/2021/05/14/quienes-son-que-piensan-que-hacen-radiografia-a-los-27-constituyentes-de-la-lista-del-pueblo/.

species – have been constitutionally recognized as forms of citizenship contribution. In this sense, it tells the story of the relevance of constitutionalism for women's citizenship as defined in male terms (that is to say, with a focus on equal rights and participation in the so-called public sphere), as well as women's ability to redefine the very understanding of citizenship to include participation in social reproduction and a life free of coercion in every domain of human interaction, including in and through the so-called domestic sphere. It starts from the hypothesis that, to a larger or lesser extent depending on context and culture-specific variables, as well as on the intersecting axis of discrimination women suffer, the gendered separation of spheres and tasks was structurally entrenched in the DNA of the modern state construct in ways that significantly limited the emancipatory promise of modern constitutionalism. Because of this, the conquest of rights and access to institutions by women on male terms, following mainstream accounts of contemporary inclusive constitutionalism, has been inadequate to sufficiently disestablish the foundational gender order.[20] In fact, as we shall see, in many

[20] Since the emergence of the "separate spheres" doctrine in the nineteenth century, feminist scholarship, including feminist legal scholarship, has made this dichotomy the center of its project of critique. See, for instance, Frances E. Olsen, "The Family and the Market: A Study of Ideology and Legal Matter," *Harvard Law Review* 96, no. 7 (1983): 1497–578; Ruth Gavison, "Feminism and the Public/Private Distinction," *Stanford Law Review* 45, no. 1 (1992): 1–45. As feminist theory has argued, the public/private distinction is basically an ideological one, and the "line between public and private is constantly renegotiated." See Joan Landes, ed., introduction to *Feminism: The Public and the Private* (London: Oxford University Press, 1998), 3. Although a significant emphasis is placed on the historical formation of the modern constitutional state in the Western world, it is important to understand the persistence of the dichotomy across time and space. As Susan Gal has forcefully argued, we need an account of how the distinction operates as "ideological communication." To do this, we need to look for "the indexical properties of the public/private distinctions" in ways that reveal that its referential content "relies on contexts of use and that the distinction is relative to those contexts." The semiotic approach she suggests invites us to think that, beyond particular configurations, "public" and "private" are not "particular places, domains, spheres of activity or even types of interaction" or a particular set of "institutions or practices." Instead, she suggests that the public/private dichotomy is best understood as a discursive phenomenon and that the "historically locatable process of developing these categories into politically and economically significant distinctions appropriates or is parasitic on the much more widespread pragmatic possibility of using, in interaction, a variety of indexical signals for more proximate versus more distanced relationships or events." This means that "public and private will have different specific definitions in different historical periods and social formations. But once a dichotomy is established, the semiotic logic forms a scaffolding for possibilities of embedding and thus for change, creativity, and argument." They can also be made "lasting and coercive, fixing and forcing such

jurisdictions and domains, this foundational constitutional gender structure has actually held back, rather than facilitated, women's emancipatory claims. Only since the turn of the century do we find that women's empowerment, expressed in their increased participation in international and national decision-making (including through constitution-making, litigation, and interpretation), is allowing for a significant expansion of the domain of application or coverage of the constitutional egalitarian ethos in ways that have increasingly challenged the political relevance of the separate spheres, of gender roles, and, more recently, of sexual and gender identity.

In terms of its organizing structure, chapter 1 begins with the birth of written constitutionalism, which, it is argued, entrenched a two-track citizenship model for men and women. It will take us through the times and conquest of women's suffrage and its limited, yet highly significant, impact on women's constitutional equality, given that voting rights did not produce the overall subversion of the gender order, as the old "head-and-master" rules coexisted virtually everywhere with women's newly conquered political voice. Chapter 1 also takes us to interwar and post–World War II constitutionalism and shows how, despite the gradual acceptance of the principle of sex equality as a constitutional principle, the pervasive nature of the head-and-master regime – whether or not it was given explicit constitutional expression, and certainly modulated by additional axes of domination – created a sort of "family exceptionalism" that limited women's full and egalitarian constitutional membership. Chapter 2 explores the impact of second-wave feminism in constitutionalism since the 1970s. It describes its meaningful impact on women's constitutional citizenship, with the ideal of a gender-neutral legal order becoming the new norm, replacing the *pater familias* or the head-and-master regime, challenging the multiple forms through which marital status had conditioned women's constitutional standing. Courts gradually began to challenge gender stereotypes, helping women join the marketplace on ever more equal terms with men (although never on

distinctions, binding social actors through arrangement such as legal regulation and other forms of ritualization and institutionalization." See Susan Gal, "A Semiotics of the Public/Private Distinction" in *Differences: A Journal of Feminist Cultural Studies* 13, no. 1 (2002): 79–81, 85. This conception might help us understand the different political and economic configurations that the distinction has lent itself to, and it may account for some of the variations across time and space but also for the different roles it has played in shaping the meaning of femininity for different subgroups of women and different types of activities, or the same activities when performed in different locations.

fully equal terms, given the insufficiency of either ignoring, as one strand of constitutionalism did, or simply accepting – and only partially accommodating – as the other strand did, the fact that women have continued to bear the brunt of reproductive labor both in and outside their homes). This chapter also describes the first constitutional affirmations of women's reproductive autonomy by discussing how both the assimilationist and maternalist strands of gender constitutionalism started approaching the abortion debate when it first became constitutionalized. With the single exception of abortion constitutionalism, the selective focus on formal marital and market equality and the insufficient prioritization of other forms of gender subordination show the limits of this more promising, but still limited, form of constitutionalism. This is, however, still the most representative form of constitutionalism today, placing most emphasis on rights rather than on ensuring opportunities for women's equal participation and on formal rather than substantive gender equality.[21]

Chapter 3 brings us to more contemporary times, carrying us through what I call the "women's participatory turn," beginning in the late 1980s and flourishing since the mid-1990s, a participatory turn that sees women's claims shifting from equal rights to equal participation – not only in the employment domain but also in the domain of politics. More generally, this shift is also evident in women's access to positions of authority and decision-making, calling on constitutional doctrines and norms of substantive equality to legitimize or even demand affirmative action, parity democracy measures, and a stronger list of socioeconomic rights. This participatory turn, which also accompanied the spread of more inclusive constitution-making processes, refers to women ultimately joining these processes in more significant (though by no means

[21] Out of the 194 written constitutions around the world, almost all guarantee equality in explicit terms; almost two-thirds entrench equality or nondiscrimination guarantees on the basis of sex; and almost one-third make explicit reference to gender. See Katharine G. Young, "Introduction: A Public Law of Gender?," in Rubenstein and Young, *The Public Law of Gender*, 2 (citing various sources). We can thus assume that most constitutional systems are committed today to some form of inclusive constitutionalism, which is not at all irrelevant, given the fact that formal inequalities persist in several countries' legislations. That said, the extent to which these constitutional provisions are effectively used to promote gender-neutral legal orders depends on whether the provisions are enforceable; the various tests relied by courts in drawing distinctions between legitimate and discriminatory differential treatment; and whether some jurisdictional domains, including family, religious, customary, or tribal law are exempt from (full) constitutional sex equality scrutiny.

equal) ways, both through official bodies and sites (such as constitution-making assemblies and constitutional courts, or as judges and litigants) and, most emphatically, grassroots mobilization. Coinciding in time with the blooming of theories of multiculturalism, women's participatory turn also helped bring to the fore the complexity of intersectional forms of discrimination and the opportunities and challenges that must be confronted by women – including those whose religious, cultural, ethnic, or racial(ized) identities might place them outside the hegemonic frame of decision-making and self-government in the eyes of either the majority society, their own communities, or both. In particular, as we shall see, the participatory lenses foreground the possibility of enhancing women's agencies to resolve the possible set of tensions and conflicts in contexts of legal pluralism or devolved structures of power.

As I discuss in Chapter 4, in recent years, this participatory form of gender constitutionalism, with its emphasis on women's agency and its ensuing invitation to take intersectional agendas on board, has been gradually contributing to the expansion of constitutional agendas and helping shape the contours of "new millennium" gender constitutionalism. This new millennium constitutionalism finds expression in new constitutional doctrines and texts drafted in recent constitution-making processes after the third wave of democratization and with particular strength since the beginning of the new century.[22] It is gradually coming to terms with the need to fully disestablish the foundational gender order; to constitutionally recognize the centrality of social reproduction; and to craft more egalitarian, plural, and democratic family structures as a constitutional imperative, meaning those in which patriarchal power structures are overcome, gender roles challenged, and severe and systematic forms of autonomy limitation and exploitation identified as constitutionally relevant. Building on the maternalist constitutional tradition and its recognition of the centrality of care, but going beyond it by challenging traditional gender roles, this new millennium gender constitutionalism manifests itself in a rich constitutional agenda, which includes same-sex partnerships and marriage; an expanded array of sexual and reproductive rights and new understandings of abortion rights; the recognition of the constitutional dimensions of domestic and other forms of gender violence; the need to enhance coresponsibility and

[22] Since the 1990s, at least 110 countries around the globe have been engaged in writing new constitutions or major revisions of old ones (see ibid., 3). In many of these new texts, issues of gender equality have been a central concern during the constitutional process.

the collective assumption of the costs of human reproduction (built around notions of "positive motherhood" and "new fatherhood"); and the social construction and fluidity of the concept of gender itself, as exemplified by the claims of trans persons. I briefly discuss all these manifestations in Chapter 5, under the banner of transformative gender constitutionalism (suggesting that this form of constitutionalism has the potential to better go to the roots of the normalized gender order than inclusive constitutionalism). This last form of gender constitutionalism, however timidly accepted in the real world so far, has the potential to be truly revolutionary by challenging the gender order in the DNA of modern constitutionalism. We, therefore, cannot be fully surprised if its agenda is not proceeding without major resistance. This is why Chapter 5 ends with a brief description of a growing and increasingly globally orchestrated antigender equality agenda that is finding expression in many parts of the world and that attempts to reassert – including through constitutional means – the validity of the contours of the so-called traditional family, which is felt under threat, including the gender binary, the gendered division of roles, and a heterosexual conception of the family, all of which are heralded as basic pillars of society capable of holding together increasingly fragile states and insecure citizens in a globalized world.

In crafting the periodization that structures the book, it is important to note that I have paid particular attention to the moment when the various claims around gender equality entered constitutionalism (and experienced either contraction or expansion under it). The book cannot, therefore, be read as suggesting an evolutionary path that must sequentially repeat itself in the advancement toward women's constitutional equality in every single jurisdiction. Ultimately, it might be best to think of these categories as forms of constitutionalism rather than stages in constitutionalism and to think of them as forms that can be present or absent in different constitutional regimes, which can also vary in time and sequence among national jurisdictions – not being, for the most part, mutually exclusive. Also, some jurisdictions will present some, but not all, of the features that I put together as falling under one typology. These are, after all, constructed and somewhat idealized, oversimplified typologies. In sum, the forms identified are (1) *exclusionary gender constitutionalism*, where constitutional law significantly fails to consider sex equality a constitutional concern; (2) *inclusive gender constitutionalism*, which seeks to grant women rights equal to those of men, redeeming women from their otherwise decimated citizenship status (often shaped by their marital status), yet without fundamentally challenging the structure of the underlying gender order conceptually built around traditional and patriarchal family schemes; (3) *participatory gender constitutionalism*, which is receptive to the idea that gender justice requires going beyond equal rights and calls for facilitating women's equal participation in the male-dominated public sphere, including in the world of constitution-making, by calling on notions of substantive equality, parity democracy, and what we can identify as feminist multiculturalism; and, as of recently, (4) *transformative gender constitutionalism*, which expects constitutional law to advance the agenda of radically subverting the original constitutional gender order by taking the domestic sphere and the types of activities centrally associated with it as a relevant domain of citizenship contribution and by defending the need to fully expand the constitutional ethos of democratic equality and individual autonomy to the various "private spheres," ultimately contributing to the full disestablishment of gender roles and fixed gender identities and concepts.

These four forms are defined on the basis of the role that constitutional law has played in women's citizenship claims. Whether and when they are adopted in various jurisdictions will depend on a wide set of factors, not all of which are gender-specific. These factors include, at the very least, the moment a constitution was drafted and the dominant conception of women's citizenship at that time; whether its drafting or interpretation has been influenced by women in different capacities (as constitution-makers, justices, litigants, or through civil society organizations promoting constitutional change for women); the claims that women and different groups of women have constitutionally articulated (courts respond to claims before them); whether a constitution reflects a minimalist or a maximalist conception of the state in terms of its role in ensuring intergroup equality (including as mediated through private interactions); how constitutions regulate the sources, hierarchy, and conflicts of norms and jurisdictions in contexts of legal pluralism; and whether constitutions create synergies with regional and international sources of normativity, facilitating the incorporation of evolving human rights standards or failing to do so.

I further make an effort to include or refer to the wide array of women's constitutional imaginations, narratives, and aspirations, including in the various instances in which they were not monochromatic or when constitutional systems failed to take them fully or partially into account, in the conviction that expressed desires and failed attempts should be incorporated much more frequently than they commonly are to our national and global accounts of constitutional history. In doing so, I drew inspiration from a fairly recent experience in Egypt. As many scholars enthused by the possibility of an Arab Spring that would consolidate a fourth wave of democratic transitions, I found myself in Cairo in the spring of 2014 interviewing scholars and activists to get a sense of women's involvement in the country's constitutional moment, which had seen the passing of two constitutions in a short time following the fall of the Mubarak regime, the coming to power of the Muslim Brotherhood under Morsi's presidency, and his ousting from power aided by military intervention. Like so many others, I have of course been saddened by the evolutions in the country since and the limited reach of the democratic reforms that were being advanced at the time. I was also made acutely aware that, in contexts in which political power is not fully secularized, democratically elected religious majorities can bring about limitations to, rather than expansion of, women's autonomy. Yet, at the same time, nothing, I feel, detracts from the extraordinary dimensions of what I learned about the experience of Egyptian women during my stay, including the ways women had mobilized to craft women's constitutional aspirations. Drawing from their own constitutional history and the experience of feminist pioneers to make connections between Egypt's past and present (and avoid accusations of being westernized), activists and academic coalitions of women had taken on themselves to study comparative experiences in order to foreground gender equality in constitution-making processes; more or less managed to negotiate some differences between religious and secular women; and, through innovative and participatory methods, encouraged thousands of women in the country, including in remote villages, to think of themselves as constitution-makers drafting documents that synthesized their views.[23] This, I thought, was in and of itself worth learning and sharing with the rest of the world, and this eye-opening experience lies at the basis of my attempt to recover women's voices and aspirations, in all their manifestations and regardless of the outcomes ultimately achieved.

In other words, the (her)story of constitutionalism should include women's agency in all its breadth and complexity, and not only their access to official sites of decision-making or their success record, even if, for limits of space, I could only hint at some of the many forms in which such agency has expressed itself around the world. Those who believe in

[23] Hala Kamal, "Inserting Women's Rights in the Egyptian Constitution: Personal Reflections," *Journal for Cultural Research* 19, no. 2 (2015): 150–61.

the concept of democratic constitutionalism will probably approve of the choice and help us develop it further by recovering much of what has been so far neglected to the margins or to complete silence.

I.3 The Limits and Limitations

The phrase "around the globe" is a big concept, so allow me to introduce some nuances and disclaimers. In terms of the geographic scope of the book, the reader will notice that, whereas I could not minimally pretend to be exhaustive, I have made an effort to draw from many jurisdictions, identifying regional trends whenever I could, in order to exemplify certain themes and in an attempt to give due credit and recognition to diverse realities and constitutional dynamics. Inevitably also, my choice has been shaped by existing secondary literature and my rich yet limited linguistic skills, certainly not rich enough to access primary or secondary sources in most existing languages.

In trying to overcome geographical bias, I have made several conscious choices. First, I have purposefully tried to ensure that the struggles to bring gender justice considerations to bear on the way constitutions are drafted and interpreted, while being true to history, do not overrepresent the importance and achievements of countries from the Global North, although the importance of colonial pasts in shaping postcolonial constitutional dynamics around the world certainly cannot be denied. I have also tried to compensate for the Anglo-Saxon dominance in some of the existing literature in the field. Surely, one cannot be fully surprised that the English-speaking world writes about English-speaking countries, with which it naturally shares historical connections, but we must be mindful that the relative academic hegemony of the English-speaking world may then have the effect of shaping academic fields in particular ways. The same can be said about the relative disciplinary hegemony of European constitutionalism and, within Europe, of some countries in the North – such as Germany, often taken as a key reference in continental European constitutionalism – over others from the South or in the East, which might also have influenced transnational constitutional dynamics. The book thus tries to draw from many rich regional experiences, including those currently taking place in the Arab world, Latin America, Asia, and Central and Eastern Europe. It also brings to the fore experiences of relatively small and underexplored countries, even if just to challenge the Global North/Global South line of division that is reproduced when the examples chosen to illustrate a field systematically or predominantly come from the Global North, leaving the Global South either entirely out or, at best, relegated to the condition of exotic footnotes. Of course, I am absolutely mindful that such an ambitious goal will always carry inherent flaws. I have surely left out more than I was able to include. The ambition to be geographically and thematically comprehensive, while theoretically analytical, has also come at the expense of much decontextualizing and a significant amount of oversimplifying. And whereas I have at least tried to ensure the accuracy of the sources and of my interpretations of them (relying on what I considered authoritative local sources as well as, whenever I could, the generous help of friends in the relevant academic communities who have revised earlier drafts), in the end, the achieved result can only be the beginning of an exercise, which, I am sure, will be challenged, enriched, nuanced, and amplified by members of the global academic community that I consider myself a part of. Sometimes, I suspect, we just need to dare and think big. After all, haven't we been passing on canonical and inevitably limited and biased versions of the (hi)story of local and global constitutionalism to our students again and again? Why not attempt a few of the (her)stories in the coming decades?

As I have mentioned above, the reader should not read this book as suggesting an evolutionary or normative sequence in the advancement toward women's constitutional equality in every jurisdiction. Similarly, we should be fully aware that, in many jurisdictions (such as those with a stronger parliamentary tradition or weaker forms of rights-based, court-led constitutionalism), similar evolutions in terms of advancing or resisting the advancement of women's equal citizenship have taken place mostly through political struggles and legislative milestones, with written constitutions playing a minimal, if any, role at all. The central questions this book seeks to address are therefore more modest: to the extent that constitutional texts, actors, litigation, and doctrines have played a role in shaping the dynamics of inclusion or exclusion of women (and, to a certain degree, that of gender and sexual minorities) as full and equal citizens, which was that role, how has it changed over time, and, possibly, why? As the reader will be able to anticipate, the answers to these questions must certainly be connected to various existing gender regimes (especially as they may affect constitutional texts coming to life in time and space, to some extent, "freezing the conceptual imagination"[24] as to the forms of injustice that deserve constitutional redress) but also to

[24] Irving, *Gender and the Constitution*, 165.

many other variables related to the general features of the different constitutional systems. These variables comprise the different powers and composition of constitutional or supreme courts; the richness or paucity of rights in constitutions as well as their scope (whether they only limit state action or also bind private powers), the theories of interpretation, and the system of guarantees that sustain them; and, more broadly, the rules and conditions that have shaped the possibility for women and other minorities to access constitutional justice (such as standing rules, rules on the participation of amicus curiae, or support for public interest litigation). After all, it is always constitutional doctrine that fills constitutional clauses with substance, for it responds to the various claims and arguments that reach the courts.

In assessing change, and sometimes celebrating progress, I have focused on constitutional claims, texts, and jurisprudence and limited myself, also for reasons of space, to the higher ranks or special courts in the judiciary with the function of constitutional interpretation, as representing the most authoritative voice in settling constitutional meaning in each jurisdiction. I will of course concede to those who have claimed that "constitutionalism is too narrow and formalistic a container for addressing the problems feminism identifies" and that "custom, habit, norms, roles, and other dominant regularities powerfully constitute the law for women, that is, the real rules to which they are held."[25] I may be particularly challenged by those who rightly point to problems of the "gap in enforcement," if not in "sincerity,"[26] of what all too often appear as cosmetic, if not "sham," constitutions,[27] which, in the many scenarios in which political elites co-opt the energies of and support for women's movements internally to secure foreign approval externally, might in fact be called "cynical constitutions." Nothing new under the sun: "The goal of gender equality has been coopted by various other projects – nationalism, socialism, and most pressing now, neoliberalism and

[25] MacKinnon, foreword to *Feminist Constitutionalism*, xi.

[26] Young, "Introduction: A Public Law of Gender?," in Rubenstein and Young, *The Public Law of Gender*, 3.

[27] See David S. Law and Mila Versteeg, "Sham Constitutions," *California Law Review* 101, no. 4 (2013): 863. See also Alexandra Huneeus, Javier Couso, and Rachel Sieder, "Cultures of Legality: Judicialization and Political Activism in Contemporary Latin America," in Javier Couso, Alexandra Huneeus, and Rachel Sieder, eds., *Cultures of Legality: Judicialization and Political Activism in Latin America, Cambridge Studies in Law and Society* (Cambridge: Cambridge University Press, 2010).

securitisation."[28] At the same time, it is important to underline that new provisions offer a new moral and political vocabulary that often reflects the aspirations of women and encourage legal battles to come. They also have an expressive and educating function across the channels through which the migration of public law ideas around the world operates, such as borrowing and transplants.[29]

At the end of the day, it is legitimate to question the real impact of increasingly gender-responsive constitutions.[30] Constitution-drafting and litigation will, for the most part, offer inevitably narrow sites of transformation, being as they are, out of reach for the majority of women and certainly, with some notorious exceptions, of otherwise marginalized groups. Moreover, liberal democratic constitutionalism of the kind that has become increasingly hegemonic and that has accompanied the consolidation of market economies in advanced capitalist societies is also a product of its time. And, despite variations, it has a limited capacity to channel claims of radical transformation through the support of meaningful measures of dignitary and material predistribution or redistribution – measures that would arguably be needed to make our societies more radically egalitarian. Ironically – or perhaps not so much – the family may prove less impenetrable in certain ways than the market when it comes to fully freeing every site of power from domination patterns contradicting the constitutional ethos.

For this reason, I should make clear from the outset that I doubt that any form of gender constitutionalism will be able to achieve truly transformative goals unless it is accompanied by meaningful political action, which, whether or not constitutionally inspired, should prove able to tackle the intersecting axes of discrimination and disadvantage that shape existing hierarchies and domination patterns, as well as the growing

[28] See Young, "Introduction: A Public Law of Gender?," in Rubenstein and Young, *The Public Law of Gender*, 3, citing Kumari Jayawardena, *Feminism and Nationalism in the Third World* (London: Zed Books, 1986); Penny Griffin, "Gender, Governance and the Global Political Economy," *Australian Journal of International Affairs* 64, no. 1 (2010): 86–104.

[29] On this topic, see Sujit Choudhry, ed., *The Migration of Constitutional Ideas* (Cambridge: Cambridge University Press, 2006); Günther Frankenberg, ed., *Order from Transfer: Comparative Constitutional Design and Legal Culture* (Cheltenham, UK: Edward Elgar, 2013); Vicki C. Jackson, *Constitutional Engagement in a Transnational Era* (Oxford: Oxford University Press, 2010).

[30] See, for instance, Priscilla A. Lambert and Druscilla L. Scribner, "A Politics of Difference versus a Politics of Equality: Do Constitutions Matter?," *Comparative Politics* 41, no. 3 (2009): 337–57.

socioeconomic inequality that currently threatens the sustainability of our democratic societies. How to do this while making sure that the environmental threats that also question the sustainability of our existence on this planet are addressed is certainly one of the most pressing questions of our times. Both tasks require rethinking in a serious way how to organize our political communities placing the sustainability of the species and the planet, and, hence, care and life, at the center stage. It is my basic contention that, in so doing, we can draw from the lessons that global gender constitutionalism can teach us so far.

1

The Constitutional Establishment of the Gender Order

Revolutionary Times and Exclusionary Constitutionalism

1.1 The Revolutionary Moment and Women's Citizenship

In France, after the March on Versailles on October 5, 1789, women presented the Women's Petition to the National Assembly, proposing a decree that would give women equal rights. Only two years later, in 1791, in her Declaration of the Rights of Women and the Female Citizen, Olympe de Gouges affirmed that a "woman is born free and remains equal to man in rights" in a text advocating not only universal suffrage but also women's access to public office, equal property rights, and decision-making powers for husbands and wives. Six decades later, in 1848, on the other side of the Atlantic, the Declaration of Sentiments was adopted at the Seneca Falls Convention, the first women's rights convention organized by women. Its words offered a testimony of the failure of previous women's revolutionary emancipatory ambitions against men: "Having deprived her of this first right of a citizen, the elected franchise, thereby leaving her without representation in the halls of legislation, he has oppressed her on all sites. He has made her, if married, in the eye of the law, civilly dead."[1]

The revolutionary emancipatory ambitions that succeeded had been primarily the ambitions of men. Whereas in 1776 the American Declaration of Independence proclaimed that "governments are instituted among *men*, deriving their just powers from the consent of the governed" after affirming that "all *men* are created equal ... and endowed by their Creator with certain unalienable rights," it would not be until 1789 that the French Declaration of the Rights of *Man* and of the

[1] Cited in Reva Siegel, "The Nineteenth Amendment and the Democratization of the Family," *Yale Law Journal Forum* 129 (2020): 459.

Citizen would declare the "freedom and equality of *men* at birth" (italics are mine). Both documents, signaling the birth of modern rights-based constitutionalism resulting from the French and American Revolutions, clearly used a universalist language, inspired as they were, by enlightened theories of natural rights and human reason. Yet both were also using the word "men" literally and not simply as a generic and disembodied expression of the universal person. No woman was included in the drafting bodies of these declarations. Women were simply intended to be excluded from the consenting sovereign: they were denied both political rights and independence as well as equality in the domestic sphere of marriage. It would take more than a century for women's suffrage to start to become a reality, and even so, this would be limited to a few places around the world and would leave, for the most part, no constitutional traces. The ideals of liberty and equality were eclipsed by fraternity and were given "masculine features."[2] Moreover, the term "men" in the declarations was not meant to include all men but rather only white people and property owners; that is, a small minority of the population in both nations, the minority considered suited for citizenship. Women had to rely on their husbands' goodwill – something that Abigail Adams (the wife of John Adams, drafter of the Massachusetts Constitution and future United States president) knew well when, in March 1776, anticipating the Declaration of Independence, she famously wrote a letter to her husband begging him to "remember the Ladies, and be more generous and favorable to them than your ancestors. Do not put such unlimited power into the hands of the Husbands. Remember all Men would be tyrants if they could."[3] How much of his wife's advice John Adams intended to follow or could take on, we do not know. What we do know, however, is that Samuel Chase, signatory to the Declaration of Independence and future Supreme Court justice, wrote in his treatise *Baron and Feme* that "the law of nature has put [a wife] under the obedience of her husband."[4]

[2] See Joan B. Landes, *Women and the Public Sphere in the Age of the French Revolution* (Cornell: Cornell University Press, 1988), 158.

[3] See Helen Irving, *Gender and the Constitution: Equity and Agency in Comparative Constitutional Design* (Cambridge: Cambridge University Press, 2008), 5, in which she cites Abigail Adams, cited in L. H. Butterfield et al., eds., *The Book of Abigail and John: Selected Letters of the Adams Family, 1762–1784* (Cambridge, MA: Harvard University Press, 1975).

[4] See John Kang, "Patriarchy and Constitutional Origins," in *Constitutions and Gender*, ed. Helen Irving (Cheltenham, UK: Edward Elgar, 2017), 513, in which he cites Carol Berkin,

It is in fact an irony that the arrival of written, rights-based constitutionalism signaled a moment of regression rather than an advancement in women's political entitlements. In many European jurisdictions, the modern legal order deprived women of the suffrage rights they had enjoyed under the political institutions of the *ancien régime*, where feudal notions of status or property ownership had allowed for a limited recognition of political rights – usually restricted to municipal or provincial elections – to some noble and taxpaying women.[5] Starting in the early nineteenth century, women were also denied independent and equal citizenship by legislation that made their nationality dependent on their husbands.[6] Sometimes, these regressions required the explicit underscoring that the gender-neutral formulation of the new concept of citizenship in fact only encompassed men. This was so despite women's undeniable involvement in the revolutionary struggles of the time on both sides of the Atlantic.[7]

Women's disenfranchisement was not a minor issue or an easy one to overcome. In the United States, women were first granted suffrage in the state of Wyoming in 1890, when it joined the federation, and only achieved suffrage at a federal level in 1920 through constitutional reform embodied in the Nineteenth Amendment, whereas French women had to wait until 1944 after World War II to become politically entitled. If political equality was hard to conquer even in the Western world, full

Revolutionary Mothers: Women in the Struggle for America's Independence (New York, NY: Alfred A. Knopf, 2005).

5 Ruth Rubio-Marín, "The Achievement of Female Suffrage in Europe: On Women's Citizenship," *International Journal of Constitutional Law* 12, no. 1 (2014), 8–9.

6 See Helen Irving, "Citizenship and Nationality," in Irving, *Constitutions and Gender*, 387–413. See also Jo Shaw, *The People in Question: Citizens and Constitutions in Uncertain Times* (Bristol: Bristol University Press, 2020), on gender discrimination, 131, 141–43, 147–48, and on ethnicity-based discrimination, 107–9, 114–15, 234–35, 140–41, 143–44. Note that naturalization and citizenship rules exemplified also the intersection between race and sex discrimination: "If a woman was not white, she was ineligible for naturalization and could not, regardless of coverture, take on the citizenship of an American husband. On the other hand, even if eligible, she could not be naturalized if her husband was ineligible." See Nancy F. Cott, *Public Vows: A History of Marriage and the Nation* (Cambridge: Harvard University Press, 2000), 165.

7 In fact, a number of publications refer to the "founding mothers" when describing the various ways in which women supported the revolution in North America. See, for instance, Cokie Roberts, *Founding Mothers: The Women Who Raised Our Nation* (New York: William Morrow, 2004). On women in the French Revolution, see Shirley Elson Roessler, *Out of the Shadows: Women and Politics in the French Revolution* (New York: P. Lang, 1996).

equality in rights was even harder: it took over a century and a half since the dawn of revolutionary constitutionalism to kick-start the process of overruling head-and-master laws that rendered women legal minors within the household and fully affirming women's equal civil status. Only in the 1960s and 1970s, under the influence of second-wave feminism's challenge to the patriarchal household-state model, did this process, which is still ongoing in many parts of the world, begin in the countries that are widely considered the cradle of constitutionalism.

None of this is truly surprising, however, if we bear in mind that sex inequality was central to both the liberal and the republican traditions of citizenship that modern constitutionalism inherited. In the modern republican tradition, with its roots in antiquity, citizens were expected to contribute to the common good, although this meant different things for men and women. While men were expected to focus on soldiering and government, inhabiting the realm of human freedom, women were to channel their contribution through motherhood, guarding the republican virtues and morals in the so-called private sphere.[8] Yet women did not fare much better under the liberal tradition, since in the bourgeois societies in which the liberal discourse of universal freedoms and rights flourished, subjects and rights holders were only those endowed with property (including that of the self), those who could sustain themselves – those who, in other words, were subjected to no one. Certainly, these could only be some men and not women, who were typically denied full property rights. Slave men and women were literally owned by their masters as part of the household property; most "free" women depended on their husbands,[9] and all women were said to be destined to taking care of others. In short, both republicanism and liberalism constructed the myth of the independence and self-sufficiency of free, propertied men by relegating women to their private sphere, a sphere in which they would devote themselves to the task of human and social reproduction, enjoying a legal status that, in many ways, brought them closer to property than to a status of property holders.[10]

[8] Ruth Lister, *Citizenship: Feminist Perspectives*, 2nd ed. (New York: New York University Press, 2003), 71.

[9] Ruth Lister et al., *Gendering Citizenship in Western Europe: New Challenges for Citizenship in a Cross-National Context* (Bristol, UK: The Policy Press, 2007), 21.

[10] Revolutionary France abolished slavery throughout its conquered territories in 1794, following the 1971 Haitian Revolution, and the United Kingdom's Slavery Abolition Act of 1833 abolished slavery in many parts of the British Empire. Nevertheless, the

Unlike slaves and other racialized persons, women were not denied full humanity during revolutionary times, but the new constitutions were often silent about their political status. Thus, an obvious question comes to mind to anyone trained to admire the enlightened and liberal philosophical seeds on which the modern order was built: how could women's subjection be reconciled with the egalitarian promise that was foundational to modern constitutionalism? The institution of the marital family, based on the marital contract and central to the household-based political order, holds the answer. In modern times, the order of status was to be replaced by one based on contract, and marriage was to embody a woman's consent to her place in both society and the political community, hence shaping her distinctive form of modern citizenship. Understanding this requires us to take a look at the transformation of marriage as an institution in the revolutionary period and in modern times.

1.2 The Enlightened Marital Contract and the Modern State

In her fascinating account of the history of marriage (*Marriage, a History: How Love Conquered Marriage*) on which I draw in this book to describe the evolution of the institution of marriage, historian Stephanie Coontz explains the profound changes to marriage brought about by the spread of the market economy and the advent of the Enlightenment. From being a system of political and economic alliances in its first five thousand years of existence, during the eighteenth century, the institution of marriage came to be seen as a private relationship between two individuals.[11] For the very first time in history, people came to be expected to marry freely for love and companionship. Behind this evolution, Coontz explains, lie a series of political, economic, and cultural changes that, from their inception in Europe in the seventeenth century,

institution of slavery remained central to the economy of the Southern states in the United States until its complete abolition at the end of the American Civil War. The original constitution had expressed the view that Blacks (or, for that matter, Indians) were not fully human, and so their disenfranchisement had naturally followed. Slavery and the inferior political status of Blacks for representation purposes was, if not explicitly written into the US Constitution, then at least acknowledged in its Apportionment Clause and the Fugitive Slave Clause. This had to be overcome by the Thirteenth, Fourteenth, and Fifteenth Amendments, also known as the Reconstruction Amendments.

11 Stephanie Coontz, *Marriage, a History: How Love Conquered Marriage* (New York: Penguin Books, 2006), 145–46.

began to erode the older functions of marriage. Only in the late eighteenth century, and then only in Western Europe and North America, did the notion of free choice and marriage for love succeed as a cultural idea. Among the economic and political preconditions that made what she calls the "marriage revolution" possible, Coontz underlines the spread of wage labor in the growing market economy and a new industrialist social order. It was this increase in wage labor that made newlywed couples less dependent on their parents and, in turn, facilitated the historical transformation of the household into a nuclear family, where husband and wife were seen as complementing each other.[12] The husband, once the overseer of the family labor force, gradually came to be seen as the person who inhabited the public sphere and who, by himself, had to provide for the family through income that was generated outside the household. The wife, once a companion in the farming economy, became instead the source of emotional, moral, and physical nurturing for both the husband and the progeny and was relegated to the private sphere. This is how, during the nineteenth century, most Europeans and Americans came to accept a new view of husbands as providers and wives as caretaking homebodies, entrusting the husband with a duty to protect her and grating him an entitlement to control her and her autonomy. It is interesting to note that this ideal, to which we shall return further on, could not be achieved by a majority of families in the mid-twentieth century, and even then, it was mostly white families who did. This model ignored the ways in which racial patriarchy – expressed through slavery, expropriation, and confinement of indigenous peoples, colonized populations, and otherwise marginalized racial minorities – created a public sphere as a "white male creation."[13] The model also implied the existence of a stable marital relationship and the possibility of surviving on the earnings of a single breadwinner, thus giving way to the advent of the family wage that many failed to achieve. However elusive, though, this culturally hegemonic model was exported abroad, forcing poor, single white women and nonwhite men and women to live under its shadow.[14]

[12] Ibid., 146.

[13] Charles W. Mills, "Intersecting Contracts," in *Contract and Domination*, eds. Carole Pateman and Charles W. Mills (Cambridge: Polity Press, 2007), 187.

[14] It has been noted that colonization transformed not only the material lives of colonized people but also their sense of what it meant to be female and male. See Margaret Strobel, "Women's History, Gender History, and European Colonialism," in *Colonialism and the Modern World: Selected Studies*, eds. Gregory Blue, Martin Bunton, and Ralph Croizier (Armonk, NY: M. E. Sharpe, 2002), 57. On the imposition of European domestic life and

The freedoms afforded by the market economy had their parallel in new political and philosophical ideas, and these, too, had an impact on the deep alteration of the marital institution. Political absolutism had sustained the idea of the family as a miniature monarchy until the late seventeenth century and made the husband king over his dependents.[15] The new political ideals stoked by the Glorious Revolution in England in 1688, and the even more ambitious revolutions in America and France at the end of the eighteenth century, came to question the traditional and classic defense of patriarchal authority.[16] Eighteenth-century Enlightenment thinkers defended the notion of individual rights and insisted that social relationships, including those between men and women, be organized "on the basis of consent, rather than force, and on transactions rather than in-born status."[17] Thus, "consent-based" marriage as contract replaced the natural subjection of women to their husbands and became the legitimating instrument of the new family order.

This, however, did not automatically entail the overcoming of sex inequality, which was said to be grounded in nature. Only a small minority of female and male thinkers in both Europe and America, including Olympe de Gouges, the marquis de Condorcet, and Mary Wollstonecraft, went so far as to call for complete equality within marriage. Most enlightened thinkers simultaneously defended the ideas of universal freedom and equality, as well as the subordinate position of women. It was the contractual fiction of free and consent-based marriage that allowed the notions of hierarchy and community, which the modern project was supposed to replace, to go unchallenged when it came to women. Love gradually displaced obedience as the dominant narrative to support the need for an identity of interests ensuring family unity, whereas in fact it gave cover, under the pretense of family privacy, to the most abusive forms of subordination of women, including through

morals at family level and as central to validate the whole colonial enterprise, see also Amy Kaler, "Visions of Domesticity in the African Women's Homecraft Movement in Rhodesia," *Social Science History* 23, no. 3 (1999): 269–309.

15 Kang, "Patriarchy and Constitutional Origins," 501.

16 Coontz, *Marriage, a History*, 148.

17 Ibid., 146–47. If old forms of subordination were legitimized by God's words, nature, tradition, and ascription, civil subordination was to be generated through contracts about property in the person. See Carole Pateman, "On Critics and Contract," in Pateman and Mills, *Contract and Domination*, 209–10.

the use of violence.[18] Since these enlightened thinkers provided the philosophical underpinnings of modern constitutionalism, it is worth pausing to reflect on their vision of the place of women in the new social and political order.

Take John Locke, for instance. In the late seventeenth century, Locke had argued that governmental authority was simply a contract between ruler and ruled. It followed that, if a ruler exceeded the authority his subjects granted him, he could be replaced. Under the same logic, he suggested that marriage, too, could be seen as a contract between equals.[19] Yet he still believed that men would normally rule their families because of their greater strength and ability, which he took to be indisputable natural facts. This idea that physical differences between the sexes should be reflected in a distinct legal status for men and women – and, essentially, in women's subordination to men – was a thought that later contractarian and enlightened authors would also share and that seems to represent a concession to nature in tension with the notion that any form of political subordination needed to find its ultimate justification in human-made arrangements. In fact, a paradigmatic expression of this understanding of women as naturally dependent and subjugated to men can be found in Jean-Jacques Rousseau's writings, which, by contrast, also reflect his perception of men as independent beings. Like Locke, Rousseau based his theory on the different natures of men and women. For Rousseau, men are naturally free, whereas women are made to please men and be subjugated by them, including by being trained to endure a certain amount of violence as would be needed to domesticate them and have them abandon the temptation to ever situate themselves above men.[20] This is because nature has made one sex stronger and another one weaker, which explains why only men have a natural inclination to be free and why justice, reason, and the public arena are the exclusive territory of men.[21] Women, Rousseau claimed, lacking theoretical intelligence and being rather endowed with practical reason, chastity, modesty, sweetness, wit, and beauty, are to remain away from the public sphere and put their virtues at the service of the private,

[18] See Reva B. Siegel, "'The Rule of Love': Wife Beating as Prerogative and Privacy," *Yale Law Journal* 105, no. 8 (1996): 2117–207.

[19] Coontz, *Marriage, a History*, 148.

[20] Jean-Jacques Rousseau, *Emile or On Education*, trans. Allan Bloom (New York: Basic Books, 1979), 412, 425–26.

[21] Jean-Jacques Rousseau, "The Social Contract," in *The Social Contract and The First and Second Discourses*, trans. Susan Dunn (New Haven, CT: Yale University Press, 2002), 149.

domestic realm.[22] These thoughts provided ammunition to politicians of the time. In the words of Rousseau's fellow citizen and prime minister, Charles-Maurice de Talleyrand, "The delicate constitution of women, their peaceful inclinations, the numerous duties of maternity, constantly estrange them from public concerns. . . . Let us teach women that the less they participate in law-making, the greater the protection and strength they will derive from the law."[23]

In accounting for how egalitarian contractualism could justify women's ongoing subjection to men, Carole Pateman's seminal book, *The Sexual Contract*,[24] on which I rely, brilliantly describes that the answer lies precisely in the construction of the separate spheres on which the modern project was grounded since its inception.[25] Pateman examines how the embedding of a sexual contract within modernity, supplementary to the social contract, was a step to simultaneously affirm and overcome women's characteristic order of status in premodern times. In other words, the marriage contract allowed the subjection of wives to be both theoretically rejected and practically entrenched in the new political system. The replacement of an order of status by one of contract defined modernity. In the new modern imaginary, Pateman explains, contract is what allows the individual to believe that their relations with others are based on freedom and equality instead of natural subjection and hierarchy. Contract is also what men use in the public sphere, be it civil society or the public arena, when interacting with other equals. At the same time, modernity conceptualized this contractarian male individual, and hence the modern citizen, on the basis of an implicit subordination of women naturally deemed unfit for the public realm. Because the idea of human equality – the very essence of the new social and political order – could not be entirely compromised, this fiction-based "sexual contract," embodied in the marital institution, was paramount.

Marriage allowed women to "contract into," and thus "consent to," an institution that sealed patriarchy, affirming their obedience to men. The upshot of this is that women's incorporation into civil society in the modern political order became a gender-specific one: women were

22 Ibid.

23 Cited in Barbara Taylor, "Mary Wollstonecraft, sobre mujer y vida pública," in *Mujeres para la historia: figuras destacadas del primer feminismo*, ed. Rosa María Capel (Madrid: Abada Editores, 2004), 59.

24 Carole Pateman, *The Sexual Contract* (Stanford: Stanford University Press, 1988).

25 In this regard, see also Susan Moller Okin, *Women in Western Political Thought* (Princeton, NJ: Princeton University Press, 1979).

incorporated as women, and not simply as persons, as are the parties to the original social contract, meaning that they were added as natural subordinates to men through a pact of protection/subordination.[26] The incorporation of women through the sexual contract, therefore, enabled the affirmation of the public spheres of market and state to be crafted as quintessentially male domains of interpersonal liberty, equality, and fraternity.

At the same time, a growing body of literature has explored how the social contract was built on a sexual contract (which in theory regarded women as equal and complementary to men) but also on a racial contract that regarded people of color (whether Native American and Australian "savages," African slaves, or colonial peoples in European empires) as "subpersons,"[27] as less than equal and not so worthy to be included as free individuals in the white polity, and hence as noncitizens or at best second-class citizens in racialized, patriarchal, and imperial sociopolitical structures.[28] And although the racial contract in many ways trumped the marital contract, taken to paradigmatically define the relations between the sexes along the public/private division, "human reproduction, sex and anti-miscegenation" were also at the heart of the racial contract in ways that shaped the sexual and reproductive appropriation of nonwhite women. In other words, the social, sexual, and racial contracts reinforced each other in the household-based polities of patriarchal, racial, and imperial states.[29]

[26] Pateman, *The Sexual Contract*, 181.

[27] Indeed, "from the early modern period onward, 'race' became the vehicle through which certain groups of humans were deemed to be inferior, to be at the margins of humankind or even outside of humanity altogether," with modern conceptions of race in the seventeenth and eighteenth century built around theories about the stages of "civilization." See Carole Pateman, "Race, Sex, and Indifference," in Pateman and Mills, *Contract and Domination*, 136.

[28] See David Theo Goldberg, *The Racial State* (Maiden, MA: Blackwell Publishers, 2002); Charles W. Mills, *The Racial Contract* (Ithaca: Cornell University Press, 1997).

[29] For instance, Pateman recalls that, since race required purity of the bloodline, the interrelation between the sexual and racial contracts meant that the sexuality of whites and Blacks was seen quite differently. The white race was protected through prohibitions, both formal and informal, against interracial sexual relations, including through the lynching of Black men for the alleged "rape" of white women. Slaves were prohibited from marrying (although their unions were regularized after emancipation), and white men had an unconstrained access to women slaves who would pass their lifetime bondage onto their joint children. See Pateman, "Race, Sex, and Indifference," 134–35, 142–44. The forceful incorporation of nonwhites into the whiteman's patriarchal household deprived nonwhite men of the citizenship standing of the social contract as well as of

Despite some variations around the specific understanding of the marriage contract, not only contract theorists but also modern philosophers in general came to embrace the separate spheres tradition, defining distinct places for men and women in society and in relation to the state, thus shaping women's specific citizenship in the sense of belonging or contributing to the community. The dispute over the proper understanding of the marriage contract between Immanuel Kant and Georg Hegel, beautifully portrayed in Pateman's book, is particularly interesting because it reflects the dominance of the contract logic but also the witty efforts to make it compatible with the modern understanding of romantic marriage. For Kant, Pateman explains, marriage was the "Union of two Persons of different sex for life-long reciprocal possession of the sexual faculties,"[30] a vision that, by the way, is not radically different from Locke's own views on the marriage contract, "consist[ing] chiefly in the spouses' Communion and Right in one another's Bodies."[31] Kant also argues that women have no civil personality[32] and must, therefore, be kept away from the state and subject to their husbands – their masters – in marriage. Kant sees no contradiction in affirming women's lack of civil personality and, at the same time, their capacity to enter marriage[33] because for him the marriage contract is sui generis: in the marriage contract, an individual acquires a right to a person – or, more exactly, as

"the right to their wives" that the sexual contract would have otherwise secured, while also depriving nonwhite women of the possibility to inhabit "their private sphere" instead of being forcefully incorporated into their owners'. On the ways in which the racial contract trumped the sexual contract, see, for instance, Pauline E. Schloesser, *The Fair Sex: White Women and Racial Patriarchy in the Early American Republic* (New York: New York University Press, 2002), 33. Here Schloesser explains how one's status in slavery nullified the protections of coverture, for if either husband or wife was enslaved, the owner retained his right to treat his or her slave as property. See also Mills, "Intersecting Contracts," 182. Mills explains how, in the colonial enterprise, "nonwhite women in the *public* sphere are in the *private* sphere of the white patriarch, as minors subject to their paternal rule," in an extended colonial family model where white women were "simultaneously subordinated individually in their private families and privileged collectively as co-rulers" of the white colonial family household. See Mills, "Intersecting Contracts," 182.

30 Immanuel Kant, *The Philosophy of Law*, trans. W. Hastie (Edinburgh: T. & T. Clark, 1887), §24, 110, cited in Pateman, *The Sexual Contract*, 168, n. 38.

31 John Locke, *Two Treatises of Government*, ed. P. Laslett (Cambridge: Cambridge University Press, 1967), II, §78, cited in Pateman, *The Sexual Contract*, 168, n. 39.

32 Immanuel Kant, *Political Writings*, ed. H. Reiss (Cambridge: Cambridge University Press, 1970), 139, cited in Pateman, *The Sexual Contract*, 169, n. 43.

33 Pateman, *The Sexual Contract*, 169.

Kant states, revealing his bias, "the Man acquires a Wife"[34] – who thus becomes a thing, a commodity, or a piece of property. But, because both parties become things (back to a neutral framing!) and each is the possession of the other, they both regain their standing as rational personalities and make use of each other as persons, not property,[35] whereby the mutual use of sexual desire implies disposing over the person as a whole, including "the welfare and happiness and generally over all the circumstances of that person."[36]

Hegel would later rebel against Kant's conception of the marriage contract as one for reciprocal use,[37] claiming that this represented a degraded understanding of marriage. Instead, marriage was to be seen as a distinct form of ethical life, nothing less than a "contract to transcend the standpoint of contract."[38] For Hegel, the end of marriage was not mutual sexual use. Rather, being at the origin of the family, the marriage contract created a substantive relation constituted by "love, trust, and common sharing of their entire existence as individuals"[39] and represented a breeding laboratory of citizenship and the necessary private foundation for public life.[40] In other words, the marital family signified a space for the formation of human consciousness in which children learned and adults were continually reminded of what it means to be a member of a small association based on love and trust, something they needed to be adequately prepared for to participate in the universal public sphere of civil society and the state.[41]

Notice that, in spite of this significant disagreement in their perception of the marriage contract, both Kant and Hegel still considered that it was women's destiny to remain in the natural private sphere of the family, with sexual difference necessarily entailing a patriarchal division of labor.[42] This is because, in essence, and not unlike Rousseau, both Kant

[34] Kant, *Philosophy of Law*, chap. 2, sec. 3, §23, 109, cited in Pateman, *The Sexual Contract*, 170, n. 46.

[35] Pateman, *The Sexual Contract*, 170.

[36] Immanuel Kant, *Lectures on Ethics*, trans. L. Infield (New York: Harper and Row, 1963), 166–67, cited in Pateman, *The Sexual Contract*, 170, n. 49.

[37] G. W. F. Hegel, *Philosophy of Right*, trans. T. M. Knox (Oxford: Clarendon Press, 1952), §75, and addition to §161, cited in Pateman, *The Sexual Contract*, 173, n. 56.

[38] Ibid., §163, cited in Pateman, *The Sexual Contract*, 174, n. 58.

[39] Ibid., cited in Pateman, *The Sexual Contract*, 174, n. 60.

[40] Pateman, *The Sexual Contract*, 175.

[41] Ibid., 176.

[42] These philosophical theories were in turn supported by scientific research on the biology/nature of women developed in the second half of the eighteenth century, which produced

and Hegel shared a vision of women's nature as unfit for public, political, or civil reason. Women's lack of civil personality, alluded to by Kant, would explain why they must be kept away from the state and subject to their husbands – their natural superiors and masters[43] – in and through marriage, and women's capacity to enter the marriage contract would simply represent a concession to his maxim that all human beings have the rational capacity to act according to universal moral principles.[44] But even Hegel, who criticized both Rousseau's social contract theory and Kant's marriage contract, still shared their patriarchal understanding of masculinity and femininity and, therefore, of the public and private division of spheres and labor.[45] For Hegel, the "difference in the physical characteristics of the two sexes has a rational basis and consequently acquires an intellectual and ethical significance,"[46] dictating women's substantive destiny in the family, where they must cultivate family piety as their ethical frame of mind. Lacking in the capacity to submit to "the demands of universality,"[47] women cannot enter into civil public life and must remain in the natural private sphere of the family.[48] The husband has the "prerogative to go out and work for the [family's] living to attend to its needs, and to control and administer its capital."[49]

One century after Rousseau, John Stuart Mill – the liberal thinker who, out of commitment to the principles of liberty and equality, most explicitly and actively rebelled against the subjection of women to men – was still accepting and justifying the separation of spheres as well as the system of gender roles articulated around it. A strong defender of sex equality, Mill had come a long way compared to his enlightened predecessors, and he specifically argued for the reform of existing marriage law, rejecting the conferral of legal power and control by the husband on the person, property, and freedom of action of the wife. And yet, he still saw no contradiction between affirming women's equality and

a new discourse on the fundamental differences between the two sexes. See Andrea Maihofer, *Geschlecht als Exiszenzweise* (Frankfurt: Ulrike Helmer Verlag, 1995) 22ff, 91ff.

43 Kant, *Philosophy of Law*, chap. 2, sec. 3, §26, 111–12, cited in Pateman, *The Sexual Contract*, 172, n. 53.

44 Pateman, *The Sexual Contract*, 171.

45 Ibid., 176.

46 Hegel, *Philosophy of Right*, §165, cited in Pateman, *The Sexual Contract*, 176, n. 65.

47 Ibid., §166, and addition, cited in Pateman, *The Sexual Contract*, 176, n. 66.

48 Pateman, *The Sexual Contract*, 176.

49 Hegel, *Philosophy of Right*, §171, cited in Pateman, *The Sexual Contract*, 177, n. 67.

accepting women's position as housewives and economic dependents.[50] Like the classical social contract theorists, Mill also assumed that sexual difference would necessarily lead to a sexual division of labor.[51] For Mill, the husband, being usually older than his wife, would typically have more authority in decision-making.[52] As a result, even when women are recognized equal opportunity in education and the "power of earning," and marriage is reformed in egalitarian terms – as he argued should be the case – a woman, by virtue of becoming a wife, will still choose to remain in the home, protected by her husband, as if that were her "career." In sum, choice, consent, and contract were still acknowledged to be at the basis of women's legitimized condition of subjection now that patriarchy could no longer be affirmed as a man's natural right. This, then, is how the division of roles and women's subordination to men through the institution of marriage came to be part of the DNA of modern constitutionalism. Concessions to "nature" were thus made to justify both the racial and the sexual contracts that underlay the modern order.

1.3 Women's Struggle in Revolutionary Constitutionalism and the Birth of Modern Patriarchal Family Law

The philosophically imbued common sense of the time and the dominant notions of femininity built around it explain why, in revolutionary constitutionalism, women's political disenfranchisement was, for the most part, not constitutionally articulated but simply assumed as the natural order of things on which the new order was built. At the same time, this should not mislead us into thinking that there was no resistance on the side of women against this purportedly natural order of things. Indeed, a vivid debate about women's rights – unduly silenced in most constitutional law textbooks to date – did take place in those revolutionary times. Unsurprisingly, the debate had the challenging of the marital institution at its core, and calls to reorganize marriage were expressed in academic, political, and popular circles. Women's

50 *Essays on Sex Equality*, ed. Alice S. Rossi (Chicago: University of Chicago Press, 1970), 45–46, cited in Pateman, *The Sexual Contract*, 161, n. 23.
51 Pateman, *The Sexual Contract*, 162.
52 John Stuart Mill, "The Subjection of Women," in Rossi, *Essays on Sex Equality*, 168–70, cited in Pateman, *The Sexual Contract*, 162, n. 25.

participation in governance was also contested.[53] For women, the idea of distinguishing emancipatory claims pertaining to the so-called private sphere from those affecting the public sphere never made sense, as their lives were too clear a testimony to their intertwined nature and the complexity of the resulting limitations.

The revolutions in America and France inspired calls to vindicate women's rights and reorganize marriage as part of the same emancipatory agenda.[54] Mary Wollstonecraft's *Vindication of the Rights of Women*, published in England in 1792, would inspire the constitutional campaigns of women for decades to come. A year earlier, in 1791, Olympe de Gouges wrote her Declaration of the Rights of Women and the Female Citizen, claiming that the revolution would only take effect when all women became fully aware of their deplorable condition and of the rights they had lost in society. The declaration replicated the rights granted to men, point by point, now including women, but also added a reference to women's reproductive autonomy and a postscript, a "Form for a Social Contract between Man and Woman" – essentially, a manifesto of equality in marriage.[55] Many decades later, Elizabeth Cady

[53] Coontz, *Marriage, a History*, 151.

[54] The fact that women were major and active political actors during the revolution is best captured by the label "les tricoteuses," or "knitters," which was coined to qualify those women who were involved in revolutionary politics, as their political participation often meant that they had to bring along domestic work that they could not afford to interrupt or set aside. See Dominique Godineau, *Les citoyennes tricoteuses: Les femmes du peuple à Paris pendant la Révolution française* (Aix-en-Provence: Alinéa, 1988) cited in Stéphanie Hennette-Vauchez and Ruth Rubio-Marín, "The Political Subject: A Gendered Enterprise," in *The Cambridge Companion on Law and Gender*, eds. Stéphanie Hennette-Vauchez and Ruth Rubio-Marín (forthcoming). Also, it is important to recall that revolutionary women were extremely vocal in their claim to the right to bear arms and be members of the national guard; in fact, although they were never formally admitted, some actually joined the army. See Dominique Godineau, "De la guerrière à la citoyenne. Porter les armes pendant l'Ancien Régime et la Révolution française," *Clio. Femmes, Genre, Histoire*, no. 20 (2004): 43–69.

[55] Irving, *Gender and the Constitution*, 7. It is worth noting that legislative drafts in revolutionary France, which were discarded under Napoleonic influence, embodied a genuine attempt to actively apply an egalitarian lens to the family, which would cancel any notion of marital authority, and to promote one of equality between the spouses in terms of assets management and patrimonial decision-making. See Hugues Fulchiron, "La femme, mère et épouse dans le droit révolutionnaire," in *Les femmes et la Révolution française*, vol. 1, ed. Marie-France Brive (Toulouse: Presses universitaires du Mirail, 1989), 377, cited in Hennette-Vauchez and Rubio-Marín, "The Political Subject," in Hennette-Vauchez and Rubio-Marín, *The Cambridge Companion on Law and Gender* (forthcoming).

Stanton would repeat the exercise by recasting the text of the American Declaration of Independence as a Declaration of Sentiments, adopted at the Seneca Falls Convention in 1848. Convened by Cady Stanton and Lucretia Mott to discuss the social, civil, and religious condition of women, the convention demanded the admission of women to all the rights and privileges that belonged to women as citizens, including the franchise and the legal rights to property.[56] Although these expressions are the most visible, claims for women's rights were not limited to the centers of political revolution. Instead, similar demands were also expressed in the 1790s in Germany and Italy.[57]

Despite these feminist expressions of revolutionary fervor, hierarchy and paternalism prevailed in the end, and in a conservative reaction to the revolutions, American and French legislators rolled back on the political freedoms that women and children had gained at the height of revolutionary activity, backing away from far-reaching interpretations of individual rights.[58] Indeed, in order to suppress women's claims during the postrevolutionary period, most states passed their first explicit prohibitions on women's political rights.[59] In so doing, they evinced the dominant fear that revolutionary agitation for the "rights" of women would ultimately undermine all family ties.[60] This suggests that, notwithstanding the revolutionary exaltation of the rights of the individual, as opposed to those that were conditioned by group belonging, the heterosexual reproductive family was taken as the foundational societal group, unchallenged in its capacity to shape the status of individual rights and

[56] At the same time, it has been observed that, throughout the nineteenth century and into the first decade of the twentieth century, it was very difficult for white women to see Black women as political equals in a context of widespread racism and colonialism and that white women, who attacked the sexual contract, could still compare their position favorably to that of the women of "lesser races." See Mills, "Intersecting Contracts," 147–48. See also Schloesser, *The Fair Sex*, 80–82, on how, in the United States, Mercy Otis Warren, Abigail Smith Adams, and Judith Sargent Murray – leading female intellectuals in the revolutionary period – all ended up by acquiescing to the terms of racial patriarchy, embracing a vision of themselves as possessing distinctive virtues in a particular civilizing mission in the early days of the republic. On the need to challenge "imperial feminism," meaning the way the movement for female emancipation in Britain was closely linked to theories of racial superiority and empire, see Valerie Amos and Pratibha Parmar, "Challenging Imperial Feminism," in *Feminism and "Race,"* ed. Kum-Kum Bhavnani (Oxford: Oxford University Press: 2001), 19.

[57] Coontz, *Marriage, a History*, 152.

[58] Ibid.

[59] Coontz, *Marriage, a History*, 153.

[60] Ibid., 152.

obligations pertaining to the household.[61] The new democracies were thus better understood as household democracies.

Interestingly, men were not the only ones who feared the possibly destructive effects of women joining the public sphere. This apprehension was also understandably shared by many women who cared not only about family ties but also about the system of dependencies built around it. In the time following the revolution, women worried that, in the context of their actual economic dependence on men, full legal equality would expose them to more risks than secure new opportunities.[62] Full equal rights without enough opportunities in the marketplace and without men's involvement in the domain of care were, at the time and would remain throughout the history of women's constitutionalism, a threatening combination pushing many women – out of pragmatism, if not in principle – to be eager to retain "women's prerogatives," especially when seen as protection rather than outright subordination and when referred to those women for whom the household system, because of class and race, entailed a certain degree of protection.

Modern family law, as a separate body of positive law, consolidated precisely during this time.[63] And it did so in ways that entrenched and regulated women's hierarchical subordination within the domestic sphere, becoming thus the cornerstone of women's distinctive citizenship. The French Civil Code, or *Code Napoléon*, widely praised as the first realization of liberal principles in private law and exported to many other countries in Europe and the French colonies, was adopted in 1804 and embodied the preservation of "the traits of medieval patriarchy the longest and in its purest form."[64] The leading rule that "the man owes his wife protection; the wife owes the husband obedience" (article 213) was generally interpreted to mean that, although a wife could formally own property, she was under the legal guardianship of her husband, who also held legal custody over their descendants, including unwed

[61] See Anne Verjus, *Le cens de la famille. Les femmes et le vote* (Paris: Éditions Belin, 2002); Jennifer Heuer, *The Family and the Nation: Gender and Citizenship in Revolutionary France, 1789–1830* (Ithaca: Cornell University Press, 2005); Suzanne Desan, *The Family on Trial in Revolutionary France* (Berkeley: University of California Press, 2006).

[62] Coontz, *Marriage, a History*, 153.

[63] Janet Halley and Kerry Rittich, "Critical Directions in Comparative Family Law: Genealogies and Contemporary Studies of Family Law Exceptionalism," *American Journal of Comparative Law* 58, no. 4 (2010): 756.

[64] See Marianne Weber, *Ehefrau und Mutter in der Rechtsentwicklung* (Tübingen: J. C. B. Mohr, 1907), cited in Lister et al., *Gendering Citizenship in Western Europe*, 32.

daughters, who were not authorized to abandon the paternal household even after coming of age. Forever a minor according to the code, the wife had to request her husband's authorization for a number of acts, including being a party to legal proceedings, signing contracts, setting herself up in a profession, doing financial transactions, and joining a political party or trade union. The revolutionary goal of guaranteeing all children, including those born out of wedlock, equal claims on their parents was also abandoned, with Napoleon famously stating that the nation had no interest in recognizing bastards.[65] This code had a great impact on all countries subjected to the French empire during the Napoleonic Wars, including Belgium and the Netherlands, and left its mark even after those countries or regions gained independence. The cultural impact of French liberalism went beyond its territorial domains and was, for instance, exported to the French colonies and to the colonies of other European countries that, like Spain, had also been affected by it. This would naturally carry repercussions on Latin America.[66]

However, the *Code Napoléon* was not an exception. The German Civil Code, in fact, was quite similar. Coming into force in 1900, it reestablished paternal authority and reasserted a husband's right to decide in "all matters affecting communal life of the couple."[67] Moreover, the husband was in principle granted the exclusive right to manage property, including his wife's, and to intervene and even end his wife's employment contracts.[68] In English common law, also exported to the British colonies, the so-called coverture doctrine remained the dominant paradigm. As described in William Blackstone's commentaries on English common law, a marriage license was something like "a certificate of ownership of the wife, entitling the husband to her property, her body and its products, including the labour she engaged in for wages and the labour that produced offsprings; obliging him to provide for her care and feeding; giving him a cause of action against those who injured her or his interests

[65] Coontz, *Marriage, a History*, 153.

[66] See Jorge L. Esquirol, "René David: At the Head of the Legal Family," *Rethinking the Masters of Comparative Law*, ed. Annelise Riles (Oxford: Hart Publishing, 2001).

[67] See Bürgerlichen Gesetzbuches, § 1354 BGB, in force until 1953. For the (unsuccessful) protests against the German Civil Code, see Ute Gerhard, *Unerhört: Die Geschichte der deutschen Frauenbewegung* (Hamburg: Rowohlt Verlag, 1990), 225ff.

[68] Bürgerlichen Gesetzbuches, § 1358 BGB.

in her; making him responsible for her actions; and giving him the rights to control her."[69]

In sum, the synthesis of the revolutionary outbreak was a unique middle way between egalitarian and patriarchal views of marriage whereby people came to view each sex as having a distinctive and complementary role, based on an underlying racialized power structure that trumped the sexual contract built around marriage. Leaving aside the few male and female "radicals" who, consistent with the logic of the Enlightenment, defended the idea that men and women should have the same rights, most people accepted the general view that the family should remain the main domain of women's activity, a sphere attached with a unique moral quality that had to be "protected from contamination by involvement in men's mundane spheres of activity."[70] A family exceptionalism, so to speak, was built into the constitutional project since its very inception, carving out what in federal terms we could visualize as a space of white male supremacy and governance. It is within this space where appeals to the law of nature (and men and women's distinct biology) still dictated the norms, with slavery, in some instances, and the artifact of contract and consent, in others, legitimating various degrees and forms of exploitation of women's productive and reproductive labor – a labor that would sustain the new market economy – and a new legal discipline, family law, providing the relevant legal architecture.

1.4 The Constitutional Embedding of the Breadwinner Family Order

Throughout the nineteenth century and the first half of the twentieth century, the male breadwinner heterosexual marriage only gained cultural hegemony in Europe and North America even though it continued to represent an unachievable ideal for many. As wage-earning work and commerce gradually moved out of the household and into separate work sites, the division between a husband's wage-earning activities and a wife's household activities grew, as did the sense that women and men

[69] See William Blackstone, "Of Husband and Wife," in *Commentaries on the Laws of England*, ed. Wayne Morrison (London: Routledge-Cavendish, 2001), vol. 1, chap. 15. Master of the household, the husband could command his wife's obedience even through the use of "moderate correction" (i.e., corporal punishment or "chastisement") if she defied his authority.

[70] Coontz, *Marriage, a History*, 153.

lived in separate spheres: women overseeing that of domesticity and men that of the economy and governance.[71] Removed from the sphere of the cash economy, women homemakers were doomed to financial dependence on their husbands. Culturally, the home became the sanctuary in which women could be protected from "the turmoil and contamination of economic and political life" and men could escape the "materialistic preoccupations of their daily workday."[72]

Many women, whose mothers had embraced the revolutionary feminist demands of the 1790s, abandoned earlier calls for equality and fully advocated the doctrine of separate spheres for men and women.[73] As a result, by the middle of the nineteenth century, there was a growing consensus throughout Western Europe and North America that the love-based marriage, in which the wife stayed at home protected and supported by her husband, was the path to happiness. In real life, this ideal was still difficult to achieve, especially for lower-class wives and, in the United States, African American women. Since the beginning, the male breadwinner/female homemaker family model for the middle and upper classes had rested on the existence of large sections of the lower class who could not live up to it[74] and for whom the growing cultural hegemony of femininity notions defined around this model entailed dignitary and material forms of harm. At the same time, the duality between productive and reproductive work was established, and women's labor and productive tasks within the household were culturally transformed into acts of "homemaking" and expressions of "love" rather than work. In the world of cash transactions, women's care labor became increasingly undervalued.[75] To the extent that women were still expected to perform a role in the public world, this would occur either as an extension of their caretaking duties to the wider, and typically local, community (as in their involvement in poverty relief programs) or through the influence they could have on their husbands and children.[76]

This social and political gender order found some constitutional manifestations both in the Old and the New Worlds. However, most of the revolutionary constitutional texts remained silent about women, the

[71] Ibid., 154.
[72] Ibid., 156.
[73] Ibid., 161.
[74] Ibid., 169.
[75] Ibid., 156.
[76] Ibid., 163.

family, or the gender order articulated around it. This is not surprising, considering the emphasis placed during the revolutionary period on foregrounding the individual and breaking away from the ancien régime's privileging of intermediate bodies. Some revolutionary constitutions, though, contained indirect traces of the dominant gender order that affected not only women but also all those destined to domestic chores. Spain's first constitution in the revolutionary period, that of 1812, for instance, included a clause (article 25) providing that men devoted to the domestic service should have their privileges of citizenship suspended.[77] The more commonly shared silence around the family and the underlying gender order was instead a reflection of the "normalization," "naturalization," or "depolitization" of the marital family–based political order. Still, despite the silence of the early constitutional texts, there is no doubt that the heteronormative procreative family as a foundational unit of society was the hegemonic construct built into sex-silent texts during the first constitutionalism. In this family-based political order, "state law looked to the head of household to govern and represent his legal dependents, not only children, but adults affiliated through institutions including slavery, employment and marriage" (slaves, servants, and wives).[78]

Because of its historical continuity and the permanence of its text, the United States Constitution, and American constitutionalism in particular, offers a wonderful vantage point from which to observe the gendered construction of this new political and economic order as well as of the central role of marriage and the traditional family, especially in the latter's articulation as a natural repository of care and human interdependence. In its original text, dating back to 1787, the US Constitution did not contain any reference to family or marriage. Yet the direct link between the construction of the family organization and marriage, on the one hand, and the exclusion of women from the public sphere, on the other – interpreted as including both the market and the domain of civic and political rights and duties – can be confirmed through the gendered subtexts present in many of the Supreme Court's decisions. In 1872, Justice Bradley, concurring in the denial of the right to practice law to women in general, focused on the petitioner's status as a married woman

[77] Raquel Rico Linage, *Constituciones históricas* (Sevilla: Universidad de Sevilla, 1989), 23.

[78] Siegel, "The Nineteenth Amendment," 456. See also Hendrik Hartog, *Man and Wife in America: A History* (Cambridge, MA: Harvard University Press, 2000), 101.

and bluntly stated this now infamous opinion that simply reflected the order of the day:

> The constitution of the family organization, which is founded in the divine ordinance, as well as in the nature of things, indicates the domestic sphere as that which properly belongs to the domain and functions of womanhood. The harmony, not to say identity, of interests and views which belong, or should belong, to the family institution is repugnant to the idea of a woman adopting a distinct and independent career from that of her husband. . . . It is true that many women are unmarried and not affected by any of the duties, complications, and incapacities arising out of the married state, but these are exceptions to the general rule. The paramount destiny and mission of woman are to fulfil the noble and benign offices of wife and mother. This is the law of the Creator. And the rules of civil society must be adapted to the general constitution of things, and cannot be based upon exceptional cases. (Bradwell v. Illinois, 83 U.S. 130, 141–42 [1872])

Just a few years after deciding *Bradwell* in 1873, a case on polygamy gave the Supreme Court the opportunity to explicitly recognize the centrality of marriage, not only as the foundational relationship for the nuclear family but also as the very basis of society itself in "civilized nations," in a language that plainly gives visibility to the racial undertones of the sexual contract. In Justice Waite's words, "Marriage, while from its very nature a sacred obligation, is nevertheless, in most civilized nations, a civil contract, and usually regulated by law. Upon it society may be said to be built, and out of its fruits spring social relations and social obligations and duties with which government is necessarily required to deal."[79] Over thirty years later, in 1908, by upholding a state law limiting women's work hours (meaning only those outside the home, of course!), the Supreme Court would still insist that "a proper discharge of [a woman's] maternal functions – having in view not merely her own health, but the wellbeing of the race – justif[ies] legislation to protect her from the greed, as well as the passion, of man."[80]

1.5 First-Wave Feminism and Women's Constitutional Engagements

Despite their constitutional erasure and political disenfranchisement, by the mid-nineteenth century, women were organizing, often in clubs and

[79] See Reynolds v. United States, 98 U.S. 145, 165 (1878).
[80] See Muller v. Oregon, 208 U.S. 412, 422 (1908).

associations, around a growing feminist conscience to react against their constitutional silencing and their political disenfranchisement,[81] but also against the oppressive and often violent family structure that they understood to be the backbone of their subordination. They did so in a global movement known as first-wave feminism (even though those recognizing the attempts of women in the early revolutionary times might disagree with this label). The turn of the century would finally see women's first important victories materialize in constitutional law.

The struggles for transformation were many and more or less peaceful in nature and certainly limited if we take the position of racialized women into account, with the women's movement between the 1870s and 1920s largely segregated.[82] As regards the realm of constitutionalism and the various fights to turn emancipatory ideals into a constitutional reality, women relied both on the constitutional interpretation of sex-silent texts as well as on attempts to bring about new constitutional norms. In all instances, women never limited themselves to a women's rights agenda, though this was certainly a key part of their demands. Rather, women sought to advance their broader views on what constituted a just society, a vision undeniably shaped by their experiences as women. Because these experiences were in fact different for different women, in their various struggles, women faced the obstacle of speaking with one voice, not only because of the natural difficulty of setting a priority order between the competing emancipatory causes of the time, or their different positionalities, but also, once again, because of the natural fear for the costs that a process of gender roles disestablishment could entail for women themselves, especially for those who were both

[81] The women's movement was divided along class lines from the start, and not all of women's groups placed the same importance in achieving suffrage. In Germany, for instance, the *Allgemeine Deutsche Frauenverein* (German Association of Female Citizens) was founded in 1865 and is perceived as the beginning of the German (bourgeois) women's movement. The ADF claimed a right to work for (bourgeois) women. The women's worker movement began in 1869 with the *Verein zur Fortbildung und geistigen Anregung der Arbeiterfrau* (Association for the Lifelong Training and Intellectual Stimulation of Working Women). One of the most important representatives of the more radical wing of the women's movement was Hedwig Dohm (1813–1919), along with Clara Zetkin (1857–1933). Already in 1876, Dohm demanded comprehensive and full equality of women in legal, economic, and political terms, as well as the right to vote for women. See Hedwig Dohm, *Der Frauen Natur und Recht: Zur Frauenfrage zwei Abhandlungen über Eigenschaften und Stimmrecht der Frauen* (Berlin: Wedekind & Schwieger, 1876).

[82] See Louise Michele Newman, *White Women's Rights: The Racial Origins of Feminism in the United States* (New York: Oxford University Press, 1999).

subordinated and comparatively privileged by it. Tellingly, however, in crafting their demands, most women challenged the idea of the family as a natural order free from the demands or aspirations of justice. Instead, women typically identified abuse and exploitation wherever they encountered it in their own lives, including, and often beginning, in the domestic sphere, whether in their own or in that of others.

The fight for women's suffrage has come to epitomize women's mobilization and transnational coalition-building during the nineteenth century, but this struggle was not always fought for with constitutional tools (even though it did have an explicit constitutional dimension in several countries). The fact is that women were engaged in various other constitutional causes that concerned their own status in the political community as well as in other causes of public interest they thought worth pursuing.

In the nineteenth-century United States, for instance, many women were active abolitionists who drew analogies between their experiences of domestic servitude and the enforced servitude of slavery and underlined the dual exploitation of slave women, who were exploited for their labor and also subjected to sexual abuse by their masters. In this sense, it has been said that women were both in large part "the agents and the subjects of the Thirteenth Amendment to the US Constitution," which was ratified at the close of the Civil War in 1865 and prohibited slavery.[83] Also, in 1873, the Women's Christian Temperance Union was established with the aim of prohibiting and politicizing family abandonment, domestic violence, and sexual abuse, which at the time were primarily attributed to the consumption of alcohol by unruly husbands. The US Supreme Court's interpretation of the commerce clause had been contrary to the goal of prohibition, and therefore an amendment was successfully sought in 1919 with the ratification of the Eighteenth Amendment, allowing federal powers to mandate prohibition at a national level. This decision, however, would be reversed through the Twenty-First Amendment in 1933, when it became clear that the amendment had not succeeded in its initial goal, thus returning control to state jurisdiction. And in 1920, the Nineteenth Amendment to the US

[83] See Akhil Reed Amar, "Women and the Constitution," *Harvard Journal of Law and Public Policy* 18, no. 2 (1995): 465–74, at 465–67. Middle-class women were at the heart of the British antislavery movement, and after the British ended slavery in 1833, they turned their attention to the United States. That said, it has been noted that "women antislavery activists commonly came to the movement out of Christian duty... and a sense of cultural superiority." See Pateman, "Race, Sex, and Indifference," 148.

Constitution was finally passed, an achievement that ratified the enfranchisement of women.

In Australia, the scenario was different. Women's involvement in the constitutional process during the 1890s, which would lead to the adoption of the country's constitution in 1900, had already centered on securing women's franchise (recognized already in two colonies at the time of drafting), with women's suffrage leagues proving incredibly active. Yet the Woman's Christian Temperance Union also played a leading role in another early constitutional cause, whereby women sought to ensure that the prohibition of the sale and trade of liquor, which they hoped would help overcome domestic violence and abandonment, remained within state jurisdiction.[84]

Participation in constitution-making and reform was not, however, the only early expression of constitutional engagement by and for women at the time. In several countries, court litigation and constitutional interpretation to ensure women's inclusion were tried first. In the United States, the adoption of the Fourteenth Amendment in 1868, whose historical purpose was to force former slave states to recognize the legal citizenship of emancipated slaves, seemed to open a window of opportunities for women when it recognized citizenship to "all persons born or naturalized in the United States and subject to the jurisdiction thereof," compelling states not to make or enforce any law that should "abridge the privileges or immunities of citizens of the United States." This new provision prompted people like Myra Bradwell to approach the Supreme Court to claim equal privilege as a US citizen and the ability to earn a livelihood by obtaining a license to practice as a lawyer, only to be told by the court that the privileges referred to did not include her claim and be subsequently sent home to do a woman's work.[85]

There were several attempts at accessing voting rights through constitutional litigation and interpretation, taking advantage of the fact that women's political disenfranchisement was often (though not always)[86] not explicitly articulated in the constitutions of the time. These attempts would not achieve positive outcomes, however. For instance, a systematic approach to constitutional interpretation was unsuccessfully tried by Susan B. Anthony in 1872 in the context of her trial for the federal crime

[84] Irving, *Gender and the Constitution*, 76–78.

[85] See Bradwell v. Illinois, 83 U.S. 130 (1872).

[86] In Canada, for instance, article 41 of the Constitution Act of 1867 specifically limited voting to "every male British subject."

of voting without the right to vote, only to find that such interpretation did not support her claim to be granted suffrage as a "citizen privilege" because the Fifteenth Amendment, ratified in 1870, had not listed gender or sex (only race, color, or previous condition of servitude) among the prohibited grounds for denying the right to vote.[87] Likewise – and to the horror of many women suffragists, at least of those who had also fought for abolition – section 2 of the Fourteenth Amendment (adopted only two years before and reducing the number of members of the House of Representatives to which a state was entitled if it disenfranchised any *male* inhabitant of such state) introduced for the first time the word "male" into the constitution, linking it to the franchise and thus rendering explicit what had so far remained an implicit provision; that is, that the constitution only covered male suffrage.[88] In spite of this, in 1874, Virginia Minor, a leader of the women's suffrage movement who had failed to register to vote in Missouri elections, unsuccessfully tried her constitutional luck under the Fourteenth Amendment's Privileges and Immunities Clause.[89] Little did she know that Maria Montessori, the famous Italian pedagogue,[90] or Julieta Lanteri,[91] one of Argentina's feminist pioneers, would years later also unsuccessfully try theirs, only to find the constitutional doors in their countries still equally shut to their suffragist demands.

1.6 The Struggle for Women's Suffrage and the Separate Spheres Tradition

Soon enough, it became obvious that, in those settings in which creative constitutional interpretation would not open the door to women's political enfranchisement, the only conducive way was to turn to law reform,

[87] Irving, *Gender and the Constitution*, 10–11.

[88] See Kathleen M. Sullivan, "Constitutionalizing Women's Equality," *California Law Review* 90, no. 3 (2002): 736.

[89] See Minor v. Happersett, 88 U.S. 162 (1874).

[90] See Susanna Mancini, "From the Struggle for Suffrage to the Construction of a Fragile Gender Citizenship: Italy 1861–2009," in *The Struggle for Female Suffrage in Europe: Voting to Become Citizens*, eds. Blanca Rodríguez-Ruiz and Ruth Rubio-Marín (Leide-Boston: Brill, 2012), 378, citing R. Romanelli, "Circa l'ammissibilità delle donne al suffragio politico nell'Italia liberale. Le sentenze pronunciate dalla magistrature nel 1905–1907," in *Laboratorio di storia. Studi in onore di Claudio Pavone*, eds. Paolo Pezzino and Gabriele Ranzato (Milano: Franco Angeli, 1994).

[91] Corte Suprema de Justicia de la Nación [CSJN] [National Supreme Court of Justice], 15/05/1929, "Don Julieta Lanteri Renshaw, solicita se ordene su enrolamiento en su carácter de argentina naturalizada," Fallos de la Corte Suprema de la Nación, t. 154, 283.

constitutional or otherwise. In the United States, a campaign began for what was hoped would be the Sixteenth Amendment, recognizing that the right of citizens to vote should not be abridged by the nation or by any state on account of sex. Although the proposal was first introduced in Congress in 1878, more than forty years were to pass before it succeeded with the ratification of the Nineteenth Amendment in 1920. Notice that this achievement came after women had already gained suffrage on equal terms with men and in many other parts of the world through nonconstitutional means:[92] Australia (1902), Finland (1905), Norway (1907), and Canada (1918). Because at the time none of these countries had a bill of rights that could be interpreted to entrench women's exclusion from the public sphere, constitutional amendment was unnecessary and legal reform sufficient. As a matter of fact, two colonies in Australia (South Australia and Western Australia) had already enfranchised women before the country's constitution was finally adopted in 1900, and this created an opening for women's involvement in the constitutional process, even in colonies where they still lacked the right to vote.[93] Although the suffragists' lobbying efforts did not succeed in guaranteeing women's suffrage in federal elections, a provision (section 41) was included in the constitution whereby women who were already entitled to vote in their colonies would be ensured the right to vote in federal elections. This then created pressure for women's

[92] Limited voting rights had been gained by women in Sweden, Finland, and some western US states in the late nineteenth century. See Ellen Carol DuBois, "Women Suffrage around the World: Three Phases of Suffragist Internationalism," in *Suffrage and Beyond: International Feminist Perspectives*, eds. Caroline Daley and Melanie Nolan (New York: New York University Press, 1994), 252–76. In 1893, New Zealand, then a self-governing British colony, granted adult women the right to vote, and the self-governing British colony of South Australia did the same in 1895. Australia federated in 1901, and women acquired the right to vote and stand in federal elections in 1902. See Allison Sneider, "The New Suffrage History: Voting Rights in International Perspective," *History Compass* 8, no. 7 (2010): 692–703. The first European country to introduce women's suffrage in 1907 was the Grand Duchy of Finland, then part of the Russian Empire. Norway followed suit in 1913. In 1918, the United Kingdom enfranchised women over the age of thirty who met a property qualification; equal voting rights would not come, however, until 1928. The Irish Free State provided equal voting rights from its inception in 1922 until its dissolution in 1937. Still, most European, Asian, and African countries did not pass women's suffrage until after the World War I and several European countries only did so after World War II, including France (1944), Greece (1952), Italy (1946), Switzerland (1971), and Liechtenstein (1984). See Blanca Rodríguez Ruiz and Ruth Rubio-Marín, eds., *The Struggle for Female Suffrage in Europe: Voting to Become Citizens* (Leiden: Brill, 2012).

[93] Irving, *Gender and the Constitution*, 15.

enfranchisement in the other colonies and resulted in the granting of female suffrage in 1902 in the first federal Franchise Act.[94] This story, as many others that we will recount, seems to suggest that, where it was affirmed, rights-based constitutionalism could be more of an obstacle than a facilitator of the assertion of women's equality. Why? Because it implicitly entrenched a male-dominated family order.

Whether fought for through constitutional means or otherwise, women's access to suffrage had an undeniable constitutional dimension. It was fought for and won on the basis of a new conscience of women as political actors, exasperated by the relatively little importance attached to the cause by traditional political parties and even by women's bourgeois associations. Suffragist organizations, proliferating at the turn of the century, took the lead through a movement with international ambitions, which consolidated with the formation of the International Women Suffrage Association between 1899 and 1902, recruiting women from all walks of life and challenging dominant definitions of womanhood articulated around domesticity.[95] Women's access to voting rights also came to define, in each country, the "consenting" body that would henceforth be entitled to participate in constitution-making or reform. More importantly, women had a difficult time claiming their equal stature as regards the enjoyment of all other rights and freedoms constitutionally enshrined for as long as the right to political participation was formally denied to them. In essence, both symbolically and practically, the denial of women's suffrage represented the confirmation of the gender order that the constitutions were built on – namely, one entrenching the separate spheres ideology and women's motherhood-citizenship. No surprise, then, that in the struggle for women's franchise the arguments used for and against suffrage, including those by women who mobilized against it, were all reflective of the dominance of the separate spheres both as a reality and, just as importantly, as an ideological construct.

Clearly, there were many reasons why women faced the challenge of speaking with one voice in the struggle for suffrage. Divisions along class lines (with bourgeois women leading the feminist movement in most countries, sometimes fearing suffrage would be granted to insufficiently educated women) and political lines (with progressive forces sometimes claiming that women would vote more conservative under the influence

[94] Ibid.
[95] Rubio-Marín, "The Achievement of Female Suffrage in Europe," 12–13.

of tradition and religion, and conservative forces making strategic considerations along similar lines) entrenched the conflict, although there were also divisions along ethnocultural and racial lines.[96] Nationalist struggles of various kinds also got in the way of women on both sides of the Atlantic. In the complex social and political context of Habsburg Austria, for instance, ethnic and nationalistic loyalties impeded a united suffrage movement. And much the same happened in Switzerland, where cultural differences and language barriers between the different regions made a unified effort difficult to achieve. The language question also caused a division within the Finnish Women's Association. And in Ireland, membership in suffrage societies was depleted by defections to newly formed female nationalist or unionist organizations. In the United States, the National Woman Suffrage Association broke with the abolition tradition, advocating women's rights first and foremost, as they opposed the ratification of the Fifteenth Amendment, whereas the more moderate American Woman Suffrage Association maintained its alliance with the old abolition cause throughout.[97]

Yet, both in Europe and America, women's disagreement also revolved around the possible effects that granting women the right to suffrage

[96] These divisions were not only connected to struggles as to whether race or sex-based disenfranchisement deserved the greatest concern but also to the relative importance that should be attached to the cause of suffrage and the challenge to the separate spheres tradition in the creation of a truly comprehensive women's movement. Many Black women resented the fact that white leaders dismissed their concerns – such as miscegenation, interracial rape, lynching, and their admittance to race segregated public spaces – as "race questions," irrelevant to the foremost goal of "political equality of women" of the women's movement. See Louise Newman, *White Women's Rights*, 6, 7, 134. At the same time, the separate spheres ideology and the rebellion against women's motherhood-only citizenship could not resonate fully with those women who had never been confined to the "private sphere" and to normative motherhood but were rather expected to work outside their home, often in precarious or exploitative conditions.

[97] See Janet Zollinger Giele, *Two Paths to Women's Equality: Temperance, Suffrage, and the Origins of Modern Feminism* (Woodbridge, CT: Twayne Publishers, 1995), 114. See also Ellen Carol Dubois, *Feminism and Suffrage: The Emergence of an Independent Women's Movement in America, 1848–1860* (Ithaca: Cornell University Press, 1999), 162–202. The difficult political dilemma arose around the passing of the Fifteenth Amendment, which would grant suffrage rights to freed male slaves, despite the fact that Black and white women continued to be excluded from the ballot box. The two most prominent white leaders, Elizabeth Cady Stanton and Susan B. Anthony, opposed the amendment and the controversy would split the movement for a generation. By the 1890s, white suffragists would enter into "extremely unsavory alliances with racist Southern politicians." See Pateman, "Race, Sex, and Indifference," 149.

might have on the traditional family.[98] Conservative forces in particular considered female suffrage to be politically contentious because it could erode family harmony and generate social instability. Antisuffragists stressed that women were especially suited and exclusively destined for the work of family maintenance. Lacking the capacity for managing public affairs, suffrage rights would simply distract women from their obligations as wives and mothers.[99] Instead, women were to be represented by men as the heads of the family household. Two contradictory arguments were thus lumped together – namely, that women's suffrage was unnecessary, because a unity of interests (which the male head of household could defend) was presumed, and that it could disrupt family harmony in case of a clash of interests, making the subordination of women the only solution.[100] In Sweden, for instance, a parliamentary commission was formed and put in charge of investigating the potential consequences of female suffrage on birth rates and marriage. And, in the United Kingdom, one of the arguments that liberal Prime Minister William Gladstone held in stubborn resistance to female suffrage was that women could be potentially corrupted by politics and thereby threaten the family.[101] In fact, it was also in Britain that the National League for Opposing Women's Suffrage was founded in 1910.

At stake was not just ideology but a reasonable concern. After all, the separate spheres tradition held out the promise of economic subsistence for a subset of women and a defined social place as a wife to women from "all respectable classes." True, women's economic opportunities had improved by the end of the nineteenth century, but they were still very limited. In this context, working-class women, and not only middle-upper class women, had reasons to fear, for they would have to compete economically against men, as antisuffragists claimed they would be compelled to do if the sexed order of society came to be challenged and the system of subsidiary protections for women in the incipient welfare state were entirely dismantled in the name of full equality.[102] "Middle-class husbands could offer their wives a more comfortable existence than spinsters could provide for themselves."[103]

98 Rubio-Marín, "The Achievement of Female Suffrage in Europe," 15–17.
99 Reva B. Siegel, "She the People: The Nineteenth Amendment, Sex Equality, Federalism, and the Family," *Harvard Law Review* 115, no. 4 (2002): 947–1046, at 979.
100 Ibid., 981.
101 Rubio-Marín, "The Achievement of Female Suffrage in Europe," 16.
102 Coontz, *Marriage, a History*, 182.
103 Carole Pateman, "Three Questions about Womanhood Suffrage," in *Suffrage and Beyond: International Feminist Perspectives*, eds. Caroline Daley and Melanie Nolan (New York: New York University Press, 1994), 341.

While some feared that women's suffrage would disrupt family life, the argument that, as mothers and providers of care, women were unsuited for political concerns was sometimes turned on its head.[104] Not only did suffragists draw on the examples of Australia and New Zealand to show that female suffrage had not led to a neglect of homes and families, but they also sustained that, on the contrary, motherhood made for good and caring citizens particularly suited to act in local politics.[105] It was argued that the nation would benefit if women's natural inclinations to care were put to public service, especially at a time when the legislative concern with social welfare was increasing. If women were included in the public sphere, they would stand for patriotic motherhood. The enfranchisement of women thus came to be defended as a means of "social housekeeping," giving women a say in the regulation of municipal services and in the industrial conditions that they and their children had to endure.[106]

These were not just conservative or male voices, or both. Many women and activists shared the view that men's and women's contributions to the nation were of a different kind. In other words, there was a key dividing line between egalitarians and "maternalists" among those fighting for suffrage. Egalitarians relied on considerations of justice, calling on the universal language of individual freedom and equality. They also underscored the fact that what prevented women from participating in the public world was not nature itself but men's monopoly on education, training, paid employment, and suffrage. Maternalists, on the other hand, based their claims on the particular role and different needs of women, emphasizing maternal values and women's caring approach to life, which, they said, could and should be used to advance the national interest. There were also divisions in regard to the relevance of women's suffrage for the subversion of the separate spheres tradition. Many middle-class and working-class suffragists linked the vote to women's economic independence, regarding it as a way to improve their conditions and their positions as workers in male-dominated workplaces. However, for other suffragists, including those who were recruited from the women's temperance movement, suffrage was vital to strengthen the position of women in private life and eliminate men's domestic tyranny.

[104] Rubio-Marín, "The Achievement of Female Suffrage in Europe," 17.

[105] Krista Cowman, "Female Suffrage in Great Britain," in Rodríguez Ruiz and Rubio-Marín, *The Struggle for Female Suffrage in Europe*, 275–76.

[106] See Eileen Boris, "The Power of Motherhood: Black and White Activist Women Redefine the 'Political,'" *Yale Journal of Law & Feminism* 2, no. 1 (1989): 25–49.

It seems that, in the end, pro-suffrage voices often managed to successfully combine several types of arguments in making their case, some affirming and some subverting the separate spheres ideology.

Compelling and important as the campaign for women's suffrage was, it would not be the only effort for women's full political membership. The campaign to acquire, retain, and transmit citizenship/nationality in their own right and on equal terms to men was also waged for decades. Delayed for almost a hundred years, independent and equal constitutional citizenship was denied to women in most countries until well into the twentieth century, in some cases, even after World War II. And like the suffrage campaign, it also concerned the recognition of women as independent and autonomous members of a nation state in their own right, as lack of nationality entailed deprivation of equal political rights and residential security, something that epitomized the lack of recognition of the full membership in one's constitutional community.[107] In fact, women's suffrage organizations were expanded to incorporate the goal of citizenship equality. The fact that the practice of tying women's nationality to that of their husbands was supported by the international community and defended on the need to ensure family unity comes as no surprise.[108]

1.7 Sex Equality Enters Constitutionalism and So Does Motherhood and the Protection of the Family

Given the preponderance of the gender order on which modernity was built, it is not surprising that the conquest of female suffrage, even in those cases in which it was clearly enshrined in the constitution, did not automatically lead to an overall reinterpretation of the text nor was it able to dismantle the many legal distinctions between men and women on which the dominant ideologies around the breadwinner family model were based. In fact, just as women's attempt to use the Fourteenth Amendment's Equal Protection Clause to rule out sex-based privileges had systematically failed in the United States, so did their attempts to rely on the Citizenship Clause of the same amendment to challenge conditional marital nationality laws[109] and to use the newly conquered

[107] See Irving, "Citizenship and Nationality," 387.

[108] Ibid., 389.

[109] See Mackenzie v. Hare, 239 U.S. 312 (1915), in which Ethel Mackenzie unsuccessfully challenged the legal provision in the Expatriation Act of 1907, which had deprived her of

Nineteenth Amendment as a broader litigating tool to claim access to other domains of citizenship, including citizenship duties such as jury service in front of state courts.[110] Suffrage was conquered, but first-wave feminism had not yet defeated the paramount family model and the political order based on it. Thus, with the single exception of short-lived and unsuccessful attempts to impose special occupational safety and hour regulations on establishments employing women (which, in the time of the economic laissez-faire heyday of the *Lochner* era,[111] were seen as unduly infringing against liberty of contract), the expansive reading of the revolutionary changes embodied in the Nineteenth Amendment's suffrage clause was systematically unsuccessful, despite some of the

the possibility to be registered in the California electoral roll following the enfranchisement of women in that state in 1911. The court reminded her that "[t]he identity of husband and wife is an ancient principle of our jurisprudence" and that a foreign marriage was voluntarily entered into "with notice of the consequences," therefore concurring that "marriage of an American woman with a foreigner is made tantamount to voluntary expatriation."

110 See Jennifer K. Brown, "The Nineteenth Amendment and Women's Equality," *Yale Law Journal* 102, no. 8 (1993): 2194–201. Similarly, in other countries, the legislative conquest of suffrage generally gave little significance to the broader interpretation of the constitution with respect to defending women's political rights. The Canadian Persons Case best exemplifies this. Women had gained suffrage in Manitoba, Saskatchewan, and Alberta in 1916 and, at the federal level, in 1918. However, this did not include *all* women. The Dominion Elections Act of 1920 excluded people disfranchised by a province "for reasons of race" from the federal franchise. This meant people of Japanese, Chinese, and Hindu (meaning any non-Anglo-Saxons from the Indian subcontinent) origin were excluded from federal elections in British Columbia and Saskatchewan. This would last until 1948 and, needless to say, included women as well as men. Also, under Canada's Indian Act, "status Indians" were denied the right to vote, while aboriginal people were enfranchised in 1960. In 1928, the Canadian Supreme Court was confronted with the question as to whether, for the purpose of being appointed to the Canadian Senate, the word "persons" in section 24 of the Canadian Constitution (the 1867 British North America Act) should be read as including women too. The Supreme Court denied it, relying on an originalist interpretation that reasserted the fact that, in 1867 and under common law, women were incapable of holding public office. See Edwards v. Attorney General of Canada, [1928] S.C.R. 276 (Can.). Fortunately, on appeal, the Privy Council (the highest court of appeals in the British Empire) reversed the decision based on a liberal interpretation that came from seeing the Canadian Constitution as a living tree capable of growth and expansion to match the evolution of societal values. See Edwards v. Attorney General of Canada, [1930] C.A. 124 (Can.). For a detailed history of the case, see Robert J. Sharpe and Patricia I. McMahon, *The Persons Case: The Origins and Legacy of the Fight for Legal Personhood* (University of Toronto Press, 2007).

111 Lochner v. New York, 198 U.S. 45 (1905).

Supreme Court's more celebratory rhetoric.[112] In fact, as we shall see, this dominant family model and the social order built around it were some of the main reasons behind the failure of the US Constitution to incorporate, by way of amendment, a direct ban on sex discrimination, something that was first proposed in 1923 soon after the granting of female suffrage.[113]

If, in the United States, the breadwinner family ideology shaped constitutionalism in spite of the absence of explicit traces in the constitutional text (as the constitution did not include any reference to the family or marriage other than for the purpose of federalism),[114] in

112 See Adkins v. Children's Hospital, 261 U.S. 525, 553 (1923): "In view of the great – not to say revolutionary – changes which have taken place . . . in the contractual, political and civil status of women, culminating in the Nineteenth Amendment . . . the ancient inequality of the sexes, otherwise than physical . . . has continued with diminishing intensity."

113 After the conquest of the right to suffrage, the women's movement splintered. Under the leadership of Alice Paul, the National Women's Party decided to focus more narrowly on removing sex-based disabilities from the law of marriage and other legislation, pursuing formal equality in the law without addressing law and norms governing sex, reproduction, and the relation of market and family labor. This led to the introduction of state legislation and, in 1923, the first Equal Rights Amendment or ERA. And, although by focusing on discrimination on account of sex or marriage, both Paul and Florence Kelley had sought to avoid invalidating sex-based protective labor legislation, by mid-decade, Paul's drive for the ERA divided the movement, with social welfare-feminists concerned that it would invalidate the sex-based protective labor legislation on which working women with family responsibilities depended at a time when unions would not organize women. Birth control and the rights of Negro women were also postponed, and many women interested in the rights of Black people, pacifism, and birth control departed the NWP. See Siegel, "The Nineteenth Amendment," 472–71.

114 It was on the basis of the *Lochner* era concept of contractual and economic liberty that the Supreme Court recognized for the first time in the 1920s some protection for parental prerogatives in the education and raising of children, grounding it on the Fourteenth Amendment's substantive due process guarantees. See Meyer v. Nebraska, 262 U.S. 390 (1923), and Pierce v. Society of Sisters, 268 U.S. 510 (1925). The right to family life (understood, even then, as autonomy and privacy, and not as an institution deserving the active support of the state) was only affirmed for the first time in *Griswold v. Connecticut*, 381 U.S. 479 (1965), with the protection of marital privacy and the married couple's use of contraceptives. It has since expanded to cover a whole set of family-related autonomy rights (sometimes recognized as pertaining to the individual and sometimes to the family, but always framed as negative or noninterference rights), including the right to marry, procreate, terminate pregnancy, cohabitate with extended family, raise children, and engage in sexual intimacy. The family was simply assumed to be the underlying unit in the social structure of the US constitutional system, and this is supported by the fact that *Griswold* (where the Supreme Court first asserted the notion of marital privacy) referred to it as a zone of privacy derived from several constitutional amendments – that is, as (an implicit) "right older than the Bill of Rights," thus

Europe, where, for the most part, democratic constitutionalism failed to establish itself solidly until the second half of the twentieth century – first, against monarchical reactionary forces, and then, against fascist and totalitarian movements – the same ideology shaped and limited women's citizenship. European enlightenment constitutions had also remained silent about the family and women's constitutional status, providing at best, general equality clauses with no specific mention to sex.[115] Contrary to the United States, though, where the original constitutional text has remained valid and amendments have been difficult to achieve, Europe's tormented constitutional history and the proliferation of constitutional texts that characterized it have allowed for a textual reception of changing understandings regarding women's status and the ways this status came to be shaped by prevailing conceptions of the family. In several European countries, women's newly conquered voting rights opened women's access to constitution-making for the first time during the interwar period. In every site, the number of women present remained token, yet, whenever they could, women used their newly gained powers to ensure a sex equality provision but also, tellingly, to include the protection of motherhood and the family under the constitution. In other words, equality of rights and women's specific protections as mothers were, from the start, seen not only as complementing but also qualifying each other, given the relatively unchallenged dominant gender ideology.

Germany's 1919 landmark Weimar Constitution, which governed Germany during the Weimar Republic (1919–1933), provides a good illustration of the coexistence of constitutional sex equality provisions, harvesting the fruits of first-wave feminism, the dominant family ideology, and women's involvement in constitution-making. Indeed, the forty-one women (i.e., 10 percent) that had been elected thanks to the newly conquered right to vote (first recognized in 1918) participated in the drafting of the Weimar Constitution, which recognized men and women "fundamentally" the same *civic* rights and duties (under article 109) as well as women's equal access to the civil service (article 128). The text also contained a clause reflecting the social centrality and political relevance of the family structure in general and of motherhood in

suggesting its foundational and natural character. See also David D. Meyer, "The Paradox of Family Privacy," *Vanderbilt Law Review* 53, no. 2 (2000): 527.

115 This was, for instance, the case of the French Declaration of the Rights of Man and of the Citizen, proclaiming "all to be equal under the law" (article 6).

particular. Thus, under a chapter devoted to life in community, article 119 recognized that the marital family, based on the equality of both genders, enjoyed the special protection of the constitution and entrusted both the state and the community to protect the welfare of families and mothers.[116]

In the constituent assembly drafting the Weimar Constitution, women from different political parties had disagreed as to whether the protection of motherhood should be limited to cover marital children only (something conservative women saw as necessary to protect the marital family) or should instead encompass unwed mothers and their out-of-wedlock children, a debate with obvious class undertones that the postwar context and the general increase of single-headed households allowed to minimize somewhat.[117] There was also disagreement about whether the role of motherhood was really compatible with women joining public office. Interestingly, though, the need for motherhood and the family to be protected for the sake of women's well-being gathered consensus across the board and was key to the German socialist women's understanding of the constitutional protection that women required.[118] In other words, the generalized assumption about distinct gender roles, backed by the reality of the time, survived the constitutional recognition of equality, which helps explain why the sex equality provision was qualified with two caveats: the limitation to civic rights and duties and the reference to men and women enjoying "fundamentally" (*grundsätzlich*) the same rights and duties. Such qualification was especially justified on the basis

[116] More specifically, article 119 provided that "Marriage, as the foundation of the family and the preservation and expansion of the nation, enjoys the special protection of the constitution. It is based on the equality of both genders. It is the task of both the state and the communities to strengthen and socially promote the family. Large families may claim social welfare. Motherhood is placed under state protection and welfare."

[117] In the end, the Weimar Constitution also offered some protection for children born out of wedlock, whose welfare had been a concern for many German feminists, especially during World War I. The Weimar text (article 119) kept a separate sentence referring to mothers' claims to special care, suggesting that all mothers, and not only those bound by marriage, deserved such special protection.

[118] See Julie C. Suk, "Feminist Constitutionalism and the Entrenchment of Motherhood," in *Special Issue: Law and the Imagining of Difference*, ed. Austin Sarat (Bingley: Emerald Publishing Limited, 2018), 119. In fact, several of the women present in the assembly had taken an active part in social movements to protect mothers in the two decades preceding this constitutional moment. Different groups of women certainly differed as to the reasons why mothers deserved special protection, but the fact that this protection was needed so that family and mothers alike could meet their various obligations was widely shared by both liberal bourgeois feminists and social democrats.

of men's distinctive military obligations, despite the fact that, following Germany's defeat in World War I, the Treaty of Versailles had imposed severe restrictions on the German military, essentially prohibiting compulsory military service.[119] Tellingly, although the qualifier would be kept in the end, it was deemed unnecessary even by the strongest supporters of the constitutional sex equality provision, since "women were fulfilling similar obligations of citizenship, such as educating and raising children" and this seemed to be uncontroversially accepted by all.[120]

The German Constitution was not an isolated case. Other constitutions of the interwar period, especially constitutions of socialist inspiration and greater expectation of state involvement, also mentioned protections of motherhood and social reproduction[121] as well as the termination of "sex-based privileges." This was, for instance, the case of article 25 of the 1931 Constitution of the Second Spanish Republic, which also added the qualifier "fundamentally" when referring to men and women's equal rights. In some instances, this general cancellation of sex-based privileges came hand in hand with the granting of equal political rights to women for the first time. This was true of the 1931 Spanish Constitution but also of others, including the 1920 Czech

[119] Ibid.

[120] Ibid. Some neighboring constitutions followed the German example: for instance, the 1920 Czech Constitution acknowledged that "privileges due to sex, birth, or occupation shall not be recognised" (article 106.1) while enshrining the notion that "wedlock, family, and motherhood should be under the special protection of the law" (article 126).

[121] In particular, constitutions of socialist inspiration were often explicit on the need to provide for social reproduction directly and not just by protecting mothers and families. This was the case of the 1936 Constitution of the Soviet Union, with article 122 providing that "Women in the U.S.S.R. are accorded equal rights with men in all spheres of economic, state, cultural, social and political life. The possibility of exercising these rights is ensured to women by granting them an equal right with men to work, payment for work, rest and leisure, social insurance and education, and by state protection of the interests of mother and child, prematernity and maternity leave with full pay, and the provision of a wide network of maternity homes, nurseries and kindergartens." This feature would be a constant in countries of socialist tradition, both during and after the Soviet empire. In this regard, we should note that the most influential work that touched on the issue of women's oppression influencing Eastern European policies was Engels's *On the Origin of Family, Private Property and the State* published in 1884, in which Engels claims that women's oppression has its roots in the emergence of the monogamous family, which in its turn emerged because of the development of private property accumulated by men through a surplus of production, hence the need to significantly move women's household tasks under the responsibility of the community. See Friedrich Engels, *On the Origin of Family, Private Property and the State* (London: Penguin Books, 2010).

Constitution, the 1920 Austrian Constitution, and the 1921 Polish Constitution. Nevertheless, the full abolition of sex-based privileges and distinctions was not a general feature of European interwar constitutionalism, and some countries would go back and forth on the matter. Some constitutional provisions specifically recognized women's political status as being inferior to men's (such as article 6 of the 1923 Romanian Constitution), while others simply allowed the legislator to elaborate on the distinctions between men and women that they deemed justified according to "the specific functions" of each (such as article 16.2 of the 1934 Austrian Constitution). In fact, it was rather illusory to proclaim an unqualified equal status as long as the dominant breadwinner family model ideology, and the legal order which articulated it, continued attaching different functions to men and women, with family codes in particular drawing all kinds of distinctions between husband and wife and, in that sense, defining, more than constitutions themselves, the confines of women's constitutional membership.

An important reason why the family ideology left a clear constitutional imprimatur in Western Europe has to do with the early formation of the welfare state model.[122] It certainly helps explain the growing preoccupation with the protection of both the institution of the family, to which the social function of care was primarily assigned, and motherhood, as a valued role but also a potentially vulnerable condition (especially in situations of "family failure," where the figure of the male head of the household was missing). Initial programs of social provision – established across the West in the formative period of the welfare state, approximately from the 1880s to the onset of World War I – were designed to fit and reinforce the family wage system, with men acting as breadwinners and women as primary caretakers, domestic workers, and secondary wage earners. This model of women's social citizenship, built around a "two-channel" or "patriarchal" welfare state,[123] entrenched women's dependent citizenship by retaining them as objects of protection owing to their weak or dependent nature, or else to their

[122] In the welfare literature, there is however some variation as to the role expected of the family and the breadwinner model in different European countries. See, for instance, Gøsta Esping-Andersen, *Three Worlds of Welfare Capitalism* (Princeton, NJ: Princeton University Press, 1990).

[123] See Ann Shola Orloff, "Gender and the Social Rights of Citizenship: The Comparative Analysis of Gender Relations and Welfare States," *American Sociological Review* 58, no. 3 (1993): 323.

roles as mothers and caretakers.[124] In this light, constitutional references to the dominant family model and to the role of the state in supporting it were not necessarily seen as in contradiction with the abolition of sex-based distinctions or privileges but rather as necessary protections owed to women in their expected roles as caretakers. After all, the system of protections was also, of course, a reflection of the political economy of the time, when women were offered mostly domestic or manufacturing jobs that were extremely poorly paid and that only those in dire need would take, amid rampant job segregation and pay discrimination.[125]

The breadwinner family model was indeed so widely accepted that it conditioned the emancipatory horizon of many forms of activism. Thus, a "maternalist" strand of welfare politics developed in the first half of the twentieth century, proposing full state support to widowed or abandoned mothers. The intended aim was to allow these women in "broken" or "failed families" to stay at home and care for their children. Some reformers went as far as to demand a general "endowment of motherhood" for all mothers, in the belief that this would express a political recognition on the work of mothering and independent income.[126] Yet, as a matter of fact, this general approach did not succeed, except in a weak form as children's allowances that most states paid to mothers but that were never sufficient to support a woman without a husband. This is how "maternalist" programs came to be primarily a back-up for the "failures" of the family wage system, and most benefits were restricted to single mothers, usually widows but sometimes also divorced, separated, or unmarried women. Parity between benefits for stay-at-home mothers and benefits for wage earners, as well as a standard of living for single mothers comparable to their married counterparts, remained elusive goals – a reality that was not free of stigmatizing effects on women, often poor and racialized.

[124] See Nancy Fraser, "After the Family Wage," in *Justice Interruptus: Critical Reflections on the "Postsocialist" Condition* (New York: Routledge, 1996), 41–66. Fraser explains how, when women accessed the rights of citizenship, the latter had already a masculine profile and how, when they accessed social citizenship, they did so through a rhetoric that entrenched their dependent citizenship – that is, as objects of protection because of their weak and dependent nature, or in their roles as mothers and protectors. "In this way, women's social citizenship appears anchored in the rhetoric of domestic needs, rather than civil or political citizenship, that dominate the rights discourse in the public sphere."

[125] Coontz, *Marriage, a History*, 209.

[126] Orloff, "Gender and the Social Rights of Citizenship," 323.

It was in this context that many Western European constitutions came to recognize the social centrality of the family structure, making direct reference to the need to attach special protection to motherhood and inaugurating a maternalist tradition in constitutionalism that was then exported to many corners of the world. In fact, some European constitutions of the interwar period were quite thorough in terms of the entrenchment of the breadwinner marital family model, with its distinctive gender roles and its implications with respect to the differentiated expected contributions to the common good. In this regard, perhaps the bluntest example of the period is the 1937 Irish Constitution (replacing the 1922 text and still in force today), which, infused with a politicized Catholic ethos, glorified the sanctity of the family. Article 41, devoted to the family, reads:

> (1.1) The State recognises the Family as the natural primary and fundamental unit group of Society, and as a moral institution possessing inalienable and imprescriptible rights, antecedent and superior to all positive law.
>
> (1.2) The State, therefore, guarantees to protect the Family in its constitution and authority, as the necessary basis of social order and as indispensable to the welfare of the Nation and the State.
>
> (2.1) In particular, the State recognises that by her life within the home, woman gives to the State a support without which the common good cannot be achieved.
>
> (2.2) The State shall, therefore, endeavour to ensure that mothers shall not be obliged by economic necessity to engage in labour to the neglect of their duties in the home.
>
> (3.1) The State pledges itself to guard with special care the institution of Marriage, on which the Family is founded, and to protect it against attack.

That this provision could be reconciled with the generically expressed principle of equality, also contained in the Irish Constitution, is better understood if we look at the exact framing of the equality clause (article 40.1), which affirms equality but also recognizes the possibility of legitimate distinctions on the basis of different physical and moral natures or social functions.[127]

In any event, in Europe, the abolition of sex-based privileges through some form of sex equality clause was seen from the start, and to a greater or lesser extent, as compatible with the preservation of the traditional

[127] Article 40.1 provides that "all citizens shall, as human persons, be held equal before the law. This shall not be held to mean that the State shall not in its enactments have due regard to differences of capacity, physical and moral, and of social function."

family order. However, the fear that women's proclaimed constitutional equality might threaten both the established gender order and the system of protections put into place for women as mothers and dependent spouses provoked different results in other contexts. Notably, it contributed to the failure of the Equal Rights Amendment (ERA) in the United States. This amendment, which galvanized efforts of formidable women,[128] would have recognized that "equality of rights under the law shall not be denied or abridged by the United States or by any State on account of sex." It was first proposed in 1922 – around the same time that equal rights provisions were starting to flourish in European constitutionalism – precisely by those who saw in it a natural sequence after the conquest of suffrage through the Nineteenth Amendment. Yet it took almost fifty years for Congress to finally adopt it in 1972, yielding to the pressure of second-wave feminist activism. Within the following two years, thirty of the required thirty-eight states had ratified it, but thereafter the pace of ratification slowed dramatically and then grounded to a halt. It ultimately faded away in 1982, since proponents were unable to secure the necessary state ratifications despite strenuous advocacy and a three-year extension.[129]

At the time, the ERA's ultimate failure was the result of conservatism appealing to caution. There were those who saw the amendment (just as suffrage opponents had done in the past) as a threat to the family structure. Their success, though, relied on appealing to those who instead feared the wiping out of special protections for women workers or dependent spouses in the context of a labor market in which women could still not be expected to compete on equal terms. In her narrative, Phyllis Schlafly, the strongest anti-ERA advocate, uplifted the role of motherhood to that of "home executive," arguing that marriage and motherhood were the most reliable security the world could offer to women.[130] Schlafly, as well as, more generally, the members of the STOP ERA movement, argued that the ERA would invalidate state laws that made it the obligation of the husband to support his wife financially, wiping out the right of a wife to receive social security benefits based on

[128] See Julie C. Suk, *We the Women: the Unstoppable Mothers of the Equal Rights Amendment* (New York: Skyhork Publishing, 2020).

[129] In March 2017, the ratification process resumed, and Nevada became the first state in thirty-five years to ratify the ERA. The last ratification needed was achieved on Jan. 15, 2020, in Virginia with, as of yet, uncertain legal consequences.

[130] See Susan Marshall, "Ladies against Women: Mobilization Dilemmas of Anti-feminist Movements," *Social Problems* 32, no. 4 (1985): 357.

her husband's earnings. One thing is clear: their primary concern was certainly not with women (including many Black women and other racialized minorities), for whom a supportive husband was not in the picture or who were married to men with very little income. These were women, in other words, who were already destined to care and homemaking, although not of their own children or of their own homes, as well as to other menial and underpaid jobs.

By comparing the constitutional evolution in both Europe and the United States, we can only hypothesize that the US Constitution's lack of European-style motherhood and family protection clauses allowed the equal rights provision to be perceived as much more threatening to traditional family roles and the system of protections for the legally enforced dependency of women than the equality provisions of the interwar and, as we shall see, postwar European constitutions. In the end, few of those who opposed the ERA argued for women's inequality: instead, they urged the importance of preserving women's traditional family roles and what they called "traditional family," which, for many, had in fact never been more than a cultural construct.[131] Timing was also a crucial factor, since by the time the amendment was finally passed, the New Right had begun to focus on the family as a source of political mobilization, facilitating the drawing of links between the amendment and abortion and homosexuality in ways that ultimately helped sustain the argument of the threat to the traditional family, thus blocking its adoption.[132]

1.8 Post–World War II Constitutionalism: Between Continuation and Rupture, toward Inclusive Gender Constitutionalism

The embracing of sex equality became a defining feature of liberal democratic constitutionalism in the context of the human rights revolution and the second wave of democratic constitutionalism led by Western European countries coming out of the ashes of World War II. This constitutionalism would be exported to much of the world in the context of decolonization and also inspire constitutions in later waves of democratization. This is also the time when those European countries that came

[131] Reva B. Siegel, "Constitutional Culture, Social Movement Conflict and Constitutional Change: The Case of De Facto ERA; 2005–06 Brennan Centre Symposium Lecture," *California Law Review* 94, no. 5 (2006): 1379.

[132] Siegel, "Constitutional Culture," 1390.

to solidly embrace democratic constitutionalism but had not enfranchised women, including France, finally felt the urge to do so.[133] The first international convention focusing specifically on women, the Convention of the Political Rights of Women, adopted in 1952, similarly addressed many of the inequalities that women had enjoyed thus far in accessing and transmitting their nationality, although women's equal citizenship still remains unrealized in many countries of the world.[134] More crucially, the endorsement of either the equality between men and women, the ban on discrimination on the grounds of sex as well as of race, or the recognition of some notion of marital equality became a feature in all the main human rights instruments and constitutions adopted at the time.[135] A legally ordained hierarchy between the sexes or the races came to be seen increasingly in contradiction with the egalitarian ethos of liberal democratic constitutionalism and the new human rights order. Some of the postwar constitutions also added a reference to sex equality when referring to several of the domains and

[133] See Sylvie Chaperon, "The Difficult Struggle for Women's Political Rights in France," in Rodríguez Ruiz and Rubio-Marín, *The Struggle for Female Suffrage in Europe*, 305.

[134] National legislation does not allow women to confer their nationality on an equal basis with men in many countries in the Middle East, North Africa, and sub-Saharan Africa.

[135] See article 2 of the Universal Declaration of Human Rights, which guarantees the right of every human being to enjoy the rights enshrined in its provisions without distinction of any kind, including sex and race. Article 7, moreover, provides that "all are equal before the law and are entitled without any discrimination to equal protection of the law" and that "all are entitled to equal protection against any discrimination in violation of this Declaration and against any incitement to such discrimination." The International Covenant on Civil and Political Rights envisages a broad right to equality and non-discrimination in relation to the enjoyment of the rights laid down by its provisions and set forth in article 2.1. It also establishes an obligation for states parties to "ensure the equal right of men and women to the enjoyment of all civil and political rights set forth in the present Covenant" (article 3). Similarly, in article 23, it provides that the free and full consent of both parties to marriage is required. Similar provisions are also described by the International Covenant on Economic, Social and Cultural Rights in articles 2.2 and 3. At a regional level, the European Convention on Human Rights sets a prohibition of discrimination in article 14, whereby "the enjoyment of the rights and freedoms set forth [in the Convention] shall be secured without discrimination on any ground such as sex, race, colour, language, religion, political or other opinion, national or social origin, association with a national minority, property, birth or other status." Italy's 1947 constitution recognized citizens to have equal social dignity and be equal before the law without regard to their sex (article 3). Germany's 1949 Basic Law (*Grundgesetz* [GG]) also mentioned equality between men and women (article 3 [2] GG) and prohibited disadvantages on the basis of sex (article 3 [3] GG). The Preamble to the Constitution of 1946 that the current 1958 French Constitution refers to (which has been legally binding since 1971) also recognized equality of men and women before the law.

institutions in which women had traditionally been relegated to a lesser legal status, such as marriage, the working place, or the educational system.[136]

Although all of these signs expressed a commitment to remove the traces of sexual subordination from the legal realm by promising to deliver, at best, a gender-neutral order, some sex-based differentiations would linger for years to come, including some explicitly entrenched in constitutional texts, shaping women's differential constitutional membership. Moreover, the axis of gender differentiation was tackled to a lesser extent or only implicitly, and this limited the actual scope of the affirmation of "sex equality" as a feature of the new constitutional order. In other words, the basis of the sexual contract was not radically shattered: the active disestablishment of the separate spheres tradition, which dictated men's and women's distinctive roles in society, was not a core element of the early agenda of post–World War II constitutionalism.

After all, timewise, this was the heyday of the breadwinner family model. The 1950s and early 1960s in fact coincided with a strong postwar pronatalist movement encouraged by the relief that the end of two decades of depression and war had brought and the "delights at the benefits of the first real mass consumer economy, with millions of new houses built and furnished with comforts and time-saving appliances that would have been unthinkable just a few years earlier."[137] In this context, the idea that marriage should provide both husband and wife with "sexual gratification, personal intimacy, and self-fulfillment" reached its peak,[138] and divorce rates declined. When wives and mothers did take paid employment, it was generally part-time or in seasonal jobs. Gender and pay inequality in the labor market was rampant at the time and in fact grew during the 1950s and 1960s.[139] And, although African American and immigrant women were much more likely than whites to work outside the home – including in white homes – they were hugely underrepresented in mass media and popular culture.[140]

[136] For instance, the 1947 Italian Constitution, still in force, recognizes that marriage entails the moral and legal equality of the spouses (article 29.2) and that working women are entitled to equal rights and, for comparable jobs, equal pay as men are (article 37.1).

[137] Coontz, *Marriage, a History*, 230.

[138] Ibid., 233.

[139] Ibid., 236.

[140] Ibid. In fact, the "male breadwinner marriage" seemed so pervasive and so popular that social scientists of the time speculated that it was an inevitable result of modernization, since industrial societies relied on a necessary division of labor. This idea was articulated

Also, despite criticism of the bourgeois family in the dominant philosophy under state socialism, the persistent reference in constitutional texts to the need for public provisions of care,[141] and the insistence of women joining the sphere of production, many countries of the Eastern Block strongly promoted women both as mothers and coworkers with men through measures that encouraged women to bear children, influenced by a demographic concern (especially since the late 1960s). Apart from propagandistic means, such as different honorary titles for bearing and rising children, these measures included long maternity leaves, the criminalizing of abortion in the most extreme cases, and financial incentives for mothers. Given that communism had not been accompanied by a significant revisitation of hegemonic masculinity encouraging men to be more involved in the private sphere and in caretaking, this then translated more often than not in women having a double shift.[142]

These conditions were, to some extent, reflected in the constitutional gender order of the time. It therefore makes better sense to think of the postwar constitutional moment as representing a mix between continuity and progressive change rather than a moment of full rupture as far as the gender order is concerned. Tellingly, and in spite of women's political emancipation through enfranchisement, some evident sex-based distinctions remained, reminding of women's traditional exclusion from the public sphere of citizenship functions and duties. These included, paradigmatically, women's differential treatment regarding military duties,[143]

in 1963 in a hugely influential book by American sociologist William J. Goode entitled *World Revolution and Family Patterns*.

141 See, for instance, article 24 of the 1946 Yugoslav Constitution, which reads: "Women have equal rights with men in all fields of state, economic and social-political life. Women have the right to the same pay as that received by men for the same work, and as workers or employees they enjoy special protection. The state especially protects the interests of mothers and children by the establishment of maternity hospitals, children's homes and day nurseries and by the right of mothers to a leave with pay before and after childbirth."

142 Hilda Scott, *Women and Socialism: Experiences from Eastern Europe* (London: Alison & Busby, 1976), 212–13; Raluca Maria Popa, "Socialism and Gender (In)equality: Gender Relations in Socialist Theory and in the Context of Late Socialist Family and Reproductive Policies in Hungary, Poland and Romania," (master's thesis, CEU, Budapest College, 2003), 43–44. See also Barbara Einhorn, *Cinderella Goes to Market: Citizenship, Gender, and Women's Movements in East Central Europe* (London: Verso, 1993), 18–19.

143 Thus, in 1956, when Germany finally came to have an army, the constitution was amended. Article 12 (4), however, exempted women from being required by law to render service in any unit of the armed forces and prohibited them from being employed

but also, for instance, sex discriminatory rules on the succession of the Crown in some parliamentary monarchies, as in the case of Spain.[144] More importantly, human rights treaties,[145] European constitutions of the time, and those that, in the context of decolonization, emulated them, acknowledged the need to protect mothers and the institution of the family (oftentimes explicitly referred to as heterosexual or marital) as the foundational unit of society, the old repository of care and dependence, deserving of state recognition and protection. Within this family domain, the specific centrality of motherhood was also generally acknowledged. In fact, some of the new postwar constitutions were still quite specific about women's expected roles within the breadwinner family model, the dominant cultural symbol of the time, and demanded state assistance and support.

In this framework, post–World War II European constitutionalism continued with the maternalist strand of interwar European constitutionalism and replicated its combination of constitutional sex equality, motherhood, and family protection. Not everyone, however, had expected this coexistence to be peaceful. In fact, Germany's 1949 constitution or Basic Law (*Grundgesetz* [GG]), resulting from a constitution-making process in which women had less participation than in the former 1919 Weimar Constitution, had first been drafted without a sex equality provision, precisely because conservative forces feared that a constitutional guarantee of equality for women could be deployed to

in any service involving the use of arms. Subsequently, in a 1968 amendment, article 12 (4) was replaced by article 12a (4), providing that women could be obliged to serve in the armed forces, especially in medical care units, but would not be allowed to serve in any units involving the use of arms. Since Dec. 23, 2000, the text only makes reference to the prohibition of *forcing* women to serve in the armed units of the military, something they are nonetheless *allowed* to do since Jan. 1, 2001. Notice that also article 13 of the 1974 Swedish Constitution's equality clause, under the fundamental rights and freedoms chapter, provides that "no act of law or other provision may imply the unfavourable treatment of anyone on grounds of gender, unless the provision forms part of efforts to promote equality between men and women or relates to compulsory military service or other equivalent official duties."

144 See article 57.1 of the Spanish Constitution (1978).

145 See Wendy Lacey, "Gender Equality: International Law and National Constitutions," in Irving, *Constituions and Gender*, 140. Article 25.2 of the Universal Declaration of Human Rights establishes that both motherhood and childhood are to be given special protection. Article 10.2 of the International Covenant on Economic, Social and Cultural Rights provides that "Special protection should be accorded to mothers during a reasonable period before and after childbirth. During such period, working mothers should be accorded paid leave or leave with adequate social security benefits."

harm women by depriving them of their "special protections."[146] In the end, it fell on one of the only four women selected to participate in the constituent assembly, Elisabeth Selbert, to travel the country to advocate in favor of including an equality provision specifically referencing men and women.[147] Yet notice that one of the arguments Selbert would often put forward in making her case was that the equal rights provision was quite consistent with the law's different treatment of men and women and that the "husband's obligation to support [the family] was equivalent to the wife's obligation to educate the children and run the household." This, then, was the confined gender equality vision of the time.

As we have seen, the Grundgesetz eventually included an equality clause with a sex discrimination ban (articles 3 [2] and 3 [3], now with no restriction to the realm of civic rights compared to the Weimar Constitution, thus rendering the patriarchal family law in the German Civil Code unconstitutional). But, not surprisingly, Germany's Basic Law also included a provision referring to the protection of the family and mothers (article 6).[148] The precise scope of the latter and the question of whether or not it should protect out-of-wedlock children and unwed mothers, of which there were many after the war, once again divided women from different political perspectives and class sensibilities. Still, the German Constitution was not the only text, nor the most explicit one, addressing the dominant breadwinner family model in the postwar period. Italy's 1947 constitution (drafted with only a small participation of women – 21 out of 556 elected members – after women attained suffrage in 1946) also banned discrimination on the grounds of sex while at the same time recognizing the family as "a natural association founded on marriage" (article 29.1). The text also guaranteed "the moral and legal equality of spouses" (article 29.2), foreseeing, however, that "such equality is to take place within legally defined limits to protect the unity of the family." Article 36.1 referred specifically to the family wage concept, and

146 Suk, "Feminist Constitutionalism and the Entrenchment of Motherhood," 121.

147 Susanne Baer, "The Basic Law at 60 – Equality and Difference: A Proposal for the Guest List to the Birthday Party," in "The Basic Law at 60," ed. Susan Baer et al., special issue, *German Law Journal* 11, no. 1 (2010): 67, 70, 75.

148 Article 6 (1) of the German Basic Law, devoted to the family provides that "marriage and the family shall enjoy the special protection of the state," whereas article 6 (2) acknowledges that "the care and upbringing of children is the natural right of parents and a duty primarily incumbent upon them. The state shall watch over them in the performance of this duty." Of interest for our purpose is the fact that, according to article 6 (4) "every *mother* shall be entitled to the protection and care of the community" (my emphasis).

article 37, despite recognizing in paragraph 1 that "working women are entitled to equal rights and, for comparable jobs, equal pay as men," described in paragraph 2 that "working conditions have to be such as to allow women to fulfil *their essential family duties* and ensure an adequate protection of mothers and children" (italics are ours). As in postwar Germany, women in Italy spoke with different voices during its constituent process. They agreed on the necessary protection of motherhood and the family while holding competing visions as to the normative basis on which this protection should also be extended to single mothers. And yet, they all recognized motherhood as serving a social function and deserving protection as such.[149]

In sum, this incipient post–World War II European constitutionalism, which would later travel to the rest of Europe and also inspire constitutions in much of Latin America, Africa, and Asia down the road, not only acknowledged sex equality but also the central role of marriage and family as the natural bedrock for human society, recognizing at the same time the importance of the state in supporting the family and also, more specifically, motherhood. One has only to look at some historical examples to understand the extent to which this constitutionally enshrined ideology limited the breadth of the affirmation of women's equality. This is especially true when we consider that, in many countries, a systematic reform of family, criminal, employment, or social security legislation to render it gender neutral would only take place years after the constitution had come into force. Moreover, because the line that separates discrimination from justified differentiation has always been drawn based on what were considered to be "reasonable" or "objective" distinctions between the sexes, this allowed for different interpretations of what constitutional sex equality actually meant.

The case of Italy is most telling, for it shows how a sex equality mandate like the one included under article 3 of the 1947 Italian Constitution could be subverted to justify a disparate treatment, as long as some alleged difference between the situation of men and women were defended as reasonable. Italy did not pass its sex egalitarian legal reforms until the 1970s, including the first major family code reform approved in 1975.[150] Its 1947 constitution, as we have seen, affirmed that marriage entailed the "moral and legal equality of the spouses," yet qualified this equality principle with a phrase allowing for a wide realm of discretion

[149] Suk, "Feminist Constitutionalism and the Entrenchment of Motherhood," 125–28.

[150] See Legge 19 maggio 1975, n.151, G.U. May 23, 1975, n.135 (It.).

("within legally defined limits to protect the unity of the family" [article 29.2]). Because of this, the Italian Constitutional Court was confronted several times during the 1960s by various discriminatory provisions. Its early decisions show how a patriarchal and hierarchical understanding of the family and the assumed breadwinner family model guided its interpretation of what the notion of "family unity" entailed.

Most infamously, in 1961, the Constitutional Court upheld a Criminal Code provision making a wife's adultery a criminal offense, yet qualifying a husband's as such only when it was committed within the household or "notoriously" elsewhere, considering this distinction justified on the basis of the social consensus around the different meanings of men's and women's adultery as well as on the fact, taken as self-evident, that the wife's adultery constituted a more serious attack to family unity.[151] Although the court soon departed from this precedent, it had other opportunities to confirm the family ideology that was prevalent at the time. In 1966, for instance, the court reinforced a Civil Code regulation whereby, in case of widowhood followed by a new marriage, only women – and not men – were expected to inform judicial authorities. These, in turn, could then assess whether it was necessary to deprive women of the power to administrate the property children would inherit from the first marriage (fearing that the remarrying widow might be more distracted by the new family and its needs than would a remarrying widower under equivalent circumstances).[152] And, in 1967, the court once more validated a Civil Code regulation whereby, in case of consensual separation, a husband had to provide for all of his wife's needs regardless of the latter's financial situation (the wife being only obliged to do so in case of insufficient means of subsistence). This time, the different treatment was allegedly justified by a superior status granted by the law

[151] See Sentenza 64/1961 (Nov. 28, 1961). Fortunately, the court would depart from this doctrine only a few years later. See Sentenza 126/1968 (Dec. 16, 1968); 127/1968 (Dec. 16, 1968); 147/1969 (Nov. 27, 1969). Around the same time, other courts around the world were confronted with claims about dissimilar treatment of men and women regarding the crime of adultery, including as a result of colonial legacies. This was the case of the Indian Supreme Court, which in 1954 issued a judgment upholding section 497 of the colonial Indian Code of Criminal Procedure (Act XLV of 1860), which only punished the male adulterer and only allowed the husband of the female partner to bring charges. See Yusuf Abdul Aziz v. State of Bombay, AIR 1954 SC 321.

[152] See Sentenza 49/1966 (May 4, 1966).

to the husband within the family, a superior status that was said to imply both his "marital authority" and his obligation to provide for his wife.[153]

Although perhaps less overt in its constitutional incorporation of the traditional family model than Italy, Germany's constitutional history also provides a case in point. The 1949 German Basic Law entered into force before the main sex egalitarian reforms of family law were passed in the 1970s.[154] It has to be said that, already from the start, the plain affirmation of women's hierarchical subordination came to be seen as incompatible with the new constitutional order. Yet the same could not be said about the separation/differentiation axis. Thus, when interpreting the gender equality and sex antidiscrimination clauses in the constitution, the early jurisprudence of the Federal Constitutional Court (FCC) held that a different treatment on account of sex was constitutionally forbidden, except for when it could be grounded on "objective biological or functional" sexual differences.[155] This rhetoric (which in some form survived until the 1990s) had its zenith during the 1950s and 1960s, and it allowed the court to interpret sexual equality as requiring respect for "legitimate sexual differences," be they biological or functional in nature. Particularly strong emphasis was laid on the equal worth of the roles of men and women within the family, of fathers and mothers, and of the work of breadwinners and housewives.[156] The "two-track"

[153] See Sentenza 144/1967 (Dec. 12, 1967), overturned by Sentenza 133/1970 (June 24, 1970). For a critical analysis of this case law and the way the concept of family unity was initially used by the court to entrench gender stereotypes based on a patriarchal family model, see Barbara Pezzini, "La struttura di genere della famiglia nella giurisprudenza costituzionale," in *Genere e dirittto: Come il genere costruisce il diritto e il diritto costruisce il genere*, ed. Barbara Pezzini (Bergamo: Bergamo University Press–Sestante Edizioni, 2012), 26–31.

[154] Until Mar. 31, 1953, it was foreseen that laws contrary to the gender equality clause of article 3 (2) GG would remain in force. The deadline lapsed without any major reforms. The First Equal Treatment Act (*Erstes Gleichberechtigungsgesetz*), covering civil aspects of marriage and family, entered into force on July 1, 1958. Certain patriarchal features of the Civil Code were "overlooked" in this reform, leading to several constitutional challenges. The first act comprehensively reforming marriage and family law (*Erstes Gesetz zur Reform des Ehe- und Familienrechts*) was only adopted in January 1977. See Barbelies Wiegmann, "Der Hürdenlauf der Frauen im Recht seit 1900," in *Frauen und Recht Reader*, ed. Ministerium für Gesundheit, Soziales, Frauen und Familie des Landes Nordrhein–Westfalen (Düsseldorf, 2003).

[155] See BVerfGE 3, 225, Dec. 18, 1953.

[156] For a description of the decisions of this period, see Blanca Rodríguez Ruíz and Ute Sacksofsky, "Gender in the German Constitution," in *The Gender of Constitutional Jurisprudence*, eds. Beverley Baines and Ruth Rubio-Marín (Cambridge: Cambridge University Press, 2005), 152.

citizenship model, so to speak, was constitutionally acceptable, and this allowed traditional gender stereotypes to go unchallenged. What were not acceptable, according to the FCC, were arbitrary distinctions that could only be interpreted as relics of patriarchy, such as granting the father the last word when parents could not reach an agreement on decisions concerning their children's welfare.[157] In other words, there had to be equal worth attached to men's and women's distinctive roles within the family (i.e., the breadwinner and the complementing housewife).[158] This doctrine allowed the court to uphold a rule whereby a man could be legally obliged to financially support his out-of-wedlock children, which the mother was expected to raise,[159] as well as another rule that granted widowers a pension only if the deceased wives had been the main breadwinners, whereas a widow's pension was granted regardless of similar considerations.[160]

This had a bearing on the interpretation of the family provision in Germany's Basic Law. Indeed, at the time, much of the German legal scholarship argued that only the traditional family, organized around a housewife and a breadwinner, could enjoy the protection of article 6 (1), sometimes alluding to its roots in natural law and Christianity.[161] The truth of the matter is that the court itself never went as far as explicitly articulating its preference for the breadwinner family model. Rather, this was the actual result of a doctrine exalting the equal worth of both sexes while demanding respect for the "objective natural and functional differences" between men and women. In theory, the court was simply upholding the duty of the state to remain neutral. Marital privacy, it held, should encompass the autonomy of the couple in deciding about the internal structure of the family, including whether one or both spouses should be income earners.[162] The problem, as we shall see, is that this supposed

157 See BVerfGE 10, 59, July 29, 1959.

158 See Rodríguez Ruíz and Sacksofsky, "Gender in the German Constitution," 152.

159 See BVerfGE 11, 277, July 21, 1960.

160 See BVerfGE 17, 1, July 24, 1963.

161 See Christine Franzius, *Bonner Grundgesetz und Familienrecht Die Diskussion um die Gleichberechtigung von Mann und Frau in der westdeutschen Zivilrechtslehre der Nachkriegszeit (1945–1957)* (Frankfurt: Klostermann, 2005), 92–95, referring to Friedrich Wilhelm Bosch and Günther Beitzke, two civil law professors and commentators of the time, who strongly supported the conception of the family unit as derived from natural law and Christian doctrine with a similar patriarchal structure as the one embedded in the German Constitution.

162 See, for all, BVerfGE 6, 55, Jan. 17, 1957, at 67 and 80; and BVerfGE 9, 237, Apr. 14, 1959, at 241–43. In fact, in Europe, where the institutional approach to family and

neutrality proved to be rather fictional in the face of a social reality and a legal system that clearly privileged the culturally dominant model of the separate spheres tradition and separate roles for men and women, a social reality the court ended up endorsing.

This family exceptionalism, exempting the domain of the family from a strict application of the constitutional gender equality mandate, was not an exclusive feature of European post–World War II constitutionalism. After all, this constitutionalism impacted many constitutions written for new states emerging into independence in the decades to come, sometimes copying the basic constitutional rules of their former colonial masters. In fact, such family exceptionalism was kept alive in many countries around the world for a very long time, especially, as we will discuss, in contexts in which the formal or informal influence of religious forces and traditions proved strongest or in those in which cultural norms accommodated under systems of legal pluralism survived free of constitutional sex equality scrutiny.[163]

India represents a fascinating case, given how progressive some of the provisions inserted in the Indian Constitution were for their time. The

marriage has prevailed constitutionally, post–World War II constitutional texts did not contain the notion of a right to family privacy, beyond the concept of inviolability of the home, intended to protect against undue searches and seizures (see, for instance, article 13 of the German Basic Law and article 14 of the Italian Constitution). This changed in the 1950s, when the European Convention of Human Rights recognized the right to private and family life, under article 8, as well as the right to marriage, under article 12. Other European constitutions would then follow suit and recognize marriage separately (described as a fundamental right, the right to marry) and family (expressed as an institution), with the state often being called on the protection of the latter. The 1978 Spanish Constitution is an example of this (article 39 refers to the family as an institution that deserves state protection, and article 32 refers to the fundamental right of men and women to marry).

[163] In some countries of Islamic tradition that had purposefully sought to modernize and came to share the basic structure of the postwar gender constitutional architecture (including the prohibition of sex discrimination, the protection of motherhood, and the recalling of sex equality in domains in which women had traditionally been discriminated against – e.g., education), a further constitutional reform was deemed necessary to render explicit the equality of the spouses. This was, for instance, the case of Turkey, where the 1961 constitutional scheme, which reflected the postwar model and was practically reproduced by the 1982 constitution, required an amendment in 2001 to explicitly insert interspousal equality. In 2004 and 2010, the equality provisions would be further reformed and strengthened to incorporate a substantive equality logic. See Bertil Emrah Oder, "Women and Constitution-Making in Turkey: From Ottoman Modernism to a Constitutionalism of Women's Platform," in *Women as Constitution-Makers: Case Studies for the New Democratic Era*, eds. Ruth Rubio-Marín and Helen Irving (Cambridge: Cambridge University Press, 2019), 283, 290, 298.

Constitution of India came into force on January 26, 1950, and contains both a generic right to equality (article 14) and a prohibition of discrimination on the grounds of sex (article 15 [1]). It also contains a clause, article 15 (3), allowing the state to make special provisions for women and children; one (article 16) guaranteeing equality of opportunity for all in public employment and prohibiting discrimination on the grounds of sex (article 16 [2]); one (article 325) prohibiting electoral ineligibility on grounds of sex; and yet another one (article 39) requesting the state to direct its policies toward securing, among other things, equal rights to livelihood and equal pay for equal work for men and women.[164] Yet, as has been criticized,[165] none of this impeded the courts to uphold, until 2018, criminal law provisions sanctioning different rules for male and female adultery on the basis of patriarchal understandings of women's sexuality as a male possession;[166] from disqualifying women from certain

164 Article 51A, on fundamental duties, directs citizens to renounce practices derogatory to the dignity of women but was not part of the original 1950 constitution. Instead, it was introduced by the Forty-Second Amendment Act in 1976. Interestingly, provision 51A (e) of the amendment includes the duty to "promote harmony and the spirit of common brotherhood amongst all the people of India transcending religious, linguistic and regional or sectional diversities." The term brotherhood, in connection with the duty to "renounce practices derogatory to the dignity of women," seems to refer to the fact that it falls on men (tied as brothers) to run India's public affairs. When read together, the two duties seem to recognize that the challenge of respecting women's dignity is one shared by the various cultural and religious groups reflecting women's overall subordinate position. Notice also that the preamble orientates the constitution toward certain values that include justice, liberty, equality, and "fraternity."

165 See Ratna Kapur and Brenda Cossman, "On Women, Equality and the Constitution: Through the Looking Glass of Feminism," *National Law School Journal* 1 (1993) and Gautam Bhatia, *The Transformative Constitution: A Radical Biography in Nine Acts* (New Delhi: HarperCollins, 2019), 9–11.

166 See Yusuf Abdul Aziz v. State of Bombay, AIR 1954 SC 321. Section 497 of the colonial Indian Code of Criminal Procedure (Act XLV of 1860) only punished the male adulterer and only allowed the husband of the female partner to bring charges. The court called on article 15 (3) and allowed for the enactment of "special provisions" for women in the understanding that the adultery law provided a safe harbor for women. The *Yusuf Abdul Aziz* case was upheld by the Supreme Court up to three times. See Sowmithri Vishnu v. Union of India, AIR 1985 SC 1618; V. Revathi v. Union of India, AIR 1988 SC 835; and W. Kalyani v. State, (2012) 1 SCC 358. In the 1988 decision, the court's reasoning left no room for interpretation: "The community punishes the 'outsider' who breaks into the matrimonial home and occasions the violation of the sanctity of the matrimonial tie by developing an illicit relationship with one of the spouses subject to the rider that the erring 'man' alone can be punished and not the erring woman." The provision was only struck down in 2018, after the court came to the conclusion that such legislation conferred a dubious "benefit" on women, given that it was premised on the understanding of women's sexual passivity. The concurring opinion of Justice Malhotra noted that

positions based on their different nature and functions;[167] or from justifying different retirement rules for male and female air attendants by referring to women's role as mothers and caregivers.[168] Nor was the constitution taken by the courts to "provide for an overhaul or reform of personal and religious laws which governed women's private lives at home and in families in relation to matters of marriage, guardianship, adoption or inheritance,"[169] despite the fact that the constitution contains an – as of yet – unfulfilled directive principle (article 44) mandating the state to enact a uniform civil code.[170]

In sum, modern constitutionalism was superimposed on an extractive reproductive and heteronormative family structure with racist undertones, which was naturalized and even romanticized. This is the reason why every attempt to advance toward the affirmation of women's equal citizenship, hand in hand with a more egalitarian and democratic family, would be resisted as a challenge to the very structure of the foundational constitutional order rather than as a natural step in the gradual conquest of the enlightened contractarian project of coexistence among naturally free individuals. This also explains why, in order to tell the story of women's evolving citizenship, one cannot simply tell the story of women's gradual acquisition of men's rights. Instead, the story has to include the transformation of the understanding of the roles primarily

"special provisions" for women could no longer be justified under a protective-patriarchal logic, whereas that of Justice Dhananjaya Yeshwant Chandrachud refers to the challenged provision as "grounded in paternalism, solicitous of patriarchal values," arguing that it "subjugates the woman to a position where the law disregards her sexuality." See Joseph Shine v. Union of India, AIR 2018 SC 4898.

167 See R. S. Singh v. State of Punjab, AIR 1972 Punjab and Haryana 117, where a host of assumptions about gender roles – from differing physical strength to the performance of "maternal functions" – were invoked to uphold an order disqualifying women from being appointed as superintendents in men's jails.

168 See Air India v. Nargesh Meerza, AIR 1981 SC 1829. The rule forced an air hostess to retire on the grounds of marriage, first pregnancy, or thirty-five years of age, whichever occurred earlier. The Supreme Court upheld, modified, and struck these rules down in parts. In the case of marriage, it considered that the forced retirement of the married air hostesses within four years of joining the service was reasonable, as it boosted the family planning program and the success of marriage, which were considered to be the specific responsibility of women. See Bhatia, *The Transformative Constitution*, 10–12.

169 See Shreya Atrey and Gautam Bhatia, "In Search of Principle: Seventy Years of Gender Jurisprudence in India," in *Gender, Sexuality and Constitutionalism in Asia*, eds. Wen-Chen Chang et al. (Oxford: Hart Publishing, forthcoming).

170 See State of Bombay v. Narasu Appa Mali, AIR 1952 Bom 84, upholding a provincial law that discriminated against daughters in inheritance, observing that uncodified "personal laws" were not subject to constitutional scrutiny.

assigned to women and around which different groups of women have necessarily had competing visions and anxieties, built to a greater or lesser extent their sense of identity and purpose, and managed to secure a system, however fragile, of protections.

In the United States, this dominant family ideology and the way it was portrayed as increasingly under threat would lead to a failed attempt to amend the constitution – more specifically, to the failure to incorporate a sex equality provision. In Europe and elsewhere, sex equality provisions made it into constitutional texts and were probably less threatening because the constitutions also embedded protections of women as mothers, as well as of marriage and the family as institutions. This maternalist tradition allowed the sex equality provisions to be interpreted in light of family, marriage, and motherhood protective clauses, allowing the dominant breadwinner family ideology to shape the contours of how far constitutional equality could actually go.

It would take over a century and a half since the dawn of constitutionalism in the Western world to revisit marriage and family law in order to ensure women's legal equality with men, for it was only in the 1960s and 1970s, and under the influence of second-wave feminism's attack on the patriarchal family model, that both marriage and the family, regarded as the paradigmatic realms of tradition, began to be more seriously confronted, and with them, the place of women in society and the implicit understandings of the prevalent gendered conceptions of citizenship.

2

Inclusive Constitutionalism and Its Limits

2.1 Second-Wave Feminism and Women's Equality Claims

On August 26, 1970, the National Organization of Women (NOW) staged a one-day strike in forty US cities to commemorate the half-century anniversary of the Nineteenth Amendment's ratification. The Women's Strike for Equality argued that the Nineteenth Amendment, which granted women the right to suffrage, had neither repaired the constitutional damage it was supposed to remedy nor ensured women's equal citizenship.[1] Despite their political enfranchisement, women were still second-class citizens and would remain so unless fundamental changes in employment and family life conditions were finally implemented, just as the suffragists had also claimed decades before. Voting rights were not enough. In addition to the ratification of the Equal Rights Amendment (ERA) to the Constitution, the strike sought three reforms that were seen as necessary to fulfill the promise of equal citizenship for women: equal opportunity in jobs and education, free abortion on demand, and free twenty-four-hour childcare centers.[2] In a nutshell, political rights meant little unless and until women could also be equally employable as men, free to decide whether or not and when to bear children, and free from being uniquely in charge of caretaking. For women, the conditions of their private lives and public options were inextricably linked.

The strike demands represented the crystallization of the feminist movement's advocacy of the late 1960s in the West. The central claims of what came to be known as second-wave feminism were replicated in many parts of the world and embodied a comprehensive attack on the whole 1950s package of beliefs about women's roles and marriage, with

[1] Reva B. Siegel, "The Nineteenth Amendment and the Democratization of the Family," *Yale Law Journal Forum* 129 (2020): 475.

[2] Ibid.

some feminist manifestos declaring that marriage turned women into "breeders" and "domestic servants."[3] Representative of the time was Betty Friedan's seminal book *The Feminine Mystique* (1963) and its radical critique of the devastating effects of gender stereotypes forcing women to conceive themselves primarily and quintessentially as mothers and wives. For obvious reasons, the movement's central tenets resonated better with white women's experience of oppression and dispossession than with that of nonwhite women subordinated through other racialized forms of oppression.[4]

Changes in the economy and medicine facilitated the movement's development and the demise of the traditional marital family. The expanding economy of the 1960s needed women to offer a wage and more opportunities in the growing service sector, whereas the inflation of the 1970s made it harder for a man to be the sole breadwinner in the family and live up to the breadwinner family model.[5] Increasing opportunities for women in paid employment meant more professional

[3] Stephanie Coontz, *Marriage, a History: How Love Conquered Marriage* (New York: Penguin Books, 2006), 248.

[4] Mills mentions oppression through conquest, land expropriation, slavery, regimes of colonial forced labor, segregation, and racialized occupational positions in the job marketplace among the more salient aspects of this relation, as he describes how the public/private partition did not resonate much with nonwhite women who had always inhabited "the public sphere," whether as slaves working in plantation economies, colonial laborers, domestics forced to seek employment in white households, or as workers in race- and gender-differentiated occupations. See Charles W. Mills, "Intersecting Contracts," in *Contract and Domination*, eds. Carole Pateman and Charles W. Mills (Cambridge: Polity Press, 2007), 181. Nevertheless, one must recall that the public/private dichotomy is a fractal distinction, so that "whatever the local, historically specific content of the dichotomy, the distinction between public and private can be reproduced repeatedly by projecting it onto narrower contexts or broader ones. Or it can be projected onto different social 'objects' – activities, identities, institutions, spaces and interactions – that can be further categorized into private or public parts," so that spaces that are undoubtedly public in one context can be turned into private ones through lexical gestures, allowing some distinctions to conveniently disappear. See Susan Gal, "A Semiotics of the Public/Private Distinction," *Differences: A Journal of Feminist Cultural Studies* 13, no. 1 (2002): 81. Because of this, it is possible to identify a problem of predominant attribution (without autonomy or value recognition) of sexual and reproductive work and roles, as well as the devaluation thereof (even when performed as a form of employment for others or in the homes of others), as cutting across class and race and as supported by a disciplinary male regime that subjects women to ordinary forms of violence, even if the forms and manifestations of sexual and reproductive control, extraction, dispossession, and violence may vary along these axes and additional axes of subordination added to the regular experiences of women.

[5] Coontz, *Marriage, a History*, 242.

aspirations, and for many of them, this meant postponing marriage to complete their education. Yet, more education also meant greater frustration at the persistent inequalities. This dissatisfaction formed the basis for a wider women's rights movement, contributing to women's entry into the workforce and the higher education system, with a "growing number of middle-class wives rejecting full-time homemaking as a 'woman's career.'"[6] Women's ability to plan, coupled with their newfound work lives and the introduction of the birth control pill, which had just become commercially available, resulted in greater reproductive autonomy. This contraception revolution enabled the sexual revolution, which accepted premarital sex, disconnecting sex and reproduction.[7] In turn, the increasing number of childless marriages weakened the connection between marriage and parenthood, undermining some of the traditional justifications for both while "elevating marriage over all other relationships as an institution of public relevance and limiting it to heterosexual couples."[8]

Fueled by these fundamental changes in women's work roles and reproductive rights, the social movements of the 1960s and early 1970s brought on a series of far-reaching transformations in the Western world. After 150 years of mere incremental changes, the legal status of women experienced nothing less than a true revolution. In many countries, this revolution proceeded without much intervention from rights-based constitutionalism and constitutional courts, mostly through gradual legislative reforms. This was the case of the United Kingdom, the Nordic countries, and France. Yet, in many other countries, some of the most important struggles were elevated to constitutional courts. In response, different constitutional traditions proved to be more or less receptive to women's egalitarian aspirations concerning the family and marriage, the market, and reproduction.

In those instances where constitutions were drawn into the debate, sex equality clauses and doctrines became a mechanism that, for the most part, certainly paved the way for some necessary changes, affecting both the family and the marketplace by rendering women's legal status fundamentally equal to that of men. Family exceptionalism – or the idea that, despite the egalitarian constitutional ethos, the family as society's foundational unit and the gender roles within it had to be preserved as

[6] Ibid., 253.
[7] Ibid., 254.
[8] Ibid., 255.

expressive of women's natural duties or as a distinctive form of citizenship for women – finally gave way to the promise of a gender-neutral legal order and an inclusive type of constitutionalism. This would allow women to start overcoming the laws that had enforced male household headship for so long by considering women legal minors and limiting their opportunities for financial independence. Having joined men in the public domain of suffrage, it was time for women to join men in the domain of wage labor in the marketplace on ever more equal terms and regardless of their marital status.

Nevertheless, the attempts to go further and fully engage with inequalities connected to women's reproductive capacities, aspirations, and roles had more uneven prospects. It required ensuring the social distribution of the costs of human reproduction and carving out reproductive autonomy from, for the most part, reproduction-silent constitutional texts – texts that had been built on the assumption of traditional family schemes. The lack of a "male comparator" proved a difficult obstacle in an inclusive form of constitutionalism that essentially accepted women into a domain of rights crafted by and for men's vision of autonomy. Reproductive autonomy became thus an essential element in women's emancipatory struggle. Women needed to be freed from legal limitations and gender-based stereotypes about their natural abilities and capacities – the very stereotypes on which the separate spheres ideology had been entrenched since the origins of constitutionalism. Yet their liberation also required to ensure that motherhood was not the result of undesired pregnancies, just as it was necessary to highlight the collective shouldering of the costs of childbearing, which had until then been dumped on women as a class and, more specifically, on poor or racialized women more than others.[9]

Constitutionally speaking, both the starting positions and evolutions in the United States and Western Europe were somewhat different. Although interrupted by the upsurge of authoritarian and dictatorial regimes, Europe's constitutions during the interwar period had already begun developing protective provisions on sex equality, motherhood, and family. Also, as we have seen, in the immediate postwar years, European

[9] Second-wave feminists fought for the redistribution of childbearing labor between women and men in the home, as well as the redistribution of the costs of pregnancy, childbirth, and child-rearing between family and society. See Deborah Dinner, "The Costs of Reproduction: History and the Legal Construction of Sex Equality," *Harvard Civil Rights–Civil Liberties Law Review* 46, no. 2 (2011): 415, 419.

constitutionalism had found ways to craft a sex equality doctrine that, on the basis of family exceptionalism, proceeded in a sort of "two-track citizenship" logic, denying women true equality. Consequently, a hermeneutic shift would now be required to retain the value of motherhood and its protections without letting it justify the curtailment of women's rights in other domains.

In the United States, the constitutional amendment to establish sex equality through the ERA was approved in Congress in 1972 with broad-based support of the women's movement of the time and sent to the states for ratification. Nevertheless, by the mid-1970s, an organized movement against the changes brought about on gender roles and sexual norms was in full swing, and right-wing activist Phyllis Schlafly was leading a successful fight against the ratification of the ERA. Not unlike Selbert in postwar Germany, ERA proponents tried to explain that its adoption did not necessarily invalidate women's exemption from compulsory military service or measures designed to promote the economic welfare of women, nor did it prevent them from "performing their duties as homemakers or mothers."[10] Equal rights did not have to entail strictly equal treatment. But what had been possible in 1949 in Germany became impossible in the convoluted 1970s in the United States, which were witnessing a gender revolution of greater dimensions and on multiple fronts, along with the discussion of abortion rights. This meant that, in the United States, overcoming sex-based discrimination had to become the primary work of legislators and litigators relying on constitutional interpretation to push their egalitarian goals rather than being based on a formal constitutional amendment.

2.2 Overcoming the Head-and-Master Regime: Toward Women's Equal Legal Status and Transitional Queries

While the repeal of sex-based disabilities from the law of marriage and other legislation proceeded without much constitutional input in the pursuit of formal equality in countries with a strong parliamentary tradition or weak forms of judicial review, constitutions did help trigger

[10] Reva B. Siegel, "Constitutional Culture, Social Movement Conflict and Constitutional Change: The Case of De Facto ERA; 2005–06 Brennan Centre Symposium Lecture," *California Law Review* 94, no. 5 (2006): 1380.

the necessary legislative reforms in those countries with a tradition of rights-based constitutionalism and an enforceable right to sex equality (whether textually or jurisprudentially affirmed in the constitution). In one way or another, in the 1970s, legislators in consolidated democracies across the West started a process of repealing all kinds of explicit sex-based discriminations and gradually producing what, for the most part, turned into gender-neutral legal orders, with only some areas closely linked to a gendered and patriarchal understanding of citizenship (such as military duties, nationality rules, and even family names), proving particularly resilient to sex-differentiated conceptions of citizenship. The new wave of legislative amendments entailed, paradigmatically, the reform of family codes to reframe marriage as "an association of two equal individuals rather than as the union of two distinct and specialized roles"[11] – and, subsequently, reforms to tax, social security, and employment legislation to account for women's increasing independence and participation in the market and commercial transactions regardless of their marital status. Yet it also involved the reform of criminal laws that had thus far combined paternalism and the patrimonialization of women by turning them into objects of protection: not as holders of sexual freedom but rather as instrumentally linked to men's honor and reputation. In Western countries and beyond,[12] this gradual equalization

[11] Coontz, *Marriage, a History*, 255.

[12] In India, for instance, the explicit sex equality provisions contained in the 1950 constitution would give rise to constitutional challenges framed under formal equality and focused upon "colonial holdovers" that seemed starkly at odds with the constitutional guarantee against sex discrimination, as well as post-colonial laws, rules, and regulations that were mechanically modelled upon their colonial antecedents. These ranged across civil law, criminal law, and employment law (to name just a few legal domains), and included, for example, different rules to determine when plaintiffs in legal proceedings could be compelled to furnish securities; different rules governing the consequences of marriage for employment in the civil services; outright prohibitions upon certain forms of employment, such as a jail superintendent or a nurse; and different punishments for "adultery." See Shreya Atrey and Gautam Bhatia, "In Search of Principle: Seventy Years of Gender Jurisprudence in India," in *Gender, Sexuality and Constitutionalism in Asia*, eds. Wen-Chen Chang et al. (Oxford: Hart Publishing, forthcoming). See, for instance, Bombay Labour Union v. Messrs International Franchises, AIR 1966 SC 942 (1965), striking down a rule requiring an unmarried woman to give up her employment upon marriage, even though the court continued to assume that the woman was the primary caregiver for children on the basis that widows were just as likely to have such responsibilities and, therefore, it could not be said that married women posed a greater absenteeism problem; C. B. Muthamma v. Union of India, AIR 1979 SC 1868 (1979), endorsing a formal equality analysis to strike down the Indian Foreign Service's restrictions on the appointment of married women; and Maya Devi v. State of Maharashtra

process under the umbrella of the formal equality rule was accompanied by interesting, though very often rather formalistic, constitutional rulings, especially in the 1970s, 1980s, and 1990s, presenting the multiplicity of claims that one can expect to find in a gender order transition.[13]

(1986) 1 SCR 743, striking down the requirement that married women obtain their husbands' consent before applying for public employment.

[13] In other geographical areas, the cultural, social, and political changes necessary to overcome the head-and-master regime would take much longer to come about, and in some regions they are still ongoing. In many Asian countries, for instance, women's use of constitutional litigation began mostly in the mid-1990s and early 2000s, as the relevant legal and judicial strategies became available only after social and political reforms in the 1980s and 1990s. Lack of democratic stability, as well as Cold War polarization, prevented some of the reforms from taking place sooner in time. See Ruth Rubio-Marín and Wen-Cheng Chang, "Sites of Constitutional Struggle for Women's Equality," in *Routledge Handbook of Constitutional Law*, eds. Mark Tushnet, Thomas Fleiner, and Cheryl Saunders (London: Routledge, 2015), 303–4. Since the turn of the century, we observe inclusive gender constitutionalism being increasingly displayed elsewhere. For Taiwan, see Judicial Yuan [JY] [Constitutional Court], Interpretation No. 365 (Sept. 23, 1994), holding unconstitutional a provision of the Civil Code that accorded the power of final decision to the father if there was disagreement over the exercise of parental rights in relation to the child; Interpretation No. 452 (Apr. 10, 1998), invalidating another provision in the Civil Code that required the wife to take over the residence of the husband after marriage; and Interpretation No. 457 (June 12, 1998), striking down a government regulation that deprived veterans' married daughters, but not married sons, of their equal right to inheritance of government leased property. For Nepal, see Meera Dhungana v. Ministry of Law and Justice, 2052, 37(6) NKP 462 (1995), in which activist lawyers successfully challenged the validity of section 16 of the chapter on inheritance for daughters in the Muluki Ain or National Code, even though the Supreme Court did not exercise its power of judicial review to strike down the impugned provision, issuing instead a mandamus to the government to introduce an appropriate bill in parliament in consultation with the various competent organizations. The tendency to declare inequalities contrary to the constitution while ordering the government to introduce amendments instead of directly striking down a decision has been confirmed in other cases concerning, for instance, different marital ages for men and women (Sapana Pradhan Malla v. Office of the Prime Minister, 2063, 48[3] NKP 289 [2006]) and sex-differentiated conditions allowing husbands to remarry when the wife is affected by incurable veneral disease or serious mental disability (Sapana Pradhan Malla v. Office of the Prime Minister, 2065, 50[8] NKP 917 [2008]). For South Korea, see the case related to the use of the paternal family name (17-2 KCCR 544) (Hunbeobjaepanso [Const. Ct.], Dec. 22, 2005, 2003Hun-Ka5), striking down as unconstitutional the provision of the Civil Code that required adoption of the paternal family name; and the case related to the house head system (17-1 KCCR 1) (Hunbeobjaepanso [Const. Ct.], Feb. 3, 2005, 2001Hun-Ka9), holding unconstitutional the century-long family law whereby husbands and fathers were always registered as house heads and children were required to be registered with the household of the father rather than the mother after divorce. This was a family law that made a female citizen belong to her father when she was born, to her husband when she married, and then to her son when her husband died, reflecting the "three rules of obedience" that the Confucian tradition imposed on women. See Yoon Jin Shin

Thus, in many parts of the world, protectionist norms that had limited women's legal capacity and employment opportunities began to be challenged for the first time (including norms that restricted their access to dangerous, physically strenuous, or male-dominated professions, prohibited night shifts, or established maximum hours for women only).[14] The same was true of norms that, stereotypically assuming their dependency on men, had limited women's ability to generate work-related benefits to support their dependent husbands – a form of dignitary harm that also had economic implications for women.[15] However, some of the claims challenging these norms came from women for whom the letting go of the protections they had once been granted came too late to hold any emancipatory promise, even if they had formed part of a broader scheme entrenching their dependence on men. In Spain, for instance,

"Gender Equality, Individual Empowerment, and Constitutional Rights Review: South Korea's Dynamic Development," in Chang et al., *Gender, Sexuality and Constitutionalism in Asia*.

[14] See, for instance, the landmark decision BVerfGE 85, 191, Jan. 28, 1992, in which the German Federal Constitutional Court found paternalistic the prohibition of women's night work and condemned it for perpetuating the stereotype of women as indefensible creatures – an image that served women's subordination. See also Corte Constitucional [C.C.] [Constitutional Court], noviembre 27, 1997, Sentencia No. C-622/97 (Colom.), striking down a labor code provision prohibiting women factory workers from working at night in Colombia.

[15] See, for instance, Alkotmánybíróság (AB) [Constitutional Court], 10/1990. (IV. 27.) (Hung.), abolishing widow's pensions that were granted only to women; Corte Constitucional [C.C.] [Constitutional Court], marzo 7, 1994, Sentencia No. T-098/94 (Colom.), declaring unconstitutional a social security scheme providing medical benefits to wives or permanent companions of male employees but not to husbands or companions of female employees; and Corte Constitucional [C.C.] [Constitutional Court], julio 11, 1996, Sentencia No. C-309/96 (Colom.), striking down a law that terminated survivor benefits of a worker's widow if she remarried. See also Costa Rica's Constitutional Chamber of the Supreme Court, decision No. 0629-94, Jan. 31, 1994, striking down a social security norm whereby should an insured man wish to cover his wife, all he had to do was to prove the existence of the marriage, whereas if the insured woman wanted to do the same, she had to comply with a series of additional requirements, such as proving that her spouse was sick, unable to work, a student, unemployed, or otherwise economically dependent on her. More recently, see Amparo en revisión 664/2008, Suprema Corte de Justicia de la Nación [SCJN], septiembre 17, 2008, Semanario Judicial de la Federación y su Gaceta, Novena Época, febrero de 2009, Tomo XXIX, Tesis 2a. VII/2009, página 470 (Mex.), where the Mexican Supreme Court struck down a social security provision requiring a widower – but not a widow – to prove economic dependency on his deceased working wife or partner in order to access a pension. See, along similar lines, Amparo en revisión 364/2018, Suprema Corte de Justicia de la Nación [SCJN], junio 20, 2018, Semanario Judicial de la Federación y su Gaceta, Décima Época, Libro 57, agosto de 2018, Tomo I, Tesis 2a. LXX/2018 (10a.), página 1250.

after the 1978 constitution came into force with a prohibition of discrimination on the grounds of sex (article 14), the Constitutional Court was seized by women who had been subject to a system of mandatory or voluntary "marital leaves" under Franco's regime. This system had first forced and later on given incentives to women who left their employment at the time of marriage (unless and until the deaths of their husbands), only to find employers and courts denying their claims to recover their positions on the basis that the preconstitutional scheme had become invalid – as sex discriminatory – after 1978.[16]

Also, under a new doctrine of sex neutrality, many of the battles were first led to the benefit of men seeking access to those "privileges" or "benefits" that women had enjoyed as actual or assumed dependent caregivers or that could, at best, be considered double-edged. These included, and in some legal systems continue to include, topics such as care-related tax exemptions reserved for women and women's access to, or preferential treatment in, orphanage or survivors' pensions, or else earlier retirement. The rule of lower age for retirement and pension eligibility was the norm in most countries at some point in time and has given rise to similar legal battles.[17] Allegedly, this rule sought to compensate women for the double shift that work inside and outside the home had demanded from them throughout life, even though, in practice, it often meant that they had to abandon their employment in time to care for their somewhat older retired husbands. The differential scheme also often translated into a smaller pension fund for women, for pension benefits were usually calculated based on the overall employment time, the pay level achieved during the final years, or both. But leaving aside

[16] See Ruth Rubio-Marín, "Women and the Cost of Transition to Democratic Constitutionalism in Spain," *International Sociology* 18, no. 1 (2003): 245–63.

[17] For Colombia, see Corte Constitucional [C.C.] [Constitutional Court], septiembre 15, 1994, Sentencia No. C-410/94, upholding differential retirement and pension eligibility ages in favor of women as a legitimate means to compensate for women's continuing inferior position in the labor force and for the physical and mental burdens placed on them because of their double workload as members of the paid labor force and as responsible for society's unpaid domestic work. For similar legislation and reasonings, see also Costa Rica's Constitutional Chamber of the Supreme Court, decision No. 06472-99, Aug. 18, 1999. For Japan, see Nissan Motors, Inc. v. Nakamoto (1981), in which the Supreme Court of Japan struck down a private company regulation that stipulated different mandatory retirement ages for men and women as an irrational discrimination against women. For Nepal, see Rina Bajracharya v. HM Government Secretariat of the Council of Ministers, 2057, 42(5) NKP 376 (2000), striking down a gender-discriminatory provision in regard to the retirement age of Royal Nepal Airlines Corporation employees.

the complexities around the rule and the challenge of the double-bind situation that women often confronted, the fact is that a doctrine that promised a gender-neutral legal order and strict sex equality simply invited all to come forward and claim equal treatment, and men, as a class, were best equipped to undertake long legal battles.[18] Granted, as we shall see, sometimes it was women who strategically sought men-led causes in an effort to appeal to what men, too, had to win by leaving behind gender-based stereotypes that assumed that men could never depend on their wives or be caregivers, something that was blatantly wrong. The fact that high courts in the 1970s and 1980s were mostly a male preserve certainly encouraged this strategy. Yet whether the way to remedy inequality was leveling up or down was often left open for legislators or courts to decide.

Beneath many of the legal battles that come coupled with leaving behind an exclusionary type of constitutionalism and embracing an inclusive one, there is often the question of how to best address the needs of a generation of women caught in between, especially as long as the gap between the aspiration of the new egalitarian order and the underlying social reality remains unbridged. This generation of "in-between" women is unlikely to benefit from the normative shift toward a more egalitarian system during its life course, which has shaped expectations around the now "old system" that typically contained severe limitations to their autonomy but also some "protections" or "remedies" to account for women's legally enforced dependence on men and their imposed care-giving roles. Relatedly, and given the limited power of the law to change social reality in the short term, courts in every jurisdiction have had to struggle with the question of where exactly to draw the boundaries between protective/paternalist outdated norms (which primarily limit women's opportunities while, typically, entrenching old gender

[18] See Judith A. Baer, "Women's Rights and the Limits of Constitutional Doctrine," *Western Political Quarterly* 44, no. 4 (1991): 821, 823, table 1, indicating that men brought eighteen of the twenty-six constitutional cases decided by the US Supreme Court between 1971 and 1984. See also Beverley Baines, "Using the Canadian Charter of Rights and Freedoms," in *The Gender of Constitutional Jurisprudence*, eds. Beverley Baines and Ruth Rubio-Marín (Cambridge: Cambridge University Press, 2005), 52, arguing that, of all the sex discrimination cases decided during the first three years after the equality provision in the Canadian Charter (section 15) became effective, thirty-five were brought by or on behalf of men and only nine by or on behalf of women. See also Saras Jagwanth and Christina Murray, "No Nation Can Be Free When One Half of It Is Enslaved," in Baines and Rubio-Marín, *The Gender of Constitutional Jurisprudence*, 243, making a similar claim concerning the South African Constitution.

stereotypes) and compensatory sex-based differentiations responding to women's lingering disadvantages, a judgment that requires careful reflection about the role of the courts vis-à-vis the legislator in bringing about change and social transformation.[19] Although some constitutions, aware of these and other transition challenges, have foreseen the gradual entering into force of newly proclaimed sex equality provisions or the possibility of exceptions,[20] this is not very common, and courts have often failed to openly confront these complexities by creatively designing a doctrine that would not put the burden of the primary costs of the transition toward the new order on the "generation caught in between." For instance, in the example just mentioned, the Spanish Constitutional Court denied the claims of women seeking reinstatement in their jobs after their husbands had gone missing, on the understanding that they should have reacted immediately after the constitution came into effect and not wait until they were widows, as the old legislation required.[21]

Dealing with the legacy of the past has also meant that courts around the world have had to decide whether measures could be used to compensate for past and enduring inequalities (even in those cases in which doing so could contribute to perpetuating old gender-based stereotypes) or whether removing the norms perpetuating gender stereotypes was instead the paramount role of constitutional sex equality, even if it meant ignoring sex-based distinctions that were still much alive in society.[22]

19 For instance, the Federal Constitutional Court in Germany has, on repeated occasions, upheld the legal rule making a widower's pension, but not a widow's, dependent on whether the deceased spouse had mostly supported the family. The court reasoned that the rule merely mirrored a division of roles between the sexes that was predominant at the time, acknowledging the ongoing evolution of social norms in order to undermine that very division of roles, declaring it, however, to be the future task of lawmakers to translate such an evolution into law. See BVerfGE 39, 169, Mar. 12, 1975, at 185 et seq.

20 Section 37 in the South African Constitution permits emergency derogation from the constitutional protection of equality with respect to gender, though not sex, and has been said to reflect a certain reticence on the part of the constitutional drafters to upset prevailing stereotypes about the role and status of women. See Penelope E. Andrews, "From Gender Apartheid to Non-Sexism: The Pursuit of Women's Rights in South Africa," *North Carolina Journal of International Law* 26, no. 3 (2000): 693–722, at 700.

21 See Rubio-Marín, "Women and the Cost of Transition," 239–57.

22 In The President of the Republic of South Africa and the Minister of Correctional Services v. John Phillip Peter Hugo 1997 (4) SA 1 (CC) (S. Afr.), the South African Constitutional Court upheld a presidential pardon in favor of women prisoners with young children, which had been challenged by male prisioners. While the court majority accepted that the presidential act was discriminatory between men and women, it held

Often, instead of openly confronting these tensions to articulate transitional approaches or to self-reflectively elaborate on the need for a more or less interventionist role on the part of courts vis-à-vis the legislator, and in view of delayed, ongoing, or expected social change, some decisions relied on substantive equality/affirmative action doctrines that gained a foothold, especially since the 1980s and 1990s, to uphold "compensatory privileges for women" while failing to pay due consideration to the stereotyping effect that such privileges continued to have.[23] Some courts, however, have more directly confronted those tensions and, at least in theory, made an effort to draw relevant distinctions before upholding protective measures.[24]

Whether or not proving sensitive to transitional considerations, in responding to the various claims under the new equality doctrine, courts have not been able to claim that all differences between men and women are irrelevant to the law, for some biological distinctions have commonly been accepted as reasonably requiring specific treatment. As we are about to see, it was both the narrower or broader interpretation of what the law deemed relevant "sex-based differences" (whether biological or socially constructed) and the dissimilar conceptions of what those differences determined that ended up crafting different understandings of constitutional sex equality since the 1980s. In the United States, for instance,

that it recognized a social reality and gave relief to a third group, that of the children who suffered by being deprived of their mothers who were their primary caretakers.

[23] See, for instance, Corte Constitucional [C.C.] [Constitutional Court], noviembre 12, 1992, Sentencia No. C-588/92 (Colom.), upholding a law granting single daughters of military officials, but not their sons, special social welfare rights in the name of real and effective equality, in view of women's frequent economic dependency on men. By contrast, the same court rejected a municipality's attempt to rely on positive discrimination to reserve certain housekeeping and maintenance positions exclusively for women. See Corte Constitucional [C.C.] [Constitutional Court], enero 26, 1996, Sentencia No. T-026/96.

[24] The Spanish Constitutional Court, for instance, soon declared the need to ensure that, irrespective of whether the examined norm favored women, it was important to make sure that it did not curtail women's overall equal opportunities. See S.T.C., Mar. 9, 1992 (No. 28/1992); Mar. 25, 1993 (No. 109/1993); and Nov. 28, 1994 (No. 317/1994) – all declaring the unconstitutionality of norms that allowed only women to take indefinite employment leaves while married. Also, according to the court, it is necessary to make sure that the measures at stake have not lost their original meaning and do not help perpetuate cultural stereotypes that contribute to consolidating discriminatory practices and that assume women's greater vocation or obligation to care in the family. See S.T.C., Feb. 14, 1983 (No. 7/1983) and S.T.C., July 16, 1987 (No. 128/1987). See Ruth Rubio-Marín, "Engendering the Constitution: The Spanish Experience," in Baines and Rubio-Marín, *Gender of Constitutional Jurisprudence*, 260.

the male norm became the standard, and any departure from strictly equal legal treatment was seen as suspicious for fear that it would entrench, rather than subvert, the gender roles ideology. In Europe, instead, where the importance of motherhood protections had long since been constitutionally entrenched, the challenge became that of ensuring – increasingly under a logic of substantive, real, or de facto equality – that women could retain their motherhood functions while enjoying equal opportunities in the job market. As we will now discuss in more depth, none of these two approaches, however, could deliver true equality in the marketplace or elsewhere, as men and society did not simultaneously come to share the cost of social reproduction. It would take much longer before the true constitutional dimension of this agenda began to be recognized.

2.3 Women and the Market: The Fruits and Limits of Assimilationist Workerism[25]

In the United States, second-wave feminists had argued that policies premised on the assumption that all women were dependent caregivers inflicted "dignitary harm," but they had also argued that social arrangements that produced caregiver dependency entailed "distributive injustices."[26] As it turns out, the movement was very successful in many ways but, at a constitutional level, the success was greater at tackling the dignitary rather than the distributive wrongs women had experienced. Congress responded to the movement's wide-ranging constitutional appeal by enacting the ERA in 1972, as well as other legislation to combat discrimination and ensure some federal coverage of childcare.[27] And

[25] This and the following sections rely heavily on and partly reproduce sections of Ruth Rubio-Marín, "The (Dis)establishment of Gender: Care and Gender Roles in the Family as a Constitutional Matter," *International Journal of Constitutional Law* 13, no. 4 (2015): 787–818, at 796–805.

[26] Siegel, "Constitutional Culture," 1376.

[27] In particular, Congress succeeded in passing legislation to ensure that sex discrimination provisions (Title VII of the 1964 Civil Rights Act) would be enforced as seriously as its race discrimination provisions, as well as civil rights laws prohibiting sex discrimination in other institutional settings (such as Title IX of the 1972 Education Act, which prohibited discrimination by sex in any program receiving federal aid). It also approved funding and tax credits for childcare programs on the universal coverage model; however, this fell short of the coverage for care that working women were asking for. See ibid., 1377. As Siegel explains, "support for the federal childcare program grew from the civil-rights, antipoverty, and women's movements; and the program attracted opposition

although the ERA never saw the light of day, the Supreme Court started developing jurisprudence that reflected its central tenets. This prompted a transition toward a gender-inclusive constitutionalism that, for the first time in the country's history, ensured that women's claims to equality could be brought under the constitutional umbrella.

It was women's rights advocates, including the famous Ruth Bader Ginsburg (US Supreme Court justice since her appointment in 1993 until her death in 2020, founder of the Women's Rights Project, and, at the time, lawyer for the American Civil Liberties Union), Dorothy Kenyon, and Pauli Murray, who in the 1970s persuaded the Supreme Court to begin to read guarantees of sex equality into the Equal Protection Clause of the Fourteenth Amendment of the US Constitution. In 1971, the Supreme Court decided on *Reed v. Reed*[28] and struck down an Idaho statute that preferred men over women as estate administrators, holding it irrational and thus unconstitutional under the Equal Protection Clause. Two years later, in *Frontiero v. Richardson*,[29] the court articulated for the first time the now orthodox view that laws based on sex stereotypes are constitutionally impermissible, calling for strict scrutiny as a standard of review. This time, the case was brought by a wage-earning wife in the nonstereotypical position of lieutenant in the US Air Force seeking a range of benefits, including housing and medical insurance for her husband. Giving the court the occasion to recognize the fundamental role that the law of marriage had played in keeping women subordinate to men, the court then acknowledged that, throughout much of the nineteenth century, the position of women had been comparable to that of Blacks under pre-Civil War slave codes, since neither slaves nor women could hold office, serve on juries, or bring suit in their own names, and that married women had been traditionally denied the legal capacity to hold or convey property or serve as legal guardians of their own children.[30] The court also acknowledged how the "pedestal" on which women (seen as in need of protection) had often been placed could easily become a "cage" and how much of the history of the separate

accordingly. Its defeat over the course of the decade was tied to the rise of the new right," resisting "communal approaches to child rearing" over the family-centered model. See Siegel, "The Nineteenth Amendment," 477.

[28] 404 U.S. 71 (1971).

[29] 411 U.S. 677 (1973).

[30] Ibid., at 685.

spheres for women and men, with the division of labor it enforced, was rooted in nothing but "romantic paternalism."[31]

This new doctrine, which was certainly influenced by the Supreme Court's color-blindness approach to racial discrimination claims,[32] had a rapid impact, turning the battle against state action that enforced the separate spheres reasoning – and thus gender antistereotyping – into the essence of the sex equality principle that had just been assigned to the constitution, making gender neutrality the ultimate goal of a legal system to the benefit of both women and men. Indeed, in 1975, the court held in *Wiesenfeld* that denying survivor benefits to a widower would have discriminated against both his deceased wife as wage earner and him as surviving caregiver to their child.[33] The net effect of the new cases was to dismantle, as a matter of constitutional law, the legally enforced sex-role differentiation in marriage. Of course, couples were still free to have a role-differentiated marriage. The law, however, could neither require nor even assume that, as a norm, breadwinners were male and homemakers female.[34] Reflecting the changing spirit of the time, the court was rather explicit about what needed to change in some of its decisions. For instance, in *Stanton v. Stanton* (a 1975 decision striking down differential ages of majority for boys and girls for the purposes of determining a divorced father's support obligations), the court remarked that "no longer [was] the female destined solely for the home and the rearing of the family, and only the male for the marketplace and the world of ideas."[35]

Certainly, the constitutional rejection of sex-role differentiation did not automatically alter the fact that women continued to bear most of the child-rearing and family care responsibilities, as it is still the case today. Yet, from then on, whatever the statistical evidence could say about these

31 Ibid., at 684.

32 See Reva B. Siegel, "Equality Talk: Antisubordination and Anticlassification Values in Constitutional Struggles over Brown," *Harvard Law Review* 117, no. 5 (2004): 1470–547.

33 See Weinberger v. Wiesenfeld, 420 U.S. 636 (1975), which held unconstitutional the provision granting social security survivor benefits only to mothers and not to fathers.

34 See Mary Anne Case, "The Very Stereotype the Law Condemns: Constitutional Sex Discrimination Law as a Quest for Perfect Proxies," *Cornell Law Review* 85, no. 5 (2000): 1447–91.

35 See Stanton v. Stanton, 421 U.S. 7, 14–15 (1975). See also Orr v. Orr, 440 U.S. 268, 278–80 (1979), declaring that husbands had to be eligible for alimony equally with wives and that the state's purpose for reinforcing a model of "allocation of family responsibilities under which the wife plays a dependent role [was] no longer valid to justify a statute that discriminates on the basis of gender."

enduring differences between the sexes, any law that generalized on the basis of such evidence would be interpreted as "normalizing," sanctioning, or entrenching different sex roles, and hence, discriminatory. Given this disconnect between the aspirational theory and the enduring reality, it has been claimed that the new legal doctrine ended up serving the exceptional man and woman (i.e., those breaking away from expected gender stereotypes) more than the norm.[36] In other words, the doctrine became an engine of transformation but was much less useful when it came to accommodating the complex needs of real women who continued to bear the brunt of caretaking. This is because the task given to the equal protection norm concerning sex equality was not to reflect and accommodate functional differences between the sexes but rather to ignore them as a way to free the individual from normative sex-based expectations. In 1996, in *United States v. Virginia* (still, to this day, the court's leading decision on heightened scrutiny of sex classifications), it became clear that overbroad generalizations about talents and capacities based on sex were no longer acceptable, not even in the paradigmatic domain of male citizenship as traditionally conceived, i.e., the military.[37] Functional de facto differences could not be accommodated, only "real differences," typically grounded on biological distinctions and narrowly interpreted.[38]

36 Julie C. Suk, "Are Gender Stereotypes Bad for Women? Rethinking Antidiscrimination Law and Work-Family Conflict," *Columbia Law Review* 110, no. 1 (2010): 16, 55.

37 See United States v. Virginia, 518 U.S. 515, 533 (1996), which struck down a scheme placing female would-be cadets in a separate but decidedly unequal girls' school lacking Virginia Military Institute's funding and prestige.

38 For instance, a statutory rape decision protecting underage girls, but not boys, was held to reflect merely a natural asymmetry: the heavy burdens of possible pregnancy would deter girls from underage sex but boys needed the added disincentive of criminal law (see Michael M. v. Superior Court of Sonoma County, 450 U.S. 464, 473 [1981]). Twenty years later, in *Nguyen v. INS*, 533 U.S. 53 (2001), the court again emphasized reproductive differences in rejecting an equal protection challenge to a law that conferred citizenship on the child of a US citizen when the child was born abroad and out of wedlock, depending on whether the citizen's parent was a woman or a man, and granting automatic citizenship when the parent was a woman, arguing that "the difference between men and women in relation to the birth process is a real one." Whereas the dissenters in the opinion viewed the sex-differentiated treatment as reflecting sex-role stereotypes (see O'Connor J., dissenting, 84–94), the majority accepted Congress's interest in ensuring that parents transmit citizenship to children born out of wedlock only when a tie develops between them, a relationship opportunity that birth affords the mother but not the father. The way the court has relied on the distinction between biological versus nonbiological facts in deciding the level of scrutiny to be applied has been criticized for obscuring the manifold ways in which judgments about a woman's distinct biology can in turn be shaped by social roles. Siegel

This antistereotyping sex discrimination doctrine became and remains the dominant model in US constitutionalism. Under it, and given its emphasis on fighting gender stereotypes, it is not surprising that men have often been successful in bringing antidiscrimination claims forward, especially during the years in which the doctrine was being formed. The empowerment of women required freeing both men and women from the gender roles in which historical socialization had trapped them. After all, challenging "preferences" given to women (such as those excluding them from hard jobs and civic duties) meant questioning the stereotype that depicted women as fragile and dependent and men as aggressors and providers.[39] The belief, then, was that disaggregating the biology of sex from the culture of gender was what equality actually required.[40] And although the court did not rule out that differential treatment could sometimes be established as a form of compensation for past discrimination,[41] its symmetrical approach to the Equal Protection Clause made formal equality the norm and affirmative or ameliorative action the exception under a heightened scrutiny standard. In other words, the preference for formal equality, gender neutrality, and antistereotyping set the presumption that differential treatment could always hide preferences that are "confining," "protectionist," or "paternalistic" (described by some as affirmative action for "ladies").[42] At the end of the day, and in

calls this phenomenon "physiological naturalism," which she defines as the belief that objective facts about reproductive differences – rather than judgments about social roles – motivate and justify regulations that uniquely burden one sex. See Reva Siegel, "Reasoning from the Body: A Historical Perspective on Abortion Regulation and Questions of Equal Protection," *Stanford Law Review* 44, no. 2 (1992): 267–77.

39 See Kathleen M. Sullivan, "Constitutionalizing Women's Equality," *California Law Review* 90, no. 3 (2002): 752.

40 See Mary Anne Case, "Disaggregating Gender from Sex and Sexual Orientation: The Effeminate Man in the Law and Feminist Jurisprudence," *Yale Law Journal* 105, no. 1 (1995): 9–13; and Katherine M. Franke, "The Central Mistake of Sex Discrimination Law: The Disaggregation of Sex from Gender," *University of Pennsylvania Law Review* 144, no. 1 (1995): 1–99.

41 Thus applying an intermediate scrutiny test, see Schlesinger v. Ballard, 419 U.S. 313 (1975), in which the court upheld a preference by allowing women more years to prove their worth in an up-or-out naval officer promotion scheme, literally stating that "the different treatment of men and women under [the challenged provisions] does not reflect archaic and overbroad generalization, but instead, the demonstrable fact that male and female line officers in the navy are not similarly situated with respect to opportunities for professional service." See also Califano v. Webster, 430 U.S. 498 (1977), upholding the preference of counting fewer of women's low-wage years when calculating social security retirement payouts to compensate for common wage discrimination.

42 Sullivan, "Constitutionalizing Women's Equality," 753.

almost every instance, it can be argued that the benefits that a specific subgroup of women, however numerically significant, might draw from protective measures (think of pregnant women or women with young children) can always be seen as in tension with the prejudice that gender stereotypes impose on all women.

Despite its noble emancipatory promise and the undoubted victories it delivered, this formalistic take on sex equality has been said to account for some of the most criticized shortcomings of the protection of women under the US Constitution. It is noteworthy that, since its 1974 decision in *Geduldig v. Aiello*,[43] the Supreme Court rejected the claim that pregnancy-based discrimination amounts to gender discrimination, requiring heightened scrutiny and arguing that, although only women can be pregnant, not all women become pregnant, and that pregnancy is a real sexual difference.[44] This was partly offset by the 1978 Pregnancy Discrimination Act, which defined this type of prejudice as sex discrimination under the nation's employment discrimination law.[45] As a

[43] See Geduldig v. Aiello, 417 U.S. 484 (1974). The case was brought by pregnant employees alleging that California's disability insurance system violated the Equal Protection Clause because it excluded pregnancy-related disabilities from normal pregnancies while covering all work-disabling conditions, whether incurred on the job or off the job. "Pregnancy and childbirth, unlike illness and injury, often result in a decision to leave the work force," the court reasoned, while deferring, under rational basis scrutiny, to the policy as a rational way of saving public monies.

[44] Several US scholars today question whether Geduldig v. Aiello can still be considered valid. Siegel argues that there have been important doctrinal developments since *Geduldig* – in particular, through two cases of the Rehnquist Court; namely, United States v. Virginia, 518 U.S. 515 (1996), and Nevada Department of Human Resources v. Hibbs, 538 U.S. 721 (2003), showing that equal protection law has evolved in its approach to pregnancy so that laws concerning pregnancy-based, sex-role stereotypes, rather than any sound physiological consideration, should be deemed as violating equal protection under heightened scrutiny standards of review. See Reva B. Siegel, "The Pregnant Citizen, from Suffrage to the Present," in "Nineteenth Amendment Edition," ed. Grace Paras, special issue, *The Georgetown Law Journal* 108 (2020): 167–230. See also Deborah Dinner, "Sex Equality and the U.S. Welfare Regime: The Story of *Geduldig v. Aiello*," in *Reproductive Rights and Justice Stories*, eds. Melissa Murray, Katherine Shaw, and Reva B. Siegel (St. Paul, MN: West Academic–Foundation Press, 2019), 94. In any event, the *Geduldig* view that pregnancy discrimination was not sex discrimination was not unique to the United States; it also appeared in Canada (see Bliss v. Canada, [1979] 1 S.C.R. 18), only to be overruled in 1992 when the Canadian Supreme Court finally concluded that pregnancy-based discrimination was indeed sex discrimination. See also Brooks v. Canada Safeway Ltd., [1992] 1 S.C.R. 1219.

[45] At the same time, the Pregnancy Discrimination Act, following an assimilationist and formalistic logic, also tied employers' treatment of pregnancy to their treatment of other disabilities in the workplace. In this sense, the act has been said to rest on the premises of

constitutional (though not legislative) matter, invidious intent (and not just impact) has been required to prove sex-based discrimination, mimicking racial discrimination standards. This, coupled with a strict application of the state action doctrine (making private discrimination fall outside of the purview of the constitution), has also limited the scope of the kinds of norms and treatments that could be considered sex discriminatory from a constitutional point of view.

There is a large body of literature describing how these stringent limitations to the forms of constitutionally valid protections under the still dominant antistereotyping and formalistic interpretation of the sex equality doctrine have, for the longest time, affected the possibility of protecting pregnancy and motherhood under the US Constitution, a text that unlike most other constitutions in the world, still does not mention either. Pregnancy and motherhood protections, according to Justice Ginsburg, one of the main protagonists in the crafting of the antistereotyping doctrine, were not to be necessarily rejected. However, a troubling concern was raised: "Patriarchal rules long sequestered women at home.... It is not always easy to separate rules that genuinely assist mothers and their children by facilitating a woman's pursuit of both paid work and parenting from laws that operate to confine women to their traditional subordinate status."[46] And, although much of the feminist movement of the time insisted on the need to cater to the specific needs of women as mothers and mothers-to-be against a history of labor legislation restricting women's and mothers' capacity to be employed, the universalist and assimilationist strategy prevailed in the 1960s and

feminist universalism or sameness feminism, a form of feminism that was, however, not endorsed by most feminists at the time, who also wanted to "change the social structures that created the context for workplace and other inequalities – in particular, the social structures that gave women sole or primary responsibility for childrearing." Yet, as Bagenstos notes, while attempts to secure public funding for abortion failed and the push for a national childcare program stalled, this sameness model remained the most viable, albeit limited, strategy. See Samuel R. Bagenstos, "Nevada Department of Human Resources v. Hibbs: Universalism and Reproductive Justice," in Murray et al., *Reproductive Rights and Justice Stories*, 186–87.

46 Ruth Bader Ginsburg and Deborah Jones Merritt, "Affirmative Action: An International Human Rights Dialogue," *Cardozo Law Review* 21 (1999–2000): 253–82. This is not to say that Justice Ginsburg endorsed the narrow concept of sex discrimination that the court went for. In the early 1970s, Ginsburg authored briefs and law review articles arguing that laws according differential treatment on the basis of pregnancy should be subject to strict scrutiny under the Equal Protection Clause. See Siegel, "The Nineteenth Amendment," 183.

1970s, thus underplaying the differences between men and women but also, to a large extent, between different groups of women.[47]

As a result, protections for motherhood have always remained rather minimal in the United States, often disadvantaging racialized and single mothers, and have had to be crafted in gender-neutral terms by assimilating pregnancy, motherhood, and parenting needs to any other gender-neutral leaves related to sickness or family care. Equality in terms of sameness of treatment – or, in other words, assimilationist equality taking men as the point of reference – thus gave birth to a form of "assimilationist workerism," which entailed not only assimilating women to the same treatment enjoyed by men but also prioritizing the domains thus far inhabited by men, like the marketplace, as the relevant realm for constitutional justice and equality struggles. In fact, even today, despite many states and employers having adopted these measures across the country, the United States, unlike most other countries in the world, continues to lack general, mandatory, and paid maternity leave for all workers.[48]

Although much of the protection of pregnant women, working mothers, and parents in the United States has come through legislative

[47] See Martha Albertson Fineman, *The Neutered Mother, the Sexual Family and Other Twentieth Century Tragedies* (New York: Routledge, 1995), 37.

[48] It is the Family and Medical Leave Act (FMLA), adopted in 2003, which even today provides some kind of general coverage, entitling employees to twelve weeks of unpaid leave annually to care for a newborn baby or adopted child, an ill family member, or a worker's own serious health condition. See 29 U.S. Code § 2612 (a) (1), upheld by the Supreme Court in *Nevada Department of Human Resources v. Hibbs*, 538 U.S. 721, 731 (2003), because of its gender-neutral framing. Yet, many have criticized the fact that the FMLA only covers a small percentage of those employed in the United States and offers a kind of unpaid leave that many women cannot afford to take. See also Joan Williams, *Unbending Gender: Why Family and Work Conflict and What to Do about It* (Oxford: Oxford University Press, 2000), 237. Bagenstos has also criticized what he identifies as the FMLA's universalist approach because, despite its neutral framing, it does not deal with the fact that female workers continue to take the leave far more frequently than male workers. As we will see, in other countries, fathers are specifically required to take certain periods of the leave, periods are set aside for each parent, or both. These periods may not be transferred to the other part and may be forfeited if the assigned parent does not take them. Also, Bagenstos argues, the statute ties self-care leaves together with parental and family leaves, which has generated employer discontent with self-care leaves (likely to be taken intermittently and unpredictably). In turn, this has fed a backlash against the FMLA as a whole, making the adoption of paid family leave policies embraced by the majority of industrialized countries even more unlikely. For further details, see Bagenstos, "Nevada Department of Human Resources v. Hibbs," 202–3. Policy debates around the topic have resumed under the Biden administration.

means and court intervention,[49] it seems that the US constitutional tradition of antistereotyping or assimilationist workerism made it fundamentally more difficult to reclaim the centrality of motherhood and care as one of constitutional substance. In fact, at least some voices in the debate have deplored the legacy of this approach by remarking that, in their discussions about motherhood, they have too often been automatically labeled as "pronatalists" and condemned as endorsing normative motherhood,[50] and that this has forced feminists to narrow their focus mostly on nonfamily circumstances. To the extent that they could be discussed, family circumstances have also been framed more as an obstacle to employment equality than as an expression of the human interdependent condition or the fulfillment of the human capability of care, which the "founding fathers" forgot to address. This doubtlessly facilitated the handing over of the agenda of "family values" to the cultural right.[51] As we shall see, to this day, this cultural right has not been willing to let go of its traditional understanding of gender roles within the family or of its central conviction that the family remains the natural repository of "inevitable dependency," a dependency that has, for the most part, been "allocated away from the state to the private grouping."[52] At the same time, this "familialization of care" has had terrible effects on those mothers who, unable to rely on the support of a breadwinner or on their class privilege, have found it impossible to combine motherhood and self-reliance through employment and have been stigmatized for it.[53]

2.4 The Working Mother: The Potential and Limitations of Maternalist Accommodationism

The European experience offers a different landscape and has resulted, broadly speaking, not in the "privatization" of motherhood or the family,

[49] Recently, Congress is considering the Pregnant Workers Fairness Act (H.R. 2694, 116th Cong. [2019–2020]), which mandates pregnancy-specific accommodations; yet, once again, the proposed pregnancy accommodation statute is itself couched in gender-neutral, not sex-specific, terms.

[50] See Fineman, *The Neutered Mother*, 87.

[51] Ibid., 88.

[52] Ibid., 161–62.

[53] As we shall see, the bare impossibility for women to replicate the male model, now taken as a universal standard, has triggered national and global dynamics of "class, ethnic and racial dumping" whereby the shortage of care is addressed thanks to poorly paid and precarious forms of care work provided mostly by immigrant women.

but rather in the adoption of measures to allow women the combination of paid employment and motherhood, thereby accommodating, instead of ignoring or subverting, women's unique role in reproduction and family sustenance. As a result, women have often experienced a separate professional track, the so-called mommy track, which includes different forms of glass ceilings and is characterized by market segregation, a prevalence in the informal sector, part-time work, and lower pay.

Legislated and often mandatory (time-limited) maternity leaves are one of the common forms of support for working parents in European countries, dating back in some cases to the nineteenth century and the formation of the welfare state. Germany adopted the first such legislation in 1883 (in the form of statutory health insurance for workers offering, among others, childbed benefits for mothers after birth), followed by Sweden in 1891 and France in 1928.[54] The early legislation was typically paternalistic in its concern for the health of the child and the mother, with prenatal and postnatal leaves being compulsory and supplementary income support of job protection seldom provided. After World War II, the pronatalist rationale became very explicit in social policies across Europe, many wishing women to return to the role of homemakers.[55] This rationale explains why many nations at the time, such as Denmark, Finland, Greece, the Netherlands, and France, mandated compulsory pregnancy leaves but failed to prohibit dismissal from jobs. Not until the late 1960s did two decades of uninterrupted change begin, during which the concept of maternity leave evolved from a prohibition on employing women during pregnancy or a period before or after labor to one of time off work to care for newborns and young children, combined with job security, as countries with compulsory leave started adding prohibitions against dismissals from employment of both pregnant workers and workers on maternal or parental leave.[56]

[54] See Christopher J. Ruhm and Jackqueline L. Teague, "Parental Leave Policies in Europe and North America," in *Gender and the Family Issues in the Workplace*, eds. Francine D. Blau and Ronald Ehrenberg (New York: The Russell Sage Foundation Press, 1997), 133–56.

[55] Even in the Eastern Bloc, where women were still expected to work shoulder to shoulder with men in factories, long maternity leaves were established as an important part of the region's pronatalist policies. See Raluca Maria Popa, "The Socialist Project for Gender (In)Equality: A Critical Discussion," *Journal for the Study of Religion and Ideologies* 2, no. 6 (2003): 49–72, at 56–57.

[56] Portugal, Spain, and Finland instituted job-protected leaves during the 1969–1971 period, and France and the Netherlands passed similar legislation in 1975 and 1976. Denmark, Ireland, and Greece ratified such laws between 1980 and 1984.

The special protections for maternity and pregnancy in Europe were not questioned or seen as in conflict with notions of gender equality, understood as gender neutrality, but rather deemed necessary by the principle of equality that, in the postwar period, also began to encompass diverse family formations and children born out of wedlock. Mothers have primarily remained the target of such measures ever since, with far longer leaves. Paternity leaves, on the other hand, while mostly voluntary in nature, are only now starting to be adopted in an increasing number of countries. So far, such leaves have often been conceptualized as subsidiary to maternity leaves, reflecting both the assumption and social reality that mothers, not fathers, are most commonly the primary caretakers.

Looking back into constitutional history, we find a moment of doctrinal convergence between the United States and Europe in the 1970s, when the role of women as housewives was increasingly questioned and the role of women in the employment market was increasingly affirmed, a process fueled by the expansion of market forces as well as the challenge of second-wave feminism to women's enforced subordination through the separate spheres ideology. This process would, in due course, allow women on both sides of the Atlantic to claim access to professions that had so far been primarily reserved for men either de jure or de facto.[57] The main difference is that, in the United States, the emphasis remained on formal equality and an antistereotyping principle – and, as we have seen, this soon led to an assimilationist logic that simply silenced and "privatized" the gendered division of roles that continued to be placed on the family realm (a realm sealed by constitutionally protected privacy notions) while inevitably pathologizing family forms that could

[57] For women constitutionally litigating to access employments traditionally held by men, see the cases decided by the Spanish Constitutional Court, S.T.C., Nov. 14, 1991 (No. 216/1991) and S.T.C., Dec. 14, 1992 (No. 229/1992) on women wanting to be employed in the mining sector; the German case BVerfGE 89, 276, Nov. 16, 1993, about a woman who was not shortlisted for a job as a mechaninc although she possessed the required qualifications; and the Argentine case, Corte Suprema de Justicia de la Nación [CSJN] [National Supreme Court of Justice], 20/05/2014, "Sisnero, Mirtha Graciela y Otros c/ Taldelva SRL y Otros s/ amparo," Fallos de la Corte Suprema de la Nación, t. 337, 611, on women fulfilling requirements but failing to be hired as drivers. Interestingly, some constitutions have in fact explicitly entrenched the idea of employments that could be reserved for the different sexes. The 1973 Pakistani Constitution, for instance, has a provision (article 27) on the safeguard against discrimination in services, which, however contemplates that "specified posts or services may be reserved for members of either sex if such posts or services entail the performance of duties and functions which cannot be adequately performed by members of the other sex."

not possibly live up to the myth of self-sufficiency. In Europe, on the other hand, while formal equality and antistereotyping provisions were adopted too, an accommodationist logic gradually unfolded, which reflected the traditional and constitutionally rooted importance attached to the social protection of motherhood, seeking to provide working women with the actual means to combine paid and unpaid labor as a way to ensure their opportunities in the marketplace, even if those still remained limited by their disproportionate share of unpaid labor in the family.

Several characteristics of the welfare state tradition merged with the liberal tradition in postwar Western European constitutionalism and account for the specific features of Europe's understanding of sex equality in the constitutions of the second democratization wave that began during the postwar period and reached its peak in the mid-1970s. First, the existence of constitutional provisions recognizing the obligation of the state to afford protection to the family, and more specifically to motherhood, an element that allowed the promotion of women's work–life balance and the reduction of the burdens of working mothers.[58] As we have seen, this trend was born in the interwar constitutional period and survived the immediate post–World War II European constitutionalism period thanks also to the contribution (however limited) of women in constitution-making processes. From there, it would be exported to other countries in Europe, including those in Southern Europe joining the third democratization wave. It would then reach the rest of the world through the constitutionalization process following Africa's decolonization (1950–1975) and the democratic transitions in Latin America and Asia Pacific in the 1980s, as well as in sub-Saharan Africa in 1989. This protection of pregnancy and maternity was not only shared but was actually even more prominent in the socialist constitutional tradition, which additionally emphasized the need for some degree of communalization of housework and reproductive labor. Indeed, the constitutions of Central and Eastern European countries,[59]

[58] Thus, paragraph 11 in the preamble of the 1946 French Constitution declares that "[the nation] shall guarantee to all, notably to children, mothers and elderly workers, protection of their health, material security, rest and leisure." See also Julie C. Suk, "Feminist Constitutionalism and the Entrenchment of Motherhood," in *Special Issue: Law and the Imagining of Difference*, ed. Austin Sarat (Bingley: Emerald Publishing Limited, 2018), 128.

[59] It is interesting to note that in this period one can clearly observe a shift in the way gender equality was generally understood in communist countries. Whereas in the first years of

those of former Soviet states, and even those in other parts of the world drawing inspiration from this socialist tradition contain quite elaborate motherhood protective clauses.[60]

An additional feature of this European constitutionalism that made it amenable to motherhood protections was the gradual qualification of formal equality notions by substantive equality clauses, making the state responsible for the removal of social and economic obstacles impeding de facto or real equality. With only some exceptions, these constitutional substantive equality clauses were primarily designed with a class axis in

communism, equality between men and women was generally understood as *sameness*, in that women were generally supposed to be, work, and lead their life in the same way as men, in the late 1960s, because of the demographic concerns in the region, communist states began to accommodate women's different role as mothers and define equality as *difference*. The 1977 USSR Constitution reflects this. Article 35 provides: "Women and men have equal rights in the USSR. Exercise of these rights is ensured by according women equal access with men to education and vocational and professional training, equal opportunities in employment, remuneration, and promotion, and in social and political, and cultural activity, and by special labour and health protection measures for women; by *providing conditions enabling mothers to work; by legal protection, and material and moral support for mothers and children, including paid leaves and other benefits for expectant mothers and mothers, and gradual reduction of working time for mothers with small children*" (italics are ours). Article 53, in turn, provides: "The family enjoys the protection of the state. Marriage is based on the free consent of the woman and the man; the spouses are completely equal in their family relations. The state helps the family by providing and developing a broad system of childcare institutions, by organising and improving communal services and public catering, by paying grants on the birth of a child, by providing children's allowances and benefits for large families, and other forms of family allowances and assistance." Constitutions adopted after the fall of communism have continued to pay attention to the special needs of working mothers. Examples include article 47 (2) of the 1991 Bulgarian Constitution, according to which "mothers shall be the object of special protection on the part of the State and shall be guaranteed prenatal and postnatal leave, free obstetric care, alleviated working conditions and other social assistance," or article 39 of the 1992 Lithuanian Constitution, according to which "the law shall provide to working mothers a paid leave before and after childbirth as well as favourable working conditions and other concessions."

60 According to Suk, the (nonexhaustive) list of countries containing a provision on the status or rights of mothers or pregnant women (or both) includes European nations such as Germany, France, Italy, Spain, Poland, Romania, Greece, Portugal, the Czech Republic, Hungary, Austria, Bulgaria, Slovakia, Ireland, Croatia, Lithuania, and Switzerland. In Latin America, the duty to protect mothers is found in the constitutions of Argentina, Bolivia, Brazil, Colombia, Costa Rica, Ecuador, Panama, Paraguay, Peru, Uruguay, and Venezuela. In Asia, the constitutions of China, South Korea, and Mongolia contain motherhood protection clauses, whereas in Africa, motherhood is specially protected in the constitutions of Ethiopia, Madagascar, and Niger. See Suk, "Feminist Constitutionalism and the Entrenchment of Motherhood," 116–17.

mind during the postwar constitutionalism period;[61] however, starting in the 1980s, and especially since the 1990s, they began to include (not only in Europe under the influence of European antidiscrimination law[62] but elsewhere as well under the influence of the Convention on the Elimination of All Forms of Discrimination against Women) a more explicit mention of the goal of women's equal opportunities or de facto equality, sometimes specifically validating the adoption of affirmative action or special measures to reach the desired result.[63] In sum, in Europe, a certain antisubordination logic, however imperfect, gradually

[61] For instance, the equality provision in the Italian Constitution contains a clause (article 3) whereby "it is the duty of the Republic to remove those obstacles of an economic or social nature which constrain the freedom and equality of citizens, thereby impeding the full individual development of the human person and the effective participation of all workers in the political, economic and social organization of the country." The 1978 Spanish Constitution drew on it (see article 9.2).

[62] In terms of European Union law, the expansion of the legal framework of the gender equality model is best epitomized by the adoption of the Treaty of Amsterdam in 1997, when gender equality between men and women was incorporated in the treaty as a fundamental community value to be promoted (article 2). Inspired by the Beijing Women's Conference, the treaty also incorporated the idea of gender mainstreaming (article 3), setting thus the basis for policies in pursuit of gender equality, preventing the confinement to an equal opportunity ghetto, and promoting integration across all fields of policy-making. The treaty also enshrined the European Council's competence to undertake proactive measures to combat discrimination based on sex, racial or ethnic origin, religion or belief, disability, age, or sexual orientation (article 6a). The principle of equal pay was defined as a principle of equal pay for work of equal value; and, despite the adoption of the principle of equal treatment, member states would not be prevented to adopt positive discrimination measures (article 119). Reaffirmed under the Lisbon Treaty, the European Union still operates under this legal framework, whose profile is now reproduced in the European Charter of Fundamental Rights (articles 20, 21, and 23). The extent to which such legal framework and policies have allowed women to make progress has been questioned. The European Court of Justice has often adopted a very formalistic understanding of equality, making affirmative action measures an exception to be interpreted narrowly, observing the inherent limitations of an antidiscrimination equality model to address structural inequalities. At best, it has been claimed, the model has accelerated the process whereby some women have entered the male domain of employment, and even so, in a segregated market where the most precarious forms of employment (unwanted part-time, underpaid, and with poor employment conditions) are overwhelmingly feminized. See, for instance, Maria Stratigaki, "The Cooptation of Gender Concepts in EU Policies: The Case of 'Reconciliation of Work and Family,'" *Social Politics: International Studies in Gender, State & Society* 11, no. 1 (2004): 30–56.

[63] Thus, article 3 (3) of the 1949 German Constitution, according to which "no one may be prejudiced or privileged because of . . . sex" was supplemented by article 3 (2.2), inserted by amendment on Oct. 27, 1994, which provides that "the state shall promote the actual implementation of equal rights for women and men and take steps to eliminate disadvantages that now exist."

came to offer the dominant interpretive grid of the sex equality provision, with some national courts validating affirmative measures that went even beyond what European law allowed for and still others explicitly recognizing that the reason why the constitution had included sex as a suspect classification criterion had less to do with the goal of gender neutrality than with "putting an end to the traditional contempt of women and removing those differences in treatment that had placed women in a situation of legal and social inferiority."[64]

Doctrinally, the accommodation of de facto gender specificity (be it biological or functional) in European constitutional tradition has also been furthered by a constitutional antidiscrimination doctrine in the making that starts from the premise that pregnancy discrimination constitutes sex discrimination (and that the failure to take pregnancy into account may also amount to discrimination); considers discriminatory impact and not only discriminatory intent; and accepts, in some instances at least, the relaxation of the state action doctrine in favor of horizontal effects, especially in the employment domain – a domain characterized by gross disparities of power – to help women overcome the real obstacles they encounter within it. In the European Union, this antidiscrimination doctrine and the ensuing need to accommodate motherhood in the employment sector have all been heavily influenced by the interaction between national law and European law, the latter enjoying primacy within its jurisdictional domains, including the employment sector.

German constitutionalism provides an illustration of the described doctrinal evolution. In the 1970s, the Federal Constitutional Court finally abandoned the "two-track" citizenship model that had normalized men and women's separate roles (while seeking to attach equal dignity to both in a different treatment–equal value logic), which it had espoused in the immediate postwar years, and came to affirm strict equality between husband and wife in the family domain. In this spirit, it struck down legislation allowing only German fathers, but not mothers married to a foreigner, to pass on their nationality,[65] as well as provisions in the German Civil Code requiring all family members to take the husband's family name (although wives wishing to keep their birth name would subsequently be required to include their husbands' name as well).[66] This

[64] See Spanish Constitutional Court's decision S.T.C., Dec. 19, 1988 (No. 241/1988), p. 6.
[65] See BVerfGE 37, 217, Mar. 21, 1974.
[66] See BVerfGE 48, 327, May 31, 1978.

jurisprudential change contributed to the first important legal reform of marriage and family law in 1976 and, with it, to the abandonment of the breadwinner family model as explicitly enshrined in the Civil Code. In 1979, a provision that had been designed to facilitate women's "double shift," by granting those women working outside the home one day of "housework" holiday per month yet denying the same advantage to men, was declared unconstitutional.[67] Likewise, the claim to make the cost of childcare a tax deduction to the advantage of women, who bore the brunt of this responsibility, was denied on the basis that, if both spouses shared the breadwinning responsibility, then they could be presumed to also share the children and the housework.[68]

Yet strict formal equality and antistereotyping discrimination did not become the paradigm in Germany, which followed instead the accommodationist path hand in hand with the tools provided by European antidiscrimination legislation. Thus, as early as the 1980s, guided by a substantive equality/antisubordination logic, the court validated differential treatment when it saw that such treatment was intended to ensure women's equal opportunities – especially in view of their role as mothers, a role that was not fundamentally questioned – and addressed the need to overcome the undervaluation of part-time employment options more frequently enjoyed by women. As we shall see, this commitment to substantive equality notions became only more evident when, in October 1994, article 3 (2) GG (declaring equal rights between men and women) was amended to explicitly incorporate the state's duty to promote the effective implementation of equality of rights for women and men.

Thus, in Germany, as much as elsewhere in Europe, while purely paternalistic measures have been rejected, the fact that mothers and pregnant women deserve special constitutional protection at work has remained uncontroversial. In fact, the German court has grounded this protection on article 6 [4] GG but also stated that this duty of protection does not fall on the state alone but on the community as a whole. Moreover, although the protections for pregnant women and working mothers have typically come through legislation, the German court, like many of its European counterparts, has not hesitated to intervene when legislative protection was inadequate, as when in 1991, after the reunification of the country, the court struck down a civil service reorganization

[67] See BVerfGE 52, 369, Nov. 13, 1979.
[68] See BVerfGE 47, 1, Oct. 11, 1977.

scheme that it deemed insufficiently protective of pregnant women.[69] Additionally, the acceptance of disparate impact discrimination under the clear influence of EU law has also allowed the court to check whether formally neutral norms or acts could have a disparate, negative impact on women, taking into account their legal and social, and not just biological, realities. This concept of "legal and social realities," which the law was expected to take into account, has included considerations as diverse as those of women's greater contribution to care labor in the household,[70] women's specific position within a sex-segregated employment market,[71] and even women's enjoyment of legal protections linked to motherhood.[72]

However, the maternalist accommodationist strand of the equality doctrine has its own complications. For one thing, distinctions between acceptable compensatory or protective measures and those that simply enshrine paternalistic prejudices thereby limiting, rather than expanding, women's options can be – but are not, as we have seen – easy to draw.[73] Also, even the best intended compensatory or accommodationist measures, especially when they single out women, may end up both perpetuating existing gender roles and backfiring against market forces in ways

[69] See BVerfGE 84, 133, Apr. 24, 1991, at 155 et seq.

[70] See BVerfGE 113, 1, Apr. 5, 2005, declaring professional pension funds of the Baden-Württemberg bar contrary to article 3 (2) insofar as they do not exempt members from paying the contribution during the time they stay at home to take care of their children.

[71] See BVerfGE 126, 29, Apr. 14, 2010, finding discriminatory, in the context of the privatization of a public hospital, the decision to exclude only cleaning staff from an employment reallocation scheme given its disparate gender impact.

[72] See BVerfGE 132, 72, July 10, 2012, striking down a legislative provision that makes it conditional for third-country nationals possessing a residence permit for humanitarian or political reasons to receive education and parental allowances by the German state only if they are integrated into the labor market. The court took into account the greater difficulty of women to fulfill the requirements, given that they are prohibited from working after giving birth. In essence, then, the concept of "sex" in the sex discrimination ban is interpreted as covering sex itself, as the biological condition of being a woman, and as encompassing also the circumstances that are said to be directly related to it. This includes not only pregnancy or breastfeeding but also the enjoyment of benefits, such as leaves, to reconcile family obligations and work life, since they are mostly required by women. See also, for instance, the Spanish Constitutional Court's decision, S.T.C., Nov. 5, 2007 (No. 233/2007).

[73] The German Federal Constitutional Court has explicitly endorsed the need to draw a distinction between paternalistic protections that de facto limit women's opportunities and proper protections, striking down, for instance, a provision that prohibited women's work at night because it perpetuated an image of women as defenseless creatures, reinforcing their subordination. See BVerfGE 85, 191, Jan. 28, 1992.

that restrict women's chances to be hired and promoted, as so many of its critics in the United States, including within the feminist camp, have long been warning. Think of maternity or parental leaves. Clearly, as long as women are their primary beneficiaries, employers will have an incentive to discriminate against them in hiring and promotion, particularly mothers or women of reproductive ages. Also, measures for the reconciliation of work and family often allow for a stratified employment market, with women's work more closely identified with part-time, precarious, and informal work, which, in turn, reinforces the traditional norm of expecting women to do a larger share of caregiving than men.[74] Aware of this, the German court eventually started to support the need to at least distribute more evenly the social costs of the protection of motherhood in the workplace.[75]

Finally, the accommodationist interpretation of the sex equality mandate, resulting from the substantive equality principle or the motherhood/family protection mandate, has also been found to be insufficient by those seeking to derive adequate motherhood protection from the constitution, given that both the substantive equality and the motherhood/family protection mandates have been most commonly framed as directive principles. An enforceable positive right to meaningful state assistance with reproduction and care burdens has not been recognized, especially when that assistance entails compromising significant public funds. Banning discrimination is important, and formulating an encompassing concept of discrimination helps too, but it leaves the question of how to distribute the costs of reproduction fundamentally unresolved. For single mothers, many of them poor, and for the many who cannot rely on an additional income source from a partner or spouse to supplement their own, the challenge can be particularly harsh.

At the root of the problem lies the fact that, even in Western European constitutionalism, when motherhood protection made it into the constitution, it was to some extent also echoing the paternalist welfare state approach.[76] This compelled the state and the wider community to assist women in taking care of the family while at the same time naturalizing

[74] Suk, "Are Gender Stereotypes Bad for Women?," 54.

[75] See BVerfGE 109, 64, Nov. 18, 2003, striking down an employer's contribution scheme to maternity leave because it had a discriminatory effect on women's employment opportunities.

[76] See Ann Shola Orloff, "Gender and the Social Rights of Citizenship: The Comparative Analysis of Gender Relations and Welfare States," *American Sociological Review* 58, no. 3 (1993): 323.

women's duties. This sense of normative motherhood sits more at odds with US antistereotyping doctrine than with European accommodationist tendencies. As we are about to see, it may also explain the different constitutional framing of the abortion question when it finally entered into the constitutional conversation around the same time and in the context of the second-wave mobilization against abortion criminalization.

Both forms of constitutionalism shared a silence around the impact of reproduction on women's life projects and hence of women's autonomy interest in deciding if and when to conceive. This lack of any mention of reproductive rights is probably the most paradigmatic example of the limits of an inclusive constitutionalism built around the male experience. Adding women to the mix meant opening the doors of political and market participation, which had been a male preserve to women. Yet, although equally central to their independence, the freedoms to decide whether or not to beget children, live through a pregnancy, give birth, and become a mother had not been considered *constitutional* in substance by the founders, despite the fundamental way in which they impacted women's bodies and life course, both then and now.

2.5 The Birth of Abortion Constitutionalism

The 1960s signaled the liberalizing abortion trend in both Europe and North America, with at least forty-two jurisdictions changing their abortion laws between 1967 and 1977 – the vast majority expanding the legal indications for abortion (i.e., the conditions under which abortion was not criminalized, including therapeutic, eugenic, ethical/juridical [rape], and socioeconomic necessities).[77] Pioneered by Scandinavian countries, the liberalization of abortion became a unifying issue for the feminist movement in Western Europe in the early 1970s, especially in countries with a strong Catholic tradition. Among the factors accounting for a change in public opinion and press coverage in favor of liberalization were the number of illegal abortions and their high mortality rate, with a traditionally higher incidence in poor and racialized women who could

[77] See Mary Ann Glendon, *Abortion and Divorce in Western Law: American Failures, European Challenges* (Cambridge, MA: Harvard University Press, 1987), 45; and Kim Lane Scheppele, "Constitutionalizing Abortion," in *Abortion Politics: Public Policy in Cross-Cultural Perspective*, eds. Marianne Githens and Dorothy McBride Stetson (New York: Routledge, 1996), 29–54.

not find ways to bypass the prohibitions. Also, despite the law, in many countries, the number of prosecutions was just minimal, and criminalization ended up mostly having a discriminatory impact against poor women who could not travel abroad to have an abortion (in countries where the procedure was legal in the 1960s, such as Japan, England, and Sweden) and had to do so by referral to an underground network of doctors providing safe abortions for a price.[78] Health problems for women who had been exposed to drugs or illnesses known to cause developmental harms to the unborn (e.g., thalidomide, measles), a growing preoccupation with overpopulation (after the best-selling book *The Population Bomb* warned in 1968 that the Earth was running out of resources),[79] and professional concerns by doctors worried about erratically enforced criminal abortion laws were also pressing issues and demanded a change.[80]

By the early 1970s, feminist arguments for the liberalization of abortion were added to these public health, professional, and populationist concerns, with youth movements also joining in and "challenging traditional sexual mores."[81] In calling for a complete repeal of laws criminalizing abortion, feminists in Europe and North America relied on "speak-out" strategies consisting on "outing" themselves in groups and acknowledging through media outlets that they had had an abortion. In France, 343 women signed a manifesto written by Simone de Beauvoir in *Le Nouvel Observateur* in April 1971; two months later, Aktion 218, a women's organization in West Germany named after the Penal Code section criminalizing abortion, followed in the French steps by publishing abortion stories and the names of 374 German women in *Der Stern*.[82] On August 4, 1971, it was now the turn of Italian women to orchestrate their own self-incrimination campaign in *Liberazione Notizie*, soon followed by a similar campaign in the United States, which was published in the spring 1972 edition of *Ms.* magazine.[83]

[78] See Machteld Nijsten, *Abortion and Constitutional Law: A Comparative European-American Study* (Florence, IT: European University Institute, 1990), 37–38; and Linda Greenhouse and Reva B. Siegel, "The Unfinished Story of *Roe v. Wade*," in Murray et al., *Reproductive Rights and Justice Stories*, 55.

[79] Greenhouse and Siegel, "The Unfinished Story of *Roe v. Wade*," 56.

[80] See Reva B. Siegel, "The Constitutionalization of Abortion," in *The Oxford Handbook of Comparative Constitutional Law*, eds. Michel Rosenfeld and András Sajó (Oxford: Oxford University Press, 2012), 1060–64.

[81] Ibid.

[82] Ibid.

[83] Ibid.

Whereas public health officials and others seeking the liberalization of abortion were calling for the need to proceed incrementally (by adding exceptions to criminalization along the indications model), feminists advocated categorical change and outright repeal, pressing for autonomy values and defying normative motherhood ideas that had thus far shaped women's citizenship and constitutionalism. On February 1969, mobilizing for decriminalization, Betty Friedan, president of the National Organization for Women, articulated these views most clearly in her address at the First National Conference on Abortion Laws:

> There is no freedom, no equality, no full human dignity and personhood possible for women until we assert and demand the control over our own bodies, over our own reproductive process [. . .]. Women are the ones who therefore must decide, and what we are in the process of doing, it seems to me, is realizing that there are certain rights that have never been defined as rights, that are essential to equality for women, and they were not defined in the Constitution of this, or any country, when that Constitution was written only by men. The right of woman to control her reproductive process must be established as a basic and valuable human civil right not to be denied or abridged by the state [. . .]. The real sexual revolution is the emergence of women from passivity, from *thing-ness* . . . to full self-determination, to full dignity.[84]

Moreover, the criminalization of abortion had a clear class and racial impact in both Europe and the United States, and abortion rights did not exhaust the scope of reproductive justice claims. Indeed, in the United States, Frances Beal, a prominent African American feminist, described the specific harms that the criminalization of abortion inflicted on women of color, calling also on the need to broaden the discussion of the reproductive harms that were inflicted on women beyond those linked to the abortion ban. Referring to the "double jeopardy" that women in Black and Puerto Rican communities experienced at the time, Beal recalled how the eugenicists' agenda added to the suffering of her people: women of color were pressured to accept sterilization in exchange for welfare benefits at the same time they were being exposed to unsafe abortions when unable to bear more children.[85] Also, although the

[84] Betty Friedan's address at the First National Conference on Abortion Laws, "Abortion: A Woman's Civil Right" (February 1969), reprinted in Linda Greenhouse and Reva B. Siegel, eds., *Before Roe v. Wade: Voices that Shaped the Abortion Debate Before the Supreme Court's Ruling* (New York, NY: Kaplan Publishing, 2010), 39–40 (brackets are ours).

[85] Frances Beal, interviewed by Loretta J. Ross, for the Voices of Feminism Oral History Project, Mar. 18, 2005, 40, https://www.smith.edu/libraries/libs/ssc/vof/transcripts/Beal.pdf.

abortion debate ended up dominating much of the scene, it is important to recall that the feminist claims for reproductive justice included "protection for women who sought to raise children" and the possibility to "postpone having them." Feminists sought "job security for working pregnant women and government support for childcare on a cross-class basis."[86]

As the abortion movement gained force in both Europe and North America, antiabortion forces started to organize countermobilizations. In their opposition, conservative Catholics led the struggle and used the modern language of constitutional and human rights to advance their claims and argue for the right to life of the fetus (described as "innocent human beings"). They became the main engines of a resistance to change, with invocations to Nazism in West Germany and to the moral fabric of the nation in the United States, as they attempted to tie the notion of human life to that of human dignity and the rule of law.[87] In this highly polarized context, governments were forced to act, but because the strongly emotive and symbolic content of the abortion issue made a political compromise difficult to reach in some countries, constitutional courts were asked to step in, mostly to help resist the liberalizing attempts.[88] This is how the first judicial decisions discussing abortion in constitutional terms saw the light of day in North America and Europe. Not surprisingly, the basic framing of the abortion question differed radically in both continents.

2.5.1 Reproductive Autonomy Becomes Constitutionally Entrenched

Proactive in nature and extremely exceptional for its time, *Roe v. Wade*[89] was a landmark case, prompting the US Supreme Court, for the first time in the world's constitutional history, to read a pregnant woman's reproductive autonomy into a silent constitutional text. The Supreme Court would rely on the right to privacy to back the claim of a pregnant woman challenging the constitutionality of a Texas statute that made it a crime to "procure an abortion except by medical advice for the purpose of saving the life of the mother." In fact, the decision, which in time would inspire

[86] Siegel, "The Nineteenth Amendment," 476–77.
[87] Siegel, "The Constitutionalization of Abortion," 1063–64.
[88] Nijsten, *Abortion and Constitutional Law*, 39, 43.
[89] 410 U.S. 113 (1973).

similar claims constitutionally articulated in other countries,[90] has been said to be more responsive to public health arguments than to the feminist claims of the time, foregrounding, above all, the autonomy of doctors rather than that of women and the physical and psychological difficulties of pregnancy for a woman rather than her autonomy to decide freely about her life path as an equal citizen.[91]

The fact is that in *Roe v. Wade*, the US Supreme Court endorsed a trimester framework, affirming a woman's and her practitioner's right to decide whether or not to terminate her pregnancy, banning any kind of state interference in the first trimester, yet allowing public powers to regulate abortion in order to protect the health and life of the pregnant woman after the first trimester and to limit or even ban abortion after the point of fetal viability, when the state's interest in the protection of fetal life could be said to have become compelling. In the universal public imaginary, it became the first articulation of a pregnant woman's constitutional subjecthood and her right to decide whether or not to continue her pregnancy; this has, to a large extent, retained the symbolism around women's self-ownership.

Later case law came to refine *Roe* in ways that gave greater recognition (though not a stronger protection) to a woman's right to autonomy. In 1992, in *Planned Parenthood v. Casey*,[92] still valid law today, the Supreme

[90] In R. v. Morgentaler, [1988] 1 S.C.R. 30 (Can.), the Canadian Supreme Court responded to the claim of a doctor prosecuted for performing abortions who argued that the law at stake, which contemplated an extremely stringent therapeutic exception (requiring the involvement of four doctors, hospitalization, and a diagnosis of danger to the woman's life or health), infringed on women's right to privacy and to make unfettered decisions about their lives. The Canadian Supreme Court indeed found the regulation to be contrary to section 7 of the Canadian Charter, but did so by calling on the right to security of the person instead, including the protection of psychological integrity (with only Justice Bertha Wilson, the only woman judge, interpreting that the provision also deprived women of the right to liberty, as it encompassed important decisions on her private life). However, unlike Roe v. Wade, the Canadian court's decision did not create a constitutional right to an abortion; rather, it upheld the legitimacy of balancing fetal interests against those of women, thus leaving the decision open for further, albeit more narrowly conditioned, regulation than the one struck down. See Baines, "Canadian Charter of Rights and Freedoms," 55.

[91] Siegel, "The Constitutionalization of Abortion," 1066.

[92] See Planned Parenthood of Southeastern Pennsylvania, et al. v. Casey, Governor of Pennsylvania, et al., 505 U.S. 833 (1992). In *Casey*, the Supreme Court analyzed the constitutionality of a Pennsylvania statute that imposed a 24-hour waiting period before abortions could be performed, required a woman seeking an abortion to receive certain information designed to persuade her to choose childbirth over abortion, required a minor to obtain parental consent, and required a woman seeking an abortion to provide

Court reaffirmed the central tenet of *Roe* (i.e., a woman's right to terminate her pregnancy before viability) but departed from *Roe*'s trimester scheme in a decision that has, nonetheless, been praised for reasserting women's constitutional autonomy through its narrative.[93] From then on, government regulation for the purpose of protecting potential life throughout the term of pregnancy would be valid as long as the law did not impose an "undue burden" on the pregnant woman's decision whether to bear a child; that is, judged on the basis of whether such regulation had "the purpose or effect of placing a substantial obstacle in the path of a woman seeking an abortion of a nonviable fetus."[94] Since then, the boundaries of the expression "undue burden" have become the object of endless and fierce constitutional struggles in a never-ending attempt to overturn *Roe* and *Casey*, a true conservative obsession we will return to in Chapter 5.

To this day, and for the rest of the world, the US constitutional abortion paradigm built since *Roe* has remained one in which the protection of the fetus is not seen as a constitutionally grounded obligation (i.e., it remains a *may* and not a *must*, an interest the state *may* legitimately want to protect), although at the point of viability the state's interest can be considered compelling enough to limit a woman's choice. At the same time, *Roe* and *Casey* embody women's successful attempts to place the reproductive rights agenda into the gender-neutral constitutional framework, with *Roe* being a pioneering case that challenged the limits of gender-inclusive constitutionalism by expanding its domain to include essential elements of autonomy that male-made constitutions had failed to consider. Unfortunately, the ability of this constitutional precedent to generate a broader reproductive and care justice agenda in tune with the claims of women's movements of the time were and remain limited. Despite *Casey*'s narrative appeals to women's equal citizenship,

notice to her spouse. Only the spousal notification requirement was struck down by the court.

93 Many have argued that "*Casey* locates its constitutional basis in evolving views of women's citizenship that give to women, rather than the state, primary authority in making decisions about their roles." See Siegel, "The Constitutionalization of Abortion," 1069. Literally, the Supreme Court stated that "[a woman's] suffering is too intimate and personal for the State to insist, without more, upon its own vision of the woman's role, however dominant that vision has been in the course of our history and our culture. The destiny of the woman must be shaped to a large extent on her own conception of her spiritual imperatives and her place in society" (*Casey*, 505 U.S. 833, 852 [1992]).

94 *Casey*, 505 U.S. 833, 877 (1992).

doctrinally, *Roe* and *Casey* crafted reproductive autonomy as a privacy-based domain, free from state interference, and not as a positive right linked to the need for the state to create a suitable environment for human procreation. This environment should begin with but also go beyond ensuring that women are not forced to bear children of unwanted pregnancies. It should require enabling measures for all women and have the support of a society that collectively responds to the challenges of social reproduction. A firmer anchoring on equality would have also considered issues of access and taken into account the situation of women bearing the brunt of intersectional discrimination along class and racial lines.[95] Yet, already in 1980, when the US Supreme Court decided *Harris v. McRae*, a case validating the restriction of federal funds for abortion, it became clear that *Roe*'s abortion right had been turned into a privilege for the better-off, leaving reproductive autonomy for many poor women and women of color without constitutional shelter.[96] Clearly, the New Right's conservative agenda of the 1980s was also not conducive to the broader recognition of the need to socially distribute the costs of human reproduction that the feminist movement had claimed all along.

[95] In fact, at the time of *Roe*, feminists were bringing lawsuits emphasizing that abortion bans violated equal protection because they discriminated on the grounds of poverty, race, and sex, violating their right to privacy. See Greenhouse and Siegel, "The Unfinished Story of *Roe v. Wade*," 53, 63–65, 68.

[96] Even before Harris v. McRae, the US Supreme Court had rejected the argument that public funding or public facilities must be provided to facilitate abortion even in the case of an indigent woman suffering from a medically abnormal pregnancy that could cripple her for life. See Peolker v. Doe, 432 U.S. 519, 521 (1977). See also Maher v. Roe, 432 U.S. 464 (1977) (no constitutional right to abortion funding in the context of medically normal pregnancy) and Webster v. Reproductive Health Services, 492 U.S. 490 (1989) (constitutionally valid to prohibit public funding to perform abortions). See also Eileen L. McDonagh, "My Body, My Consent: Securing the Constitutional Right to Abortion Funding," *Albany Law Review* 62, no. 3 (1999): 1057–118. In Harris v. McRae, 448 U.S. 297 (1980), the Supreme Court upheld the constitutionality of the Hyde Amendment, which prohibited the use of federal funds for abortions desired by Medicaid recipients, something that disproportionately burdened women of color, over-represented among those living in poverty. Author Khiara M. Bridges draws connections between advocacy against the Hyde Amendment and the growing opposition to sterilization abuse, highlighting the ways in which activists argued that, by refusing to fund indigent women's abortions, yet covering the cost of their sterilizations, the federal government was actually making it more likely that low-income women of color would choose sterilization in order to avoid unwanted pregnancies. See Khiara M. Bridges, "Elision and Erasure: Race, Class, and Gender in *Harris v. McRae*," in Murray et al., *Reproductive Rights and Justice Stories*, 120.

2.5.2 *Normative Motherhood Becomes Constitutionally Entrenched*

Europe's welfarist and maternalist constitutional tradition shaped the abortion debate in different ways from the very start, when it was taken to the courts. Similar clashes between liberalizing attempts and reactionary counterforces had taken place between 1974 and 1975, producing constitutional decisions on abortion in Austria, France, Italy, and Germany. Yet, unlike in the United States, abortion constitutionalism in Europe started off, for the most part, "reactive" in nature; that is, with those resisting liberalization taking the lead in appealing to the constitution. The only exception was Italy, where the Constitutional Court was seized by a judge who successfully challenged the country's criminalization of abortion in *all* cases (with a very narrow necessity exception) as inadequate to protecting a woman's health and life.[97] For the rest of Western European countries, abortion liberalization came about mostly through legislation, as neither women nor those defending women's reproductive rights relied on constitutional texts, which were almost entirely silent on the matter of reproduction, or constitutional courts to advance their position.[98] Conservative groups seizing the courts were adamantly opposed to legislative attempts to depart altogether from the

[97] See Corte cost., 18 febbraio 1975, n. 27, 20, in Giur. cost., 1975, 117, 43; Racc. uff. corte cost., 201, 98; Foro it. I, 515 (It.).

[98] In the communist bloc, the repression of religion allowed for a different dynamic to unfold, and some of the constitutions of the time had some provisions concerning reproduction, although not specifically referred to abortion. Article 55 of the 1991 Slovenian Constitution – which substantially reproduces the provisions contained in article 233 of the 1974 Constitution of the Socialist Republic of Slovenia – reads: "Everyone should be free to decide whether to bear children. The state shall guarantee the opportunities for exercising this freedom and shall create such conditions as will enable parents to decide to bear children." Just like in Slovenia, Croatian women won the right to abortion by virtue of the 1974 amendment to the federal Yugoslav Constitution. Although abortion during state socialism was generally legal – with the exception of Romania and partly Bulgaria – the debate was seen as inextricably linked to the question of demographic control, and, to some extent, to that of women's health but much less so to that of women's autonomy. Indeed, the coexistence of abortion with pronatalist policies glorifying motherhood, however, make this region a dubious example of early recognition of women's reproductive autonomy. Thus, whereas Russia was the first country in Europe to legalize abortion in 1920, by 1936, in the context of a demographic crisis and now part of the USSR, it criminalized abortion, only allowing it in exceptional cases. A new change took place in 1955 when, worried about the high number of illegal abortions, the USSR relegalized abortion, a trend that would be followed by most countries in the Eastern Bloc. See Alix Holt, "Marxism and Women's Oppression: Bolshevik Theory and Practice in the 1920s," in *Women in Eastern Europe and the Soviet Union*, ed. Tova Yedlin (New York: Praeger, 1980).

then narrow and dominant model – criminalization of abortion with only some exceptions through indications – or at least to expand it in ways that would widen women's interests. This was the case in Austria, France, and Germany precisely around the time of *Roe*. When appealed, rights-based constitutionalism was brought in to impede rather than expand women's emancipatory reproductive claims. Given Europe's maternalist constitutional tradition, this may not have come as a full surprise. Nevertheless, because European postwar constitutions contained, at best, a provision commending states to protect mothers and families – but not to force women, not even pregnant women, to become mothers – it took some doctrinal engineering to constitutionally ground the obligation of the state to protect the fetus and, more importantly, to derive from it pregnant women's constitutional prima facie duty to bear and give life to it.

In Austria, the constitutional court refused to grant unborn human life any constitutional standing.[99] In other countries, despite the prevalent silence on the matter in the constitutions of the time,[100] constitutional

[99] The Austrian Constitutional Court confronted the challenge of legislation exempting women from criminal punishment in those cases where they had an abortion performed within the first three months. In its decision, the court rejected arguments based on an alleged right to life of the fetus, arguing that neither the Austrian Constitution nor the European Convention of Human Rights by which it was bound recognized such a right but also that, even if one was willing to infer such a right, it would protect against state interference and not against interferences by private parties. See Verfassungsgerichtshof [VfGH] [Constitutional Court], Oct. 11, 1974, Erklaerungen und Beschlüsse des Verfassungsgerichtshofes [VfSlg] 7400/1974.

[100] Article 4.1 of the American Convention on Human Rights, adopted in 1969, refers to the need to protect life from the moment of conception. But only in the 1980s, after the abortion debate was first constitutionalized, do we find some constitutions referring explicitly to the unborn life as deserving constitutional protection. In explicit affirmation of its Catholic ethos and rejection of Roe v. Wade, the 1987 Constitution of the Republic of the Philippines included a provision undertaking to "equally protect the life of the mother and the life of the unborn from conception" (article 2, section 12). See Bryan Dennis Gabito Tiojanco, "Gender and Constitutionalism in the Philippines," in Chang et al., *Gender, Sexuality and Constitutionalism in Asia*. Similarly, under the influence of Catholicism, the Republic of Ireland underwent a constitutional amendment in 1983 whereby "the State acknowledges the right to life of the unborn and, with due regard to the equal right to life of the mother, guarantees in its laws to respect, and, as far as practicable, by its laws to defend and vindicate that right" (Ireland, Eighth Amendment of the Constitution Act, 1983 [amending Ir. Const., article 40, section 3.3]). This provision then also provided the basis for further litigation. For instance, in some cases, the courts prohibited private groups from disseminating information on abortion services available abroad. See Attorney General (Society for the Protection of the Unborn Child) v. Open Door Counselling and Dublin Well Woman Centre Ltd.

courts – heavily influenced by religious forces – came up with doctrinal constructions to support the protection of the fetus, turning this constitutional protection into a constitutional *must*, not a simple *may*. Still, not always did this construction doom liberalizing attempts to failure. For instance, in responding to the claims presented to it, the Italian Constitutional Court supported the move toward more expansive abortion laws.[101] The German Federal Constitutional Court, however, took a radically different path, setting a precedent that came to exercise a paramount influence both in Europe and beyond, especially in countries with a dominant Catholic ethos.

In 1975, the German Federal Constitutional Court handed down a landmark decision striking down a legislative attempt to decriminalize

[1988] IR 593. This article was amended in 2018 when the Thirty-Six Amendment to the Constitution was passed, which introduced a new clause that reads, "Provision may be made by law for the regulation of termination of pregnancy." Other constitutional examples explicitly referring to the protection of human life before birth include two similarly formulated provisions: article 15.1 of the 1992 Slovak Constitution ("Everyone has the right to life. Human life is worthy of protection even before birth") and article 6.1 of the Czech Charter of Fundamental Rights and Basic Freedoms ("Everybody has the right to live. Human life deserves to be protected already before birth"), part of the 1992 Czech Constitution.

101 The Constitutional Court recognized that the protection of the unborn had a constitutional foundation (pointing to appropriate protections for "the mother and child" and "the inviolable rights of the person" in articles 37 and 2 of the Italian Constitution, respectively). Nevertheless, the Italian court struck down the challenged legislation because the necessity exception (the only general exception that the law contemplated in the general Penal Code) was too narrow and rested on a wrong equivalence between the right to life and health of a pregnant woman, who is a person, and that of an embryo, which has yet to become a person. See Corte cost., 18 febbraio 1975, n. 27, 20, in Giur. cost., 1975, 117, 43; Racc. uff. corte cost., 201, 98; Foro it. I, 515. Not explicitly granting the fetus proper constitutional standing, the French Constitutional Council declared the constitutional validity of a legislative reform allowing women to have an abortion as a result of a "situation of distress" or for therapeutic reasons within the first ten weeks as not contrary to the principle of liberty of the person (in article 2 of Declaration of Rights of Man and of the Citizen). Although validating the relevance of "the principle of respect for every human being from the very commencement of life" referred to as such in the challenged statute, the Constitutional Council seemed to endorse the balancing act in the law when underscoring that the exceptions applied only in case of necessity and according to conditions strictly defined by the law. See Conseil constitutionnel [CC] [Constitutional Council] decision No. 74-54DC, Jan. 15, 1975, J.O. 671. A similar reasoning was adopted by the Constitutional Council in 2001 when validating a legislative reform that expanded from ten to twelve weeks the time of abortion for women in situation of distress, but also making the counseling procedure purely optional. See Council constitutionnel [CC] [Constitutional Council], decision No. 2001-446DC, June 27, 2001, J.O. 10828.

abortion during the first twelve weeks of pregnancy, under the only condition that women willing to have an abortion be subject to counseling in order to learn about available public and private assistance.[102] The entire decision framed the constitutional question as one about the protection of the fetus in such a way that it normalized or naturalized a pregnant woman's duty to bear a child, a duty that was explicitly referred to by the court. Unlike the French court, the German court decided that it could not allow the time-based solution that the legislation proposed by applying a proportionality analysis, balancing a woman's autonomy versus the protection owed to the fetus. For the German court, proportionality was simply out of the question. As an "unborn human being," the court held, the fetus enjoyed the protection of the right to life (article 2 [2] GG), and this ruled out the possibility of signaling different stages in the process of development of the fetus (such as viability), which could be deemed fundamentally relevant for determining the varied degrees of constitutionally required protection.[103] Similarly, the court recognized that the fetus also enjoyed the protection of human dignity (article 1 [1] GG).[104] In fact, connecting both life and dignity, the German court elevated human life to the category of supreme value in Germany's constitutional order, calling for state protection.[105] The court did admit, however – albeit only in passing – that women's self-determination could be impaired by pregnancy, birth, and child-rearing, yet these harms paled in comparison to the harm done to the unborn when destroyed, which is why the life of the fetus had to be granted priority as a matter of principle and for the entire duration of the pregnancy.[106] This meant, in other words, that pregnant women had a prima facie constitutional duty to

[102] See BVerfGE 39, 1, Feb. 25, 1975.

[103] See ibid., at 37. In the court's reasoning, it was not even necessary to decide whether a fetus is, strictly speaking, a constitutional rights bearer because, beyond providing enforceable individual rights, fundamental rights also embody an objective order of values that has to be proactively safeguarded by state action. See also ibid., at 41.

[104] Ibid., at 41.

[105] Ibid., at 42 et seq. This was the first decision in which the court established its famous and, until today, highly influential duty of the state to protect fundamental rights. Although, in this first abortion decision, the consequences the court derives from the affirmed duty to protect every human life are highly problematic from a woman's autonomy point of view, it is worth noting that the "duty to protect" doctrine has been adopted in Germany to address structural inequality and dependent, vulnerable subjectivities in German constitutional law.

[106] Ibid.

carry their pregnancy to term[107] and did not have a right to arbitrarily reject what the court called their "natural maternal duties and the self-sacrifices that came along with them."[108] Instead, public authorities had a duty to protect the unborn, even against the pregnant woman.[109] Whatever reproductive autonomy women could be said to enjoy constitutionally, it seemed to stop in principle at the point of pregnancy.

For the court, however, this decision did not mean a total erasure of women as constitutional subjects. Women's maternal duties could be superseded in extraordinary circumstances, such as those that are typically reflected in the exceptions of an indications model, including the protection of the life and health of the woman, in case the fetus has serious malformations, when pregnancy results from rape, or even when the woman lacks social means to fulfill her maternal duties.[110] Nor did it mean that the criminalization of abortion was always a necessary method to protect the unborn. For the court, it fell within the realm of legislative discretion to decide what form of protection of the unborn would be the most effective. Still, the legislator could only let off criminalization when showing that they had put into place other means that would be at least *as effective.*[111] In any event, the court stated that, even in an indications model exempting women from criminal punishment, the legal system was generally under the obligation to condemn abortion as a wrong. This is why, before having an abortion, women would still be expected to go through dissuasive counseling, be reminded of their fundamental duty to respect the life of the unborn, and be encouraged to continue with the pregnancy.[112] Thus, the decision essentially framed the abortion issue as one about pregnant women as threatening mothers versus fetuses as helpless others while endorsing both punitive (the threat of criminal sanction) and dissuasive (dissuasive counseling) means as valid forms of protection of the unborn. When a revised version of the Abortion

107 Ibid., at 44 et seq.
108 Ibid., at 56.
109 Ibid., at 48.
110 Ibid., at 48 et seq. For the court, women *must* be constitutionally exempted from criminal punishment when their lives or health are at stake. Beyond that, the legislator is free to decide what other categories of extraordinary burdens should not be imposed on pregnant women, including those represented by the eugenic, ethical, social, or emergency indications for abortion.
111 See ibid., at 55 et seq.
112 See ibid., at 61 et seq. The legislator must always signal that abortion is wrong and that it can at best be tolerated, yet never approved. See also ibid., at 52 et seq.

Reform Act was passed following the decision and broadening the indications model, the solution made no one happy. Antiabortionists objected to the high number of abortions being performed under the social hardship indication and to the public insurance coverage of such abortions, whereas pro-choice activists considered the regulation too burdensome, ineffective, and unnecessarily restrictive of a woman's decision during the early pregnancy stage.

If *Roe v. Wade* had offered the world an interpretive path to ground women's reproductive autonomy on reproductive silent constitutions, the 1975 German decision offered an example of how to derive mandatory constitutional protection in favor of the unborn and of motherhood as a duty of pregnant women. Nevertheless, in 1993, the Federal Constitutional Court was presented with yet another opportunity to refine its doctrine and would do so in a way that afforded a somewhat greater recognition of women's autonomy. In the past, the law of East Germany, unlike that of West Germany, had allowed women to make their own decisions about abortion in early pregnancy. Now, with the backdrop of the reunification of East and West Germany, the proposed solution was a new legislative attempt to introduce a periodic model decriminalizing abortion in the twelve weeks after a nonexplicitly dissuasive and open-ended counseling procedure and a three-day waiting period. The new legislation reflected the view that, instead of resorting to punitive or even dissuasive means, the state's duty to protect developing life could be better served by encouraging policies seeking to prevent unwanted pregnancies (preventive protection) and improve the social environment for women and families with children (enabling or promoting protection). Consequently, the new legislation contained a voluminous package of general social measures on education, birth control, and state assistance in matters of family planning and pregnancy. But, once again, the act was constitutionally challenged and struck down.[113]

In responding to the constitutional challenge, the Federal Constitutional Court did not oppose the abandoning of criminalization and the embracement of a periodic model per se, especially in view of the (by then) abundant evidence of the inefficiency of criminalization in its attempt to lower the number of abortions. However, for the German court, the specific counseling procedure foreseen in the law was deemed to be insufficiently dissuasive and hence insufficiently protective of the

[113] See BVerfGE 88, 203, May 28, 1993.

unborn. Preventive and promotional measures to protect unborn life were not enough. More explicit dissuasion was required to convince women to resume their natural obligations of motherhood in order to maximize the rescue options of each individually conceived fetus but also to protect women from the undue influence of those who, instead of being supportive of their decision to become mothers, could discourage them (including the husband and other family members). In other words, the protection derived from the duty to protect was owed to each individually conceived fetus and could not be reduced to a general act of expressing respect for unborn human existence and trying to reduce the number of abortions.[114] At the same time, there was a shift in the perception of the woman who typically goes for an abortion, from that of a selfish or whimsical woman to that of a desperate and vulnerable potential mother, in synchrony with the recognition of the special link tying the fetus to the woman. This relationship was described by the court as one of "duality within unity,"[115] distancing itself from the previous adversarial relationship that opposed women and threatened fetuses and that the first abortion decision had portrayed. Still, a depiction of women as responsible and sexed human beings deciding autonomously on reproduction matters was nowhere to be found. The conclusion reached in the end described that the effective protection of unborn human life was only possible with the support of the mother and not against her.

On the other hand, foregrounding Germany's maternalist and welfarist constitutional tradition, the court clearly recognized that neither dissuasive nor punitive means of protection were sufficient. Prevention and assistance were also required for those women who would embrace motherhood in principle but either lacked the means to do so or were rightly concerned about the toll on their social and professional development. For the German court, the duty of protection of the right to life had to be interpreted in light of the duty of protection of the family and motherhood enshrined under article 6 (1) and (4) of the German Basic Law. This meant that the responsibility to protect life could not *entirely* fall on the woman but was to be shared, with motherhood and the care of children being portrayed as a service done for the benefit of the entire

[114] See BVerfGE 88, 203, at 252.
[115] See ibid., at 253.

community.[116] Hence, the hypothetical validation of a system that, in seeking to protect human life, prioritized working with and not against pregnant women by providing adequate support to them while at the same time appealing to their sense of moral responsibility. Recognizing that only abortions that fell under the old indications model, and not those freely chosen, could still be publicly funded, the court – sensible to both social justice and strategic considerations – also established an exception for women who lacked sufficient financial means.[117] This then was the model the legislator tried to replicate.

The impact of the German abortion decisions on neighboring countries was noticeable, and although the doctrinal construction embraced by Germany ultimately allowed for the adoption of a periodic solution under the condition that it was accompanied by adequate dissuasive and promotional mechanisms to protect unborn human life, its original architecture remained best suited to support an indications system like the one the country had adopted after the 1975 decision. In fact, this architecture was borrowed by other countries primarily with this purpose, and in the mid-1980s, we find that constitutional courts in both Portugal[118] and Spain[119] were relying on slightly modified versions of it to defend newly introduced exceptions from reactionary Catholic and conservative forces wanting to stick to unconditional criminalization. Both these courts overcame some of the doctrinal indeterminacy of their German counterpart and defended the position that the fetus was not a rights holder, but they still thought it embodied an objective constitutional value worthy of constitutional protection. In 1998, the Hungarian Constitutional Court also relied on the German doctrinal

[116] Tellingly, in spelling out what it considered to be some of the most common causes for abortions at the time, the court included the lack of adequate housing; the lack of means to raise children while furthering an educational project or an economic activity; and the lack of material means and social discrimination against single mothers (ibid., at 259). Among the many protective actions that were called for to overcome this deficiency, the court mentioned state assistance in case of need but also legislation to ensure a children-friendly society, including the prohibition of ending lease agreements because of the birth of a child; legislation ensuring equality between men and women in employment; facilitating the compatibility between education, profession, and family responsibilities; and compensating for the ensuing losses for the person primarily in charge of raising children.

[117] See ibid., at 270 et seq. and at 315.

[118] See Tribunal Constitucional (TC) [Constitutional Court], Acórdão No. 25/84, Diário da República n.° 80/1984, Série II de 1984-04-04; and Acórdão No. 85/85, Diário da República n.° 143/1985, Série II de 1985-06-25.

[119] See Spanish Constitutional Court's decision S.T.C., Apr. 11, 1985 (No. 53/1985).

construction to set limits to an indications system that it thought went too far, leaving the fetus unduly unprotected.[120]

2.6 Inclusive Constitutionalism Revisited

The increasing incorporation of women under the umbrella of constitutional equality since the 1970s, whether textual or jurisprudentially constructed, and hand in hand with the overcoming of family exceptionalism, signals a key milestone in the history of gender constitutionalism and highlights some of the opportunities that constitutional law provides to help women consolidate their claim to equal citizenship. The constitutional ban on sex-based discrimination and the promise of a gender-neutral legal order have been instrumental in the overcoming of sex-based hierarchies of marriage and family law that had sealed women's dependency on men during nineteenth-century constitutionalism, interwar constitutionalism, and, to a significant extent also, the constitutionalism of the immediate post–World War II years. According to women and men, a different legal status of rights and duties – while ideologically confining women to the "private sphere" of the household (both their own and that of others) and allocating them the condition of legal minors within families governed by men – was no longer compatible with gender-inclusive constitutional understandings of sex equality.

At the same time, a constitutional doctrine emphasizing above all gender neutrality and formal equality limited the reach and depth of the subversion of the preexisting "sexual contract" in ways that failed to respond to the amplitude of claims put forward by women's movements during the second feminist wave. We can see this most clearly in the United States, where a concern with antistereotyping yielded significant results but also limited the possibility to attend to the gender-specific

[120] In its 1998 decision, the Hungarian Constitutional Court struck down an indications model that included, among others, the "situation of serious crisis," for which a woman's signature was to be sufficient. For the Hungarian court, a regulation that was only protective of a woman's autonomy was not constitutional. However, the court acknowledged that the decriminalization of abortion, coupled with abortion dissuasive counseling, would be a constitutionally valid method of protecting unborn life, which would also be respectful of a woman's right. See Alkotmánybíróság (AB) [Constitutional Court], 48/1998. (XI. 23.), Magyar Közlöny (MK) [Official Gazette of Hungary], 1998/105, 26.

needs of working women and mothers, including single mothers, thus keeping motherhood and care mostly relegated to the private domain and often pathologized together with dependence. By contrast, European constitutionalism – starting from a maternalist tradition and developing under the auspices of evolving international human rights standards and the influence of European law – came to embrace a more substantive understanding of sex equality notions, seeking the protection of pregnant women and working mothers through a system of accommodations that would enable women to combine work inside and outside the home, both paid and unpaid, productive and reproductive. Yet, this European model, underscoring the "special relationship between a woman and her child," had important shortcomings too, since it entrenched, rather than subverted, traditional gendered roles.

The double bind that women encountered as workers and mothers was clear to the feminists of the second wave: they were, after all, asking for equal opportunity in education and jobs while claiming free abortion on demand and free twenty-four-hour childcare centers. Nevertheless, with the limited exception of the abortion debate, once the head-and-master laws were repealed and other formal inequalities in the law mostly removed – with the assistance of constitutional litigation brought about by both men and women – Western constitutionalism during the 1970s and 1980s ended up having a dominant focus on women's limited market equality on both sides of the Atlantic, foiling the women's movement attempts to expand the boundaries of contestation beyond socioeconomic distribution in the market by including housework, sexuality, and reproduction in more meaningful ways. *Roe v. Wade* and its recognition of a woman's constitutional right to decide whether to discontinue an unwanted pregnancy was a huge milestone for the movement and found no equivalent in the European constitutionalism of the time, where abortion rights fared best when unchallenged at a constitutional level and German constitutionalism actually providing the rest of the world (especially the Catholic world) with a reading of reproduction-silent constitutions that had the effect of entrenching, rather than subverting, women's normative motherhood. Unfortunately though, *Roe*'s grounding on privacy, in lieu of equality, limited the impact of the decision, especially for those women subject to intersectional forms of discrimination. An equality framing might have also helped with the crafting of constitutional arguments to counter other forms of reproductive injustices taking place at the time, such as the forced sterilization of racialized women.

In the end, inclusive gender constitutionalism – still the dominant form of gender constitutionalism in many parts of the world – delivers some degree of equality but also has severe limitations for the emancipation of women. The problem is not merely the need to move beyond formal equality and gender neutrality in legal systems that have been crafted by and for men on the basis of the separate spheres tradition – which therefore reflect such tradition, even when not relying on explicit sex classifications – and in societies that, to a large extent, still functioned according to traditional gender codes. The challenge is how to expand the scope of the constitutional principle of sex equality so as to have it apply substantively within the market but also beyond the market, to capture the wide array of domains in which men have traditionally asserted their dominance over women, as well as the multiple institutions that have enabled such dominance. Many of the constitutional sex equality battles of the 1970s, 1980s, and even the 1990s were centered on either dismantling the head-and-master family order or ensuring women's participation in employment. With only some exceptions, other domains of socially relevant participation, such as reproduction, care in the family, or the exercise of public authority and political representation (where gender roles and inequalities, despite increasingly neutral legal language, continue unabated) were not seen as falling under the concern of constitutional equality. And, whereas formal equality certainly ensured that women could not be subject to sex-specific legal limitations in the family, employment, or education and that they were recognized as having equal rights and duties in accessing public authority, inclusive gender constitutionalism had little to say beyond what could be achieved in any of the other domains that remained deeply gendered. Making the subversion of gender roles *beyond* the recognition of formal equal rights or a limited form of equal opportunities in the marketplace, its chief preoccupation was something inclusive gender constitutionalism could not deliver. The legal world had been created by men to their image and contrary to the image of women. Inviting women to join the world of men without questioning the ways in which this world had been built, mostly at the expense of the world they had created for women, and either granting them the same rights men had granted themselves or some minimal accommodations as pregnant women or working mothers, could not deliver the justice women demanded. Not even in the marketplace, where gender dynamics continued largely unchanged despite formal equality, and much less in other domains and institutions. Women would have to join constitutionalism as norm creators in more than token numbers to begin building on what their forebearers had achieved and go beyond it, shaping an expanded agenda for the constitutional subversion of the traditional gender order.

3

Participatory Constitutionalism

Women as Norm Creators Broadening the Agenda

3.1 The Participatory Turn in Women's Equality

On November 3, 1992, twelve prominent Western European women with experience in high political office (including current and former ministers, prime ministers, and parliamentarians, such as Simone Veil, former president of the European Parliament and main promoter of the 1975 French law decriminalizing abortion) gathered in Athens under the auspices of the Commission of the European Communities for the first European Summit on Women in Power and adopted what would then be known as the Athens Declaration.[1] Affirming that equality of women and men imposed parity in the representation and the administration of nations, the declaration opened as follows:

> WE NOTE A DEMOCRATIC DEFICIT
>
> *We note* that the current position of women in the Member States of the European Communities as in other European countries is still characterised by profound inequality in all public and political decision-making authorities and bodies at every level – local, regional, national and European.
>
> *We note* with concern that women's participation in political decision-making has not improved in a number of European countries since the mid-seventies and that recent political developments have resulted in a significant decrease in the proportion of women in decision-making, particularly in the legislative assemblies in some of these countries.
>
> *We conclude* that women's access to the same formal rights as men, such as the right to vote, stand for election and apply for senior posts in public administration, has not produced equality in practice.
>
> *We therefore deplore* the lack of strategic policies to give practical reality to the principles of democracy.

[1] European Summit on Women in Power, Athens Declaration, Nov. 3, 1992, http://www.eurit.it/Eurplace/diana/ateneen.html.

> WE PROCLAIM THE NEED TO ACHIEVE A BALANCED DISTRIBUTION OF PUBLIC AND POLITICAL POWER BETWEEN WOMEN AND MEN.
>
> A democratic system should entail equal participation in public and political life by its citizens.
>
> We demand equality of participation by women and men in public and political decision-making.
>
> We underline the need for changes to the structure of decision-making procedures in order to ensure such equality in practice.

Calling on equality, democracy, the good use of human resources, the importance of satisfying the needs and interests of women, as well as the improvement of the policy-making for all, the Athens Declaration marked the beginning of a process that has been decisive for many European states and provided ammunition to women's movements advocating equal representation. There were good reasons to take action. Even in those pioneer handful of countries where women had gained suffrage at the turn of the twentieth century, by the 1960s they had, at best, crossed the 20 percent threshold in parliamentary seats, with representation stalling, if not decreasing, after the mid-1970s. To some extent, women in Europe were reiterating the plea for equal opportunities, a plea that, as we have seen, flourished in the 1980s (with positive actions justified under increasingly shared understandings of substantive or de facto equality), challenging the limits of inclusive constitutionalism and its predominant reliance on gender neutrality and formal equality. Yet the plea this time around had a more structural dimension, as it also expressed the need for women to join in and define the rules of the democratic game by ensuring their egalitarian participation in the spheres of power and decision-making writ large. Women, in other words, did not simply want to play the game in male-defined terms; they wanted to join in defining the rules of the game.

This increasing focus on women's empowerment was also facilitated by women's growing network of transnational alliances and evolving human rights standards. Departing from narrower and formalistic views previously endorsed, the Convention on the Elimination of All Forms of Discrimination against Women (CEDAW) – opened for signature in 1979 and entered into force in 1981, still to this day the most important human rights instrument for women's equality – had already echoed many of the arguments advanced by women's movements of the time. Under a mostly substantive equality model, CEDAW embraced a broad concept of discrimination, the legitimacy of temporary special measures to ensure women's equal opportunities, and the need to overcome gender stereotypes, all of which had an impact in much of the constitution-making that would take place in ratifying countries after the 1980s.[2] Yet it was the Beijing Platform of Action, emerging in 1995 from the Fourth World Conference on Women, that best epitomized women's participatory claims at a global level by including among its strategic objectives that of women's equal access to and full participation in power structures and decision-making positions, endorsing the principles of gender mainstreaming and gender balance of women and men in decision-making for the first time.[3] In its attempt to foreground women's inclusion in decision-making and empowerment as a democratic requirement, the Beijing Platform for Action advocated affirmative action measures not only as legitimate procedures, as CEDAW had done, but also as necessary means to combat underrepresentation. Linking equality in decision-making to the notions of justice and democracy, the platform called for a more accurate reflection of the composition of society in governing structures and the representation of women's perspectives and interests. It also listed the unequal division of labor and responsibilities within households as expressions of unequal power relations and among the reasons that accounted for women's persistent barriers to participation in the marketplace, politics, and wider public forums.[4]

Increasingly galvanized through international and regional women's conferences and human rights machineries,[5] by the 1990s, a clear "participatory turn" in the gender equality narrative and movement emerged, which continues to this day both at a global and regional level.[6] While

[2] See Vicki C. Jackson, "Feminisms, Pluralisms, and Transnationalism: On CEDAW and National Constitutions," in *The Public Law of Gender: From the Local to the Global*, eds. Kim Rubenstein and Katharine G. Young (Cambridge: Cambridge University Press, 2016), 437–64.

[3] Beijing Declaration and Platform for Action, Fourth World Conference on Women (Sept. 4–15, 1995, Beijing), adopted at the 16th Plenary Meeting of September 15, 1995, annex II, chapter 4, §G, ¶ 181 and G1.

[4] Beijing Declaration and Platform for Action, ¶¶ 181–83 and G1.

[5] After the Athens Declaration was signed in 1992, a Declaration on Equality between Men and Women as a Fundamental Criterion of Democracy was subsequently adopted during the Council of Europe's Fourth European Ministerial Conference on Equality between Women and Men, held in 1997 in Istanbul, which became a framework of reference for all those working to increase the participation of women in decision-making.

[6] In 2000, the United Nations General Assembly adopted the Millennium Development Goals (MDGs), which it aimed to achieve by 2015, including among them a provision related to gender calling "to promote gender equality and empower women." The revision and renewal of these objectives in 2015, with the adoption of the Sustainable Development

still reclaiming the centrality of rights, this gender equality narrative endorsed the need to go beyond equal rights to embrace substantive or de facto equality (measured in real opportunities and participation), as well as equal empowerment, with parity democracy or gender-balanced participation turning into new desired standards of political legitimacy. In terms of law reform, this participatory turn was paradigmatically expressed through the global – and still growing – spread of gender quotas (with eighty-six countries currently having a constitutional or legislative provision mandating that women constitute a certain percentage of candidates or seats). This is a move that has not stopped expanding, neither at state level (targeting legislative, executive, and increasingly judicial positions) nor in civil society governance (with a focus on political parties, employer organizations, trade unions, research and academic institutions, as well as executive and managerial positions in corporations and institutions).[7] Yet women joining constitution-making processes in more significant numbers and roles can be seen as an inherent, if no less explored, part of this participatory turn too. Both the adoption of gender quotas and the incorporation of women's voices to constitution-making processes have only gained force since the turn of the century.

The claims and agendas that women have been putting forward since joining constitution-making in more meaningful ways have been varied and context specific. At the same time, if we look back, we can certainly identify several constitutional transformations that epitomize some of their major contributions, many of which are related to women's

Goals (SDGs), saw gender equality as one of its main priorities, as it aimed to "empower women and girls and ensure their equal rights." Currently, the 2030 Agenda for Sustainable Development calls again for women's full and effective participation, as well as equal opportunities in all areas of decision-making in political, economic, and public life. Moreover, UN Women, created in 2010 (G.A. Res. 64/289) and dedicated to promoting gender equality and the empowerment of women, works on the adoption of new laws and the introduction of constitutional reforms to guarantee women's equal access to political spheres as voters, candidates, elected representatives, and public officials. The issue of women's empowerment has also been addressed by the CEDAW Committee, which, through its recommendations, has gradually come to embrace the normative standard of parity representation in an increasing number of domains in dialogue with member states. See Ruth Rubio-Marín, "Women's Participation in the Public Domain Under Human Rights Law: Towards a Participatory Equality Paradigm Shift?," in *Gender Parity and Multicultural Feminism: Towards a New Synthesis*, eds. Ruth Rubio-Marín and Will Kymlicka (Oxford: Oxford University Press, 2018), 78–85.

7 All these domains were mentioned in the Beijing Platform of Action's strategic objectives. See Beijing Declaration and Platform for Action, ¶¶ 184 and 191a, and G1.

participatory awakening since the 1980s and 1990s, both nationally and internationally, as well as to the development of regional and international human rights standards, galvanized through women's transnational networks, that were often directly or indirectly incorporated into the new constitutions. Of course, women have not limited themselves to advancing their emancipatory agendas through rights discourses and provisions in human rights treaties or constitutions. In particular, the choice between ordinary versus constitutional politics seems largely contextual and contingent on a wide set of factors, including the political culture and constitutional tradition of the country, but also on the concrete set of opportunity structures for women's movements to articulate their claims in different settings.

Regarding the latter, there seems to be one important dividing line. On the one hand, we find those scenarios in which a country's constitutional moment offered women the vision of a clean slate, signaled by either the drafting of a new constitution or a major reform process; scenarios that seemed to better enable women's input in crafting the new aspirations (especially, but not only, when they could avail themselves of standards and norms that had consolidated at a global or regional level or reproduced trends in neighboring countries). On the other, we find scenarios in which women's evolving emancipatory agendas are confronted with old constitutional texts and a well-consolidated body of case law. In these settings, we will see that constitutions, especially when they are difficult to amend, have often appeared as stumbling blocks rather than facilitators for the incorporation of women's renewed claims.

Overall, the gradual success of the participatory shift in women's gender equality has had several implications, constitutionally speaking, and was accompanied by further shifts. For one thing, it has led to the expansion of constitutional agendas, with a growing number of women in civil society organizations, parliaments, constituent assemblies, and constitutional courts articulating in constitutional terms many of the claims considered essential to women's equal citizenship status, often against a background of expanding, internationally recognized women's rights standards. Thus, we see violence against women, including domestic and gender-based violence, enter the constitutional conversation, but also clear attempts to enshrine more robust notions of substantive gender equality and women's participatory provisions expressed both legislatively and in the constitution itself.

Timewise, the participatory turn in gender equality mirrored a broader participatory turn in constitutionalism, largely justified by participatory democratic theory. Indeed, since the 1980s and 1990s (and accompanying many of the constitutional processes of the third wave of democratization), there has been a call for popular, civic, or democratic constitution-making,[8] seeking to rescue constitutionalism from the domain of "high politics"[9] and underscoring the "dynamic, transformative character of constitution-making."[10] Since then, the growing conviction that meaningful popular participation must be assessed more broadly has triggered a multiplication of mechanisms to encourage participatory constitution-making processes, adding to the traditional and fairly limited avenues for popular participation (such as electing representatives to the body responsible for debating and adopting the constitution or ratifying a constitution through a referendum once completed). These have included civic education programs, national and supranational lobbying, consultations with political parties and members of constitution-making assemblies, public debates, open meetings and channels for written public or online submissions, and publicity in the media, among others.[11] Also, since the third democratization wave, many of the constitution-making settings ensuring women's participation in reconstruction efforts have been provided by postauthoritarian and post-conflict societies, sometimes with UN intervention and often with the assistance of international agencies building on the growing normative framework of women's rights.[12] In short, these new approaches to constitution-making encouraged women to participate and adopt much

[8] Paul Blokker, "Constitutional Reform in Europe and Recourse to the People," in *Participatory Constitutional Change: The People as Amenders of the Constitution*, eds. Xenophon Contiades and Alkmene Fotiadou (London: Routledge, 2016), 40. See also Justin Blount, "Participation in Constitutional Design," in *Comparative Constitutional Law*, eds. Tom Ginsburg and Rosalind Dixon (Cheltenham, UK: Edward Elgar, 2011), 38–56; and Cheryl Saunders, "Constitution-Making in the 21st Century," *International Review of Law*, no. 1 (2012), https://doi.org/10.5339/irl.2012.4.

[9] Vivien Hart, *Democratic Constitution Making*, Special Report (Washington, DC: United States Institute of Peace, 2003), 5, https://www.usip.org/publications/2003/07/democratic-constitution-making.

[10] Helen Irving, *Gender and the Constitution: Equity and Agency in Comparative Constitutional Design* (Cambridge: Cambridge University Press, 2008), 26.

[11] New technological means in recent years have further facilitated a direct influence on the content and shape of the constitutional text. See Hélène Landemore, "When Public Participation Matters: The 2010–2013 Icelandic Constitutional Process," *International Journal of Constitutional Law* 18, no. 1 (2020): 179–205.

[12] This has especially been the case since 2000, with the adoption of the UN Security Council Resolution 1325 on women, peace, and security (S.C. Res. 1325 [Oct. 31, 2000]) and the long sequence of resolutions that followed it.

of the law reform–laden agenda of the international women's movement of that era.[13]

With both substantive and procedural implications, the constitutional and gender equality participatory turns also facilitated the incorporation of multiculturalism and intersectionality as more central constitutional concerns. Although the fight against racism, segregation, and the national liberation movements that ensued in a postcolonial world had accompanied the postwar human rights revolution, by the 1990s, multicultural theories were challenging the lingering traces of white colonizing powers, the European settler populations, including the insufficient recognition of political autonomy and protections of ethnocultural and religious groups as well as of indigenous peoples. In this regard, it is relevant to note that the gender "participatory turn" occurred alongside a "pluralism turn," challenging old assumptions about unitary conceptions of national sovereignty.[14] This is not surprising, as both the global diffusion of multiculturalism and of the participatory turn in gender equality shared much in common as "expressions of the delegitimization process of traditional race and gender hierarchies."[15] At the same time, the urge to have women overcome obstacles to participation and join decision-making processes in the hope that this would help advance women's concerns and interests certainly posed the challenge of ensuring that women's diverse voices were sufficiently represented.

Nevertheless, there was a potential for conflict between the gender participatory turn and the pluralism turn, since multicultural accommodations have not always worked to the benefit of gender equality or gender parity, a fact that minority women probably felt more legitimized to express when, in the 1990s, they sensed their communal identity to be

[13] According to Murray and Wittke, it is now probably fair to say that no process of substantial constitutional review in a democracy or emerging democracy can avoid engaging with gender issues and that this is in part related to some form of international involvement and assistance. Although they observe that most assistance does not address underlying gender power relations, they believe gender-focused assistance strengthens debates concerning women in society and can offer support and perhaps even legitimacy to local actors who seek a constitution that provides a foundation for achieving gender justice. See Christina Murray and Cindy Wittke, "International Institutions, Constitution-Making and Gender," in *Constitutions and Gender*, ed. Helen Irving (Cheltenham, UK: Edward Elgar, 2017), 107–34, at 124.

[14] See Will Kymlicka and Ruth Rubio-Marín, "The Participatory Turn in Gender Equality and its Relevance for Multicultural Feminism," in Rubio-Marín and Kymlicka, *Gender Parity and Multicultural Feminism*, 23.

[15] See Will Kymlicka, *Multicultural Odysseys* (Oxford: Oxford University Press, 2007).

less threatened than it had been before, when more blunt dynamics of racial and cultural subordination were the norm. Internationally, this concern was reflected in 1993 with the Vienna Declaration and Programme of Action, adopted by the World Conference on Human Rights, which prioritized the protection of women and girls rather than culture.[16] As we are to see, since the 1990s, constitutions and courts interpreting multiculturalism and pluralism have indeed evolved to find ways to protect women's rights and better accommodate women's voices and participation venues when it comes to deciding how to address those tensions.

In the pages to come, we explore both the expressions of women's participatory shift (by joining constitution-making and constitutional interpretation in more than token numbers) and the expanding agendas with which women started confronting constitutionalism, with an emphasis on advancing their real opportunities to participate not only in the labor market but also in society, the economy, and governance structures at state level and in their own communities. The following chapter continues to explore the growing constitutional agenda by looking into how women's and sexual citizenship claims have expanded within the traditionally defined public realm (market and state/governing bodies), within the so-called private realm, as a realm of interpersonal, intimate relations, and within the family and reproductive domain, giving way to yet another form of constitutionalism that challenges the very core of the foundational gender and sexual order and its traditional disciplinary mechanisms.

3.2 Women Joining Constitution-Making[17]

Throughout constitutional history, constituent assemblies and drafting committees have been prodigiously populated by founding fathers, leaving – with some rare exceptions – founding mothers out. As we have seen in preceding chapters, there have, of course, always been women

[16] Felicity Kaganas and Christina Murray, "The Contest Between Culture and Gender Equality Under South Africa's Interim Constitution," *Journal of Law and Society* 21, no. 4 (1994): 409–33, at 420–21.

[17] This section draws partly from Ruth Rubio-Marín, "Women and Participatory Constitutionalism," in *International Journal of Constitutional Law* 18, no. 1 (2020): 233–59, which, in turn, is largely indebted to *Women as Constitution-Makers: Case Studies from the New Democratic Era*, eds. Ruth Rubio-Marín and Helen Irving (Cambridge: Cambridge University Press, 2019), 1–30.

articulating views about what the constitution should contain and a reduced number of otherwise privileged women who actually managed to be involved in the constitution-making process. Both in interwar and postwar constitutionalism, we find women availing themselves of their newly conquered political rights to participate in constituent assemblies and even in constitution-drafting committees.[18] Yet, until the 1990s, women's representation in these bodies worldwide rarely went beyond 5 or 10 percent. This is hardly surprising if we take into account women's weak presence in representative institutions and their belated access to the legal profession, providing a relevant pool of constitutional expertise. It is only in the late 1980s, and especially in the 1990s (as the right to participation in constitution-making also gained status as an expression of the human right to political participation),[19] that women begin mobilizing and becoming active in constitution-making in more than symbolic numbers through their presence in elected or appointed institutions and, more importantly, through civil society and grassroots initiatives.

Given women's long-standing exclusion from constitution-making, it is evident that, historically, feminist mobilizations have not been primarily responsible for the initiation of constitutional reform and participatory practices, which have often originated from democratization movements and anti-colonial struggles, and, more recently, have also taken place in the aftermath of armed conflict.[20] In fact, many women's movements around the world have been and continue to be skeptical about constitutionalism and its "lofty promises of democracy, representation, accountability and equality,"[21] probably as a result of women's traditional exclusion from constitution-making and, to a large extent, from

[18] For Germany, see Ute Frevert, *Women in German History: From Bourgeois Emancipation to Sexual Liberation*, trans. Stuart McKinnon-Evans (Oxford: Berg, 1989); for Italy, Barbara Pezzini, "Donne e costituzione: le radici ed il cammino," *Studi e ricerche di storia contemporanea*, no. 68 (2007): 163 87; and for Spain, Alicia Ventura Franch, *Las mujeres y la Constitución Española de 1978* (Madrid: Instituto de la Mujer, 1999).

[19] In 1996, the United Nations Human Rights Committee confirmed participation in a constitution-making process as a legal right, in line with article 25 of the International Covenant on Civil and Political Rights. See U.N. Human Rights Committee, CCPR General Comment No. 25: Article 25 (Participation in Public Affairs and the Right to Vote), The Right to Participate in Public Affairs, Voting Rights and the Right of Equal Access to Public Service, July 12, 1996, CCPR/C/21/Rev.1/Add.7.

[20] See Hart, *Democratic Constitution Making*, 11.

[21] Alexandra Dobrowolsky et al., "Introduction: Women, New Politics and Constitutional Change," in *Women Making Constitutions: New Politics and Comparative Perspectives*, eds. Alexandra Dobrowolsky and Vivien Hart (Basingstoke: Palgrave Macmillan, 2004), 2.

constitutions themselves. And yet, although there have always been instances in which women declined participatory opportunities, especially when certain conditions suggested that the cause of gender equality was only being instrumentally embraced,[22] for the most part, women have joined the participatory wave, feeling compelled to seize the opportunity to shape their countries' constitutions whenever they could, sometimes even from exile and often at the price of difficult compromises.[23]

Some of the first experiences reporting a meaningful involvement on the side of women's movements in constitution-making processes include those of Canada (1982), Nicaragua (1987), Brazil (1987–1988), Colombia (1991), and South Africa (1994–1996), all of which took place after each of these countries had ratified CEDAW and other international and regional human rights treaties. Although this body of human rights norms seems to have clearly influenced at least some of the constitution-making processes of that time, in many ways, however, several of the emerging constitutions went beyond the tenets of CEDAW and were more attuned to local demands. Still, it is only since the mid-1990s that a noticeably growing presence of women in constitution-making bodies emerged and when we find the first cases of women's representation in constituent assemblies and constitutional review/drafting commissions crossing the 20 percent threshold.[24] This rise in the number of women

[22] In Egypt, for instance, after the fall of the Mubarak regime, various women's groups coalesced around a common platform pressing for more rights for women and further united when, after the coming into power of the Muslim Brotherhood, they experienced the threat of true backlash. However, after the Muslim Brotherhood was ousted, the movement divided. While some still witnessed the process leading up to the drafting of the 2014 constitution as an opportunity to push women's agendas, others viewed the pending threat of a military takeover as a far greater danger to women's rights as citizens, thus boycotting the constitution-writing process. See Mariz Tadros, "Egypt's Tale of Two Constitutions: Diverging Gendered Processes and Outcomes," in Rubio-Marín and Irving, *Women as Constitution-Makers*, 330.

[23] On women in exile preparing position papers for constitutional reform in Burma, see Irving, *Gender and the Constitution*, 18.

[24] Between 1990 and 2015, 100 countries around the world amended their constitutions, with women achieving an average presence of 19 percent during that period. See Nanako Tamaru and Marie O'Reilly, *How Women Influcence Constitution Making after Conflict and Unrest*, January 2018 Research Report (Washington: Inclusive Security, 2018), 52, https://www.inclusivesecurity.org/wp-content/uploads/2018/02/How-Women-Influence-Constitution-Making.pdf. To mention some examples, three of the twelve commissioners in Rwanda's 2003–2004 constituent process (25 percent) were women; seven of the twenty-nine constitution review commissioners in Kenya's 2000–2005 constituent process (24 percent) were women; and Morocco's appointed commission for the drafting of

active in constitution-making institutions reflected the natural increase of women in parliaments as they gradually partook in the participatory awakening, often assisted by quota legislation,[25] and came to inhabit the public sphere, but it also reflected their unyielding mobilization, demanding their seat at the table in processes that came to be increasingly supported by foreign actors and international institutions, especially in postconflict settings.[26] Some of the most recent participatory constitution-making experiences have, in fact, sought an even more direct involvement of ordinary citizens in constitution-drafting bodies, and it is precisely these experiences that have led women to come ever closer to true participatory parity.[27] Recent constitution-making

the constitution revision in 2011 comprised five women (26 percent). See Hart, *Democratic Constitution Making*, 10; and Sara Borrillo, "Women's Movements and the Recognition of Gender Equality in the Constitution-Making Process in Morocco and Tunisia (2011–2014)," in Rubio-Marín and Irving, *Women as Constitution-Makers*, 48.

25 Quota legislation has facilitated the presence of women in various recent constituent processes, including those in Bolivia, where quota legislation resulted in a constituent assembly with 33.7 percent of female representation in the process that led to the 2009 constitution; Ecuador, where quota legislation ensured 35.4 percent of female representation; and, more recently, Chile, where several constitutional amendments have been passed seeking to guarantee, for the first time in history, an almost perfect gender equal composition of the constituent assembly that is to enact the country's new constitution.

26 In mobilizing, women across the globe have increasingly found the support of international and regional organizations as well as of a growing number of intergovernmental and nongovernmental bodies, among them, International IDEA; Organisation internationale de la Francophonie; the United States Institute of Peace (USIP); Democracy Reporting International; the Public International Law and Policy Group; Interpeace; and the Max Planck Foundation for International Peace and the Rule of Law. See Murray and Wittke, "International Institutions, Constitution-Making and Gender," 107–34, at 122–23. Best practice instruments have also been developed to support these international interventions. See, for example, UN WOMEN, *Guidance Note: Women's Human Rights and National Constitutions, Leadership and Political Participation* (New York: 2012); and Melanie Allen, *Constitution Assessment for Women's Equality* (Stockholm: International Institute for Democracy and Electoral Assistance, 2016), https://www.idea.int/sites/default/files/publications/constitutionassessment-for-womens-equality.pdf. For examples concerning Rwanda's and Iraq's constitution-making processes, see Irving, *Gender and the Constitution*, 17–18.

27 An example of this is Ireland's Convention on the Constitution (held between 2012 and 2014), a convention intended to produce a report on eight issues worthy of constitutional amendment before concrete amendments were put to referendum. The constitutional convention consisted of 100 members, two-thirds of whom were to be "regular citizens" randomly selected from a group of volunteering individuals entitled to vote in an attempt to be representative of Irish society. The convention comprised 49 women, 33 of whom were selected randomly and 16 appointed by political parties. See Silvia Suteu, "Women and Participatory Constitution-Making," in Irving, *Constitutions and Gender*, 28.

processes show how the inclusion of diversity axes beyond the focus on gender is also likely to have an impact in the resulting texts.[28]

Beyond the question of numerical representation, which, as we know, is never a sufficient guarantee of substantive representation anyway,[29] participation in both formal and informal constitution-making processes was never easy for women and required strategies to overcome the very real legacies of women's political disenfranchisement and silencing. Even in those processes with formal channels for participation, ordinary

[28] In Nepal, the constitution-making process was articulated around two consecutive constituent assemblies (CA1: 2008–2013, and CA2: 2014–2017) leading to the 2015 constitution, which, despite some glaring contradictions, is one of the most gender-responsive constitutions in the world in terms of both women's rights and the treatment of sexual and gender-diverse persons. In the constituent assembly, female members represented about 33 percent of the total membership in both assemblies and were instrumental in promoting women's rights. Also, the process counted with the presence of Sunil Babu Pant, the first openly gay lawmaker in the country. Moreover, a Women's Caucus was formed in CA1, allowing members to go beyond party affiliations and provide written submissions by the Women's Caucus to all the CA1 committees, which would then lead to extensive discussions on gender equality in the deliberations of all the committees. The CA2 committee adopted the draft of the CA1 committee almost in its entirety, leading to the inclusion of provisions on sexual and gender-diverse persons, women's rights, and representation in the promulgated constitution. Nevertheless, gender-based discrimination in terms of citizenship endured notwithstanding the many efforts by female CA members. See Mara Malagodi, "Gender, Sexuality and Constitutionalism in Nepal," in *Gender, Sexuality and Constitutionalism in Asia*, eds. Wen-Chen Chang et al. (Oxford: Hart Publishing, forthcoming).

[29] In this regard, Egypt offers an interesting example. In the process of drawing up the 2013 constitution, there were five women representing 10 percent of the constitutional committee. From a descriptive point of view, this was only marginally better than the 2012 drafting committee in which women had 7 percent of seats. However, from a substantive point of view, the difference was dramatic. Out of the five women chosen to be on the constitutional assembly, at least four had strong track records of championing women's rights. See Tadros, "Egypt's Tale of Two Constitutions," 331–32. The religious views of women in drafting committees have also shaped the clauses related to gender issues in overwhelmingly Catholic countries. This is, for instance, the case of the Philippines, where the 1987 constitution (resulting from the People Power Revolution and leading to the government of Corazón Aquino, thanks in large part to the mobilization of women as campaign workers) was drafted by a commission composed of forty-eight members, forty of which were Catholic. Only six commissioners were women, three of them devout Catholics. President Aquino, who appointed the members of the commission, was also a devout Catholic. Only one of the female commissioners, Felicitas Aquino, a feminist legal activist and head of the commission's social justice committee, coauthored the resolution that led to a dedicated section on the rights of working women. See Bryan Dennis Gabito Tiojanco, "Gender and Constitutionalism in Philippines," in Chang et al., *Gender, Sexuality and Constitutionalism in Asia.*

women (as opposed to women who joined in the capacity of parliamentarians or legal experts) encountered particularly difficult hurdles, with ethnic, religious, and class dynamics often intersecting in generating special challenges. To counter this, gender-sensitive civic education and awareness-raising typically accompanied attempts to include women's voices, with women's groups themselves often taking the lead in educating less informed women.[30] Socioeconomic impediments, such as poverty and illiteracy, demanded innovative and imaginative outreach strategies.[31] Education campaigns were, for instance, carried out in South Africa during the 1994–1996 constitution-making process, with multiple drafts published along the way. Illiteracy was at least partially overcome by way of poster campaigns, radio programs, and other mass media campaigns.[32] In places such as Eritrea, where illiteracy surpassed 80 percent, nontraditional outreach initiatives were pursued during the process leading to the 1997 ratification of its constitution, including songs, poetry, mobile theatre, short stories, and even renditions in vernacular languages.[33]

To facilitate the crafting of constitutional aspirations, women all over the world began to rely on women's organizations and platforms to maximize their impact in constitution-making settings. The case of South Africa – which signed CEDAW in January 1993 and ratified it in 1995 – is compelling and, building on the Ugandan experience that anteceded it, is generally recognized as providing the first example of full constitution-making in which women's interests were asserted throughout.[34] The struggle for women's equality occurred within the

[30] Martha Morgan, "Founding Mothers: Women's Voices and Stories in the 1987 Nicaraguan Constitution," *Boston University Law Review* 70, no. 1 (1990): 19.

[31] See Elizabeth Katz, "Women's Involvement in International Constitution-Making," in *Feminist Constitutionalism: Global Perspectives*, eds. Beverley Baines, Daphne Barak-Erez, and Tsvi Kahana (Cambridge: Cambridge University Press, 2012), 213.

[32] Silvia Suteu and Ibrahim Draji, *ABC for a Gender Sensitive Constitution: Handbook for Engendering Constitution-Making*, trans. Abdulla Fadel (Paris: Euromed Feminist Initiative IFE–EFI, 2015), 115.

[33] Ibid.

[34] Catherine Albertyn, "Women and Constitution-Making in South Africa," in Irving, *Constitutions and Gender*, 47. As mentioned, the South African constitution-making experience was preceded and inspired by the Ugandan experience leading to the 1995 constitution. The latter represented a level of involvement of women that was unprecedented in the region, with women's organizations partaking in civil education, monitoring of and petitioning to the constituent assembly, and a women's caucus in the constituent assembly leading to the extensive recognition of women's rights in the final text. See Ali Mari Tripp, "The Politics of Constitution Making in Uganda," in *Framing the State in*

context of the struggle for national liberation, enabling South African women to mobilize the political and organizational skills acquired during the struggle against apartheid to make sure that the gender axis of subordination, and not just the race axis, got addressed in the constitution.[35] In 1992, the Women's National Coalition (WNC) was created by women leaders of the liberation struggle with the aim of intervening in the male-dominated processes that were advancing the drafting of a constitution for a democratic South Africa and overcoming the incipient bias that "race went first" (with a first interim constitution adopted in 1993 and the final constitution in 1996). A broad coalition of over 105 national and regional women's organizations, the WNC set for itself the task of coordinating "a national campaign for the development and education of women which will (1) acquire and disseminate information about women's needs and aspirations and (2) unify women in formulating and adopting a Charter to entrench equality for women in the new Constitution,"[36] prioritizing the social, economic, and cultural reality of women's lives.[37] Supported by international feminist groups, activists, and scholars engaged in similar struggles, the women's platform successfully convinced the African National Congress (ANC) to name female candidates to one-third of its electoral lists of parliamentary contenders in the 1994 election, ensuring substantial representation by women in the constitutional assembly, many of whom were prone to listen to the constitutional demands set forth by women's movements. Among their demands were the inclusion of the principle of gender equality and nonsexism as founding principles of the new state, the commitment to substantive equality (such as through affirmative action), socioeconomic rights, reproductive rights, equality trumping over culture and customary law, protections against violence toward women, the horizontal applica-

Times of Transition: Case Studies in Constitution Making, ed. Laurel E. Miller (Washington DC: United States Institutue of Peace Press, 2010), 163–67.

35 See Saras Jagwanth and Christina Murray, "'No Nation Can Be Free When One Half of It Is Enslaved': Constitutional Equality for Women in South Africa," in *The Gender of Constitutional Jurisprudence*, eds. Beverley Baines and Ruth Rubio-Marín (Cambridge: Cambridge University Press, 2005), 230–55.

36 Ronalda Murphy, "Constitutional Rights Discourse: Canadian and South African Feminist Engagement," in Dobrowolsky and Hart, *Women Making Constitutions*, 32.

37 Catherine Albertyn, "Women and the Transition to Democracy in South Africa," in *Gender and the New South African Legal Order*, ed. Christina Murray (Kenwyn: Juta & Co., Ltd., 1994), 52.

tion of the Bill of Rights over private powers, and effective enforcement mechanisms.[38]

South African women had at least some partial precedents to follow. In Canada, from the early 1980s and throughout the 1990s, the women's movement in general and the Aboriginal women's movement in particular were heavily involved in the country's constitutional struggles.[39] Prior to constitutional entrenchment, women in Canada had to rely on very narrow interpretations of equality and sex discrimination under the statutory Canadian Bill of Rights.[40] When, in the fall of 1980, the Canadian government decided to go for a new constitutional charter of rights and freedoms that provided the opportunity to constitutionally entrench women's equality, women and the organizations representing them set to work. First, women legal experts set the goals and articulated the requirements for equality between men and women as a nonnegotiable demand.[41] This goal was then picked up by established women's groups, many of which would then unite as the Ad Hoc Committee of Canadian Women on the Constitution, which convened a national conference of women across Canada gathering 1,300 attendees with the aim of discussing the constitutional changes required and passing a set of resolutions that were later endorsed by the National Action Committee on the Status of Women, a women's advocacy group composed of 160 constituent organizations from across the country.[42] Their primary goals included constitutional wording that would ensure de facto or substantive, and not only formal, equality; the explicit recognition of women's equal rights to those of men; and the rejection of language that could limit women's rights and their undermining by other constitutional provisions, including those protective of cultural rights in line with the constitution's expressed commitment to the country's multicultural heritage and composition.[43]

38 Albertyn, "Women and Constitution-Making in South Africa," 68, 70.

39 See Kerri A. Froc, "Is Originalism Bad for Women? The Curious Case of Canada's 'Equal Rights Amendment,'" *Review of Constitutional Studies* 19, no. 2 (2015): 237–79. See also Alexandra Dobrowolsky, *The Politics of Pragmatism: Women, Representation and Constitutionalism in Canada* (Ontario: Oxford University Press, 2000).

40 Froc, "Is Originalism Bad for Women?," 240.

41 See Beverley Baines, "Using the Canadian Charter of Rights and Freedoms to Constitute Women," in Baines and Rubio-Marín, *Gender of Constitutional Jurisprudence*, 50.

42 Froc, "Is Originalism Bad for Women?," 242–43.

43 Ibid., 242–47.

Less well-known are, perhaps, those examples of early involvement of women in constitution-making in Latin America. In countries coming out of dictatorships or violent conflict throughout the 1980s and 1990s, massive mobilizations were triggered for the first time on the side of women's movements in processes such as those leading to Nicaragua's constitution in 1987 or the promulgation of the constitution in Colombia in 1991. The Nicaraguan experience is a particularly appealing case study because the 1987 constitution was the product of a revolution that long counted women's rights among its fundamental principles. Formed in 1961, the Frente Sandinista de Liberación Nacional (Sandinista National Liberation Front), which in 1979 successfully led the overthrow of the forty-three-year Somoza dictatorship, committed itself to ending discrimination against women in its 1969 "Historic Program." The Asociación de Mujeres Nicaragüenses Luisa Amanda Espinoza (Luisa Amanda Espinoza Association of Nicaraguan Women), established shortly after the July 1979 overthrow of Somoza and named after the first woman to die in the fight against the dictatorship, turned into a women's movement in 1987, with secretariats of women in mass organizations. It would become a key actor in the articulation of women's claims during the constitution-making process, including in consultation sessions (or *cabildos*), some of which were specifically devoted to women. In these sessions, women from a broad base advanced their various claims and expectations around the new constitution. The concerns they expected the new constitution to address included equality in the political, employment, and family spheres; violence against women; and voluntary motherhood, including not only the right to an abortion but also the promotion of sex education, greater accessibility to contraceptives, the constitutional recognition of the social value of motherhood, and guarantees of protection for pregnant women and mothers.[44]

In Brazil, the 1987–1988 participatory process for drafting the new constitution after the military rule was permeable to civil society mobilization and included a wide set of voices such as those coming from various churches, landowners, businessmen, elites, as well as indigenous peoples, environmentalists, Black movements, women, and LGBTQI groups. The women's movement, which had emerged in the late 1970s in the context of democratization and the transition from dictatorship, managed to articulate itself nationally in the 1980s and contributed to the

[44] Morgan, "Founding Mothers," 29–65.

consolidation of the state machinery, with the creation of the Conselho Nacional dos Direitos da Mulher (CNDM – National Council on Women's Rights) in 1985, a federal institution dedicated to the advancement of women's rights. In 1985, this council launched the campaign "Women and Constituent Assembly."[45] This articulation allowed a strong and organized participation of women in the drafting of the new democratic constitution. Among other achievements, it enabled the elaboration of the Women's Letter to the Constituents ("Carta das Mulheres"), a historical text that included claims in the areas of employment, health, education, culture, family, violence, and social security and that was formally handed by feminist activists and members of the CNDM in March 1987 to Deputy Ulysses Guimarães, then president of the National Congress, and to all state legislative assemblies across the country. This would mark the beginning of the intense process of women's advocacy within the constituent assembly, coined "Lipstick Lobby" ("Lobby do Batom"), a name that was first maliciously used by the media and then resignified and used by the feminists.[46]

In Colombia, the women's movement formed a network around the constituent assembly (Red Nacional Mujer y Constituyente, or Women and Constituent Assembly National Network), which included 75 organizations around the country and garnered 15,000 signatures in support of its constitutional proposals. This network of women managed to participate in the official roundtables organized regionally and by sector; collected citizen proposals for constitutional change; and, as a result of their advocacy and lobbying (through means as varied as breakfasts with delegates and power-holders, press releases, radio advertising, and newsletters), secured widespread support for a significant part of their agenda from both men and women within the assembly.[47] This agenda reflected many of the standards included in CEDAW but also went beyond it and encompassed demands such as the freedom to choose motherhood – including abortion rights – joint parental responsibility for the education

[45] See Jacqueline Pitanguy, "Mulheres, constituinte e constituição," in *Redistribuição, reconhecimento e representação: diálogos sobre igualdade de gênero*, ed. Maria Aparecida Abreu (Brasília: IPEA, 2011), 17–46, at 22.

[46] Ibid., 23–24.

[47] See Julieta Lemaitre, "Feminist Legalism: Colombian Constitution-Making in the 1990s," in Rubio-Marín and Irving, *Women as Constitution-Makers*, 234, 259–60; and Martha I. Morgan, "Emancipatory Equality: Gender Jurisprudence under the Colombian Constitution," in Baines and Rubio-Marín, *Gender of Constitutional Jurisprudence*, 75–99.

and rearing of children, recognition of the social dimension of domestic work, equality of men and women in marriage, and the secularization of the state.[48]

The trend to mobilize around women's groups and platforms has continued in Latin America and elsewhere. In the context of the Bolivian constituent process that began in 2005 and led to the 2009 constitution, the local women's associations formed a powerful alliance through the Movimiento de Mujeres Presentes en la Historia (Movement of Women Present in History).[49] In Ecuador, the process leading to the 1998 constitution had already allowed women to push an ambitious agenda on women's rights owing to the joint strategies and unified actions of women's groups, their ability to establish political alliances with organizations represented in the constituent assembly, and the steadfast support of some of its elected members. Similarly, the most recent process leading to the 2008 constitution relied on a "preconstituent" platform of women's groups, which met in 2007 to define a set of nonnegotiable claims. This platform would later succeed in having some of the women in the constituent assembly sign on to the "Agreement on Women's Rights," which duly reflected their negotiated priorities.[50] In Tanzania, after President Kikwete's announcement of a new constitution-making process, women organized themselves and formed the Wanawake na Katiba Coalition (Women's Coalition on the Constitution) to streamline priorities, lobby, and ensure that the new constitution would be inclusive of women's political, social, and economic rights. Their demands encompassed, among other things, the need for the new constitution to provide for equal representation between men and women in order to engage in all levels of decision-making. Their actions were multifaceted and included translating the draft into Swahili so that it could be assessed by the average citizen; launching a country-wide campaign through constitutional fora to educate remote populations, including women, on the content of the draft constitution; leading an ultimately successful campaign to have the constituent assembly, in charge of drafting the final text, be composed by an almost equal number

48 Lemaitre, "Feminist Legalism," 258.

49 See Stéphanie Rousseau, "Indigenous and Feminist Movements at the Constituent Assembly in Bolivia: Locating the Representation of Indigenous Women," *Latin America Research Review* 46, no. 2 (2011): 11–22.

50 See Patricia Palacios Jaramillo, "Los derechos de las mujeres en la nueva constitución," Institut de recherche et débat sur la governance – IRG, accessed July 17, 2018, http://www.institut-gouvernance.org/es/analyse/fiche-analyse-452.html.

of men and women; and providing well-researched, factual, and evidence-based recommendations to the women on the constituent assembly to mainstream gender considerations into the drafts discussed.[51] And in Turkey, the Women's Constitutional Platform, an informal innovative and strategic network of alliances established in 2007 in the context of the failed 2012 constitution-making process triggered by the ruling Justice and Development Party (AKP), was the result of the collaboration of eighty-six major gender-based organizations representing a new form of network feminism rooted on the idea of building operational and goal-oriented coalitions. It succeeded in gathering almost all facets of otherwise fragmented women's groups, including urban women's associations, local networks, Kurdish women, anti-violence groups, business women, LGBTQI organizations, and sex workers, with Islamic conservative women's groups expressing their support for it in an informal way in the proposals that they agreed on, even if they were not among the official signatories of the platform.[52]

So we see that, despite their belated appearance, women now have a history of formal and informal involvement in constitution-making processes around the world. This allows us to step back and identify some of the common challenges that women have faced and the strategies they have developed in responding to them. One such strategy has been to take issues to the streets in ways that could have an immediate impact on the constitution-making process. This was, for instance, the case in Tunisia in 2011–2014, when the Association Tunisienne des Femmes Démocrates (ATFD – Tunisian Association of Democratic Women) reacted strongly against the National Constituent Assembly's proposal to insert gender "complementarity" in the first draft of the constitution (that of August 8, 2012).[53] Fearing what was generally perceived as a tremendous setback, many voices of protest against complementarity were heard in the national and international media, and twenty-five thousand signatures were collected. Civil society united and

[51] The process remained incomplete, however: the 2014 deadline expired because of a lack of consensus within the constituent assembly appointed for the purpose, leaving the adoption of the proposed amendments pending. See Ruth Meena, *Gender Analysis of the Proposed Constitution of the United Republic of Tanzania: Gains and Challenges* (Deventer: Women Fund Tanzania, 2014).

[52] See Bertil Emrah Oder, "Women and Constitution-Making in Turkey: From Ottoman Modernism to a Constitutionalism of Women's Platform," in Rubio-Marín and Irving, *Women as Constitution-Makers*, 271, 298, 300, and 301.

[53] See Borrillo, "Women's Movements," 64.

gathered in large demonstrations, with protests culminating in a huge rally of thousands of citizens marching for gender equality in Tunis's Habib Bourguiba Avenue on August 13, 2012, on Tunisian Women's Day.[54] Pressure was so great after the massive rally and the media debate it sparked that gender complementarity was eventually eliminated from the constitutional project.

Also, in many national contexts, one of the preferred strategies by women's groups from the very start has been to write their own constitutions, crystallizing women's needs and aspirations in a single document. This seems to have acted as a powerful catalyst for encouraging participation and forming coalitions, simultaneously advancing capacity-building and training. In South Africa, for instance, the ANC leadership issued a document in May 1990 entitled "Statement of the National Executive Committee of the African National Congress on the Emancipation of Women in South Africa," calling on its Women's League to initiate a campaign for a "charter of women's rights" in order to elaborate and reinforce a new constitution. This campaign prompted a unified women's movement (including women within and outside established organizational structures) where none had existed before, foregrounding participation as a method rather than technical rigor or perfect consistency. A draft women's charter was in fact adopted as the Women's Charter for Effective Equality at the national convention held by the WNC on February 25–27, 1994.[55] In Bolivia, the Mujeres Presentes en la Historia movement led a process of more than four hundred workshops and meetings throughout the country, and "about 20,000 women representing 1,000 women's and mixed organizations were consulted and participated in elaborating a comprehensive constitutional proposal."[56]

In some instances, women's associations produced a text as a result of civil society's organizing of a mock constituent assembly, or convention, with the intended goal of having an impact on the official process. In Australia, a "People's Convention" – made up of government appointees and elected representatives, with women occupying approximately 35 percent of those positions – was held in 1998 to debate the question of replacing the monarchy with a republic. At the same time, a Women's

[54] Ibid.

[55] See Murphy, "Constitutional Rights Discourse," 30–33.

[56] Rousseau, "Indigenous and Feminist Movements at the Constituent Assembly in Bolivia," 22.

Constitutional Convention initiated by women from several nongovernmental women's organizations was held prior to the People's Convention, the outcomes of which were presented to the chair of the government's constitutional convention and raised on the convention floor during the proceedings.[57] In Tunisia, in February 2012, the ATFD organized "La Constituante Fictive," a mock constituent assembly that produced a text entitled *The Constitution for Equality and Citizenship through Women's Eyes*, published after an extensive campaign and handed to the president and deputies of the National Constituent Assembly. The text included "recommendations for the constitutionalisation of gender equality and women's rights on a political, economic, social, cultural and environmental level,"[58] as well as an extensive reference to substantive equality. And in Egypt, in contrast to women's modest representation in the 2012 constituent assembly, there was a great deal of feminist mobilization. Several feminist initiatives combining the NGO and academic sectors undertook historical research on comparative constitutionalism and women's demands across Egyptian history; researched Islamic jurisprudence for a progressive interpretation of Islamic law but also pursued consultations in urban and rural communities to arrive at a set of demands that would represent their aspirations for Egypt's new constitution. These initiatives produced two main documents articulating women's aspirations (the "Women's Charter" and "Women Writing Their Constitution"), both of which pressed for socioeconomic rights, human security, equal pay, decent wages, the incorporation of CEDAW in the constitution, changes to discriminatory legislation (particularly family law), the establishment of a woman's machinery, and various institutional setups for gender accountability.[59]

Just like with women's suffrage, a generally crucial factor in shaping women's influence in constitution-making processes has been their capacity to join forces and overcome external and internal divides, such as to be able to speak with a single voice despite their different positionalities, which have been conditioned by factors as diverse as their ethnicity, religious sensibilities, and socioeconomic backgrounds. In South Africa, for instance, women had a long history of political activity, and "women's

[57] See Isabel Karpin and Karen O'Connell, "Speaking into a Silence: Embedded Constitutionalism, the Australian Constitution and the Rights of Women," in Baines and Rubio-Marín, *Gender of Constitutional Jurisprudence*, 31.

[58] Borrillo, "Women's Movements," 61.

[59] See Tadros, "Egypt's Tale of Two Constitutions," 324–25.

groups had experience in acting as a counterweight to the entrenched racial and partisan divisions of society."[60] This, as well as the fear of being excluded from the process, manifested itself during its early stages[61] and encouraged them to strategically seek "unity," rather than "sisterhood," when articulating and fighting for their demands.[62] In Colombia, the women's movement also managed to overcome long-held, bitter internal divisions (also permeated by class) between feminists of single and double militancy (the latter being mostly socialist feminists with long-standing ties to socialist parties) due to the formation of the Red Nacional Mujer y Constituyente.[63]

Yet, clearly, not everywhere has constitution-making proved to be a project that could help women overcome internal divisions among them. In some scenarios, the divides exacerbated instead. This seems to have been the case in constitution-making processes whereby different parties aligned around competing visions of women's roles and gender relations. In the Arab world, several recent attempts at constitutional reform have found society and women divided along a secularist/Islamist line. In Morocco, during the process leading up to its 2011 constitution, where women's associations were most actively engaged, secularist feminists and Islamists had competing ideologies concerning the state, Islam, and gender relations despite Islam not being a source of laws and normativity. Whereas secular feminists fought for a secular state where gender equality is respected, women activists in Islamist parties and associations conceived Islam as the first reference for individual identity, citizenship, and a vision of gender relations shaped around the notion of complementarity rather than equality.[64] Similarly, in Tunisia, the events of 2011 also encouraged a sharp confrontation with regard to women's rights along the Islamist–secularist divide, which affected women's associations and the possibilities of creating a common platform of action.[65] In Egypt, too, women confronted the challenge of finding common ground – not so much to overcome the religious/secular divide, as significant attempts were made to identify progressive interpretations of Islamic jurisprudence and Shari'a law, but rather to bridge the gap

60 Hart, *Democratic Constitution Making*, 7.
61 Albertyn, "Women and Constitution-Making in South Africa," 56, n. 48.
62 Murphy, "Constitutional Rights Discourse," 33.
63 Lemaitre, "Feminist Legalism," 242–43.
64 Borrillo, "Women's Movements," 45–55.
65 Ibid., 55–67.

between those who aligned with the political vision of the Islamists and those who did not.[66]

The influence of religious forces and the division among women on the grounds of religious beliefs has not been an exclusive feature of constitution-making processes in the Arab world. In Colombia, the Catholic Church appeared as a formidable adversary to feminist demands: rather than outright rejecting abortion rights or what the feminist proposals called "the freedom to choose motherhood," the Church mobilized in similar ways seeking to include a reference to life since conception in the constitution.[67] Competing conceptions of gender relations have also been an obstacle for women joining forces along ethnic and class issues, and not just religion. In Bolivia, the idea of complementarity, dear to indigenous women, was regarded with suspicion by the mestiza feminists, who perceived it as essentialist and conservative, while indigenous women looked at feminists – often mestizas as well – as ethnocentric and responsible for reproducing the class relations found in the broader society.[68] In Nepal, during the process to replace the country's 2007 interim constitution, female assembly members formed an informal women's caucus in 2009, but class and caste-based divisions prevailed, dooming efforts to promote a joint women's agenda in the constituent assembly.[69]

Whatever the challenges of articulating a shared agenda and the shortcomings in terms of an actual impact on the resulting texts, there seems to be ample evidence of some intrinsic gains that women's constitutional engagements over the last three decades have brought in their struggle for consolidating women's citizenship status, even, perhaps surprisingly, in cases where the entire constitutional process floundered. New women's organizations sprung up in Colombia after the 1991 constitution, many of them focusing on legal reform.[70] In Kenya, during the 2000–2005 constitution-making process, and after the proposed constitution was defeated in a referendum in 2005, women did not give

[66] Tadros, "Egypt's Tale of Two Constitutions," 342.

[67] For Colombia, see Lemaitre, "Feminist Legalism," 260; for Brazil, see Marta Rodriguez de Assis Machado and Débora Alves Maciel, "The Battle over Abortion Rights in Brazil's State Arenas, 1995–2006," *Health and Human Rights Journal* 19, no.1 (2017): 119–31.

[68] Rousseau, "Indigenous and Feminist Movements at the Constituent Assembly in Bolivia," 10–11.

[69] See Tamaru and O'Reilly, *How Women Influence Constitution Making after Conflict and Unrest*, 52.

[70] Lemaitre, "Feminist Legalism," 263.

up and reorganized to continue their demand for parity.[71] In Iraq, the struggle of secular activists and female politicians to amend the 2005 constitution and reintroduce Iraq's 1959 personal status law has continued ever since.[72] In Tunisia, the participatory process to draft the 2014 constitution, which promoted dialogue between deputies, civil society, and associations of women leaders and feminists, has been credited with helping build women's capacities and support the role of women in the larger process of democratic transition.[73] In Egypt, a group of committed activists formed the Institution to Defend the Constitution in 2016, a platform seeking to exert pressure on the government to enforce its obligations under the 2013 constitution and hold it accountable for its failure to allocate a minimum of 3 percent of its budget to health services and 6 percent to education (as stipulated in the constitution), also calling upon it to reform legislation that violated the constitution.[74] Thus, it would seem that the effects of women's participation in constitution-making on both women and women's movements have been overwhelmingly, though not exclusively, positive overall. In most settings, the joint effort in constitutional lobbying has actually strengthened women's ties and advanced women's political citizenship.

While women's involvement in constitutional drafting is a key dimension to understand the role of women as constitution-makers, a complete picture requires the analysis of the role of women as constitutional judges, given their active participation in formulating, through case law, the constitutional doctrine that gives life to the broadly framed provisions that are often found in a constitutional text. This role is all the more important in the case of constitutions that are either old or difficult to amend, which demands a purposive interpretation to remain in touch with the changing conceptions of equality. In this regard,

[71] Wanjiku Mukabi Kabira, "Women's Experience as Sources of Public and Legitimate Knowledge: Constitution Making in Kenya," *Pathways to African Feminism and Development, Journal of African Women's Studies Centre* 1, no. 1 (2013): 7–25, http://journals.uonbi.ac.ke/index.php/aws/article/view/1337. See also Jill Cottrell and Yash Ghai, "Constitution Making and Democratization in Kenya (2000–2005)," *Democratization* 14, no. 1 (2007): 20.

[72] See Noga Efrati, "Re-Living Yesterday's Battles: Women and Constitution-Making in Post-Saddam Iraq," in Rubio-Marín and Irving, *Women as Constitution-Makers*, 153, 183–84.

[73] Rangita de Silva de Alwis, Anwari Mnasri, and Estee Ward, "Women and the Making of the Tunisian Constitution," *Berkeley Journal of International Law* 35 (2017): 90–149, https://papers.ssrn.com/sol3/papers.cfm?abstract_id=2983803.

[74] Tadros, "Egypt's Tale of Two Constitutions," 346.

although there have been women on constitutional, supreme, or high courts since postwar constitutionalism,[75] the trend of including at least one woman, and often one woman only, became more generalized, once again, in the 1980s and 1990s, although it would reach other jurisdictions much later.[76] The 1990s also offered the first constitutional provisions making reference to the need for courts to reflect gender and racial diversity.[77]

Parity, however, has only been achieved in very few countries and only in the twenty-first century.[78] Yet several female justices have clearly endorsed gender parity for their respective courts, including Chief Justice Beverley McLachlin of the Supreme Court of Canada and Lady Brenda Hale, former president of the Supreme Court of the United Kingdom.[79] Many justices have also supported the idea that women on the bench, at least to some extent, speak with "a different voice,"[80]

[75] Beverley Baines mentions the examples of Erna Scheffler, appointed in 1951 to the German Federal Constitutional Court; Helga Pedersen, appointed in 1964 to the Danish Supreme Court; Sri Widoyati Wiratmo Soekito, appointed in 1968 to the Supreme Court of Indonesia; Annie Ruth Jiagge, appointed in 1969 to the Ghanaian Court of Appeal; and Cecilia Muñoz-Palma, appointed in 1973 to the Philippine Supreme Court. See Beverley Baines, "Women Judges on Constitutional Courts: Why Not Nine Women?," in Irving, *Constitutions and Gender*, 299.

[76] Israel appointed Miriam Ben-Porat in 1977; the United States, Sandra Day O'Connor in 1981; Spain, Gloria Begué Cantón in 1981; Canada, Bertha Wilson in 1982; Australia, Mary Gaudron in 1987; India, M. Fathima Beevi in 1989; Ghana, Joyce Bamford-Addo in 1991; France, Noëlle Lenoir in 1992; South Africa, Yvonne Mokgoro and Kate O'Regan in 1994; Peru, Delia Revoredo in 1996; the United Kingdom, Brenda Hale in 2004; Indonesia, Maria Farida Indrati in 2008 to its new Constitutional Court; and in Ireland, Susan Denham was appointed to the Irish Supreme Court in 1992, becoming its chief justice in 2011. Currently, there are at least three self-identified lesbian justices in constitutional courts, including Justice Susanne Baer in Germany, Justice Virginia Bell of the High Court of Australia, and Maite Oronoz Rodríguez, president of the Supreme Court of Puerto Rico. For further details, see ibid., 298, 310.

[77] Chapter 8, section 174 (2) of the 1996 South African Constitution reads: "The need for the judiciary to reflect broadly the racial and gender composition of South Africa must be considered when judicial officers are appointed."

[78] For the first time ever, there are more women than men on the German Federal Constitutional Court's bench – 9 out of 16, since July 2020 – although the president of the court is still a male judge. Most female judges have been nominated by the Green Party and the Social Democrats.

[79] See Baines, "Women Judges on Constitutional Courts," 291.

[80] See Irving, *Gender and the Constitution*, 143–44, in which the author makes reference to Justices Claire L'Heureux-Dubé and Ruth Bader Ginsburg, among others. See also Elizabeth Halka, "Madam Justice Bertha Wilson: A 'Different Voice' in the Supreme Court of Canada," in "Honouring the Past, Serving the Future (The Faculty of Law's 75th Anniversary)," special issue, *Alberta Law Review* 35, no. 1 (1996): 253; Claire L'Heureux-

backing the abundant literature on the matter, perhaps not so much because of their natural differences but rather because of their gendered lived experiences, which often lead them to favor a contextualized jurisprudence.[81] Others, like our beloved Ruth Bader Ginsburg, went as far as to suggest the possibility of an all-female bench that would not be seen as a constitutional oddity.[82]

3.3 Toward Substantive Gender Equality

As we have seen in Chapter 2, one of the key milestones in women's constitutionalism was the redefinition of the equality principle along substantive lines in many jurisdictions under certain forms of gender-inclusive constitutionalism, which initially placed most emphasis on the need to protect motherhood. If a strong trend to include both universal equality and gender-specific rights provisions in constitutions emerged after the coming into force of CEDAW[83] – which, in fact, mandated the explicit constitutional incorporation of the principle of equality between men and women in article 2 (a) – ever since the 1980s, but especially since the 1990s, we can observe a gradual turn toward the embracing of a

Dubé, "Outsiders on the Bench: The Continuing Struggle for Equality," *Wisconsin Women's Law Journal* 16 (2001): 30; and Bader Ginsburg, quoted in Sandra Berns, *To Speak as a Judge: Difference, Voice and Power* (Aldershot, UK: Ashgate Publishing, 1999), 199, n. 89.

81 Heather Elliot summarizes much of this literature in "The Difference Women Judges Make: Stare Decisis, Norms of Collegiality, and Feminine Jurisprudence – A Research Proposal," *Wisconsin Women's Law Journal* 16, no. 1 (2001): 41. Much research has since been done about "feminist judgments" projects rewriting case law from a feminist perspective, such as the Women's Court of Canada project. See Denise Réaume, "Rewriting Equality II," in "Rewriting Equality II/Récrire l'égalité II," special issue, *Canadian Journal of Women and the Law* 30, no. 2 (2018): i–x; Rosemary Hunter et al., *Feminist Judgments: From Theory to Practice* (Oxford: Hart Publishing, 2010); Máiréad Enright, Julie McCandless, and Aoife O'Donoghue, *Northern/Irish Feminist Judgments: Judges' Troubles and the Gendered Politics of Identity* (Oxford: Hart Publishing, 2017); Loveday Hodson and Troy Lavers, *Feminist Judgments in International Law* (Oxford: Hart Publishing, 2019); Sharon Cowan, Chloë Kennedy, and Vanessa E. Munro, *Scottish Feminist Judgments: (Re)Creating Law from the Outside In* (Oxford: Hart Publishing, 2019).

82 Ruth Bader Ginsburg posed the question "Why not nine women?" in conversation with Justice Sandra Day O' Connor at the Women's Conference in 2010. See Baines, "Women Judges on Constitutional Courts," 290.

83 See Adèle Cassola et al., "Where Do Women Stand? New Evidence on the Presence and Absence of Gender Equality in the World's Constitutions," *Politics & Gender* 10, no. 2 (2014): 200–35.

more substantive framing of gender equality conceptions in national constitutions. This turn was only preceded by some exceptional jurisdictions that, as in the case of India[84] and in the context of postcolonial constitutionalism, had adopted formulations beyond formalistic and symmetrical approaches to constitutional sex equality, although, for the longest time, they mostly served to validate protections of women as mothers, which were often infused with paternalistic overtones. In any event, the need to redefine equality in substantive terms was a clear expression of the limits of inclusive constitutionalism that, in principle, granted women equal rights without ensuring equal opportunities to allow women to actually participate or meaningfully enjoy the rights granted. Formally recognized rights were not sufficient to help women overcome the legacy of centuries of legal and societal discrimination, or the lingering effects of deep-seated gender stereotypes that constitutions could not simply undo by declaring, "Let there be equality from now on," or even less, "Let women be granted the same rights as men."

National developments on the subject were to some extent shaped by supranational evolutions. In particular, we notice that CEDAW contained several provisions pointing to a commitment to substantive conceptions of equality, which could act as triggers for legal reform in some

[84] In India, the framers of the 1950 constitution were very aware of the deeply entrenched inequalities, both those based on caste and those based on sex, and made their removal one of their central goals. Thus article 14 and 15, sanctioning equality before the law and the prohibition of discrimination based on sex, among other criteria, coexist with the Directive Principles in the constitution (which devote considerable attention to the advancement of economic equality) but also with article 15's explicit mention that "nothing in this article shall prevent the State from making any special provision for women and children" (3) or "for the advancement of any socially and educationally backward classes of citizens or for the Scheduled Castes and the Scheduled Tribes" (4), which was inserted by the Constitution (First Amendment) Act, 1951. The jurisprudence interpreting these articles, however, has been more mixed, beginning with a paternalistic, protectionist, or formalistic understanding of women's equality and only gradually moving toward an anti-hierarchical understanding of equality. See Martha C. Nussbaum, "India, Sex Equality, and Constitutional Law," in Baines and Rubio-Marín, Gender of Constitutional Jurisprudence, 177–80, where she cites the cases Marri Chandra Shekhar Rao v. Dean Seth G.S.M., (1990) 3 SCC 130 and Indra Sawhney v. Union of India, AIR 1993 SC 477 (1992) as important milestones in this process. Other authors identify the shift toward substantive equality and an antisubordination approach in much more recent case law, placing women's autonomy – rather than their need for paternalistic protections – at its core. See Shreya Atrey and Gautam Bhatia, "In Search of Principle: Seventy Years of Gender Jurisprudence in India," in Chang et al., *Gender, Sexuality and Constitutionalism in Asia.*

national settings.[85] The first refers to article 1's broad definition of discrimination against women.[86] The second element has to do with article 4's approval of positive discrimination or affirmative action by providing that temporary special measures to accelerate de facto equality of opportunities and treatment shall not be considered discrimination, as defined by the convention. Article 3 expressly charges party states to pursue all appropriate steps, including legislative measures, to ensure women's full development and progress. Worth mentioning are also articles 7 and 8, which obligate states to take all appropriate actions to eliminate discrimination against women in political and public life and which have provided a stimulus to the passage of laws endorsing quotas to enhance women's participation in electoral contests or their appointment to public positions. CEDAW also planted (in article 5[a]) the seeds of an antistereotyping conception of gender equality by specifying that states must adopt specific measures to combat gender prejudices that support either the idea of inferiority or superiority of the sexes or the stereotyped roles for men and women.[87] Finally, CEDAW also contemplated some social rights for women.[88] Given that more than half of the constitutions in the world today are said to have been drafted since the late 1970s, one cannot underestimate the importance of CEDAW in providing a referent for the new articulation of women's constitutional equality, especially in those countries in Asia, Latin America, and Africa

[85] See Sandra Fredman, "Beyond the Dichotomy of Formal and Substantive Equality: Towards a New Definition of Equal Rights," in *Temporary Special Measures: Accelerating De Facto Equality of Women under Article 4(1) UN Convention on the Elimination of All Forms of Discrimination against Women*, ed. Ineke Boerefijn et al. (Antwerpen: Intersentia, 2003), 111–18.

[86] As referring to "any distinction, exclusion or restriction made on the basis of sex which has the effect or purpose of impairing or nullifying the recognition, enjoyment or exercise by women, irrespective of their marital status, on a basis of equality of men and women, of human rights and fundamental freedoms in the political, economic, social, cultural, civil or any other field." See United Nations Convention on the Elimination of All Forms of Discrimination against Women, G.A. Res. 34/180 [XXXIV], U.N. Doc. A/34/46, article 1 (Dec. 18, 1979).

[87] The substantive equality approach has since been strengthened by the CEDAW Committee. See Committee on the Elimination of Discrimination against Women, General Recommendation No. 25: On Temporary Special Measures, U.N. Doc. CEDAW/C/GC/25 (2004).

[88] Article 14 of CEDAW gives particular attention to the social and economic rights of rural women, requiring states to ensure equal access of women to education, health care, social security, and labor rights.

that consolidated their democracies after its entering into force.[89] In older European democracies, it seems that the influence of regional standards, such as those set by European law around the same time, was probably more decisive.

In doctrinal terms, the distinction between formal and substantive equality is, to my understanding, a distinction that should probably be conceived around elements along a continuum rather than one categorical and strictly binary distinction. In this regard, it might be more accurate to describe any given jurisdiction as embracing different degrees (if not somewhat contradictory elements) of formal or substantive equality logic. If, broadly speaking, substantive understandings of equality imply that the constitutional equality principle should encompass an imperative to ensure the measures and opportunities that women require to meaningfully and equally enjoy the rights granted to them – thus being able to participate in all venues of life – then it is similarly important to recall that the relevant elements are not only connected to how a constitutional equality or antidiscrimination provision is drafted[90] but are also related to the specific wording of the different rights provisions and to other general features of the constitutional system. These might include some aspects related to the general theory of fundamental rights, the overall conception of the state, or constitutional hermeneutics, much of which can, in many cases, only be inferred from jurisprudential

[89] For a typology on the forms of impact of CEDAW on national constitutional law that looks at whether CEDAW's provisions are taken as a referent in constitution-drafting; whether constitutions enshrine the (superior or equal) normative value of human rights treaties or their interpretive value; or whether such an interpretive value is adopted by courts in their reading, regardless of the constitutional text, see Ruth Rubio-Marín and Martha I. Morgan, "Constitutional Domestication of International Gender Norms: Categorizations, Illustrations, and Reflections from the Nearside of the Bridge," in *Gender and Human Rights*, ed. Karen Knop (Oxford: Oxford University Press: 2004), 113–53.

[90] Kathleen Sullivan lays out a set of options for a constitutional draft in which she suggests choosing "(1) between a general provision favoring equality or a specific provision favoring sex equality, (2) between limiting classifications based on sex or protecting the class of women, (3) between reaching only state discrimination or reaching private discrimination as well, (4) between protecting women from discrimination or also guaranteeing affirmative rights to the material preconditions for equality, and (5) between setting forth only judicially enforceable or also broadly aspirational equality norms." See Kathleen M. Sullivan, "Constitutionalizing Women's Equality," *California Law Review* 90, no. 3 (2002): 735–64, at 763. See also Brun-Otto Bryde and Michael Ashley Stein, "General Provisions Dealing with Equality," in *Routledge Handbook of Constitutional Law*, eds. Mark Tushnet, Thomas Fleiner, and Cheryl Saunders (London: Routledge, 2013), 287.

constructions that can also be contradictory or inconsistent and that inevitably vary over time.

To this, one must add the fact that many of the obstacles that women and other disadvantaged groups encounter when it comes to enjoying the rights formally recognized to them are related to their disproportionate share in terms of socioeconomic marginalization. Also, gender inequality is multidimensional, and it is shaped by political, economic, and cultural factors that interact in complex ways.[91] Therefore, in order to assess the degree to which constitutions deliver a certain measure of substantive equality, it will be necessary to consider whether the constitution contains socioeconomic rights (either in the form of enforceable rights or directive principles); whether the courts interpreting them are willing to derive such rights from other rights (such as the right to equality or the right to life);[92] and whether they have generally been prone to affirm positive obligations to protect and ensure these rights, and not merely to

[91] See Sandra Fredman, "Engendering Social and Economic Rights," in *Women's Social and Economic Rights: Development in South Africa*, eds. Beth Goldblatt and Kirsty McLean (Cape Town: Jura), 33. In Fredman's understanding, we must therefore pay particular attention to the relationship between socioeconomic rights and the right to equality. Doing so would move us away from the conception of social and economic rights as a "fixed bundle of goods, to one which aims to enhance the range of feasible options for women, while at the same time valuing care and interdependence within a community." Given that, in the patriarchal construction of the welfare state, women's care duties were naturalized while women themselves were turned into objects of protection and control as mothers and caregivers, this reading of socioeconomic equality – which places emphasis on women's autonomy while pushing toward the collective assumption of care duties – seems indeed most promising.

[92] Socioeconomic rights are framed as nonenforceable directive principles in the Indian Constitution, except for the right to education, which was inserted as a fundamental right in 2002 (Eighty-Sixth Amendment Act, 2002). However, the Supreme Court has found other ways to make them enforceable by expanding the scope of the right to life (article 21). It was in 1985 with the Olga Tellis case (Olga Tellis v. Bombay Municipal Corporation, AIR 1986 SC 180) when the Supreme Court stated that the right to life includes the right to livelihood, gradually expanding it upon third-generation rights, including environmental rights and intergenerational equity. See Zia Mody, *10 Judgements That Changed India* (New Delhi: Shobhaa De Books, 2013), 81–91. The right to food, among others, illustrates the role undertaken by the Supreme Court as guarantor of these socioeconomic rights. The Supreme Court has stated that the right to food is a basic need (M/S. Shantistar Builders v. Narayan Khimalal Totame, AIR 1990 SC 630) and that the right to life "guaranteed in any civilised society implies the right to food, water, decent environment education, medical care and shelter" (Chameli Singh v. State of U. P., AIR 1996 SC 1051). It is also still supervising its implementation as a duty of the state (People's Union for Civil Liberties v. Union of India [Writ petition (civil) No. 196/2001]).

respect them.[93] Although the recognition of social and economic rights dates back to the eighteenth century, with its full development taking place throughout the nineteenth and early twentieth centuries (as in the constitutions of Mexico in 1917 or the USSR in 1924), and although social rights were also in the picture in the post–World War II human rights revolution and constitutionalism,[94] it is only after the Cold War that an increasing number of countries began to include social and economic rights in their constitutions.[95] By joining in participatory constitution-making, women have contributed to this trend in significant ways, for socioeconomic claims have been, and continue to be, of utmost importance to them both as vulnerable persons and as primary caretakers who will be expected to bear the brunt of "social assistance," when the state and the larger community fail to do so. However, as Sandra Fredman has argued, to engender socioeconomic rights, it is not sufficient to extend socioeconomic rights to women. Instead, "socio-economic rights and equality must form a powerful partnership," and these rights must be infused with substantive gender equality. This, she claims, requires to "take into account the power relations in which rights are exercised, in order to enhance the set of feasible options open to women, while at the same time valuing and supporting their roles within a complex network of interdependence." This is a task that places women's agency and participatory opportunities at center stage and requires "the restructuring of institutions" and the abandoning of the understanding of social rights as a bundle of goods that must be distributed among individuals,[96] an understanding that often resonates within the paternalistic and protectionist framework that is part of the patriarchal architecture.

[93] See Beth Goldblatt, "Constitutional Approaches to Gender and Social and Economic Rights," in Irving, *Constitutions and Gender*, 483.

[94] See Katharine G. Young, *Constituting Economic and Social Rights* (Oxford: Oxford University Press, 2012).

[95] A study of the constitutions of 195 countries (as of January 2013) found that more than 90 percent had at least one social and economic right, with the rights to education, to form or join a trade union, to health care, social security, child protection, and environmental protection appearing in more than half of the world's constitutional texts. Around one third of these countries saw all of their social and economic rights as justiciable rights; another third saw some rights as justiciable and some as aspirational; whereas the other third was composed of those countries that had no social economic rights in their constitutions or had them with a merely aspirational nature. See Courtney Jung, Ran Hirschl, and Evan Rosevear, "Economic and Social Rights in National Constitutions," *American Journal of Comparative Law* 62, no. 4 (2014): 1043.

[96] See Sandra Fredman, "Engendering Socio-Economic Rights," *South African Journal on Human Rights* 25, no. 3 (2009): 410–41, at 410–11.

Given their complexity, some of these variables deserve some theoretical reflection before we can better historicize and exemplify their evolution, as they specifically relate to women's citizenship. The primordial distinction between constitutional orders committed to formal and substantive understandings of sex equality seems to rest on whether one interprets that the core mandate of constitutional equality pertains to the abolition of more or less arbitrary or irrational differentiations between individuals along morally irrelevant and typically unchosen features (which would include sex but also race, etc.) – the difference or anticlassification approach – as opposed to the overcoming of structures of subordination that have traditionally and unjustly advantaged some groups over others – the antisubordination or antidominance approach.[97] The Spanish feminist legal academia frequently refers to the term "subordiscrimination" to refer to this latter vision, which is said to be more concerned with the structures that sustain the dynamics of oppression of some dominant groups over others than with attitudinal phenomena of invidious prejudice or with comparing groups of individuals in order to distinguish "relevant" from "irrelevant" differences between them.[98]

[97] This has been described as the antisubordination approach to the principle of equality. See Owen M. Fiss, "Groups and the Equal Protection Clause," *Philosophy and Public Affairs* 5, no. 1 (1976): 107, 108, 157; Laurence M. Tribe, *American Constitutional Law*, 2nd ed. (Mineola, NY: Foundation Press, 1988), 1514–21. For a description of both traditions, see also Jack M. Balkin and Reva B. Siegel, "The American Civil Rights Tradition: Anticlassification or Antisubordination?," in "Fiss' Way: The Scholarship of Owen Fiss," ed. Irwin P. Stotzky, special issue, *University of Miami Law Review* 58, no. 1 (2003): 9–33. On the failure of the US constitutional model to embrace an antisubordination approach, see Catharine A. MacKinnon, "Substantive Equality: A Perspective," in *Minnesota Law Review* 96, no. 1 (2011): 1–27.

[98] Dynamics of oppression can in turn be expressed in different forms. Iris Young argues that oppression consists of any system that reduces the potential for people to be fully human, either because they are treated in a dehumanizing way or because they are denied the opportunities that might allow them to reach their full human potential in both mind and body. Oppression has, according to Young, five faces – namely, violence, exploitation, marginalization, powerlessness, and cultural imperialism. See Iris Marion Young, *Justice and the Politics of Difference* (Princeton, NJ: Princeton University Press, 2011), 41. Ideally, a fully comprehensive and substantive equality model should offer remedies to all these forms of oppression and gradually admit to the tensions that may appear between them. It should also be crafted in such a way as to capture the specific and intersecting forms in which these faces of oppression manifest themselves for each of the subordinated groups in a given society. For an attempt to redefine the analytic framework of substantive equality, see Sandra Fredman, "Substantive Equality Revisited," *International Journal of Constitutional Law* 14, no. 3 (2016): 712–38; and Catharine A. MacKinnon's

Over the years, the consensus has become one in which the dominant concern is with sex/gender subordination, and as such, the affirmation of a prohibition of discrimination on the grounds of sex (a feature of about two-thirds of the world's constitutions today) may not be sufficient protection as long as the preconditions are not there for the meaningful enjoyment of the rights formally recognized to women, who thus continue to be overwhelmingly deprived of basic goods and realistic chances to participate in all venues of life. This is especially true because, as we have seen, no jurisdiction has ever accepted *all* distinctions on the basis of sex to be constitutionally impermissible. This, then, has invited judgment about which of the distinctions are justified and which are not along more or less stringent standards of review. As we have seen, across the world, biological and, more often than not, functional differentiations have also been accepted in the understanding that not all kinds of sex-based distinctions are invidious by nature and that some are also compensatory in purpose. Yet again, precisely because the accommodation of functional distinctions typically reflects the old system of gender roles for men and women, this accommodationist approach has run the risk of perpetuating gender stereotypes and entrenching women's subordinate position. Therefore, it is particularly important that the constitutional (sex) equality provision, and the case law elaborating on it, be qualified in ways that impede this by indicating that the real evil is not the classification on the basis of sex per se but rather the ways in which such classification has contributed to a system of structural subordination of women, undermining their full and equal citizenship status.

An incipient move to set limits to the kinds of legitimate sex-based differentiations that can be established is made when the constitution, besides banning discrimination (either in general or on a list of grounds including sex), contains a specific provision stating, by way of threshold, that men and women must be granted equal rights. Such an equal rights provision acts as a reminder that, whatever the distinctions allowed, they cannot undermine women's rights when compared to those of men. This is why, in the United States, the defenders of the thus far unsuccessful Equal Rights Amendment have continued to fight for it to this day in the understanding that it would symbolize the embracing of some form of

commentaries on Fredman, "Substantive Equality Revisited: A Reply to Sandra Fredman," in ibid., 739–46.

substantive equality that explicitly allows the government to undertake actions seeking women's real or de facto equality.[99]

Since rights can represent minimum thresholds but also be validly limited, constitutions may of course go even further in entrenching substantive equality understandings, just as they do when they endorse positive or affirmative equality by either allowing or directing state powers to adopt affirmative action, positive measures, and other promotional actions geared toward removing those obstacles that stay in the way of minorities' and women's de facto equality. This promotional narrative also fits better with those constitutional traditions that rest on a vision of the state that does not limit its role to guaranteeing negative freedom and that therefore embraces a theory of rights that derives positive and not just negative obligations for states. Besides explicitly accepting the validity of affirmative measures (as not contradicting or even fulfilling sex equality mandates), there are various ways in which constitutional systems can express their commitments to substantive understandings of equality. In certain constitutions, this commitment to substantive equality has been expressed generically as covering state action to ensure that various underprivileged groups can meaningfully participate and enjoy their rights (such as article 9.2 of the 1978 Spanish Constitution), whereas in others the provisions specifically refer to women.

Even when constitutional systems accept the legitimacy of promotional or compensatory measures for women as a disadvantaged group, they rarely discard some notion of formal equality, which means that there are still some limits to the nuances with which the substantive equality mandate can qualify the formal equality principle. In many legal orders, the relationship between the two norms is mediated by the different legal nature of the concerned provisions. Thus, whereas the formal equality principle or the sex discrimination ban in constitutions is typically crafted as an enforceable right, the substantive equality principle has typically come to be added or read into as a "legitimation mandate"

[99] Julie C. Suk, "An Equal Rights Amendment for the Twenty-First Century: Bringing Global Constitutionalism Home," *Yale Journal of Law & Feminism* 28, no. 2 (2017): 381–82. It is interesting to recall that, even the first postwar human rights conventions contained both a ban on sex discrimination and an equal rights provision. Both the International Covenant on Civil and Political Rights, Dec. 19, 1996, 999 U.N.T.S. 171 and the International Covenant on Economic, Social and Cultural Rights, Dec. 16, 1966, 993 U.N.T.S. 3 contain in article 3 a requirement for state parties to "ensure the equal right of men and women to the enjoyment" of the rights contained in the document, as a supplement to more general antidiscrimination guarantees.

whereby state authorities are either allowed or instructed (a "directive principle") to undertake remedial or compensatory promotional measures. In other words, constitutional systems have not granted individuals an enforceable right to compensatory or differential treatment for the sake of living up to substantive equality ideals. Thus, in practice, how much of such compensatory or differential treatment could be justified under the substantive equality ideal has remained uncertain and left to legislators' discretion, with theories of discrimination due to state omission (rather than action) being, if at all, very narrowly crafted, and theories of indirect discrimination often having a variable scope.

Consequently, the textual or, more often, merely doctrinal construction of the constitutional antidiscrimination rule appears as another relevant indicator in most jurisdictions.[100] In terms of substantive equality and antisubordination goals, the doctrine that acknowledges impact-based and indirect forms of discrimination is, perhaps, the most promising. In some jurisdictions, this has been constitutionally accepted, while in others this has only been true for statutory claims (as is the case in the United States). This is because men's and women's different starting positions and underlying social realities – many of which continue to be shaped by persisting gender stereotypes – can only be taken into account whenever evidence of the discriminatory impact of gender-neutral norms, and not just the underlying motive, is sought. And since indirect or impact-based discrimination can be activated by petitioners (unlike positive action mandates, except when they are constitutionally spelled out in concrete mandatory measures), it imbues this doctrine with the greatest transformative potential. However, there is still significant variation depending on the (more or less demanding) burden of proof and type of evidence required to show discriminatory impact but also on the fact that doctrines of indirect forms of discrimination often

[100] There is also great variation among jurisdictions as to the extent to which antidiscrimination law is constitutional or statutory in nature. On antidiscrimination theory, see Sandra Fredman, *Discrimination Law* (Oxford: Oxford University Press, 2002); Tarunabh Khaitan, *A Theory of Discrimination* (Oxford: Oxford University Press, 2015); Barbara Havelková and Mathias Möschel, eds., *Anti-discrimination Law in Civil Law Jurisdictions* (Oxford: Oxford University Press, 2019); Susanne Baer, "Equality," in *The Oxford Handbook of Comparative Constitutional Law*, eds. Michel Rosenfeld and András Sajó (Oxford: Oxford University Press, 2012), 982–1001. See also Norman Dorsen et al., eds., *Comparative Constitutionalism: Cases and Materials*, 3rd ed. (St. Paul, MN: West Academic Publishing, 2016).

allow for a greater margin of justification than those of direct discrimination and tend to have a more limited domain reach.

Additional doctrinal elements may also be important, including some features pertaining to a jurisdiction's general theory of fundamental rights. One such element is the vertical or horizontal application of fundamental rights (under different names in different constitutional traditions, such as state action doctrine, *Drittwirkung*, or horizontal effect).[101] Here it is essential to determine whether the rights included in the constitution are binding on private parties or only on governmental action, and in the case of the former, whether they provide actionable claims, at least in those instances in which it can be shown that the relationship between individuals is, structurally speaking, one characterized by a serious imbalance of power. This has generally been acknowledged to be the case between employers and employees, but one could argue this is also generally the case between women and men.

Hermeneutically speaking, there is also room for relevant variation.[102] The perspective that comes closest to matching the goals of the antisubordination approach, especially when the text of the constitution is old, is one whereby a constitution is not to be interpreted based on its original meaning at the time it was crafted but rather purposively, in accordance with the renewed understandings of the core values that underlie them. This "living tree" approach best lends itself to a contextualized interpretation of the norms that looks beyond the text and attempts to elucidate how these norms actually operate in real life, taking into account their interactions with societal factors. An additional relevant rule, as we have mentioned, involves endorsing the need to interpret constitutional norms in light of validly ratified human rights provisions or even giving precedence to the latter, especially when the state has ratified CEDAW or other relevant international or regional women's rights treaties that provide substantive protection to women.[103] Beyond

[101] On the horizontal effect of fundamental rights, see Colm O'Cinneide and Manfred Stelzer, "Horizontal Effect/State Action," in Tushnet, Fleiner, and Saunders, *Routledge Handbook of Constitutional Law*, 177.

[102] See Vicki C. Jackson, "Gender Equality, Interpretation, and Feminist Pluralism," in Irving, *Constitutions and Gender*, 221–51. See also Daphne Barak-Erez, "Her-meneutics: Feminism and Interpretation," in Baines, Barak-Erez, and Kahana, *Feminist Constitutionalism*, 85–97.

[103] One of the main demands of Colombian women's groups in the constitution-making process leading to the 1991 constitution was that the text should incorporate the substantive equality concept of CEDAW, something they achieved with article 13.

formal rules of interpretation, it is possible to identify different modes of reasoning of the various courts pointing to a more or less formalistic or substantive understanding of equality. On the one hand, there are courts that call on formal equality to strike down norms that seem to disadvantage men or simply to treat men and women differently, without making an effort to ponder whether those norms form part of a larger patriarchal scheme that structurally subordinates women; and, on the other, there are those that, relying on an affirmative action or compensatory logic, validate benefits granted to women under a protectionist reasoning that entrenches stereotypes around women's vulnerability and sometimes also reaffirm their dependent status.

Historically, there has been ample room for variation, yet, unsurprisingly, one can find the first expressions of more ambitious constitutional framings of the equality/antidiscrimination provisions in those constitutions that were drafted anew or significantly amended in more recent years. This is particularly the case in those instances where the constitution-making process took place in timely proximity to the country's ratification of CEDAW or under the influence of other relevant international and regional human rights standards, with women involved through official or informal channels and mobilization strategies during the process. These strategies were often inspired and supported by women's transnational networks and, in the last decade or so, have also been assisted by international governmental and nongovernmental actors pushing the agenda of gender-sensitive constitutions.

An early example of constitutional experimentation and innovation in this regard is Canada, with its 1982 Charter of Rights and Freedoms, which has counted with the active participation of feminist women in civil society, initially during the constitution-making process and, later on, as litigants.[104] At first, two sex equality provisions were included in

Women's rights activists also led successful campaigns to ensure that CEDAW norms be reflected in the 1998 Brazilian Constitution, the 1995 Ugandan Constitution, and the 1996 South African Constitution. See Rubio-Marín and Morgan, "Constitutional Domestication of International Gender Norms," 120–21.

104 See Baines, "Using the Canadian Charter of Rights and Freedoms," 50–54. Canada signed CEDAW on July 17, 1980, and ratified it on Dec. 10, 1981, after the 1982 Constitution Act had been adopted by a resolution in the Canadian House on Dec. 2, 1981, and the Senate on Dec. 8, 1981. See Anne F. Bayefsky, *Canada's Constitution Act 1982 & Amendments: A Documentary History* (Toronto, ON: MacGraw-Hill Ryerson, 1989), 924. Baines argues that it seems unlikely that any of the activist women lawyers at the time would have paid any attention to CEDAW, since Canadian courts gave little credit to international instruments and even now barely

the charter. The general equality provision (section 15) prohibits discrimination on nine listed grounds including sex (section 15 [1]) but, in expressing a commitment toward substantive equality, clarifies that the prohibition of sex-based discrimination does not preclude ameliorative programs for disadvantaged individuals or groups such as those that have been disadvantaged because of sex. The coming into effect of section 15 was delayed for three years to give the government time to review their existing legislation for consistency with its terms. The second provision (section 28) deals only with sex equality and reads, "Notwithstanding anything in this Charter, the rights and freedoms referred to in it are guaranteed equally to male and female persons." The women's movement had important expectations behind this clause, which was initially conceived as a "purpose clause" and provided Canadians with the opportunity to entrench a similar act as the ERA. The clause would have covered the need to interpret the entire charter in view of the sex equality mandate, ensuring de facto equality and compelling sex-based distinctions were taken as seriously as race-based distinctions, thus calling for equally demanding standards of review.[105] The potential of these constitutional provisions was then reinforced by the Supreme Court's general purposive approach to rights interpretation in general and its commitment to substantive readings of equality in particular, stating that the primordial purpose of section 15 was not to fight against irrational differentiations but rather to prevent "the imposition of disadvantage, stereotyping, or political or social prejudice, and to promote a society in which all persons enjoy equal recognition at law as human beings or as members of Canadian society, equally capable and equally deserving of concern, respect and consideration."[106] Substantive

consider them binding. It seems more likely that Canadians involved in the drafting process might have wanted to distance themselves from the formalistic US model in view of the challenges it posed to the adoption of otherwise enviable affirmative action policies (Beverley Baines, conversation with the author, Apr. 24, 2021).

105 A third sex equality provision (section 35 [4]) was entrenched by constitutional amendment in 1983 to ensure that aboriginal and treaty rights otherwise protected by the constitution were guaranteed equally to male and female persons as a way of recognizing the intersectional interests of aboriginal women. See also Froc, "Is Originalism Bad for Women?," 243.

106 See Fraser v. Canada (Attorney General), [2020] 450 DLR (4th) 1. See also Law v. Canada (Minister of Employment and Immigration), [1999] 1 S.C.R. 497, ¶ 51. In reality, *Law* built on Andrews v. Law Society of British Columbia, [1989] 1 S.C.R. 143, which has been recognized as setting the template for substantive equality. Yet, *Law* has been criticized by scholars and even the Supreme Court, since the dignity test it adds to

equality, the Canadian Supreme Court has recognized, requires attention to the "full context of the claimant group's situation, the actual impact of the law on that situation, and to the persistent systemic disadvantages that have operated to limit the opportunities available to that group's members."[107]

Yet probably the most sophisticated and complete early expression of a constitutionally entrenched commitment to substantive equality is the one provided by South Africa's 1996 constitution.[108] As we have mentioned,

the equality frame has been taken to be too discretionary, representing an additional burden on the plaintiff. See, for all, R. v. Kapp, [2008] 2 S.C.R. 41, ¶ 22 (Can.). Be that as it may, it seems that much of the credit for convincing the court to go in the direction of embracing substantive equality is due to the Women's Legal Education and Action Fund (LEAF), a national nonprofit organization that, because of the court's broad standing rules, has been able to participate in litigation by promoting equality for women and educating the public about such litigation. LEAF is to be credited with submitting to the court much of the contextual information and feminist analysis that is particularly relevant for assessing the impact of certain governmental actions and omissions concerning women's rights. LEAF was assisted by funds made available through the Canadian government's Court Challenges Program, which had been interrupted between 1992 and 1995, withdrawn again in 2006, and reinstated in 2017. See Irving, *Gender and the Constitution*, 159. See also Mary Eberts, "The Fight for Substantive Equality: Women's Activism and Section 15 of the Canadian Charter of Rights and Freedoms," *Atlantis: Critical Studies in Gender, Culture & Social Justice* 37, no. 2 (2015): 100–11; and Sherene Razack, *Canadian Feminism and the Law: The Women's Legal Education and Action Fund and the Pursuit of Equality* (Toronto, ON: Second Story Press, 1991).

107 See Withler v. Canada (Attorney General), [2011] 2 S.C.R. 396. See also Ontario (Attorney General) v. Fraser, [2020] 2 S.C.R. 3, ¶ 28, 42. Nevertheless, many scholars – pointing to the bleak record of cases won so far – would agree that the Supreme Court now names substantive equality as the doctrine that informs the test for section 15 (equality rights) without, for the most part, truly using a substantive equality analysis. See Jonnette Watson Hamilton and Jennifer Koshan, "Adverse Impact: The Supreme Court's Approach to Adverse Effects Discrimination under Section 15 of the Charter," *Review of Constitutional Studies* 19, no. 2 (2015): 191–235; Jennifer Koshan, "Under the Influence: Discrimination under Human Rights Legislation and Section 15 of the *Charter*," *Canadian Journal of Human Rights* 3, no. 1 (2014): 115–42; and feminist works cited therein.

108 Though not necessarily as comprehensively conceived as in the South African Constitution, the notion of substantive equality has proliferated in many other African constitutions since the 1990s. See Aili Mari Tripp, "Conflicting Agendas? Women's Rights and Customary Law in African Constitutional Reform," in *Constitutung Equality: Gender Equality and Comparative Constitutional Law*, ed. Susan H. Williams (Cambridge: Cambridge University Press, 2009), 180. Typically, the relevant clauses contain a mandate to the state to promote the development of women and guarantee their equal opportunities in order to ensure their equal participation in all spheres of society. See, for instance, article 89.7 in Ethiopia's 1994 constitution; article 36 (6) in Ghana's 1992 constitution; article 13 (a) in Malawi's 1994 constitution; article 67 in

the final text was the outcome of a process in which women activists effectively mobilized the political and organizational skills acquired during the struggle for racial equality to demand the inclusion of women's issues in the constitution, precisely around a time of intense feminist transnational mobilization that opened the way to the Beijing Platform of Action. First of all, the South African constitutional text is rather unique in expressing (in section 1) a foundational commitment not only to gender equality but also to nonsexism, clearly showing its concern with sex-based subordination dynamics.[109] Section 9 expressly guarantees the right to equality on the basis of gender in a provision that recognizes formal equality before the law and equal protection and benefit of the law (section 9 [1]); a commitment to substantive equality through the full and equal enjoyment of rights and the possibility to adopt positive equality measures to ensure it (9 [2]); and a prohibition of discrimination that specifies that direct, indirect, and intersectional forms of discrimination are prohibited (9 [3] and 9 [5]), whether perpetrated by private persons (9 [4]) or by the state. This section also contains a mandate to pass legislation to prevent such forms of prejudice (9 [3]), specifying that the discrimination ban includes not only sex-based but also gender, sexual orientation, pregnancy, and marital status discrimination, thus suggesting that it is the entire dominant gender order, and not mere specific provisions differentiating on the grounds of sex, that accounts for women's subordination. Further elements in the constitution affirm the commitment to substantive equality, including the broad mandate of the constitution for the state to respect, promote, and fulfill the Bill of Rights (section 7 [2]), something that is consistent with the overall commitment to positive rights reflected in the constitution's broad incorporation of justiciable social rights (including the right to health and housing in sections 26 [1] and 26 [2]) – rights that have often been seized upon by female plaintiffs.[110] On this basis, it is barely surprising that, in interpreting section 9, the Constitutional Court

Mozambique's 1990 constitution; article 23.3 in Namibia's 1990 constitution; and article 33 (2) in Uganda's 1995 constitution. Despite their proliferation, these clauses, which generally depend on subsequent executive and legislative actions to be filled out with content, tend to be elusive in resource-poor countries.

109 Section 1 of the South African Constitution, which sets out the values that underpin the entire system, also includes nonracialism and nonsexism alongside supremacy of the constitution, rule of law, universal suffrage, and a multiparty system.

110 On housing, see Government of the Republic of South Africa v. Grootboom 2001 (1) SA 46 (CC); on health, see Minister of Health and Others v. Treatment Action Campaign and Others (No. 2) 2002 (5) SA 721 (CC).

"stressed that a rigid, formal approach must be rejected in favour of a substantive, contextual and asymmetrical analysis" that interprets the right to equality in light of past and continuing discrimination.[111] Indeed, an impact- and context-based approach to equality has also allowed the Constitutional Court to better grasp intersectional discrimination.[112]

It would be a mistake, however, to think that constitutional commitment to substantive gender equality has been limited to countries undergoing their main "constitutional moments" in more recent times. The trend is indeed wider and has affected jurisdictions with older constitutions and bills of rights. In Europe, for instance, under the early influence of evolving European law standards,[113] the shift toward substantive conceptions of sex equality has sometimes proceeded through constitutional interpretation by relying on generic provisions that reflected a broader commitment to substantive equality goals while avoiding any

[111] See Saras Jagwanth, "Affirmative Action in a Transformative Context: The South African Experience," *Connecticut Law Review* 36 (2003–2004): 727. This approach has been confirmed through much of the case law of the South African Constitutional Court. See Prinsloo v. Van der Linde 1997 (3) SA 1012 (CC).

[112] See Harksen v. Lane 1998 (1) SA 300 (CC) at 49; and Brink v. Kitshoff 1996 (4) SA 197 (CC) at 44.

[113] Whereas positive action was endorsed very early on by European law (see article 2.4 in Council Directive 76/207/EEC of Feb. 9, 1976, on the implementation of the principle of equal treatment for men and women, and Council Recommendation 84/635/EEC of Dec. 13, 1984, on the promotion of positive action for women), the validity of gender quotas and, more generally, a stronger commitment to substantive equality, as well as the embracing of the principle of gender mainstreaming, would only begin in the 1990s. Thus, following a public outcry after a decision by the European Court of Justice striking down an affirmative action measure to the benefit of women (Case C-450/93, Kalanke v. Bremen, 1995 E.C.R. I-03051) as contrary to formal equality norms, the Treaty of Amsterdam, signed on Oct. 2, 1997, added the following paragraph (119 [4]) to the original provision on sex equality prohibiting sex discrimination regarding pay: "With a view to ensuring full equality in practice between men and women in working life, the principle of equal treatment shall not prevent any Member State from maintaining or adopting measures providing for specific advantages in order to make it easier for the underrepresented sex to pursue a vocational activity or to prevent or compensate for disadvantages in professional careers." See also article 141 (4) of the Treaty establishing the European Community, renumbered, as of December 2009, as article 157 (4) of the renamed Treaty on the Functioning of the European Union. In this new treaty provision, the references to "full equality in practice," "specific advantages," and "prevent[ion] or compensat[ion] for disadvantages" contrast with the simple reference to "equal opportunity" in prior antidiscrimination law. Reaffirmed under the Lisbon Treaty (2009), the European Union still operates under this legal framework, whose profile is now reproduced in the European Charter of Fundamental Rights (see articles 20, 21, 23.1, and 23.2, respectively).

explicit mention of sex or women as addressees. Yet, in time (and particularly since the 1990s), there has been a widely felt need to refer to women explicitly, and this has provoked a certain wave of constitutional amendments that have been crucial to back legal initiatives endorsing affirmative action for women in the employment or political domains. In each case, the specific context has been decisive as to the when and the what of the concrete amendment, although women's activism has been a determining factor in most instances.

In Germany, two articles in the German Constitution of 1949 (article 3 [2], recognizing men and women to be equal, and article 3 [3], stating that "no person shall be favoured or disfavoured because of sex") were supplemented by article 3 (2.2), a clause inserted by amendment on October 27, 1994, which provides that "the state shall promote the actual implementation of equal rights for women and men and take steps to eliminate disadvantages that now exist." This was conceived as a task or duty for the government and the legislator and not as an individually enforceable right. The inclusion of this clause allowing for affirmative action, discussed in the context of the adoption of quotas for women in the public and private sectors, was part of a constitutional reform package after German Reunification, in addition to other reforms aiming to reinforce the commitment of the constitution to social justice goals. It came to confirm the prior case law of the German Federal Constitutional Court, which had already interpreted the equal rights principle in article 3 (2) as a legitimate basis for affirmative action to ensure substantive or real equality between women and men.[114] At the time, Western and Eastern women joined forces in this effort. Western women were reacting to sheer statistical evidence showing persistent inequalities despite the constitutional affirmation of equality between the sexes. Eastern women, in turn, were expressing their concern about becoming the "socioeconomic losers of German Reunification," given that, in some ways, the level of

[114] See Ute Sacksofsky, *Das Grundrecht auf Gleichberechtigung. Eine rechtsdogmatische Untersuchung zu Artikel 3 Absatz 2 des Grundgesetzes*, 2nd ed. (Baden-Baden: Nomos, 1996), 386ff. See also Ute Sacksofsky, "Wenn Rechtfertigungen brüchig werden. Verfassungsgerichte in der Diskriminierungsbekämpfung am Beispiel der Geschlechterordnung vor dem Bundesverfassungsgericht," in Rainer Forst and Klaus Günther, eds., *Normative Ordnungen* (Berlin: Suhrkamp, 2021), 604–31. See also Juliane Kokott, "Zur Gleichstellung von Mann und Frau – Deutsches Verfassungsrecht und europäisches Gemeinschaftsrecht," *Neue Juristische Wochenschrift* 48, no. 16 (1995): 1049–57.

gender equality in the East had been higher than in the West.[115] Convincing the Common Constitutional Commission to include the new sentence in article 3 (2) GG during the constitutional reform required the efforts of a cross-party women's alliance composed of female representatives of trade unions, civil society organizations, and other women's groups, which launched a public call to the women of the general German public to send support letters to the commission. The convening of the alliance meeting in the island of Frauenchiemsee ("Frauen" being the German word for "women") had a symbolic message: in 1948, the Constitutional Convention laying down the basis for the 1949 constitution for the German Federal Republic after World War II had met in the island and palace of Herrenchiemsee ("Herren" being the German word for "gentlemen").

The Austrian Federal Constitution was also amended in a similar way just four years later than the German Basic Law. Indeed, the amendment of May 15, 1998,[116] which took place months after another constitutional amendment had been passed to enable women to serve in the military,[117] was now in charge of introducing paragraph 2 into article 7 of the Federal Constitutional Law whereby "the Federation, provinces and municipalities subscribe to the de facto equality of men and women. Measures to promote factual equality of women and men, particularly by eliminating actually existing inequalities, are admissible." The debate and logic animating the amendment were, firstly, the recognition that inequality between men and women persisted in Austrian society and, secondly, that the voices of women's movements were fading in Austrian politics. The specific context was rather unfavorable, with the Austrian government announcing a series of austerity measures that were expected to have a disparate impact on women.[118] As a result, women in politics and

[115] See Hans-Jochen Vogel, "Verfassungsreform und Geschlechterverhältnis – Zur Ergänzung des Art. 3 Abs. 2 GG durch ein Staatsziel Frauenförderung," in *Grundrechte, soziale Ordnung und Verfassungsgerichtbarkeit. Festschrift für Ernst Benda zum 70. Geburtstag*, eds. Eckart Klein, Klaus-Eckart Gebauer, and Ernst Benda (Heidelberg: C. F. Müller, 1995), 395–420.

[116] Bundes-Verfassungsgesetz [B-VG] [Constitution], BGBl No. 1/1930, as last amended by Bundes-Verfassungsgesetz [B-VG] BGBl No. 68/1998, http://www.ris.bka.gv.at/Dokumente/BgblPdf/1998_68_1/1998_68_1.pdf.

[117] Gesetz über die Ausbildung von Frauen im Bundeswehr – GAFB 1998 [Act on the Training of Women in the Armed Forces of 1998] Bundesgesetzblatt [BGBl] No. 30/1998, https://www.ris.bka.gv.at/Dokumente/BgblPdf/1998_30_1/1998_30_1.pdf.

[118] See Brigitte Geiger, "Geschlechterverhältnisse als Medienereignis: Berichterstattung und mediale Diskurse zum österreichischen FrauenVolksBegehren," in *Feministische Kommunikations- und Medienwissenschaft: Ansätze, Befunde und Perspektiven der*

civil society launched a popular petition requesting eleven legislative measures to improve women's welfare.[119] The petition was organized by the NGO *Unabhängiges Frauenforum* (UFF – Independent Women Forum) and signed by 11.17 percent of Austrian voters (three-fourths of which were women) in the period between May 7 and 14, 1997.[120] The main element in the petition was a request to enshrine substantive equality between women and men in the Austrian constitution and to impose a positive duty on provinces and municipalities to further the elimination of de facto gender discrimination. The ensuing constitutional amendment resulted from this popular petition.

In Greece, too, the women's movement deemed the constitutional architecture of the Greek Constitution insufficient to back necessary positive measures.[121] The 1975 constitution had included a general equality clause (article 4.1) as well as a sex equality provision affirming that "Greek men and women have equal rights and equal obligations" (article 4.2). And, although a provision was included at the time (article 116.2) allowing for nontemporary derogations from the sex equality principle for compelling reasons and as provided for by a statute, it had until then been interpreted as encompassing measures that in fact limited rather than expanded women's participation in certain domains (such as the military or police corps) on the basis of alleged intrinsic male and female characteristics.[122] By the late 1990s, a women's campaign (backed by over twenty-two women's organizations) sought the elimination of article 116.2, dissatisfied with the renewed interpretation of the provision that had been offered by the case law of the Council of State, and called for substantive equality in light of European law and CEDAW standards.

aktuellen Entwicklung, ed. Johanna Dorer and Brigitte Geiger (Berlin: Springer–Verlag, 2013), 120.

119 The PDF of the manifesto and further information or reactions to the popular petition can be found at http://zwanzigtausendfrauen.at/wp-content/uploads/2011/01/1997_Frauenvolksbegehren.pdf.

120 Karin Liebhart, "Gleichberechtigte Partizipation oder strukturelle Ausgrenzung? Genderpolitische Aspekte der Demokratiequalität Österreichs," in *Demokratiequalität in Österreich: Zustand und Entwicklungsperspektiven*, eds. David F. J. Campbell and Christian Schaller (Berlin: Springer–Verlag, 2013), 124.

121 See Ruth Rubio-Marín, "Women's Political Citizenship in New European Constitutionalism: Between Constitutional Amendment and Progressive Interpretation," in Irving, *Constitutions and Gender*, 337–38; and Dia Anagnostou, "Gender Constitutional Reform and Feminist Mobilization in Greece and the EU: From Formal to Substantive Equality?," *Canadian Journal of Law and Society* 28, no. 2 (2013): 133–50.

122 Anagnostou, "Gender Constitutional Reform," 139–40.

Tellingly, the campaign referred to a European constitutional tradition in the making, expressed in the growing number of national constitutions guaranteeing substantive equality and incorporating positive action provisions. In December 2000, the proposed amendment was finally incorporated in the reformed constitution, and the old 116.2 provision was replaced by a new one stating that "the State shall take measures for the elimination of actually existing inequalities, in particular to the detriment of women" and paving the way for the adoption of legislation that embraced gender quotas for women in local and national elections.[123]

It is possible to find other examples of countries reforming their constitutions around the same time to add a substantive gender equality dimension[124] or, short of constitutional amendments, of courts simply embracing the substantive reading of symmetrically framed constitutional equality provisions.[125] In sum, it appears that at the turn of the century, women were expressing dissatisfaction with how timidly the bans on discrimination that were to constitutionally protect them had been phrased in postwar constitutionalism and felt the urge that real de facto equality be mentioned as a legitimate goal. They did so aware of their persisting underrepresentation in the public spheres of the market

[123] In Portugal, the 1976 constitution (article 13.2) had merely provided that "no one may be privileged, favoured, prejudiced, deprived of any right or exempted from a duty for reasons of ... sex." This was amended in September 1997 to confer on the state the responsibility for promoting equality between men and women (new article 9). Almost two years later, in June 1999, the reform of the Finnish Constitution took place, which facilitated Finland's accession to the European Union. Section 6 of the constitution now provided that distinctions on the grounds of sex cannot be sustained "without an acceptable reason" and that no one shall "be treated differently from other persons," making explicit reference to measures to develop "the equality of the sexes ... in social activity and working life, especially in the determination of pay and the other terms of employment." Similar provisions can also be found in the constitutional texts of Central and Eastern European countries, including those of Romania (article 16.3) and Slovenia (article 14).

[124] See Constitution of the People's Republic of China (section 6, article 10 of Additional Articles to the Constitution, amended in 1990); Constitution of the Argentine Republic (article 75.23, amended in 1994); Constitution of Turkey (article 10, amended in 2004 and 2010).

[125] See the Spanish Constitutional Court's decisions: "Despite the bidirectional nature of the rule of "parification" between the sexes, it cannot be ignored that women as a group have been the victims of discriminatory treatment" (S.T.C., Dec. 14, 1992 [No. 229/1992], p. 2). If sex is included in the constitution as a suspect criterion of discrimination, it is because of the need "to put an end to the traditional postponement of women, erasing those differences that have historically placed them in a situation of inferiority in legal and social life" (S.T.C., Dec. 19., [No. 241/1988], p. 6).

and in public office, despite their constitutionally proclaimed equality. This trend has continued since and has found expression in more recently adopted constitutions.[126] Some of these constitutions contain rather complete and complex sex equality provisions,[127] elaborate on state duties vis-à-vis the fulfillment of other constitutional rights in general,[128] and better reflect the remedial needs of women who are subject to multiple forms of discrimination or are extremely poor and marginalized.[129] Similarly, women's platforms engaging in recent initiatives of constitution-making have only broadened their aspirations regarding socioeconomic justice to incorporate claims of environmental justice.[130] In the meantime, individual women across the globe continue to try their luck before constitutional courts. Examples abound, but we could mention those cases of the two Peruvian women asserting their right to

[126] See article 46 of the 2014 Tunisian Constitution.

[127] Mexico City's 2017 constitution provides a vivid example, with article 4 (C.1 and C.2) going beyond the category of sex (in itself, an increasingly problematic concept) to include a detailed list of sex- and gender-related prohibited discrimination grounds (including sexual preference, sexual orientation, gender identity, gender expression, sexual characteristics, and marital status); enshrining substantive equality and affirmative measures; and defining misogynous conduct and the denial of reasonable accommodation as forms of discrimination. Nepal's 2015 constitution includes sex, marital status, and pregnancy among the list of prohibited grounds of discrimination.

[128] Article 1 of the Mexican Constitution was reformed in 2011 and now enumerates the duties to respect, protect, and guarantee human rights and mentions the state's obligation to investigate, sanction, and remedy violations to these rights.

[129] Article 18 of the 2015 Nepalese Constitution calls for affirmative action measures for socially and culturally backward women, intended to leave out the "creamy layer" – a term which in Indian constitutional politics on affirmative action denotes the relatively better-off and more educated groups within the Other Backward Classes. Also, article 38, which contains an entirely new set of provisions to protect the rights of women, contemplates the need for affirmative action measures in education, health, employment, and social security. On a similar note, article 40 on the rights of Dalits brings into sharper focus the issue of intersectionality with regard to gender equality. Subclause 7 mandates equal distribution of the facilities provided under article 7 between Dalit men and women; article 42 on the right to social justice reiterates the right of "socially backward women" and "gender and sexual minority groups" to employment in state structures on the basis of the principle of inclusion in line with principles of redistributive justice; while article 43 identifies "helpless single women" as one of the groups entitled to the right to social security. Translations from Malagodi, "Gender, Sexuality and Constitutionalism in Nepal."

[130] Turkey's 2007 Women's Constitutional Platform, for instance, put the ideas of egalitarian citizenship, and social and environmental justice at the forefront of their claims. See Emrah Oder, "Women and Constitution-Making in Turkey," 301–2.

education and to attend a regular public school in order to avoid walking for hours and spending an additional two hours in public transport to reach alternative schooling centers;[131] the Indian girls claiming girls toilets, adequate water for sanitation, and other basic infrastructure within schools;[132] or the Argentine mother with a disabled child claiming her right to be included in a housing program.[133] Economic crises and policies of austerity have made the use of constitutional rights to address the persistent problems of poverty and wealth inequality in rich and poor countries alike only more compelling, giving a renewed life to principles of nonretrogression and nondiscrimination.[134]

3.4 Toward Parity Democracy

The emphasis on women's participation at the turn of the century brought to the forefront the need to overcome lingering inequalities linked to the gendered construction of constitutional membership and citizenship, inequalities that had survived since the postwar years in many constitutional democracies, despite the proclamation of the sex discrimination ban – including with explicit reference to the political and public spheres.[135] These inequalities concerned women in the

[131] See the Tribunal Constitucional [T.C.] [Constitutional Court], 14 de marzo 2017, file no. 00853-2013-PA/TC (ruling in *Marleni Cieza Fernández and Another*).

[132] See Environmental & Consumer Protection Foundation v. Delhi Administration, (2012) 10 SCC 197. See Parmanand Singh, "Enforcing Social Rights through Public Interest Litigation: An Overview of the Indian Experience," in *Socio-Economic Rights in Emerging Free Markets: Comparative Insights from India and China*, ed. Surya Deva (Abingdon: Routledge, 2016), 116.

[133] Corte Suprema de Justicia de la Nación [CSJN] [National Supreme Court of Justice], 24/04/2012, "Q. C., S. Y. c/ Gobierno de la Ciudad de Buenos Aires s/ amparo," Fallos de la Corte Suprema de la Nación, t. 335, 452.

[134] Arun Thiruvengadam and Gedion T. Hessebon, "Constitutionalism and Impoverishment: A Complex Dynamic," in Rosenfeld and Sajó, *Oxford Handbook of Comparative Constitutional Law*, 153.

[135] The first regional and international conventions specifically addressing women's political rights, including the Inter-American Convention on the Granting of Political Rights to Women (1948) and the Convention on the Political Rights of Women (1952), had stuck to a formal equality logic and pursued no objective other than affirming women's rights to political participation in equal terms, something that was basically reiterated in the United Nations' 1967 Declaration on the Elimination of Discrimination against Women (G.A. Res. 2263 [XXII], U.N. Doc. A/6880, article 4 [Nov. 7, 1967]). Relevant also was the 1957 United Nations Convention on the Nationality of Married Women, which declared that a woman's nationality should not be conditioned on her marriage or her husband's nationality.

military;[136] accessing, retaining, or transmitting nationality; and accessing hereditary positions of state power, of more or less symbolic nature, such as the monarchy.[137] Whereas the latter can probably be best understood as relics of a pre-egalitarian order resisting modernization, women's discrimination in the military spoke directly to the gendered construction of citizenship, according to which military duties and office were seen as a paradigmatically male form of contribution to the nation (equivalent to women's motherhood). The distinction has only become more problematic over time, however, as the military in many countries turned increasingly professionalized and the gender bias now meant that women were being deprived of a whole range of professional opportunities.[138] Similarly,

136 In fact, to the extent that it is still conceived as a citizen duty, distinctions between men and women are still to be found in many legal orders whether or not they are supported by explicit constitutional mention. Thus, in 1956, when Germany reorganized its armed forces, the 1949 constitution was amended. Article 12 (4), however, exempted women from being required by law to render service in any unit of the armed forces and prohibited them from being employed in any service involving the use of arms. Subsequently, in the 1968 constitutional amendment, 12 (4) was deleted and a new provision was inserted in 12a – 12a (4) – whereby women could be obliged to serve in the armed forces, especially in medical care units, but may not be required to serve in any units involving the use of arms. Nevertheles, beginning January 1, 2004, women were *allowed* to do so. Also, article 13 of the Swedish Constitution, dealing with protection against discrimination, provides that "No act of law or other provision may imply the unfavourable treatment of anyone on grounds of gender, unless the provision forms part of efforts to promote equality between men and women or relates to compulsory military service or other equivalent official duties." See also Colombia's 1996 Constitutional Court decision – Corte Constitucional [C.C.] [Constitutional Court], noviembre 16, 1994, Sentencia C-511/94 – in which the court, referring to biological and educational differences, rejected the argument that not subjecting women to compulsory military service but authorizing their voluntary service was unconstitutional. See also, for the United States, National Coalition for Men v. Selective Service System, 593 U.S. ___ (2021), denying certiorari against National Coalition for Men v. Selective Service System, No. 19-20272 (5th Cir. Aug. 13, 2020) (reported at 969 F.3d 546), upholding male-only military draft registration requirement.

137 In the Spanish Constitution, the rule of succession to the Crown (article 57.1) still discriminates against women. This discrimination was relied upon by those defending a similar discrimination in the order of succession to nobility titles, which gave birth to constitutional litigation and was finally overcome in 2006 through legislative change. See Ruth Rubio-Marín, "Engendering the Spanish Monarchy: Modernizing or Abolishing," *Royal Studies Journal* 7, no. 2 (2020): 80–93, at 84–86. In other countries, constitutional equality provisions as well as human rights norms on gender equality have successfully been relied upon to ensure women's equal right to succession. See, for instance, Indonesia's 2016 Constitutional Court decision 88/PUU-XIV/2016, striking down Yogyakarta's succession to the sultanate rule as violating the constitutional equality principle, the International Covenant on Civil and Political Rights, and CEDAW.

138 Indeed, the professionalized and voluntary positions in the military as well as in military training facilities have increasingly been opening up to women, a transformation that in

women's discrimination in nationality law was expressive of women's indirect form of citizenship, given that, in household-based democracies, the links between a woman and her nation were thought to be mediated through her marital status.[139] Although many of these presuppositions have gradually subsided in a process that has often included constitutional reforms or litigation,[140] in many contexts, the equality logic still caves in to

many countries around the world has in fact been facilitated by constitutional litigation. See, for Spain, the Constitutional Court's decision, S.T.C., Nov. 14, 1991 (No. 216/1991), striking down women's exclusion from the professional air force; for Israel, HCJ 4541/94 Alice Miller v. Minister of Defense, 49(4) PD 94 (1995), successfully challenging Israel's admission's policy to its combat pilot course; for Colombia, see Corte Constitucional [C.C.] [Constitutional Court], diciembre 15, 1995, Sentencia T-624/95, admitting women to Colombia's navy; diciembre 9, 1996, Sentencia T-704/96 (air force); and septiembre 20, 1996, Sentencia T-463/96 (naval officer training schools); and for the United States, see United States v. Virginia, 518 U.S. 515 (1996), a landmark case in which the Supreme Court of the United States struck down the long-standing male-only admission policy of the Virginia Military Institute. Also, women have sometimes succeeded in challenging other inequalities that resulted from their exclusion from military duties. See, for instance, South Korea's 1999 Constitutional Court decision, Hunbeobjaepanso [Const. Ct.], Dec. 23, 1999, 98Hun-Ma363, striking down a public servant entrance system granting extra points to male applicants who had fulfilled their military duty as discriminating against both women and persons with disabilities. Men, in turn, have sometimes successfully challenged some male-only duties derived from the portrayal of men as protectors and women as in need of protection. See, for instance, the German Federal Consitutional Court's decision, BVerfGE 92, 91, Jan. 24, 1995, striking down a provision that obliged men to pay a contribution to firefighting forces, a contribution aimed to replace men's previosuly recognized duty to contribute to firefighting when needed.

139 Similar assumptions reinforcing the idea of political communities built around patriarchal households seem to underlie the dominance of male family names. This has become a source of constitutional struggle, with many recent victories achieved. See, for instance, the Hungarian Constitutional Court's decision declaring unconstitutional the norm impeding men to bear their wives' names after marriage. See Alkotmánybíróság (AB) [Constitutional Court], 58/2001. (XII. 7.), Magyar Közlöny (MK) [Official Gazette of Hungary], 2001/138. See also the South Korean case 17-2 KCCR 544 (Hunbeobjaepanso [Const. Ct.], Dec. 22, 2005, 2003Hun-Ka5), in which the Constitutional Court struck down as unconstitutional the provision in the Civil Code that required adoption of the paternal family name.

140 The 1949 Constitution of Costa Rica was amended in 1999 to extend eligibility for naturalization to persons of both sexes who marry Costa Ricans (article 14 [5]) after the rule had been declared unconstitutional in 1992 under human rights standards. The 1965 Constitution of Singapore was amended in 2004 to allow Singaporean women to pass down citizenship by descent to children born overseas. For successful litigation around women's equality in this field, see, for Botswana, Attorney General v. Unity Dow (1991), successfully challenging a citizenship act providing for citizenship to be transmitted to children in a marriage through the father alone; for Canada, Benner v. Canada, [1997] 1 S.C.R. 358, striking down a rule imposing additional requirements for children

the dominant pressure of religious norms[141] or ethnocultural concerns, as the striking case of Nepal shows.[142]

Yet, in the domain of public and political membership and participation, formal equality has also failed to exhaust women's renewed participatory ambitions. Therefore, together with claims to overcome lingering open discriminations, constitutional guarantees for a balanced distribution of public and political power between women and men were sought and justified around theories claiming the need to replace the liberal unitary representation model with one of differentiated citizenship or

of Canadian mothers born abroad, as opposed to from Canadian fathers, to obtain Canadian citizenship; for Japan, Saikō Saibansho [Supreme Ct.] June 4, 2008, Hei 18 (gyō-tsu) no. 135, 62 Saikō Saibansho minji hanreishū [Minshū] 1367, where the Supreme Court interprets its nationality act to allow a child born out of wedlock to a Japanese father and a foreign mother to obtain Japanese nationality; and for South Korea, see case 12-2KCCR 167 (Hunbeobjaepanso [Const. Ct.], Aug. 31, 2000, 97Hun-Ka12), where the Supreme Court strikes down a nationality act that privileged paternal lineage in nationality. Nevertheless, see also a decision of the Lahore Court in Pakistan (Sharifan v. Federation of Pakistan, PLD 1998 Lahore 59), upholding a law that allows foreign spouses of male Pakistani citizens to acquire citizenship by marriage but denying that right to (in this case, Indian) husbands of female Pakistani citizens. The court argued that, by virtue of her marriage, a female spouse acquires the domicile of her husband, thereby obscuring discrimination against Pakistani female citizens unable to pass citizenship to their foreign husbands. Intriguingly, it also stated that "women are no longer to be treated as a property of the male members of the society."

141 In Islamic countries, the fight for equal access and transmission of citizenship has figured highly among women's priorities. For Iraq, Turkey, and Somalia references, see Ruth Rubio-Marín and Helen Irving, "Introduction: Women as Constitution-Makers: The Promises and the Challenges of Participation," in Rubio-Marín and Irving, *Women as Constitution-Makers*, 22. Some of the recent achievements for women in Middle Eastern constitutional movements include this form of equality. The 2005 Iraqi Constitution was pioneer among Arab countries in allowing mothers to transmit citizenship, and article 11 of the 2014 Egyptian Constitution also reflects this egalitarian evolution.

142 The case of Nepal is striking because, although the 2015 constitution contains an impressive array of constitutional provisions sanctioning women's rights, the chapter on citizenship still features explicit forms of gender-based discrimination against Nepali women who face constitutional restrictions on passing citizenship to their foreign spouses and offsprings conceived from the union with a foreign man. This results from citizenship being engineered with the goal of insulating the Nepali nation from India in view of the open border with India in the Terai region of southern Nepal, where the Madhesi community lives. Nevertheless, the Supreme Court has gradually adopted an increasingly activist stance with regard to women's citizenship rights, culminating with the 2011 landmark decision in Sabina Damai v. Government of Nepal et al., Writ No. 067-WO-0703 of the year 2067 (2010), ordering the government to issue citizenship documents to the petitioner on the basis of her mother's Nepali citizenship, regardless of the fact that the identity of the father was unknown. For further analysis and case law, see Malagodi in "Gender, Sexuality and Constitutionalism in Nepal."

differentiated universalism[143] – requiring to some degree a politics of presence[144] – and theories seeing the balanced distribution of power as a meaningful instrument to subvert the foundational sexual contract and the separate spheres built around it.[145] Indeed, an increasing number of constitution-making and constitution-amendment processes since the 1990s have sought constitutional provisions that would more explicitly endorse this goal, sometimes coexisting with other more generically expressed substantive equality provisions. The need for this explicit recognition is easy to understand in light of the abovementioned Athens Declaration. As the twentieth century came to an end, women – whose numbers in representative positions continued to be very low despite having gained all necessary rights (including the right to vote, run for office, and to access public office on equal terms) – were reaching out for a new understanding of gender equality and a new concept of democracy that would centrally address the legitimacy gap that their systemic underrepresentation embodied. Yet, precisely because this gender participatory turn engaged the notions of democracy and representation, in many settings it was deemed necessary that it be specifically reflected in the constitution.

Strictly speaking, the constitutional preoccupation with women's political representation is not altogether a contemporary issue. In fact, reserved seats for women in constitutions have an old tradition and can already be found in some post–World War II constitutions, especially, though not only, in the South Asia region, where they have often encompassed several marginalized groups (including lower castes and rural people) and not just women. Their existence epitomizes the struggle against the legacy of colonial stratification and subordination and served nation-building agendas in what were often multiethnic and linguistic societies. The 1947 Constitution of the People's Republic of China was the first among Asian constitutions to require quotas for women in electoral politics[146] (along with other ethnic minorities, overseas citizens,

[143] Iris Marion Young, "Polity and Group Difference: A Critique of the Ideal of Universal Citizenship," *Ethics* 99, no. 2 (1989): 250–74.

[144] Anne Phillips, *The Politics Of Presence* (Oxford: Clarendon Press, 1995).

[145] Ruth Rubio-Marín and Blanca Rodríguez Ruiz, "The Gender of Representation: On Democracy, Equality and Parity," *International Journal of Constitutional Law* 6, no. 2 (2008): 287–316.

[146] See articles 64, 134, and 135 of the Chinese Constitution. See also Ruth Rubio-Marín and Wen-Chen Chang, "Sites of Constitutional Struggle for Women's Equality," in Tushnet, Fleiner, and Saunders, *Routledge Handbook of Constitutional Law*, 308.

and occupational groups), and the ephemeral 1956 Pakistani Constitution provided ten reserved seats for women.[147] However, these early precedents of quotas linked to colonial dynamics, often not very ambitious, seem to have delayed the spread of more demanding quotas and parity goals, as exemplified by the case of India, the wider acceptance of both being a recent phenomenon in the region.

During the rise of pre-independence political movements in India, the opinion on gender quotas (which were part of the 1935 Government of India Act) supported by the leading women's organizations of the time – including the All India Women's Conference, the Women's Indian Association, and the National Council of Indian Women – was that they would be retrogressive, as they would contradict the principle of equality and would favor the British strategy of *divide and rule*.[148] Only in the 1990s did India begin to overcome this historically grounded reservation against gender quotas with the passing of the seventy-third and the seventy-fourth constitutional amendments on local governance, adding a one-third quota for women within the reserved seats for scheduled castes and tribes in local panchayats and municipalities (reserved seats for scheduled castes and tribes were already contemplated under the 1950 constitution for the union and states legislatures) and also allocating one-third of the total number of seats to be filled by women through direct election (including the number of seats reserved for women belonging to the scheduled castes and the scheduled tribes).[149]

[147] This evolved gradually until 2017, when the twenty-fourth amendment of the 1973 constitution – a constitution that encourages the government to take any affirmative action "to increase women's participation in all spheres of national life" (article 24) – took the number of reserved seats for women to sixty. See Aurat Foundation, *Legislative Quotas for Women: A Global & South Asian Overview of Types and Numbers* (Islamabad: Aurat Publication and Information Service Foundation, 2012), 28–35; Mona Lena Krook, *Quotas for Women in Politics: Gender and Candidate Selection Reform Worldwide* (Oxford: Oxford University Press, 2009), 58–83.

[148] See Mary E. John, "Alternate Modernities? Reservations and Women's Movement in Twentieth Century India," *Economic and Political Weekly* 35, no. 43/44 (2000): 3822–29.

[149] See articles 243 D (2)–(3) and 243 T (2)–(3) of the Indian Constitution. More recently, in 2008, a constitutional bill (One Hundred and Eighth Amendment) was presented to the parliament to reserve one-third of all seats in the Lok Sabha – lower house – and in the state legislative assemblies for women, allotted by rotation to different constituencies. This amendment, which was passed by the Rajya Sabha – upper house – in 2010 by an almost unanimous majority vote of 186 members in favor and 1 against, is still pending a vote in the Lok Sabha. And, although it has been supported by women's associations, it is important to note that previous amendment attempts were criticized within the feminist movements for encouraging the ghettoization of women representatives by

This evolution is not surprising, given that the wave of quota adoption (labeled as the "fast track" to equal representation)[150] started to flourish worldwide in the 1990s and has continued to this day, increasingly supported by constitutional provisions of different kinds. Moreover, bolstered, internationally and regionally, by the Beijing Declaration and Platform for Action (1995), CEDAW Committee's subsequent endorsement of women's equal participation in decision-making,[151] regional integration, and human rights institutions,[152] quotas went from being conceptualized as temporary measures seeking minimum thresholds or critical mass in the 1990s (often with a 30 percent target) to aiming, in the new century, at more ambitious goals, including "balanced participation" (often expressed as no more than a 60/40 disparity between sexes) and "equal representation" or "parity" (50/50 of each sex), seeking permanent, and not just temporary, corrections and targeting an ever-increasing number of positions of public and private power.

Democratization processes since the 1990s undoubtedly offered windows of opportunity to advance the agenda of women's empowerment. This was certainly the case in Latin America, where international spotlighting through the Beijing 1995 conference, the domestic and regional mobilization of quota proponents, and the "opportunities for

setting a women-against-women electoral battle in the reserved constituencies. See Vicky Randall, "Legislative Gender Quotas and Indian Exceptionalism: The Travails of the Women's Reservation Bill," *Comparative Politics* 39, no. 1 (2006): 63–82.

150 See Drude Dahlerup and Lenita Freidenvall, "Quotas as a 'Fast Track' to Equal Representation for Women: Why Scandinavia is No Longer the Model," *International Feminist Journal of Politics* 7, no. 1 (2005): 26–48.

151 See Ruth Rubio-Marín, "Women's Participation in the Public Domain," 66–96. Notice that, while not referring to quotas or parity, CEDAW had already compelled states to "take appropriate measures to eliminate discrimination against women in the political and public life of the countries" (article 7).

152 Human rights law has increasingly come to support the parity agenda. The 2003 Protocol to the African Charter on Human and Peoples' Rights on the Rights of Women in Africa (Maputo Protocol) represents the human rights instrument that, to date, most clearly enshrines the stated goal of equal participation and equal representation of women, as well as the obligation to adopt affirmative action measures to achieve these goals. The case law of the European Court of Human Rights has also underlined the link between women's political incorporation and the democratic credentials of a country and has endorsed the legitimacy of positive measures and quotas to achieve it. In this regard, see Méndez Pérez v. Spain, App. No. 35473/08, Eur. Ct. H.R. (Third Section, Oct. 4, 2011) (inadmissible); Staatkundig Gereformeerde Partij v. the Netherlands, App. No. 58369/10, Eur. Ct. H.R. (Third Section, July 10, 2012) (inadmissible); and, more recently, Metka Zevnik and Others v. Slovenia, App. No. 54893/18 (Dec. 5, 2019) (inadmissible), http://hudoc.echr.coe.int/eng?i=001-199209.

policy innovation sparked by the regional wave of democratization"[153] are all said to have coalesced toward the acceptance of parity standards, building on some earlier local expressions of the commitment to the agenda of women's political empowerment.[154] In fact, Latin America became the pioneer world region in the 1990s in terms of adoption of legislative gender quotas. In some cases, like Argentina, even preceding the Beijing Conference. The fact that several countries were drafting or amending their "post-transition" constitutions – coinciding with the wider trend toward participatory constitutionalism and relying on increasingly vocal national and international women's movements – explains why some of the constitutional texts in the region were also among the first to incorporate wording referring to the goal of women's equality in decision-making and access to public office.[155] New provisions explicitly underscore political equality and equal representation between women and men and are now contained in both laws and constitutions of countries like Argentina, Bolivia, Colombia, Ecuador, Nicaragua, Paraguay, and Mexico.[156]

153 See Jennifer M. Piscopo, "States as Gender Equality Activists: The Evolution of Quota Laws in Latin America," *Latin America Politics and Society* 57, no. 3 (2015): 47.

154 Article 48 of Nicaragua's 1987 constitution already provided that "Unconditional equality among all Nicaraguans in the enjoyment of political rights, in the exercise of these rights, and in the fulfillment of their duties and responsibilities is established; there exists absolute equality between men and women. It is the obligation of the State to remove obstacles that impede the actual equality among Nicaraguans and their effective participation in the political, economic and social life of the country."

155 See article 40 of the 1991 Colombian Constitution, article 117 of the 1992 Paraguayan Constitution, and article 37 of the 1994 Argentine Constitution. The latter reads: "This Constitution guarantees the full enjoyment of political rights, in accordance with the principle of popular sovereignty and with the laws dictated pursuant thereto. Suffrage shall be universal, equal, secret and mandatory. True equality of opportunity between *men and women* in running for elected and party offices shall be guaranteed through *affirmative actions* in the regulation of political parties and in the electoral system" (italics are ours).

156 In other countries, such as Costa Rica, the mandate has been read into the constitution through a creative interpretation of the generic equality principle (article 33) in view of article 7 in CEDAW (which requires state authorities to take appropriate measures to eliminate discrimination and promote women's participation in public positions) and the incorporation of international human rights law as having a "higher authority" than national constitutional law (article 7). See Alda Facio, Rodrigo Jiménez Sandoval, and Martha I. Morgan, "Gender Equality and International Human Rights in Costa Rican Constitutional Jurisprudence," in Baines and Rubio-Marín, *Gender of Constitutional Jurisprudence*, 106ff.

Although in some African countries, quotas in the form of reserved seats (targeting a low threshold) had already been introduced after independence, the African continent also saw a large majority of quotas introduced after 1995, often in postconflict settings, with donors, transnational feminist organizations, and other external actors actively involved.[157] In fact, the sub-Saharan region has been said to have experienced the "fastest and largest rate of change in women's political representation" owing, in large part, to the implementation of quotas.[158] Key factors animating constitutional reform regarding women in sub-Saharan Africa have been identified, and they include general democratization trends; the emergence of autonomous women's movements; changing international norms; the influence of global and regional women's movements; donor strategies; and the opportunity structures opened up in postconflict settings.[159] With respect to gender quotas specifically, the success of social movements in articulating first the minimum threshold representation and then the parity goals has also been attributed to the rhetorical blending of international frameworks, with local traditions of women's empowerment dating back to precolonial historical institutions revived in national campaigns.[160] And while some provisions in African constitutions contain legitimation mandates – which, in the affirmative action logic, enable or endorse the adoption of measures to guarantee women's equal participation[161] – most constitutional provisions allow for

[157] In the 1990s, twenty-eight sub-Saharan African constitutions were rewritten. After 2000, another ten were rewritten and six had major revisions.

[158] Tiffany D. Barnes and Stephanie M. Buchard, "'Engendering Politics': The Impact of Descriptive Representation on Women's Political Engagement in Sub-Saharan Africa," *Comparative Political Studies* 46, no. 7 (2013): 767–90.

[159] Tripp, "Conflicting Agendas?," 174–75.

[160] Fatou Kiné Camara, "African Women and the Gender Equality Regime in Africa: From Patriarchy to Parity," in *Black Women and International Law: Deliberate Interaction, Movements and Action*, ed. Jeremy I. Levitt (Cambridge: Cambridge University Press, 2015), 86–87.

[161] Most expressive is, perhaps, the 2005 Ethiopian Constitution: "The historical legacy of inequality and discrimination suffered by women in Ethiopia taken into account, women, in order to remedy this legacy, are entitled to affirmative measures. The purpose of such measures shall be to provide special attention to women so as to enable them to compete and participate on the basis of equality with men in political, social and economic life as well as in public and private institutions" (article 35 [3]). In contrast to this, many provisions reserve a specific number of seats for women. Article 49.4 of the 2005 Iraqi Constitution, for instance, provides "a percentage representation for women of not less than one-quarter of the members of the Council of Representatives," whereas article 75 of the Rwandan Constitution (as amended in 2015) reserves twenty-four of the

reserved seat systems that guarantee only a minimum number of women represented in parliament. In the meantime, voluntary party quotas have become the preferred and most effective mechanism in the more democratic regimes of the region,[162] where percentages of reserved seats have also increased somewhat in recent times.

In essence, then, what we see is that new constitutionalism has represented a force of change in the direction of women's parity. Not only because newly drafted or amended constitutions could incorporate provisions guaranteeing a certain threshold of representation for women, or at least legitimating or compelling state authorities to undertake actions to achieve this goal, but also because courts have more naturally understood such constitutional commitments as part of renewed and broader understandings of constitutional democracy resulting from the relevant democratization processes.[163] Only in some rare exceptions have courts expressed constitutional reservations and set boundaries to the expansion of positive measures to ensure women's public participation in such contexts.[164]

eighty seats in the Chamber of Deputies to women, and article 80 specifies that women are to represent at least 30 percent of the twenty-six members of the Senate.

162 Tripp, "Conflicting Agendas?," 176–77. For other examples of constitutional provisions for quotas in Africa, please refer to the constitutions of Burundi (article 169), Rwanda (articles 75 and 80), Sudan (article 24.2), Swaziland (article 86), and Uganda (article 180.2 [b]).

163 In Mexico, for instance, the Supreme Court withheld, in two different occasions before the constitution was amended to explicitly incorporate the parity principle, state legislation that imposed gender quotas as compatible with the principle of gender equality (under article 4 of the constitution) or the general right to equality and nondiscrimination (article 1) (see Acción de inconstitucionalidad 2/2002, Diario Oficial de la Federación [DOF] 18-03-2002; and Acciones de inconstitucionalidad acumuladas 7/2009, 8/2009, and 9/2009, Diario Oficial de la Federación [DOF] 21-12-2009). Also worth mentioning is the jurisprudential contribution of the Mexican Electoral Tribunal of the Federal Judiciary, which is competent to issue constitutional interpretations regarding certain electoral matters and which has also favored affirmative remedies to guarantee gender-balanced representation.

164 In 2000, the Colombian Constitutional Court – Corte Constitucional [C.C.] [Constitutional Court], marzo 29, 2000, Sentencia C-371/00 – struck down gender quota legislation, as it affected elections though not executive appointments. In fact, the challenged legislation had been passed precisely to implement the requirement of article 40 of the 1991 Colombian Constitution whereby "the authorities will guarantee the adequate and effective participation of women in the decision-making ranks of the public administration." To this end, the legislator had established a 30 percent quota for women in high-level, decision-making positions in the public sector. The provisions in the statute were examined and were found to be, for the most part, constitutional and conceptualized as temporary affirmative action measures compatible with the notion of

Yet the same is not necessarily true in older constitutional democracies. The agenda of political gender quotas has not taken off politically in the United States, where women's political representation has remained chronically low despite a significant increase of women in Congress as a result of the more recent elections.[165] Although not impossible, such an event seems unlikely in a country whose legal tradition significantly disregards evolving hard and soft human rights law standards – many of which, like those in CEDAW, it has not signed – nor with comparative law as a point of reference. Several elements in the country's political and constitutional culture make it also extremely improbable. Among them, we find the prevalent formal equality, anti-stereotyping interpretation of the Equal Protection Clause described in Chapter 2; the stronger individualist tradition, with its relentless faith in both autonomy and meritocracy, as expressed through the free functioning of the market and civil society forces (including political parties, whose associational rights are strongly protected by the First Amendment in the Constitution); the country's problematic racial past and present (which would make it difficult to press for a gender parity agenda without, at the same time, integrating some conception of equally pressing racial parity); and dominant narratives around the risk of essentializing women (as gender quotas are said to do). Since some of these elements reflect fears that would arguably be expressed by progressive sectors of society as well, including those opposed to the "difference" strand of feminism, a full-blown parity democracy agenda is indeed unlikely to flourish at least in the near future, and women are likely to continue looking for ways to enhance their levels of political participation other than through gender quotas.[166]

substantive equality, generically sanctioned in article 13.2 of the constitution, after surviving a proportionality scrutiny. The court, however, distinguished between executive appointments and elected positions and ruled out the possibility of mandatory electoral quotas for the latter, calling on the autonomy of political parties and the principle of popular sovereignty as prevalent in the electoral field. For an analysis of the Colombian decision, see Blanca Rodríguez-Ruiz and Ruth Rubio-Marín, "Constitutional Justifications for Parity Democracy," *Alabama Law Review* 60, no. 5 (2009): 1184–88. In 2015, the Colombian constitution was reformed to allow for parity measures in the legislative branch.

[165] For more information, see Jennifer E. Manning and Ida A. Brudnick, *Women in Congress: Statistics and Brief Overview* (Congressional Research Service Report, 2020), https://crsreports.congress.gov/product/pdf/R/R43244.

[166] See Ruth Rubio-Marín, "A New European Parity-Democracy Sex Equality Model and Why It Won't Fly in the United States," *American Journal of Comparative Law* 60, no. 1 (2012): 121–24.

It is interesting that even in Western Europe – where the wave of quota adoption (first of a voluntary and then of a mandatory nature) has indeed deployed its effects since the 1980s, and especially since the 1990s, and continues to this day (characterized by both domain expansion and increasing ambition with regard to the desired numerical goals)[167] – constitutions have, for the most part, either been irrelevant or represented a force of resistance against the changing understandings of gender equality and democracy underlying the gender quotas movement and the gender equality participatory shift. Without a doubt, the European country in which legislated gender quotas have triggered the most lively constitutional battles has been France.[168] Already in 1982, the National Assembly passed an act that obliged electoral ballots in municipal elections to have at least 25 percent of candidates of each gender. The act was successfully challenged before the Constitutional Council, which (ignoring the potential relevance of the provision stating that the law guarantees women equal rights to those of men in all spheres) struck it down, calling on the principle of equality before the law but also on the principles of national sovereignty and the indivisibility of the electoral body, something that indicates that the Constitutional Council was aware that the changing nature of representation was being compromised.[169] Whereas the Constitutional Council

[167] See Eleonore Lépinard and Ruth Rubio-Marín, eds., *Transforming Gender Citizenship: The Irresistible Rise of Gender Quotas in Europe* (Cambridge: Cambridge University Press, 2018). As for Eastern Europe, gender quotas existed in communist countries like Yugoslavia, Poland, Romania, or Hungary, although given the very limited powers of parliament, the presence of women in them was rather a sign of tokenism, with real power residing instead in the Communist Party apparatus. For this reason, gender quotas were initially linked to the communist regime and regarded with suspicion after the Cold War ended. That said, they have been gradually expanding in the region. See Milica G. Antic and Sonja Lokar "The Balkans: From Total Rejection to Gradual Acceptance of Gender Quotas," in *Women, Quotas and Politics*, ed. Drude Dahlerup (London: Routledge, 2006), 138–68.

[168] For accounts on the parity debate in France, see Joan Wallach Scott, *Parité! Sexual Equality and the Crisis of French Universalism* (Chicago: Chicago University Press, 2005); Eléonore Lépinard, *L'égalité introuvable. La parité, les féministes et la République* (Paris: Presses de Sciences Po, 2007); Laure Bereni, *La bataille pour la parité. Mobilisations pour la féminisation du pouvoir* (Paris: Economica, 2015).

[169] See Conseil constitutionnel [CC] [Constitutional Council] decision No. 82-146DC, Nov. 18, 1982, J.O. 3469, 3475. For a discussion of the French debate, see Blanca Rodríguez Ruiz and Ruth Rubio-Marín, "The Gender of Representation: On Democarcy, Equality, and Parity," *International Journal of Constitutional Law* 6, no. 2 (2008): 287–316, at 290–93. See also Nadia Urbinati, "Why *Parité* Is a Better Goal than Quotas," *International Journal of Constitutional Law* 10, no. 2 (2012): 465–76, at 470.

has never stopped regarding quotas with suspicion,[170] it has not been alone among its European counterparts. Sometimes dominant formal equality conceptions have prevailed.[171] Other times, even substantive equality has not been sufficient. In 1995, the Italian Constitutional Court,[172] and in 1997, the Swiss Federal Supreme Court,[173] similarly struck down gender quota legislation and initiatives, showing that even when substantive equality mandates are constitutionally enshrined, as they are in Italy and Switzerland,[174] the resistance against subverting the principle of general, free, and equal voting rights through quotas remains intact. This can only be explained by the connection drawn between such principles and the constitutionally enshrined model of representative democracy, especially in connection with principles such as formal equality (of the potentially affected men) and noninterference in the autonomy of political parties. In this regard, Spain represents an interesting European counterexample. Its Constitutional Court relied on a generic substantive equality mandate to validate legislative electoral

[170] See Eléonore Lépinard, "The French Parity Reform: The Never-Ending Quest for a New Gender Equality Principle," in Lépinard and Rubio-Marín, *Transforming Gender Citizenship*, 62–94. See also Joan Wallach Scott, "French Universalism in the Nineties," *differences: A Journal of Feminist Cultural Studies* 15, no. 2 (2004): 32–53, at 32, 47.

[171] In the United Kingdom, an employment tribunal ruled that Labour's use of all-women shortlists represented unlawful sex discrimination. See Jepson and Dyas-Elliott v. The Labour Party [1996] IRLR 116. Parliament responded with the Sex Discrimination (Election Candidates) Act 2002, which permits political parties to use all-women shortlists but does not mandate it. The act was subject to a sunset clause and due to expire in 2015 but has been extended to 2030, and only the Labour Party has made extensive use of this possibility. In 2021, 34 percent of the House of Commons are women – a record high.

[172] See Corte cost., 6–12 settembre 1995, n. 422, Foro it, I. For a thorough discussion of the Italian debate, see Rodríguez Ruiz and Rubio-Marín, "The Gender of Representation," 294–96.

[173] See Bundesgericht [BGer] [Federal Supreme Court] Mar. 19, 1997, 123 Entscheidungen des Schweizerischen Bundesgerichts [BGE] I 152. For a discussion of the Swiss case, see Blanca Rodríguez-Ruiz and Ruth Rubio-Marín, "On Parity, Interdependence, and Women's Democracy," in Baines, Barak-Erez, and Kahana, *Feminist Constitutionalism*, 188–203.

[174] Article 3 in the Italian Constitution provides that "It shall be the duty of the Republic to remove those obstacles of an economic or social nature which constrain the freedom and equality of citizens, thereby impeding the full development of the human person and the effective participation of all workers in the political, economic and social organisation of the country." Moreover, the decision rested also on the distinction between equality of opportunities and equality of results, as well as the argument that the challenged quotas in fact tried to illegitimately guarantee equality of results and not just of opportunities.

quotas, in a reasoning that also underscores the value of pluralism in democracies,[175] a logic that was also displayed in an Indonesian decision constitutionally upholding gender quotas.[176] In any event, the debate is far from settled in Western Europe; in fact, constitutional contestation is currently taking place in Germany.[177]

175 See S.T.C., Jan. 29, 2008 [No. 12/2008]) of the Spanish Constitutional Court, which in 2008 upheld mandatory electoral gender quotas, ensuring that electoral lists include no less than 40 percent of candidates from each gender and relying mostly on the substantive equality reasoning, even though this constitutes a rare exception when combined with democratic concerns around necessary pluralism. See Rodríguez Ruiz and Rubio-Marín, "The Gender of Representation," 296–300.

176 In its decision 22-24/PUU-VI/2008, the Constitutional Court of Indonesia also validated a law imposing at least one female prospective candidate in every three prospective candidates in party lists, referring to a generic substantive equality mandate contained in the second amendment (2000) to the 1945 State Constitution of the Republic of Indonesia (namely, article 28H [2]: "Each person has the right to receive facilitation and special treatment to have the same opportunities and advantages in order to achieve equality and fairness"). It also called on validly ratified international human rights instruments, including CEDAW, conceptualizing the measure as an affirmative action or a temporary special measure. The logic of substantive equality has also been crucial for upholding quota legislation in Mexico, although in the Mexican case, the constitution has been amended three times (in 2014, 2019, and 2021) and now compels the legislator to enact measures to ensure parity in both executive and legislative office (article 41) as well as in the judiciary (article 100). Interestingly, the case law has validated parity legislation on the basis of diversified rationales, from considering parity laws as temporary affirmative action measures seeking equality of results (see Acción de inconstitucionalidad 45/2014 y sus acumuladas 46/2014, 66/2014, 67/2014, 68/2014, 69/2014, and 75/2014, Diario Oficial de la Federación [DOF] 12-03-2015), or as permanent measures aiming at equality of opportunities only (see Tribunal Electoral del Poder Judicial de la Federación [Electoral Court of the Judiciary of the Federation] [TEPJF], decision No. SUP-JDC-1236/2015, Aug. 26, 2015), to underscoring their permanent nature and equality of results ambition, something no other constitutional court had done so far (see Contradicción de tesis 275/2015, Suprema Corte de Justicia de la Nación [SCJN], June 4, 2019, Décima Época, Libro 71, octubre 2019, Tomo I, Tesis P./J. 11/2019 [10A.], página 5).

177 In Germany, parity laws are being discussed at both state and federal levels in view of the fact that, in recent years, the numbers of female representatives in parliaments have either decreased or remained stagnant at low levels. On July 15, 2020, the Constitutional Court of Thuringia declared unconstitutional a state parity law that required political parties standing for elections to state and local parliaments to provide a zipper list system alternating between men and women with the aim of improving women's overall parliamentary representation primarily on the basis of undue interference with political party autonomy. See ThürVerfGHG 2/20, July 30, 2019 (Thüringen). For a similar result achieved in front of the Brandenburg Constitutional Court, see VfgBbg 9/19, VfgBbg 55/19, Oct. 23, 2020. Most recently, there has been a Federal Constitutional Court decision that struck down, on admissibility grounds, an application that requested the court to

Fortunately, constitutional hurdles have not proved insurmountable obstacles, and a series of constitutional amendments have successfully been passed over the last three decades not only, as we have seen, in countries joining the democratization wave but also in countries with more consolidated constitutional regimes. Interestingly, whereas in some jurisdictions, including Portugal (in 1997)[178] or Slovenia (in 2004),[179] constitutional amendments preceded the passing of legislation or came right after it as a form of constitutional backing, in most cases, the reforms were strictly needed to overcome the objections expressed by the courts. This was the case in France (1999) and Italy (2001 and 2003).[180] And, although some of the new wording inserted into these constitutions suggests a "substantive equality" or "equal opportunities" framing, some of the European reforms, like that in Portugal, make more direct reference to democracy,[181] thus inviting the reflection that ensuring women's empowerment is necessary to tackle the democratic deficit linked to the original sexual contract that modern constitutionalism entrenched.

hold that the government violated its constitutional duty to guarantee equality between men and women by not adopting parity laws. This decision, however, left open the question of whether a federal law adopting a parity requirement would be constitutional if justified as affirmative action of the kind that could compensate women for gender-specific disadvantages in political nomination processes. See BVerfG, 2 BvC 46/19, Dec. 15, 2020. On the general topic, see Louise K. Davidson-Schmich, *Gender Quotas and Democratic Participation: Recruiting Candidates for Elective Offices in Germany* (Ann Arbor: University of Michigan Press, 2016).

178 Portugal experienced a constitutional revision in 1997 that came to alter the wording of articles 109 and article 9 (h) in the constitution.

179 A new paragraph was added to article 43 of the Slovenian Constitution, which recognizes the universal and equal right to vote, whereas at the same time allowing for legal measures to encourage equal opportunities of women and men in standing for election to state and local community authorities.

180 In France, the Loi constitutionnelle 99-569 du 8 juillet 1999 relative à l'égalité entre les femmes et les hommes [Constitutional Law 99-959 of July 8, 1999, relative to the equality between women and men], Journal Officiel de la République Francaise [J.O.] [Official Gazzete of France], July 9, 1999, p. 10175, introduced a fourth paragraph in article 1 of the French Constitution whereby "Statutes shall promote equal access by women and men to elective offices and posts." It also amended article 4 so as to provide that political parties "shall contribute to the implementation of the principle set out in the second paragraph of article 1 as provided for by statute." On the wave of constitutional amendments in Europe, see Rubio-Marín, "Women's Political Citizenship in New European Constitutionalism," 323–56.

181 For instance, Portugal's 1997 constitutional revision altered the wording of article 109, which now states that "the direct and active participation in politics by men and women is a fundamental instrument in the consolidation of the democratic system."

In this respect, probably one of the most interesting evolutions in recent times is the growing awareness that the empowerment of women must take place not just through political office but rather in every sphere of male-dominated power and authority, including, if necessary, through the adoption of mandatory gender quotas in the corporate world. As a matter of fact, several European countries have already adopted legislation to such effect, such as Belgium, France, Germany, Iceland, Italy, the Netherlands, Norway, and Spain. Unsurprisingly, this move has also triggered constitutional contestation[182] and, in some cases, as in France, even made a second constitutional reform necessary.[183]

Although many of the provisions that are being incorporated to facilitate women's equal representation retain the form of directive principles rather than enforceable subjective rights, some courts have been willing to accept the possibility of judicially enforceable unconstitutional omissions.[184] Similarly, several courts around the world have been willing to provide directions as to how relevant electoral norms should be properly interpreted in order to optimize the effectiveness of parity rules, including by suggesting that women's quotas constitute only minimum thresholds and not top ceilings or by endorsing the use of rules to ensure that women candidates are listed in electable positions.[185] Concerns around effectiveness have also triggered recent constitutional

182 See Conseil constitutionnel [CC] [Constitutional Council] decision No. 2006-533DC, Mar. 16, 2006, J.O. 4425, 4446 (Fr.), striking down a law that requires gender corporate quotas (Loi relative a l'égalité salariale entre les femmes et les homes).

183 After this reform, article 1 of the French Constitution now incorporates, among the grand principles of the French Republic (hence among the other defining features of the French state), a provision stating that the French Republic must promote equal access for women and men to elective offices and posts as well as to positions of professional and social responsibility. Loi 2008-724 du 23 juillet 2008 de modernization des institutions de la Vème République [Law 2008-724 of July 23, 2008, on the modernization of the institutions of the Fifth Republic], Journal Officiel de la République Francaise [J.O.] [Official Gazzete of France], July 24, 2008, p. 11890.

184 See Constitutional Chamber of the Supreme Court, decision No. 00716-98, Feb. 6, 1998 (Costa Rica), declaring unconstitutional the failure by the president of the republic and the president of the legislative assembly to propose and accept a list of candidates, including women candidates, for political appointment to the board of directors of a public service regulatory body. But see Conseil constitutionnel [CC] [Constitutional Council] decision No. 2015-465QPC, Apr. 24, 2015, J.O. 7337, 7355 (Fr.), clarifying that the parity principle is not a directly enforceable right or freedom protected by the constitution. See also, for Germany, BVerfG, 2 BvC 46/19, Dec. 15, 2020.

185 On the need to ensure that women are placed in electable positions, see Tribunal Supremo de Elecciones [Supreme Electoral Tribunal], resolutions Nos. 1863-1999 and 2837-1999 (Costa Rica).

amendments reflecting increased awareness that electoral parity should be permanent and that it does not necessarily translate into women being elected in the same proportion as they appear in the electoral lists. This is due to, among other things, patriarchal legacies within political parties and the design of the electoral system itself. With proportional representation schemes being more gender-quota friendly, the size of electoral districts, the design of party lists, the possible imposition of placement mandates, and a sanction system for nonabidance may play a decisive role in the ultimate outcome.[186] Concerns around legitimacy, in turn, have widened to include other marginalized groups, such as gays and lesbians,[187] and to better reflect intersectional discrimination dynamics.[188]

Until recently, the notion of parity democracy and the requirement of gender-balanced representation, or equal participation, seems to be gaining a foothold in contemporary constitution-making in ways that are more reflective of its centrality in defining the overall features of the political system and the necessity of domain expansion. Bolivia's 2009 constitution, when defining the country's form of democracy, includes a

[186] In Peru, gender electoral quotas appeared as temporary measures in the law but were constitutionalized as permanent in 2002. In Taiwan, where the Chinese Constitution came to be implemented, a constitutional revision in 2005 changed the electoral method of the national legislature to enhance women's representation. The new rules specify that the number of elected female members on each party's list should not be less than one-half of the total number (section 2, article 4 of the Additional Articles to the Constitution of the People's Republic of China). See Wen-Chen Chang, "The Convergence of Constitutions and International Human Rights: Taiwan and South Korea in Comparison," *North Carolina Journal of International Law and Commercial Regulations* 36, no. 3 (2011): 593–624, at 539ff. Mexico's constitution, as amended in 2015, explicitly contemplates the obligation of political parties to establish rules to guarantee parity in candidacies to federal and state elections (article 41).

[187] The 1987 Constitution of the Philippines reserves one-half of the seats allocated to party-list representatives for various minorities, including women, workers, peasants, urban poor, indigenous cultural communities, and the youth (see article 4, section 5 [2] of the constitution). This list has been recently extended by the Supreme Court to include gays and lesbians. See Ang Ladlad LGBT Party v. Commission on Elections, G.R. No. 190582 (Apr. 8, 2010).

[188] Nepal's 2015 constitution contains special measures to ensure the representation of women as well as other historically marginalized groups such as the Dalit, Adivasi Janajati, Khas Arya, Madhesi, Tharu, Muslims, and backward regions (article 84 [2]). In this regard, it is also important to point at the wider spread of nested quotas combining gender and ethnic quotas. See Melanie M. Hughes, "The Combination of Gender and Ethnic Quotas in Electoral Politics," in Rubio-Marín and Kymlicka, *Gender Parity and Multicultural Feminism*, 97.

direct reference to men's and women's equality.[189] Consistent with this, the constitutional mandate of women's representation is also gradually expanding to other domains of norm creation and decision-making, among them, the different levels of legislative power,[190] the executive branches, including specific top positions,[191] and the judiciary,[192] while courts are being asked to validate the constitutional compatibility of further domain expansion, including that of universities,[193] unions, and associations.[194] Similarly, institutions are being constitutionally designed with the explicit mandate to ensure that the rules for inclusion of women

[189] See article 8, "The State is based on the values of ... social and gender equality in participation" and article 11.I, "The Republic of Bolivia adopts a participatory democratic, representative and communal form of government, with equal conditions for men and women." The idea is then picked up under article 26.I (on political rights), which provides that "all citizens have the right to participate freely in the formation, exercise and control of political power, directly or through their representatives, individually or collectively. Participation shall be equitable and under equal conditions for men and women," and article 147.I (on the legislative assembly), according to which "the equal participation of men and women shall be guaranteed in the election of the members of the assembly."

[190] Nepal's 2015 constitution includes quotas for the federal parliament (article 84), the provincial assembly (article 176), and the village and municipal assemblies (articles 222 and 223, respectively).

[191] Nepal's 2015 constitution (article 70) mandates that the president and vice president of Nepal must belong to different genders and communities. It also provides (article 91) that either the speaker or deputy speaker of the House of Representatives must be a woman and that either the chairperson or vice chairperson of the House of Representatives must be a woman (article 92).

[192] Ecuador probably offers one of the best examples. In its 2008 constitution, article 176 provides that "the requirements and procedures for designating public servants of the judiciary must involve a competitive merit-based examination, subject to challenge and social monitoring; *parity between men and women* shall be fostered." Moreover, article 65 contemplates that "the State shall promote *equality* with respect to the *representation of women and men* in publicly appointed or elected office, in its executive and decision-making institutions, and political parties and movements" (italics are ours). Earlier precedents exist. The "Fundamental Principles" of the Rwandan Constitution (chapter III, article 10) include a commitment to "equality of all Rwandans and between men and women which is affirmed by women occupying at least thirty percent (30%) of positions of decision-making organs." Section 174 (2) of the South African Constitution provides the need for the judiciary to reflect broadly the racial and gender composition of the country.

[193] See Conseil constitutionnel [CC] [Constitutional Council] decision No. 2015-465QPC, Apr. 24, 2015, J.O. 7337, 7355 (Fr.), validating a rule forcing academic councils to implement parity in public universities.

[194] See Constitutional Chamber of the Supreme Court, decision No. 04630–2014, Apr. 2, 2014 (Costa Rica).

and other underrepresented groups are duly respected.[195] While this task seems useful, it does certainly not render irrelevant the auditing of the whole institutional architecture in the configuration of all state powers and models of governance for its gender impact, including by considering whether competing designs may translate into women's better numerical and substantive representation.[196]

3.5 Toward Women's Multinational and Multicultural Equality

Historically, the participatory gender equality turn described so far developed in parallel to a pluralism turn. This pluralism turn put on the table the need to overcome the remaining legacies of processes of white domination in imperial and settler societies.[197] The multicultural theories that accompanied the pluralism turn started to vindicate not only respect for the religious, cultural, ethnic, and linguistic diversity in contemporary societies but also the need to address the fundamental problems of political legitimacy through various forms of autonomy systems, whether of a territorial or of a jurisdictional nature.[198]

In constitutional terms, this meant that older assumptions that states must have a unitary conception of national sovereignty began to be challenged and replaced by new models of "multicultural

[195] The 2018 Constitution of the Republic of Burundi requires the independent national electoral commission to "Assure the respect of the provisions of the present Constitution in regard to multiethnicity and gender, and understand the disputes regarding these (categories)" (article 92.h). This provision was already present in the 2005 text, albeit in a different section and with similar wording (article 91.g). Also, Morocco's 2011 constitution (article 19) orders the state to ensure parity between men and women, creating to this effect an "authority for parity" with the task of fighting against all forms of discrimination. Earlier, though more generic, precedents include South Africa's Commission for Gender Equality, with the mandate to "promote respect for gender equality and the protection, development and attainment of gender equality" (chapter 9).

[196] See Paula A. Monopoli, "Gender and Constitutional Design," *Yale Law Journal* 115, no. 9 (2006): 2643–51.

[197] In particular, Pateman notices that, while "the process of decolonization and national self-determination that began after World War II has swept away all but tiny remnants of the colonies of the European powers, but the Native peoples of the two New Worlds, living within the boundaries of the states constructed from the plantation of settlers, have never been seen as candidates for sovereignty," something that raises concerns about the fundamental political legitimacy of the resulting arrangements. See Carole Pateman, "The Settler Contract," in *Contract and Domination*, eds. Carole Pateman and Charles W. Mills (Cambridge: Polity Press, 2007), 73.

[198] Rubio-Marín and Kymlicka, *Gender Parity and Multicultural Feminism*, 23.

constitutionalism"[199] involving some degree of minority autonomy and allowing minorities to govern some of their internal affairs according to their own norms. Such autonomy could be the result of territorial self-government in those instances in which political subunits are created, allowing the minority to form a local majority, as when indigenous jurisdictions are recognized, or it could involve acknowledging a minority's legal order to prevail according to some subject matter divide, as in various forms of "customary" or "personal law" in pluralistic legal systems.[200]

Like the participatory turn in gender equality, the multicultural turn also began in the 1980s and has flourished since the 1990s. It, too, relied on a combination of "local mobilization and the spread of global models and discourses."[201] This convergence, whose primary result has been the production of overlapping normative and institutional orders with increasing constitutional recognition,[202] is to be celebrated, especially if, from an intersectional approach, we come to recognize the tortuous path that not only men but also women belonging to nonhegemonic racial, religious, or cultural groups have had to travel to affirm their equal citizenship status under modern constitutionalism. This is exemplified by the arduous struggles of indigenous women to thrive within the

199 Donna Lee Van Cott, "Indigenous Peoples' Politics in Latin America," *Annual Review of Political Science* 13 (2010): 385–405. The shifting conceptions of the state have been particularly pronounced in Latin America where, prior to the reforms in the 1990s, "official rhetoric proclaimed the homogeneous nature of Latin American societies." See Donna Lee Van Cott, "Latin America: Constitutional Reform and Ethnic Right," *Parliamentary Affairs* 53, no. 1 (2000): 41–54, at 41, 43, and "Indigenous Peoples' Politics in Latin America," 385–405. Since the 1990s, constitutions in several countries began to define their nations as multiethnic and multicultural, with the constituent processes in Bolivia and Ecuador in the current century taking one step further by suggesting "the existence of a nation of peoples or a multinational state and constitutionaliz(ing) conceptions from indigenous tradition," giving way to a system that, going beyond liberal constitutionalism, explores a different form of constitutionalism dubbed multinational, intercultural, and experimental. See Rodrigo Uprimny, "The Recent Transformation of Constitutional Law in Latin America: Trends and Challenges," *Texas Law Review* 89, no. 7 (2011), 1587–609, at 1590–91.

200 Rubio-Marín and Kymlicka, *Gender Parity and Multicultural Feminism*, 23.

201 Ibid., 24.

202 See James Tully, *Strange Multiplicity: Constitutionalism in an Age of Diversity* (Cambridge: Cambridge University Press, 1995); Boaventura de Sousa Santos, *Refundación del Estado en América Latina: perspectivas desde una epistemología del sur* (Bogotá: Plural, 2010).

modern constitutional architecture even today[203] or by that of women around the world who fight to retain autonomy about their religious dress codes rather than being "rescued" (sometimes only selectively) by secular conceptions of autonomy that are said to be constitutionally enshrined.[204]

Nevertheless, despite the common dynamics and shared sources, there was a potential for conflict between the gender participatory turn and the pluralism turn from the beginning; more specifically, the potential for multicultural recognition to cover women's interests related to cultural or religious belonging, but only at the expense of their equal citizenship status. Indeed, in societies embracing liberal democratic

[203] See Megan Davis, "Indigenous Women and Constitutional Recognition," in Irving, *Constitutions and Gender*, 357–86. More generally, see Joyce Green, ed., *Making Space for Indigenous Feminism* (Halifax: Fernwood Publishing, 2007).

[204] See, for example, Hilal Elver, "Gender Equality from a Constitutional Perspective: The Case of Turkey," in Baines and Rubio-Marín, *Gender of Constitutional Jurisprudence*, 291–98; and Hilal Elver, "Secular Constitutionalism and Muslim Women's Rights: The Turkish Headscarf Controversy and Its Impact on the European Court of Human Rights," in Baines, Barak-Erez, and Kahana, *Feminist Constitutionalism*, 413–32. Pateman sees "shades of old debates about civilization and lesser races, and of previous claims about the poor treatment of women in colonial possessions compared to the position of women at home" as hanging over controversies about immigration and exemplifies this by pointing to how the hijab and other female Islamic dresses have become a "battleground for the defense of European culture," even though "much of the concern appears to have less to do with women" than with "presenting the communities concerned as alien and inferior." See Carole Pateman, "Race, Sex, and Indifference," in Pateman and Mills, *Contract and Domination*, 163. Wearing a headscarf, generally not in the university setting but in the school setting, has stirred animated debates in several Western countries, including France, the United Kingdom, Switzerland, and Germany, where arguments around gender equality, the need for religious neutrality of the state, positive and negative religious freedoms of students, involvement of both parents and teachers, as well as the need to ensure social peace converge with different results and several high courts involved in their resolution. See Leyla Sahin v. Turkey, App. No. 44774/98, 41 Eur. H.R. Rep. 8 (2005), a decision by the European Court of Human Rights, which contrasts with the pro-ban position of the Turkish courts in the name of secularism described in Elver's texts. See also the German Federal Constitutional Court's decision in BVerfGE 102, 288 (2003), upholding a public schoolteacher's right to wear a headscarf on the basis of the principle of pluralism. This decision was upheld on the grounds that the veil could be assigned different meanings beyond the religious one. On the different positions on the wearing of a headscarf at school, see, among many others, Adriene Katherine Wing and Monica Nigh Smith, "Critical Race Feminism Lifts the Veil?: Muslim Omen, France, and the Headscarf Ban," *UC Davis Law Review* 39, no. 3 (2006): 743–90, at 743, 767–70; Bronwyn Winter, *Hijab & the Republic: Uncovering the French Scarf Debate* (Syracuse, NY: Syracuse University Press, 2008), 21ff.

constitutionalism, albeit composed of different collectivities claiming jurisdictional domains, there have been tensions between the affirmation of women's equal citizenship and religious, customary, or tribal norms. These tensions are even greater in societies that reject the fully secular option component of liberal constitutionalism, affirming the complex coexistence between secular and religious norms as legitimate sources of authority when those religious norms do not endorse equality between the sexes.

A phenomenon described as the "paradox of multicultural vulnerability" has been widely debated whereby multicultural recognition of legal pluralism would put women in jeopardy of being subject to laws that most often they have no role in authoring, interpreting, or contesting and that, more generally speaking, would undermine rights that are otherwise constitutionally protected.[205] Because jurisdiction is often claimed over issues pertaining to women's status within their families and communities and centrally concern women's autonomy vis-à-vis the men in the family, starting with the spouse – an autonomy that is denied when cultural or religious norms treat women as male property or when norms on marriage, divorce, the transmission of property, and the custody of children enforce their total dependency on men – it was feared that not only theocratic regimes but also some forms of liberal multicultural accommodations within otherwise secular orders could amount to nothing but the most grotesque (re)affirmation of "family exceptionalism," meaning the shielding off of such family relations from the egalitarian constitutional logic to the sacrifice of women's equal citizenship status.[206] In the African continent, for instance, it has been noted that the least challenging constitutional reforms from a women's rights perspective have been provisions related to the terms and conditions of employment, legislative quotas, citizenship rights, and even positive rights, and that it is the provisions that touch on matters that pertain to the family, clan, and custom that have proved to be more controversial, including in countries where the constitutions affirmed the primacy of women's rights and equality.[207] This suggests the possibility of a scenario in which the

[205] Rubio-Marín and Kymlicka, *Gender Parity and Multicultural Feminism*, 25. More generally, see Shachar, *Multicultural Jurisdictions*.

[206] See Susan Moller Okin, *Is Multiculturalism Bad for Women?*, eds. Joshua Cohen, Matthew Howard, and Martha C. Nussbaum (Princeton, NJ: Princeton University, 1999), 13.

[207] Tripp, "Conflicting Agendas?," 179.

guarantees of constitutional equality are then emptied through the carving out of areas of the law that, in the name of culture or religion, are labeled "personal" or "private" and hence exempt from constitutional scrutiny,[208] representing a de facto retention of exclusionary gender constitutionalism.[209]

Constitutionally speaking, then, the starting point would be the degree to which customary or religious law is recognized as a source of law and, if so, its rank within the normative pyramid and the designation of the authorities in charge of interpreting and applying it. Linked to this is also the question of the jurisdictional divide between state/secular authorities and indigenous, tribal, or religious authorities, a jurisdictional attribution that is also likely to have a great impact on women's rights, especially regarding personal law and family matters. After all, as Jill Vickers claims, "the mechanism of legal pluralism, territorial and non-territorial, is the 'federal arrangement,'" which has the greatest potential to obstruct family law reform.[210] This explains why in many countries of Islamic tradition, including Egypt, Tunisia, Iraq, and Morocco, we have witnessed many women, including religious women,[211] engage in constitution-making struggles for secularism, first and foremost, and, short of that, for a limited or subordinate rather than hierarchically superior status of Shari'a law; it also explains why, where secularism is

[208] Johanna Bond, "Gender and Post-Colonial Constitutions in Sub-Saharan Africa," in Irving, *Constitutions and Gender*, 97.

[209] On India, see Catharine A. MacKinnon, "Sex Equality Under the Constitution of India: Problems, Prospects, and 'Personal Laws,'" *International Journal of Constitutional Law* 4, no. 2 (2006): 181–97. According to Bond, however, racism and Eurocentrism (and not just sexism) played an important role in rendering African personal law external to the constitution. The African woman was located at the "intersection of mutually reinforcing colonial biases: the belief that the African colonized subject is unworthy of the public sphere of law and the belief that women must occupy the private sphere free from state intervention." See Bond, "Gender and Post-Colonial Constitutions," 97.

[210] Jill Vickers, "'Gendering' Federal Constitutions," in Irving, *Constitutions and Gender*, 166.

[211] Needless to say, neither feminism nor Islam can be conceived of as homogeneous categories, and a plurality of individual and collective agencies exist in each process arising from different approaches to the interpretation of both feminism and Islam or to the influence of different historical, political, and cultural experiences that must be duly acknowledged. See, for all, Leila Ahmed, *Women and Gender in Islam: Historical Roots for a Modern Debate* (New Haven: Yale Univeristy Press, 1992); Lila Abu-Lughod, ed., *Remaking Women: Feminism and Modernity in the Middle East* (Princeton, NJ: Princeton University Press, 1988).

not guaranteed, personal status law reform becomes the most common battlefield for reformist women.[212]

Only after the secular/religious nature of a country has been defined and after the jurisdictional split has determined which areas fall within the realm of the state – as opposed to indigenous, tribal, or religious authorities[213] – do we reach the question of whether the recognition of women's constitutional rights should prevail or trump over certain or all forms of jurisdictions and other sources of law. In this regard, constitutions can include explicit exclusionary clauses either exempting customary law or religious law from constitutional equality scrutiny or excluding personal or family law issues from constitutional nondiscrimination scrutiny.[214] In fact, this was common in the independence constitutions in the sub-Saharan African region in the 1960s following the end of colonial rule, when allegiance to custom was presented as an expression of national identity that is still reflected in a handful of constitutional provisions.[215] Such provisions have had the effect of limiting the

212 On women's struggle to have the 2005 Iraqi Constitution recognize Islam as "a basic source of legislation" rather than "the basic source of legislations" and to retain the option of nonsectarian personal status law, see Efrati, "Re-Living Yesterday's Battles."

213 For an example of the relevance of the constitutional position of Islam for women, the federalized arrangement in administering Islam, and the civil/Shari'a jurisdictional separation, see Dian A. Shah, "Gender and Constitutionalism in Malaysia," in Chang et al., *Gender, Sexuality and Constitutionalism in Asia.*

214 Section 27 of the 1991 Constitution of Sierra Leone provides that "no law shall make any provision which is discriminatory either of itself or in its effect," but then, in section 27 (4), it goes on to make exceptions related to "adoption, marriage, divorce, burial, devolution of property on death or other interests of personal law." Section 18, subsection 4 of Lesotho's 1993 constitution qualifies the nondiscrimination provision in subsection 1 as follows: "Subsection (1) shall not apply to any law to the extent that that law makes provision . . . (b) . . . with respect to adoption, marriage, divorce, burial, devolution of property on death or other like matters which is the personal law of persons . . .; or (c) for the application of the customary law of Lesotho with respect to any matter in the case of persons who, under that law, are subject to that law." Many constitutions around the world also protect Muslim personal law from constitutional equality scrutiny. See, for instance, article 12 (3) (a) of the 1965 Constitution of Singapore and article 8 (5) (a) of the 1957 Constitution of Malaysia.

215 As has been noted, in the anti-colonial struggles and national liberation movements of the twentieth century, it was the white colonizing power and the European settler population who were seen as the primary enemies. Even for postcolonial, post-1960s, second-wave feminism, feminists of color "rejected the idea that their relationships with the men in their communities were, or should be, equivalent to those that existed between white women and white men." Community as such was conceptualized as "the entire racial/ethnic community in battle against white America's domination." See Benita Roth, *Separate Roads to Feminism: Black, Chicana, and White Feminist*

usefulness of constitutional equality guarantees and insulating customary law from constitutional challenge, thus thwarting the evolution of customary law over time.[216] For this reason, they have been analogized to the frequent CEDAW reservations regarding the nonapplicability of the convention to certain family matters.[217] Nevertheless, in the 1990s, postcolonial Africa's first ever pro-democracy "constitutional moment" finally arrived and, with it, a wave of postindependence constitutional reform.[218] It is in this context, and coinciding with the gender participatory shift, that we observe a process of gradual (though not unanimous) rejection of such exclusionary clauses in the constitutions of several countries that now recognize legal pluralism but also make explicit the fact that it cannot be read as limiting women's otherwise entrenched rights by making the latter preeminent. Expressions of this shift, connected to participatory constitution-making processes, can be found in Uganda's 1995 constitution, which makes direct reference to women and

Movements in America's Second Wave (New York, NY: Cambridge University Press, 2004), 43, 70.

216 See Bond, "Gender and Post-Colonial Constitutions," 81–84, 86–87, where she describes how the history of colonialism in the region created a plural legal system in which multiple systems of law, such as statutory, customary, and religious law, operated simultaneously in an effort to preserve indigenous custom and appease traditional leaders who were granted control over the private sphere, particularly with respect to family or personal laws. She also explains that, when colonial administrators brought customary law into the colonial court system, they "filtered the law through the lens of British understandings," establishing a version of customary law that "suited the white administrators and African male elders who ruled colonial society," doing so in ways that resonated with British conceptions of the family that discriminated against women and applying only a "repugnancy" test to filter out what they considered to be "oppressive traditional practices." Allegiance to custom, as an expression of national identity, then became part of a renewed cultural pride during the independence period, which continues today, sometimes taking the form of radically nationalistic rhetoric. Bond names Botswana, Gambia, Lesotho, Mauritious, Sierra Leone, and Zambia among those countries retaining exclusionary clauses in their constitutions. See ibid., 89.

217 See Wendy Lacey, "Gender Equality: International Law and National Constitutions," in Irving, *Constitutions and Gender*, 143–44, providing a list of countries that have held reservations to CEDAW, with the effect, in many cases, of bracketing out family and marriage law from gender equality rights, explaining that the most common justification for this is that various articles (including article 2 on nondiscrimination and article 16 on nondiscrimination in marriage and family life) conflict with Shari'a law. In spite of this, she argues, it is important to remember that CEDAW itself only permits reservations that are consistent with the object and purpose of the convention (article 28.2) and that the CEDAW Committee considers both article 2 and article 16 to represent the core principles of the convention.

218 See H. Kwasi Prempeh, "Africa's 'Constitutionalism Revival': False Start or New Dawn?," *International Journal of Constitutional Law* 5, no. 3 (2007): 469.

other marginalized groups,[219] as well as in South Africa's 1996 constitution, with a more generically worded affirmation of the prevalence of the Bill of Rights over customary law.[220] More recent expressions include provisions in the constitutions of Kenya (2010) and Zimbabwe (2013), once again, adopted under the heavy influence of women's rights activists supported by international actors and, to some extent, against a background of public uproar produced by prior case law applying the exclusionary clause in ways that involved discrimination against women.[221]

Leaving aside textual variations, controversy has emerged when constitutions explicitly recognize both women's and customary rights but fail to clearly spell out how they will act in case of conflict, or simply because, in the end, there are bound to be competing interpretations by the different authorities concerned as to which norms violate or do not violate women's equal rights in an unjustified manner. This has often brought attention to the courts addressing such conflicts in ways that raise concerns because of the difficulty of large parts of the population to access the formal court system.[222] Even in countries that have tried to harmonize these contradictory impulses by directly addressing the tension, as in the case of Uganda, conflict has been unavoidable. The same is

[219] Uganda's 1995 constitution provides an example of this when it states in its National Objectives and Directives of State Policy (XXIV, Cultural Objectives) that "cultural and customary values which are consistent with fundamental rights and freedoms, human dignity, democracy and with the Constitution may be developed and incorporated in aspects of Ugandan life." Article 33 (6) also specifies that "laws, cultures, customs or traditions which are against the dignity, welfare or interest of women, or which undermine their status, are prohibited by this Constitution." Yet none of this prevented the huge pushback in defense of the clan and customary practices when the 1998 Land Act was passed recognizing common property in land inheritance in favor of women. See also Tripp, "Conflicting Agendas?," 187–88.

[220] Section 15 (Bill of Rights) of the South African Constitution acknowledges traditional or religious marriages, or marriages concluded under personal or family law, but requires any system of marriage to be consistent with the entire constitution. Similarly, cultural and religious rights are recognized under section 31, yet the constitution acknowledges that such rights "may not be exercised in a manner inconsistent with any provision of the Bill of Rights."

[221] See Bond, "Gender and Post-Colonial Constitutions," 89–92, referring to the *Magaya* decision in Zimbabwe, where the exclusionary clause was applied to deny a woman's right to inherit from her deceased father – a case that was heavily contested across the country.

[222] See, generally, Wieland Lehnert, "The Role of the Courts in the Conflict between African Customary Law and Human Rights," *South African Journal on Human Rights* 21, no. 2 (2005): 241; Muna Ndulo, "African Customary Law, Customs, and Women's Rights," *Indiana Journal of Global Legal Studies* 18, no. 1 (2011): 87.

true of the South African experience, where efforts to include an exclusionary clause by traditional leaders during the postapartheid constitution-making process were successfully defeated, largely thanks to feminist advocacy campaigns to subject personal and customary law to constitutional equality provisions.[223] Public controversy, however, has not subsided. Both the legislator and the courts, including the Constitutional Court, have retained a central role in settling conflicts between customary law and constitutional equality,[224] responding, at times, to actions brought in the public interest by women's organizations[225] and trying to strike a fair balance that does justice to women while giving due recognition to African law and legal thinking, to which the court has also referred as "a source of legal ideas, values and practice . . . that have long been suppressed or marginalized."[226]

Beyond the question of jurisdictional disputes, it has been noted that the mechanism for affirming women's rights – in contrast to community norms and to courts that are not necessarily pluralistic enough in their composition – has a limited potential because, in a real-life scenario, it forces women to choose between their rights and their culture. This choice, however, seems both unfair and largely unfeasible. Women have a right to their culture, as well as a right to equality, and the challenge is to secure both rights. Moreover, the exit option implicit in the

223 Felicitas Kaganas and Christina Murray, "The Contest between Culture and Gender Equality under South Africa's Interim Constitution," *Journal of Law and Society* 21, no. 4 (1994): 409–33.

224 See Chuma Himonga, "Constitutional Rights of Women under Customary Law in Southern Africa: Dominant Interventions and 'Old Pathways,'" in Baines, Barak-Erez, and Kahana, *Feminist Constitutionalism*, 321, 325. Overall, the South African Constitutional Court has maintained the stance adopted in 2005 in the *Bhe* decision against discriminatory customary law. In *Bhe and Others v. Khayelitsha Magistrate and Others*, 2005 (1) SA 580 (CC), both section 23 of the Black Administration Act of 1927 and the customary law rule of primogeniture were declared unconstitutional, allowing Bhe's widow to inherit his deceased spouse's estate in the midst of much controversy. Within three years of *Bhe*, the Constitutional Court struck down two other core elements of customary law in the areas of marriage and succession to status in *Gumede v. President of the Republic of South Africa and Others (Women's Legal Centre Trust as Amicus Curiae)*, 2009 (3) SA 152 (CC), and *Shilubana and Others v. Namitwa (National Movement of Rural Women and Commission for Gender Equality as Amici Curiae)*, 2007 (5) SA 620 (CC).

225 This was the case of *South African Human Rights Commission and Another v. President of the Republic of South Africa and Another*, 2005 (1) SA 580 (CC), a companion case to *Bhe*. See Bond, "Gender and Post-Colonial Constitutions," 93.

226 See Justice Albie Sachs's decision in *S. v. Makwanyane*, 1995 (3) SA 391 (CC) at 190 para. 365.

proposition ("either your rights or your culture") also ignores that the exit must be practically and not just theoretically possible, and this requires taking into account the difficulty posed by economic, social, and emotional realities that often make this exit a less than meaningful option for women and other vulnerable people.[227] In particular, when affirming one's state-granted rights through state courts is the only option to have one's rights protected against local patriarchal practices, women who seek recourse are still likely to be seen as being disloyal, and this, in turn, may trigger a defensive reaction within such group and encourage it to reaffirm the challenged dimensions of their culture. This move was labeled by Ayelet Shachar as "reactive culturalism," whereby, in response to external pressure, group members become more intransigent in their defense of (what they come to deem) "authentic" or even "sacred" practices.[228] Sadly enough, given women's all-too-common infrarepresentation in both majority and minority societies, this has often rendered them witnesses to the traditional type of fight in which a group of men step in as their "legitimate protectors" vis-à-vis another group of men.

The almost canonical example that illustrates this risk in constitutional law is the *Shah Bano* decision from India, concerning the application of religious norms potentially in conflict with women's constitutional rights.[229] Although the constitution in India protects sex equality, free choice of religion, and even a certain conception of secularism,[230] the pluralistic legal system inherited from colonial times has retained plural systems of personal law that govern family and some minor matters of property law (such as inheritance).[231] This decentralized situation dates

[227] See Sarah Song, *Justice, Gender and the Politics of Multiculturalism* (Cambridge: Cambridge University Press, 2007), 161–62; Ayelet Shachar, *Multicultural Jurisdictions: Cultural Differences and Women's Rights* (Cambridge: Cambridge University Press, 2001), 70–71.

[228] Shachar, *Multicultural Jurisdictions*, 35–37.

[229] See Nussbaum, "India, Sex Equality, and Constitutional Law," 174–204; Zia Mody, "Whose Law Is It Anyway?: A Flashpoint in Religion Fundamentalism," in *10 Judgements That Changed India*, 49–73; Marc Galanter and Jayanth Krishnan, "Personal Law Systems and Religious Conflict: A Comparison of India and Israel," in *Religion and Personal Law in India: A Call to Judgement*, ed. Gerald James Larson (Bloomington, IN; Indiana University Press, 2001), 272–80.

[230] According to its preamble, amended in 1976 (42nd Amendment).

[231] See Flavia Agnes, "Personal Laws," in *The Oxford Handbook of the Indian Constitution*, eds. Sujit Choudhry, Madhav Khosla, and Pratap Bhanu Mehta (Oxford: Oxford University Press, 2016), 903–5. Article 13 of the Indian Constitution declares "all laws

back to the British Raj. And, whereas the idea of a uniform civil code (which appears in aspirational terms under article 44 of the Indian Constitution) was contemplated in the postindependence moment and has been the object of much feminist activism,[232] it has increasingly been opposed by Muslim and other minorities, fearing that it would make them second-class citizens. A turning point in the debate was the *Shah Bano* judgment, with the ensuing backlash and the rise to power of the Hindu nationalist Bharatiya Janata Party (BJP).[233] In *Mohamed Ahmed Khan v. Shah Bano Begum & Others*,[234] the Indian Supreme Court ordered a Muslim man to pay maintenance to his elderly, divorced, and poor wife beyond the Islamic Iddat period of about three months on the grounds that the woman had no one else to support her and relying on a provision in India's secular Code of Criminal Procedure fighting destitution.[235] Her claims were successful, and in a decision by Chief Justice Chandrachud, a Hindu judge heading a Hindu-majority, five-judge bench, the court not only affirmed Shah Bano's constitutional claims but went as far as criticizing Islamic practices and proposing alternative interpretations of Islamist texts to show that this grant of

in force" that contradict fundamental rights to be null and void. Courts have held different views as to whether this includes personal laws, something that has forced feminists to address equality issues within each separate religious system, with varying degrees of success. In *Narasu Appa Mali* (State of Bombay v. Narasu Appa Mali, AIR 1952 Bom 84), the court considered that uncodified personal laws were not "laws in force" under article 13 and consequently immune to constitutional scrutiny. Despite *Narasu*, courts have increasingly tested personal law against fundamental rights by either reading down a statutory provision, reinterpreting it, or striking down the offending section, although avoiding the declaration of their unconstitutionality. See Agnes, "Personal Laws," 911–15. However, the *Narasu* doctrine might have come to an end with the so-called Sabarimala judgment (Indian Young Lawyers Association v. State of Kerala, [2019] 11 SCC 1), still under review, recognizing that "the decision in Narasu, in restricting the definition of the term 'laws in force' detracts from the transformative vision of the Constitution" (Justice Dhananjaya Yeshwant Chandrachud, concurring).

232 See Lakshmi Arya, "The Uniform Civil Code: The Politics of the Universal in Postcolonial India," *Feminist Legal Studies* 14, no. 3 (2006): 293–328; Archana Parashar, *Women and Family Law Reform in India: Uniform Civil Code and Gender Equality* (New Delhi: Sage Publications, 1992).

233 See Nussbaum, "India, Sex Equality and Constitutional Law," 190–91.

234 See Mohamed Ahmed Khan v. Shah Bano Begum & Others, AIR 1985 SC 945.

235 Article 125 of the Indian Code of Criminal Procedure refers to a maintenance order for wives, children, and parents. In the *Shah Bano* case, the Indian Supreme Court upheld the Muslim divorced woman's rights to a lifetime maintenance stating that, in case of conflict, religious neutrality of Article 125 CrPC overrides the provisions of personal law in favor of women's rights.

maintenance to the widow was in fact consistent with Islamic norms. The case was given great publicity and a virulent reaction followed, with the Muslim community rallying around the cause of denying women maintenance and Shah Bano herself feeling compelled to publicly apologize and renounce the maintenance she had obtained in court. In this context, the Muslim leadership persuaded the government to pass a law (Muslim Women [Protection of Rights on Divorce] Act of 1986) depriving Muslim women of the opportunity to win maintenance under the secular Code of Criminal Procedure. The legislation was then challenged again in court, which resulted in a decision that, instead of striking down the legislation, dictated a constitutionally conform interpretation thereof. Nevertheless, the decision included the statement of a general principle whereby decisions that touch "basic human rights, culture, dignity and decency of life and dictates of necessity in the pursuit of social justice should be invariably left to be decided on considerations other than religion or religious faith or beliefs or national, sectarian, racial or communal constraints."[236]

Recently, the Islamic "triple talaq" (talaq-e-biddat) – instant, unilateral, and irrevocable divorce performed exclusively by the husband, stating three times the word *talaq*, which means divorce in Arabic, in any format – was constitutionally and legally challenged by Shayara Bano, an aggrieved divorced Muslim woman, in the 2017 *Shayara Bano* case.[237] The five-judge constitutional bench in *Shayara Bano* was composed of judges from five different religions (Islam, Sikhism, Hinduism, Zoroastrianism, and Christianity) to avoid the controversial interpretation of Shari'a made by the Hindu-based bench that judged the *Shah Bano* case. In the landmark judgment, the Supreme Court deemed instant triple talaq unconstitutional (under article 14, read together with article 13 [1]).[238] As a consequence of the *Shayara Bano* judgment, the Muslim Women (Protection of Rights on Marriage) Act (2019) was enacted, declaring all forms of instant triple talaq void and illegal, and entitling the divorced wife to a subsistence allowance and to seek custody of her minor children.

236 See Danial Latifi & Another v. Union of India, AIR 2001 SC 3958.

237 See Shayara Bano v. Union of India, AIR 2017 SC 4609.

238 The majority judgment considered triple talaq as an arbitrary and capricious action against the principle of equality, since it was recognized and enforced in the Muslim Personal Law (Shariat) Application Act of 1937. This judgment concluded that the regulation was a law in force before the commencement of the constitution and inconsistent with fundamental rights. It also considered that, although personal law is protected under Article 25 – freedom of religion – triple talaq is not essential to the practice of Islam, following relevant Shari'a precedents and Islamic scholarship.

In view of these types of foreseeable dynamics, since the turn of the century, feminist multiculturalists have started placing more and more emphasis on the potential of reinforcing women's agency and participation within their own cultures instead of relying exclusively on state-generated rights and state courts.[239] Thus, multicultural feminists have sought a way of overcoming the paradox of multicultural vulnerability, not by rejecting multiculturalism and relying on external laws and courts, but rather by facilitating processes of debate and reform within minority groups.[240] This has led to what we might call a second "participatory turn," this time in relation to the internal decision-making processes of minority groups. Several concrete proposals have been advanced to strengthen the voices of women within minority groups, and some of them are in line with enhanced models of democratic deliberation that pay particular attention to the conditions for nondomination in intercultural conversations.[241] A constructionist approach to culture is often implicit, which starts from the fluid and changing nature of culture and

[239] It has been claimed that the state-generated rights model needs to be supplemented by other mechanisms because these rights are said to be "predicated upon decontextualization and the severance of women from their contexts," when in fact the aim should be to "strengthen women's position within the existing contexts." See Mary Maboreke, "Understanding Law in Zimbabwe," in *Gender and Social Justice*, ed. Ann Stewart (London: London Blackstone Press, 2000), 112. Beyond the problem of access to courts, Chuma Himonga identifies other reasons as to why the state-generated rights model (through legislative and judicial interventions) will not benefit many women in the African context, among them: "1) the reluctance of States to enforce court judgments in favor of women; 2) the fact that judicial interventions focus on official customary law, as opposed to living customary law; 3) the inaccessibility, complexity and alien nature of the laws they generate; and 4) the contestation about the use of Eurocentric solutions." See Chuma Himonga, "Constitutional Rights of Women under Customary Law in Southern Africa," 326. See also Susan Williams, "Religion, Custom, and Legal Pluralism," in Irving, *Constitutions and Gender*, exploring design strategies that can be used to help promote internal cultural development toward gender equality.

[240] For central contributions to this multicultural feminist literature, see Monique Devaux, *Gender and Justice in Multicultural Liberal States* (Oxford: Oxford University Press, 2006); Anne Phillips, *Multiculturalism without Culture* (Princeton, NJ: Princeton University Press, 2007); Shachar, *Multicultural Jurisdictions*; Song, *Justice, Gender and the Politics of Multiculturalism*; Leti Volpp, "Feminism Versus Multiculturalism," *Columbia Law Review* 101, no. 5 (2001): 1181–218.

[241] See Seyla Benhabib, *The Claims of Culture: Equality and Diversity in the Global Era* (Princeton, NJ: Princeton University Press, 2002). For a particular emphasis on mechanisms to strengthen the recognition, voice, and resources of internal minorities, see Susan Williams, "Democratic Theory, Feminist Theory, and Constitutionalism," in Baines, Barak-Erez, and Kahana, *Feminist Constitutionalism*, 393–410.

pays specific attention to the "politics of cultural construction, change and maintenance."[242]

There are indeed growing and promising manifestations of a participatory turn within minority groups.[243] This means that, when minority women feel disadvantaged by existing community norms, they do not merely look to external state courts to provide rights protection or exit options. Rather, they increasingly seek to be recognized as agents struggling for the right to participate in the creation, interpretation, and execution of communal norms. This participatory turn within minority communities has not always taken the form of mandatory gender quotas or parity goals (even though, in some cases, minority women have also been active in broader coalitions to seek parity and gender quotas at state level, such as in Bolivia and Ecuador).[244] In some cases, this may only be a concession to political realism recommending a gradualist approach. Where sex-based discrimination is deeply rooted, parity or gender-balanced participation may be too far removed from the starting baseline within religious or customary law jurisdictions to be a viable option in the foreseeable future. But the decision not to invoke parity may also reflect different normative values and visions of justice. In any event, any attempt to assess women's public engagement should take into account both formal and informal systems of governance and justice, for it is the latter that are most accessible to women in most contexts.[245]

[242] See Song, *Justice, Gender and the Politics of Multiculturalism*, 32; Susan Williams, "Democratic Theory," 402–10; Phillips, *Multiculturalism without Culture*, 161–62.

[243] See Kymlicka and Rubio-Marín, "The Participatory Turn in Gender Equality," exploring how women in minority cultures have, ever since the participatory turn, identified ways to strengthen their agency in norm creation and not just rights assertions, doing so in ways that do not exclusively depend on state courts for protection. Examples include those of Orthodox Jewish women fighting for the right to elect judges on rabbinical courts, but not the right to themselves serve as judges – let alone a rule requiring that 50 percent of judges be women – and women in Tanzania fighting to serve as paralegal experts in customary law disputes, rather than demanding 50/50 quotas for judges. For the former, see Meital Pinto, "Gender Parity in the Religious and Political Sphere of Israel," in Rubio-Marín and Kymlicka, *Gender Parity and Multicultural Feminism*, 119–49; and for the latter, see Johanna Bond, "The Challenges of Parity: Increasing Women's Participation in Informal Justice Systems within Sub-Saharan Africa," in ibid., 175–98.

[244] See Rachel Sieder and Anna Barrera Vivero, "Challenging Male Dominance in Norm-Making in Contexts of Legal Pluralism: Insights from the Andes," in Rubio-Marín and Kymlicka, *Gender Parity and Multicultural Feminism*, 238–73.

[245] See, for instance, Bond, "The Challenges of Parity," 175–99.

In the realm of constitutional law, all of this may suggest that, ideally, the rights and values that are constitutionally affirmed should be incorporated by all governing authorities in pluralistic legal systems, and not only or primarily by state courts or institutions. Short of this, however, the state cannot simply abandon internal minorities, not only because their rights cannot be ignored but also because internal minorities should be recognized as sources of legitimate interpretations of cultural and religious norms too. After all, some constitutions explicitly recognize everyone's fundamental right to participate in the cultural life of their choice.[246] Moreover, it is precisely the existence of constitutional norms and state courts enforcing them around the world that has enabled women (sometimes more successfully than others) to react against discriminatory norms regarding membership in their communities;[247] to claim an equal right to be present in all spaces;[248] equal participation in communal practices and rituals;[249] authority and decision-making within

[246] See, for instance, section 30 in the South African Constitution.

[247] See A.G. Canada v. Lavell, [1974] S.C.R. 1349 (Can.), unsuccessfully challenging the loss of aboriginal status due to intermarriage, a kind of struggle that ultimately succeeded in the form of a UN Human Rights Committee decision. See Sandra Lovelace v. Canada, Comm. 24/1977, U.N. Doc. CCPR/C/OP/1, at 10 (Aug. 14, 1979).

[248] On a successful challenge to the statutory rule prohibiting the entry of women of menstruating age into the famous South Indian Sabarimala Temple, see the Indian Supreme Court's decision in Indian Young Lawyers Association v. The State of Kerala, 11 SCC 1 (2019), and in particular Justice D. Y. Chandrachud's concurring opinion rebutting the criticism coming from those who saw in the ruling an undue interference in the internal autonomy of a religious group by elaborating on "the social and structural role of menstruation in the subordination of women, and how its integration into a symbolic universe of purity and pollution had been historically used to exclude women from equal access to public spaces, as well as to justify discrimination (and even violence)" against them. See Atrey and Bhatia, "In Search of Principle," in Chang et al., *Gender, Sexuality and Constitutionalism in Asia*. For another decision invalidating practices that consider menstruating women as polluting the space, see the Nepalese Supreme Court's decision in Dil Bahadur Bishwakarma v. Office of the Prime Minister, Writ No. 3303 of the year 2061 BS (2004). Decided in 2062 BS (2005), the Supreme Court held that the practice of *chhaupadi* was contrary to women's equality in the constitution. This is a practice whereby women, after childbirth and during menstruation, are forced by family members to leave the family home and live in a cowshed or hut, exposing them to a severe risk of sexual violence and attacks by animals.

[249] There have been various legal battles by women in Israel to have more equal roles in religious functions and rituals. This was best epitomized by the *Women of the Wall* cases. In the 1980s, women started to pray in a group, wearing tallits (praying shawls), and reading aloud from a Torah scroll, a practice that, before then, had only been performed by men in the men's section of the Wall plaza. This distinction had been justified on the basis of religious norms regarding the role of women as wives and caretakers, who are to

their communities;[250] and representation of the "voice of the community" to the outside world,[251] thereby challenging static interpretations of culture and the hermeneutic privilege of traditional authorities. This is, for instance, the case in Israel, where women have been increasingly successful in convincing the High Court of Justice to support a narrow interpretation of the concept of "religious" (exclusion of women from the judicial religious sphere is allowed by section 7 c of Israel's Women's Equal Rights Law) when confronting their claims to increase their participation in various positions within the religious community.[252]

be confined to the private sphere and pray silently and individually. In the end, what is at stake is the interpretation of what types of practices are in accordance with "custom" and whether this notion is to be interpreted in accordance with a pluralistic, secular approach that recognizes all the Jewish denominations and respects equality between the sexes and freedom of worship as the Jerusalem District Court ruled in 2013. See AdminC (Jer.) 23834-04-13 State of Israel v. Bonnie Riva Ras, Nevo Legal Database (Apr. 24, 2013) (Isr.), indirectly challenging prior decisions on the matter by the High Court of Justice, which were not gender equality responsive – HCJ 257/89 Hoffman v. Commissioner of the Western Wall, 48(2) PD 265 (1994); HCJ 3358/95 Hoffman v. Director General of Prime Minister Office, 54(2) PD 345 (2000); HCJFH 4128/00 Director General of Prime Minister's Office v. Hoffman, 57(3) PD 289 (2003). See Pinto, "Gender Parity in the Religious and Political Sphere of Israel," 141–45; Frances Raday, "The Fight against Being Silenced," in *Women of the Wall: Claiming Sacred Ground at Judaism's Holy Site*, eds. Phyllis Chesler and Rivka Hauts (Woodstock, VT: Jewish Lights Publishing, 2002).

250 See, for instance, Shilubana v. Nwamitwa, where the South African Supreme Court rejected opposition to the status of Hosi (a form of traditional authority), from which the plaintiff had been excluded after her father's death on account of her being a woman. Instead, the court reasoned, the Valoyi, Ms. Shilubana's ethnic group, had – through the decision of the royal family to install a woman as traditional leader – validly developed its customary law in accordance with the constitution. See Shilubana v. Namitwa 2009 (2) SA 66 (CC) at 49, 55, 73, and 75.

251 See, for instance, Native Women's Association of Canada v. Canada, [1994] 3 S.C.R. 627 (Can.), where the NWAC asked to be funded during the 1992 constitutional negotiations in Canada on the basis that they did not feel represented by the four traditional male-dominated organizations that the government had recognized and funded.

252 This has included their participation in the committees that elect judges for the rabbinical courts. See HCJ 8670/11 Emuna – the National Religious Women's Movement v. the Committee for Appointing Rabbinic Court Judges (2012), and HCJ 933/12 The Center for Women's Justice v. The Committee for Appointing Rabbinic Court Judges (2013). For their possibility to act as advocates and represent clients (mostly in divorce procedures) in rabbinical courts, see HCJ 6300/93 The Institution for Rabbinical Advocates Training v. The Minister of Religion, 48(4) PD 441 (1994); to be elected to local religious services councils, HCJ 153/87 Leah Shakdiel v. Minister of Religious Affairs et al., 42(2) PD 221 (1988), and HCJ 953/87 Poraz v. Lahat, Mayor of Tel Aviv-Jaffa, 41(2) PD 309 (1990); or appointed as directors in the administrative management of the rabbinic court systems, HCJ 8213/14 Dror v. Minister of Religious Services (2017). See also Pinto, "Gender Parity in the Religious and Political Sphere of Israel," 136–41.

In the end, internal reform, combined with court pressure that facilitates such reform, may in many contexts be the best option. For this reason, we should particularly celebrate the recent constitutional inclusion of norms or mechanisms to incorporate women's voices in all sites of decision-making, as this facilitates a liberal and de-essentialized construction of the "voice of the group" in contexts of legal pluralism. We could mention those contained in the recent constitutions of Ecuador and Mexico, which seek to ensure both the respect of fundamental rights and women's participation in decision-making in the exercise of indigenous jurisdiction.[253] Also worth mentioning is Chile's constitutional reform process, which aims to guarantee a number of seats for indigenous peoples within the constituent assembly while imposing the rule of parity on reserved seats. Evolutions of this kind suggest that, in one way or another, the participatory turn in gender equality seems unstoppable.

[253] In Latin America, growing recognition of indigenous rights have also come coupled with an explicit recognition that gender equality prevails. But new provisions have recently been added to go a step further by including women's voices in indigenous legal systems. The Constitution of Ecuador recognizes the need to ensure women's participation in decision-making in the exercise of indigenous jurisdiction (article 171), and the Constitution of Mexico (as amended in 2015) refers to women's participation under equitable conditions with men when electing indigenous authorities (article 2.A.III). Unfortunately, the emergence of an international legal right to indigenous self-determination has been mostly silent on the position of women. See Davis, "Indigenous Women and Constitutional Recognition," 359.

4

Transformative Gender Constitutionalism

Toward an Egalitarian Family Structure and Sexual and Reproductive Order

Since at least the time of the suffragists, feminists have been problematizing men's insufficient involvement in household and care work. To challenge sex roles so that working wives were not obliged to perform a double shift, feminists had to "institute a revolution in the early training and education of boys and girls." Crystal Eastman urged: "It must be womanly as well as manly to earn your own living, to stand on your own feet. And it must be manly as well as womanly to know how to cook and sew and clean and take care of yourself in the ordinary exigencies of life." Across classes, "bread-winning wives have not yet developed home-making husbands." "We must bring up feminist sons."[1] Second-wave feminists too, as we have seen in Chapter 2, had been well aware of the limitations imposed on women because of their undue share of domestic duties and saw the unequal division of labor and responsibilities within households as expressions of unequal power relations and among the reasons that accounted for women's persistent barriers to participation in politics and wider public forums. Moreover, if the "forceful confinement" of women to the private sphere spoke more clearly to some women (along racial and class lines) than to others, women's overburdening with unrecognized, undervalued, and unsupported care and reproductive work certainly resonated across the board. Yet race and class privileges have always allowed some women to share their burden with other less privileged women, as continues to be the case today, and heteronormative, biopolitical, and eugenicist approaches to reproduction have also had a disparate impact on the reproductive lives of various groups of women and men, including gays, lesbians, trans, and differently abled and racialized persons.

[1] See Crystal Eastman, "Now We Can Begin," *Liberator* 3, no. 12 (1920): 23–24, http://mc.dlib.nyu.edu/files/books/lib000037/lib000037_hi.pdf.

Early attempts to seize constitution-making to express discomfort with the unfair gendered distribution of care work can be observed in certain cases. In the national consultation process leading up to Nicaragua's 1987 constitution, carried out with the active involvement of women's associations, activist María Zúñiga complained: "Men are used to being waited on. For women who work outside the home, society has imposed a double workday on us. Housework should be recognized as socially useful and should, therefore, be shared by all family members."[2] But it is only in the twenty-first century that constitutional law has more broadly come to be perceived as a battlefield for distributive claims around care and social reproduction.

As we have seen so far, the end of the century witnessed constitutionalism being confronted with the expression of participatory claims and interventions that sought women's increased presence in the public domain and in decision-making. And although, to this day, we are far from achieving full participatory parity as measured by any standard, the general and gradual increase in numbers of women in various institutions, such as legislatures, courts, executive cabinets, and constitution-making bodies, all started to point in the right direction. We have also seen how, partly as a result of women's increased participation in different capacities (as activists, constitution-makers, judges, and litigators) in both the national and the international scene, an equal rights model, ensuring women the same rights as men, came to be challenged as inadequate to guarantee women's equal opportunities to participate in the market and in state governance structures, giving way to substantive and participatory accounts of equality. In time, it has come to be more generally recognized that full participation in public life cannot be achieved unless the inequalities that are entrenched in the so-called private sphere are also tackled. This recognition has also expanded constitutional agendas.

The "constitutionalization of the private sphere" is proceeding in a piecemeal way. Multiple agendas have flourished since the 1990s,

[2] Intercontinental Press, "Women's Rights and the New Constitution: Town Meeting Discusses Abortion, Housework, Equal Pay," *Intercontinental Press* 24, no. 15 (1986): 465, https://www.themilitant.com/Intercontinental_Press/1986/IP2415.pdf#. Similar claims around the need to ensure shared family domestic work and joint parental responsibility for the education and raising of children were expressed by women in Colombia's 1991 constitution-making process. See Julieta Lemaitre, "Feminist Legalism," *Women as Constitution-Makers: Case Studies from the New Democratic Era*, eds. Ruth Rubio-Marín and Helen Irving (Cambridge: Cambridge University Press, 2019), 252.

fundamentally challenging the structural role that the traditional family (understood as a domain of male authority and domination – marital, procreative, and heteronormative in nature) was asked to play since the birth of modern democracies for the sake of a new and more egalitarian understanding of family relations built around the overcoming of old gender stereotypes and fixed gender roles. Only when we step back and look at the various items of this agenda that has sought to democratize the family by letting the ethos of constitutional values pervade it, we become aware of their contribution to yet another form of gender constitutionalism. I call this "transformative gender constitutionalism,"[3] for it aims to transform, rather than reflect or accommodate, old understandings of gender relations and roles as well as institutional structures and practices built around them. In doing so, it contains the promise to overcome the remaining traces of "family exceptionalism" of the modern political project.

Among the first examples of transformative gender constitutionalism accompanying women's participatory moment since the 1990s we find the vindication of women's right to a life free of violence, including in the private sphere, a claim that is radical in its affirmation of fundamental rights as applicable to domestic and otherwise intimate relations, in due recognition that those relations are often mediated by gendered power dynamics. Another expression of transformative gender

[3] The term "transformative constitutionalism" has long been used to describe the South African constitution or at least some of its ambitions in terms of racial and social justice goals. See Karl E. Klare, "Legal Culture and Transformative Constitutionalism," *South African Journal on Human Rights* 14, no. 1 (1998): 146; Saras Jagwanth, "Affirmative Action in a Transformative Context: The South African Experience," *Connecticut Law Review* 36 (2004): 725–46. The transformative vision of constitutionalism has also informed Indian constitutionalism. Although the notion was already mentioned by the Indian Supreme Court in the 2007 *Anuj Garg* case (Anuj Garg v. Hotel Association of India, AIR 2008 SC 663), a new era of transformative constitutionalism has emerged in recent years. See Gautam Bhatia, *The Transformative Constitution: A Radical Biography in Nine Acts* (Noida: Harper Collins Publishers India, 2019), 33–37. Following the steps of South African constitutional jurisprudence, the Indian Supreme Court has adopted transformative constitutionalism as "the ability of the Constitution to adapt and transform with the changing needs of the times," endorsing the need for the constitution to be enforced through a "progressive and pragmatic interpretation to combat the evils of inequality and injustice that try to creep into the society" (Navtej Singh Johar v. Union of India, AIR 2018 SC 4321) and "to challenge hegemonic structures of power and secure the values of dignity and equality for its citizens" (Joseph Shine v. Union of India, AIR 2018 SC 4898). This refers specifically to the gender axis of inequality and identity, as do the other forms of constitutionalism around which this book is organized.

constitutionalism and of the challenge to the (selective) confinement of women to the domestic sphere and to normative motherhood has been the gradual, though still imperfect, affirmation of women's sexual and reproductive autonomy as constitutionally grounded, something that, as we have seen, relied on some early but rather exceptional precedents that were also very limited in scope. Such affirmation entails the importance that women's reproductive roles not be simply assumed or normalized, that women be freed from unwanted motherhood while being proactively protected in their reproductive and mothering capacities and desires without discrimination. From a life free of violence and a life free of unwanted or denied motherhood, we come to tackle the claim of a life free of exploitation, as we discuss how, over the last decades, constitutionalism has grown receptive to the fact that, if women's private and family lives are not to be an obstacle to their full participation in the public sphere and if social reproduction is to be recognized both as a collective responsibility and as something intrinsically valuable, the degree to which men and the wider community are both expected and allowed to contribute to it must also be addressed. The most recent expression of transformative gender constitutionalism is therefore related – perhaps most radically – to the extent to which constitutions have come to be seen as norms that have a bearing on how domestic and care work, essential for social reproduction and human nurturing, is split between the sexes as well as between the family unit and the rest of society, when adequately backed by the state.[4] This agenda touches not only on the deconstruction of gender roles but also on the proper identification and prioritization of public goods or human capabilities as objects of constitutional protection, including, arguably, the right to care and be taken care of. As we are about to see, it also defies traditional and hegemonic constructions of masculinity.

4.1 Destabilizing the Public/Private Divide: Intimate Partner Violence and Violence against Women as a Constitutional Concern

Besides fighting for substantive equality – mostly in the marketplace – and equal representation – mostly in the political sphere – since the turn of the

[4] See Jennifer Nedelsky, "The Gendered Division of Household Labor: An Issue of Constitutional Rights," in *Feminist Constitutionalism: Global Perspectives*, eds. Beverley Baines, Daphne Barak-Erez, and Tsvi Kahana (Cambridge: Cambridge University Press, 2012), 15–47.

twentieth century, women's movements have also gained momentum in their challenge to the limited nature of the domains in which the constitutional order of rights had, until then, been applied. In particular, they came to defend the need that the most egregious infringements against their most basic fundamental rights be considered as such and not as private or insignificant matters, whether those violations were perpetrated by state officials or private parties, in the domestic sphere, or simply in society. The 1993 Vienna Declaration, when affirming that the human rights of women and of the girl-child were an "inalienable, integral and indivisible part of universal human rights,"[5] despite stating something obvious, was radical: the violation of women's rights was exactly that, a flagrant violation of human rights. Putting the label of "cultural exceptions" or "private matters" to let such violations go unchallenged in domains of unfettered male authority was no longer acceptable. The impact of this reconceptualization in constitutionalism became clear, especially in countries drafting their constitutions since 1990.

It was indeed in the 1990s when the international human rights community truly started to deem violence against women a human rights concern. Surprisingly, the most important international women's convention, CEDAW, had not attached a central importance to violence against women, even though, since 1989, the CEDAW Committee had begun to consider gender-based violence as a form of discrimination, requiring states to take positive measures to eliminate it.[6] It was the Declaration on the Elimination of Violence against Women, adopted by the United Nations General Assembly in 1993, that came to recognize violence against women as a manifestation of historically unequal power relations between men and women and as a means of subordination of women, anchoring its meaning within patriarchy. That same year, at a regional level and as the first of its kind, the Inter-American Convention on the Prevention, Punishment, and Eradication of Violence against Women[7] was adopted by the Organization of American States, endorsing

[5] World Conference on Human Rights, *Vienna Declaration and Programme of Action*, ¶ 18, U.N. Doc. A/CONF.157/23 (June 25, 1993).

[6] See General Recommendation No. 19: Violence against Women, in Report of the Committee on the Elimination of Discrimination against Women, U.N. Doc. A/44/38 (1989).

[7] Organization of American States, Inter-American Convention on the Prevention, Punishment, and Eradication of Violence Against Women (Convention of Belém do Pará), June 6, 1994.

state due diligence standards regarding violence against women.[8] If liberal theory had primarily concerned itself with abuses of state, rather than private, power, by the 1990s, international feminists were transforming human rights law in a profound way, foregrounding an expanded notion of state accountability for human rights violations and rendering states accountable for systemically failing to act with due diligence to prevent, investigate, or punish the acts of private actors.

None of this is to suggest that violence against women had been categorically excluded from the realm of women's constitutional concerns before that time. Instead, when articulating their visions of justice, women have traditionally resisted drawing rigid divisions between the "private" and the "public." Rather, they have been inclined to identify the complex and interrelated nature of the various sources of oppression. In fact, as we have seen, already in the first constitutionalism of the nineteenth century, the temperance movement had advocated for a "Home Protection Ballot," connecting alcohol consumption to the issues of domestic violence, sexual abuse, and women's need for empowerment in the household and the public sphere.[9] The same was true, at least to a large extent, for the abolitionist movement, which was not indifferent to gender-specific forms of violence, including sexual violence, that men and women of color endured.

Previously, the understanding had at best been that some broadly framed provisions, including those appealing to life, dignity, or the right to physical, psychological, and moral integrity, could be interpreted as encompassing the prohibition of violence against women without the

[8] A few years later, in 2003, came the first key regional milestone in the African continent: The Protocol to the African Charter on Human and Peoples' Rights on the Rights of Women in Africa (Maputo Protocol). As for Europe, the Council of Europe Convention on Preventing and Combating Violence against Women and Domestic Violence (Istanbul Convention) was only adopted in 2011, entering into force in 2014. Prior to this, the European Court of Human Rights, which took a very long time to address gender violence, started to rely on the positive obligations doctrine to require states to protect persons from violence by private parties, with the famous case Opuz v. Turkey finding a violation of the convention's right to life because of Turkey's inadequate efforts to combat domestic violence, labeling domestic violence as gender discrimination. See Opuz v. Turkey, App. No. 33401/02, 50 Eur. Ct. H.R. 28 (2010). See also Ronagh J. A. McQuigg, *International Human Rights Law and Domestic Violence: The Effectiveness of International Human Rights Law* (London: Routledge, 2011). These conventions have developed standards that have, to a greater or lesser extent, impacted constitutional cultures and texts.

[9] See Erin M. Masson, "The Woman's Christian Temperance Union, 1874–1898: Combating Domestic Violence," *William and Mary Journal of Women and the Law* 3, no. 1 (1997): 163–88, at 173.

need of further specification.[10] But in the 1990s women's claims started to fare better. Certainly, the 1996 South African Constitution provides one of the earliest and fullest expressions of what it means to explicitly take on board violence against women as a constitutionally relevant concern. Chapter 2, section 7, for instance, obliges the state not only to respect but also to protect and fulfill the Bill of Rights. Pertinent is also the courts' tradition – in interpreting equality rights under section 9 – whereby a formalistic approach to equality must give way to a contextual, substantive, and asymmetrical analysis.[11] Even more directly relevant is section 12 (1), granting everyone the right to freedom from "all forms of violence from either public or private sources"; section 12 (2), granting everyone "the right to bodily and psychological integrity"; and section 16 (2) (c), excluding from the realm of validly protected freedom of expression "advocacy of hatred that is based on race, ethnicity, gender or religion, and that constitutes incitement to cause harm." Relying on these elements, the Constitutional Court of South Africa has interpreted that the constitution provides women with the right to be free of interpersonal violence and that the state has an affirmative obligation to prevent and eliminate such violence. Adopting a nuanced and contextual analysis of violence against women, the court has recognized in it a form of gender subordination, anchored in patriarchy, curtailing women's equality, liberty, and other fundamental rights. Further, the court has also considered the interrelationship between the right to equality and other rights guaranteed in the Bill of Rights, such as the right to security of the

[10] In Nicaragua, for instance, in the process leading to the 1987 Nicaraguan Constitution, those women actively involved in the constitution-making process had raised their concerns around domestic violence but framed their arguments in relation to the "dignity" owed to women. Ultimately, women did not succeed in giving special visibility to their problem. In turn, the winning argument ended up being that article 36's generic wording ("All persons shall have the right to have their physical, psychological and moral integrity respected") should also be read as protecting against gender-based violence in the domestic sphere, a thesis that was, however, challenged by those who saw this constitutional provision as binding only on state power. See Martha Morgan, "Founding Mothers: Women's Voices and Stories in the 1987 Nicaraguan Constitution," *Boston University Law Review* 70, no. 1 (1990): 49. In fact, the constitution also included a provision, section 130, that states that "No one may be subjected to slavery, servitude or forced labour," without explicitly mentioning trafficking in women or prostitution, which were, however, the main topics of discussion regarding such provision.

[11] See Saras Jagwanth, "Affirmative Action in a Transformative Context: The South African Experience," *Connecticut Law Review* 36, no. 3 (2004): 725–46, at 727.

person and the right to dignity, and has shown how violence against women has impacted all of them.[12]

The explicit reference to the constitutional provisions binding private parties is, of course, one key factor to enable this agenda (although it is important to bear in mind that nothing impedes constitutional provisions binding on private actors to also be interpreted as *limiting* women's rights). In other jurisdictions, more loyal to the traditional understanding of constitutional rights as binding only on state actors, the doctrine of state action remains an insurmountable hurdle for affected women to claim constitutional protection. Where this is the case, even when no longer providing constitutional protection to violent conduct on the basis of privacy (interpreted as noninterference in the family domain),[13] constitutions have been of little assistance to women subjected to violence.

[12] See Valorie K. Vojdik, "Conceptualizing Intimate Violence and Gender Equality: A Comparative Approach," *Fordham International Law Journal* 31, no. 2 (2007): 487–527, at 516. For a selection of the rich case law, see Carmichele v. Minister of Safety and Security and Another 2001 (10) SA 995 (CC), imposing positive duties upon the state to take preventive measures to protect individuals whose lives are at risk from the criminal acts of others; State v. Baloyi (Minister of Justice and Another Intervening) 2000 (2) SA 425 (CC), recognizing the fact that "what distinguishes domestic violence is its hidden, repetitive character and immeasurable ripple effects on our society and, in particular, on family life" (at 11) and invoking a document drafted by US National Council of Juvenile and Family Court Judges that underscores the devastating social and economic costs of domestic violence for victims and communities. It also affirmed that domestic violence involves the constitutional right to gender equality because domestic violence is "systemic, pervasive and overwhelmingly gender-specific" (at 12) and because notions of patriarchy, autonomy and privacy have been used to justify noninterference by the state into what is perceived as a private or intimate matter (at 16). As a result, nonenforcement violates the foundational commitment to nonsexism and the right to gender equality under the constitution (at 12). See also Omar v. The Government of the Republic of South Africa and Others 2006 (2) SA 253 (CC), holding that domestic violence goes against several rights protected in the constitution, such as "the right to freedom and security of the person, which includes the right to be free from all forms of violence from public or private sources" in conjunction with the rights to dignity, life, equality, and privacy (at 17), and affirming the state's positive duty to prevent and eliminate violence against women (at 11). This would involve employing a contextualized analysis of domestic violence that recognizes the state's role in creating and perpetuating women's historical subordination and vulnerability to gender-based violence.

[13] See Reva B. Siegel, "'The Rule of Love': Wife Beating as Prerogative and Privacy," *Yale Law Journal* 105, no. 8 (1996): 2117, where she explains how, until the late nineteenth century, Anglo-American common law structured marriage to give a husband superiority over his wife, granting him the right to corporal punishment, or "chastisement," if she defied his authority. She also details how, even as the chastisement doctrine was abandoned, violence in marriage was routinely condoned in the name of privacy of the home,

The US tradition provides an example, as the application of fundamental rights (with the single exception of the badges and incidents of slavery) remains limited to state rather than private action, a fact that in this particular case is compounded by other features of the US constitutional system.[14] Such features include the facts that a negative conception of rights prevails, that only intentional discrimination is constitutionally prohibited, and that the equal protection guarantee has been interpreted, for the most part and despite persistent objections by critical scholars, rather formalistically, with a focus on eliminating difference in treatment rather than overcoming subordination.[15]

Given the traditional silence of constitutional texts around violence against women, it is hardly surprising that, in several jurisdictions, constitutional rights have been seized less often by women seeking protection than by men accused of violent crimes invoking their fair trial rights. Some authors have in fact claimed that the entrenchment of constitutional rights in their jurisdictions has had an overall detrimental effect on women fighting against violence. Beverley Baines has argued

except when perpetrated by oppressed minorities, such as immigrants or African Americans.

[14] See Catharine MacKinnon, "The Supreme Court, 1999 Term – Disputing Male Sovereignty: On *United States v. Morrison*," *Harvard Law Review* 114, no. 1 (2000): 23–408, at 170; Judith Resnik, "Reconstructing Equality: Of Justice, Justicia, and the Gender of Jurisdiction," *Yale Journal of Law and Feminism* 14, no. 1 (2002): 393–418; Judith Resnik, "Categorical Federalism: Jurisdiction, Gender, and the Globe," *Yale Law Journal* 111, no. 3 (2001): 619–80.

[15] See Vojdik, "Conceptualizing Intimate Violence and Gender Equality," 499–500. Thus, in DeShaney v. Winnebago County Department of Social Services, the United States Supreme Court held that the Due Process Clause of the Fourteenth Amendment did not impose an affirmative duty upon the state to protect the life, liberty, and property of citizens against invasion from other citizens. The petitioners, Joshua DeShaney and his mother, sued to recover damages sustained by Joshua, when at four years of age suffered severe brain damage at the hands of his father, whom a state social service agency had investigated for suspected child abuse without taking further action (De Shaney v. Winnebago County Department of Social Services, 489 U.S. 189 [1989]). See also Castle Rock v. Gonzales, where, once again, the court held that the state had no affirmative duty as a matter of substantive due process to protect women from private violence (Town of Castle Rock v. Gonzales, 545 U.S. 748, 768 [2005]). And see also United States v. Morrison, 529 U.S. 598 (2000), where the United States Supreme Court struck down section 13981 of the Violence against Women Act, which created a federal civil remedy for victims of domestic violence, who would then be able to ask for compensatory and punitive damages as well as injunctive and declaratory relief in the understanding that Congress lacked the authority to create a federal cause of action under the Commerce Clause or in view of its remedial power under section 5 of the Fourteenth Amendment because such powers do not extend to the conduct of private actors.

that, for the longest time, this has been the case in Canada, for instance, regarding criminalization or regulation of sexual offenses.[16] She claims that "sexual offences – including rape, sexual assault, prostitution, pornography, hate speech, sexist speech, and sexual harassment – have created much constitutional litigation opportunities for the criminal defense bar" and that "relying on traditional legal rights such as the presumption of innocence, the right to a fair trial, and the right not to be subject to cruel and unusual punishment, as well as on freedom of expression, equality rights, and the right to life, liberty, and security of the person, male defendants have not hesitated to challenge the constitutionality of various sexual offences and the evidentiary or procedural rules pertaining to them."[17]

It is important to note, however, that several of the claims raised by defendants in Canada were not successful[18] and that, as of late, courts elsewhere have also confirmed procedural standards and rules to avoid secondary victimization and ensure victims' access to justice.[19] More

[16] See Beverley Baines, "Using the Canadian Charter of Rights and Freedoms," in *The Gender of Constitutional Jurisprudence*, eds. Beverley Baines and Ruth Rubio-Marín (Cambridge: Cambridge University Press, 2005), 56–60. For case law on rules contained in legislation or judicial practice, which came to be constitutionally challenged, see challenge of statutory rape legislation (R. v. Hess; R. v. Nguyen, [1990] 2 S.C.R. 906); of rules limiting the admissibility of evidentiary rules such as disclosure of sexual assault victims' prior sexual history (R. v. Seaboyer, [1991] 2 S.C.R. 577; R v. O'Connor, [1995] 4 SCR 41) or personal records (A. L. L. v. Beharriell, [1995] 4 S.C.R. 536; R. v. Carosella, [1997] 1 S.C.R. 80; R. v Mills, [1999] 3 S.C.R. 668); or defense, including drunkenness as a defense (R. v. Daviault, [1994] 3 S.C.R. 63), and consent rules (R. v. M. [M. L.], [1994] 2 S.C.R. 3, and R. v. Ewanchuk, [1999] 1 S.C.R. 330). In an early Human Rights Act case in the United Kingdom, an all-male panel of the House of Lords used the act to narrow the protections offered by a rape shield provision. See R. v. A. [2001] UKHL 25, [2001] 2 WLR 1546 (Eng.). And, in 2006, the Irish Supreme Court (in an all-male panel) held invalid the law on unlawful carnal knowledge of a girl under fifteen, as it did not provide an exception if the defendant reasonably believed the victim to have been of age, provoking a public outcry. See C.C. v. Ireland [2006] IESC 33 [2006] 4 IR 1 (Ir.).

[17] See Beverley Baines and Ruth Rubio-Marín, "Feminist Constitutionalism in Canada," in *The Oxford Handbook of the Canadian Constitution*, eds. Peter Oliver, Patrick Macklem, and Nathalie Des Rosiers (Oxford: Oxford University Press, 2017), 968.

[18] See, for instance, R. v. Butler, [1992] 1 S.C.R. 452.

[19] See Corte Suprema de Justicia de la Nación [CSJN] [National Supreme Court of Justice], 15/10/2015. "Ortega, Daniel Héctor s/ causa n° 1011/2013," Fallos de la Corte Suprema de la Nación, t. 338, 1021 (Arg.), affirming preliminary probatory value of victims' testimony in cases of violence against women; Corte Constitucional [C.C.] [Constitutional Court], noviembre 18, 2014, Sentencia T-878/14 (Colom.), granting an amparo to the plaintiff, a university employee, who had been dismissed after reporting her partner, a student in the university, to the police for beating her; and Jyoti Poudel v. Office of the Prime Minister,

specifically, in recent years, courts around the world are advancing in the direction of rejecting many of the constitutional objections raised by defendants against progressive judicial interpretations or more ambitious legislation.[20] Thanks in part to tireless efforts of national and transnational women's mobilizations over the last decades, it seems that courts are becoming increasingly aware of the structural dimension of violence against women, the problems surrounding impunity and the underreporting of these crimes, the hurdles of traditional evidentiary standards, and the terrible harms linked to secondary procedural victimization and, therefore, also seem more prone to accept asymmetrical responses to a phenomenon that is indeed asymmetrical in nature.[21] This increased

2067, 52(11) NKP 1903 (2010) (Nepal), where the Supreme Court issued an order of mandamus to the government to establish a fast-track court presided by female judges to hear cases on violence against women, especially domestic violence, and make arrangements to safeguard the privacy of the victims. See also Meera Dhungana v. Ministry of Law and Justice, Writ No. 2068-WS-0046 of year 2068 BS (2011). The Nepalese court pronounced its decision in 2069 BS (2012), striking down a provision criminalizing the noncooperation of human trafficking victims - mostly women - in proceedings against traffickers.

[20] See, for South Africa, State v. Baloyi (Minister of Justice and Another Intervening) 2000 (2) SA 425 (CC), upholding a provision in the prevention of family violence act, which was challenged as reversing the burden of proof and thus violating the right of an accused person to be presumed innocent. For Peru, see Tribunal Constitucional [T.C.] [Constitutional Court], Mar. 5, 2020, file No. 03378-2019-PA/TC, upholding the validity of imposing protection orders without the need to listen in every instance to the offender's testimony against the claim that this defeated the plaintiff's right to a defense.

[21] See, among others, Constitutional Chamber of the Supreme Court, decision No. 03441–2004, Mar. 31, 2004 (Costa Rica), upholding the constitutionality against discrimination claims of legal provisions that criminalize physical, psychological, sexual, and economic violence against adult women only, in the understanding that such violence, given its structural nature, amounts to a form of discrimination against women that the law is trying to address; Spanish Constitutional Court's decision S.T.C., May 14, 2008 (No. 59/2008), for an unsuccessful challenge of the distinction introduced in criminal law to punish more severely those acts of psychological mistreatment or physical violence not resulting in injury when the offended is or has been a wife or a woman who is or has been linked to a man by an analogous affective relationship, on the basis that such conduct is more serious because it corresponds to a deep-rooted type of violence that is "a manifestation of discrimination, a situation of inequality and the power relations of men over women"; the decision by the Supreme Court of the Republic of the Philippines, Garcia v. Drilon, G.R. No. 178267 (June 25, 2013), unsuccessfully challenging an act passed in 2004, after years of spirited advocacy by women's groups, as violating due process and providing protection orders from the barangay and for the courts to prevent the commission of further acts of violence against women and children; Corte Constitucional [C.C.] [Constitutional Court], noviembre 8, 2016, Sentencia C-297/16 (Colom.), for an unsuccessful challenge of the proposed legal concept of femicide as an autonomous crime in Colombia, on the basis that it violates the principle of legality and the right to due

awareness has translated into a growing number of courts, especially in Latin America, underscoring the importance of embracing a gender perspective in the administration of justice when dealing with gender violence and linking this obligation to the constitutional principle of gender equality.[22] At the same time, we find that the overreliance on criminalization as a way to combat violence against women, though increasingly validated by courts, has become an object of criticism by a sector of the feminist community rightly concerned with the limits of criminal law to address the phenomenon of violence against women, as well as survivors' needs and concerns.[23] The same has occurred with measures that have been deemed overly paternalistic and thus potentially

process; and the two decisions of the Federal Supreme Court of Brazil upholding the Maria da Penha Law, which enhances the criminal response to domestic violence suffered by women as well as violence against women (Supremo Tribunal Federal [S.T.F.] [Federal Supreme Court], Ação Declaratória de Constitucionalidade [ADC] [Declaratory Action of Constitutionality] No. 19, Relator: Min. Marco Aurélio, 09.02.2012, Díario da Justiça Eletrônico [D.J.e], 17.02.2012, 24, and Ação Direta de Inconstitucionalidade [ADI] [Direct Action of Unconstitutionality] No. 4424, Relator: Min. Marco Aurélio, 09.02.2012, Díario da Justiça Eletrônico [D.J.e], 17.02.2012, 24, 25).

22 For Peru, see Tribunal Constitucional [T.C.] [Constitutional Court], Mar. 5, 2019, file No. 01479/2018-PA/TC, arguing that if courts do not embrace a gender perspective in the administration of justice, they become complicit with the societal violence victims endure. For Argentina, see Corte Suprema de Justicia de la Nación [CSJN] [National Supreme Court of Justice], 29/10/2019, "R., C. E. s/ recurso extraordinario de inaplicabilidad de ley en causa n° 63.006 del Tribunal de Casación Penal, Sala IV," Fallos de la Corte Suprema de la Nación, t. 342, 1827, relying on standards developed in the Inter-American system to affirm the need to overcome gender stereotypes and incorporate a gender perspective in the assessment of facts and the interpretation of requirements concerning legitimate defense in a context of gender violence. And for Mexico, see Amparo directo en revisión 2655/2013, Suprema Corte de Justicia de la Nación [SCJN], noviembre 6, 2013, Semanario Judicial de la Federación y su Gaceta, Décima Época, Libro 4, marzo de 2014, Tomo I, Tesis 1a. C/2014 (10a.) and 1a. XCIX/2014 (10a.), páginas 523–25, on domestic violence and custodial disputes; and Amparo en revisión 554/2013, Suprema Corte de Justicia de la Nación [SCJN], marzo 25, 2015, Semanario Judicial de la Federación y su Gaceta, Décima Época, Libro 18, mayo de 2015, Tomo I, Tesis 1a. CLXI/2015 (10a.), páginas 439–40, on the crime of femicide, establishing that, when investigating the violent death of a woman, the investigating bodies must analyze whether there were gendered reasons behind the crime and look for specific evidence to determine whether sexual violence had anteceded the killing and whether the victim was immersed in a context of generalized violence.

23 In South Korea, for instance, Yoon Jin Shin explains how criminal law has increased the severity of criminal punishment of sexual violence and has imposed "additional security measures against convicts, including the attachment of a GPS device to offenders, the disclosure of convicts' personal information, and the ordering of pharmacologic treatment." In a series of decisions, South Korea's Constitutional Court upheld most of these special measures, including aggravated punishment, as proportional, considering the

contributing to the care/control paradigm that women have traditionally been subject to.[24]

It is also important to underscore that constitutions have not been seized by defendants alone. Constitutional texts and supreme/constitutional courts interpreting them have also opened new channels for the proactive articulation of women's wrongs, the latter often relying on old texts or generic provisions without any explicit reference to gender violence. In India, the constitution has been key in the long fight against gender-based violence, even though the 1950 text does not mention violence against women. Thus, despite some greatly contested early decisions,[25] the Supreme Court came to acknowledge that rape constitutes a violation of a woman's right to life and personal liberty under article 21[26] and has condemned procedures that are insufficiently protective of women's rights.[27] And, in Nepal, legislation immunizing husbands from the crime of raping their wives was struck down as

public interest in suppressing sexual violence. See Hunbeobjaepanso [Const. Ct.], Dec. 29, 2016, 2015Hun-Ba196, 222, 343; Jul. 24, 2014, 2013Hun-Ma423, 426; Jul. 26, 2012, 2012Hun-Ba144; and May 31, 2012, 2010Hun-Ba401, cited in Yoon Jin Shin, "Gender Equality, Individual Empowerment and Constitutional Rights Review: South Korea's Dynamic Development," in Wen-Chen Chang et al., *Gender, Sexuality and Constitutionalism in Asia* (Oxford: Hart Publishing, forthcoming). Shin also notices how concerns have been raised about the potentially limited effects of this legislation in deterring sexual violence.

24 See, for instance, the Spanish Constitutional Court's decision S.T.C., Oct. 29, 2010 (No. 60/2010), in which it upheld the constitutionality of legislation imposing the sanction of distancing orders in domestic violence cases, removing any judicial discretion to consider factors such as the desire of the victims, the seriousness of the crime, or the potential danger of the perpetrator. This decision is examined and criticized in Blanca Rodríguez Ruiz, *Género y Constitución: Mujeres y Varones en el Orden Constitucional Español* (Lisboa: Juruá, 2017), 120.

25 In particular, the protests ensuing in response to the Supreme Court's decision in Tukaram v. State of Maharashtra, AIR 1979 SC 185, where it acquitted police officers of rape in custody and provoked an influential open letter by leading legal academics, including Upendra Baxi, Vasudha Dhagamwar, Raghunath Kelkar, and Lotika Sarkar. This signaled "a key moment in the fight against gender-based violence" in India, which has been linked to the fate of India's constitutionalism and to the discourse of postcolonial constitutionalism. See Shreya Atrey and Gautam Bhatia, "In Search of Principle: Seventy Years of Gender Jurisprudence in India," in Chang et al., *Gender, Sexuality and Constitutionalism in Asia*.

26 See Bodhisattwa Gautam v. Miss Subhra Chakraborty, (1996) 1 SCC 490; and Chairman, Railway Board v. Mrs. Chandrima Das, AIR 2000 SC 988.

27 See Bharwada Bhoginbhai Hirjibhai v. State of Gujarat, AIR 1983 SC 753, holding that the refusal to act on the testimony of a victim of sexual assault in the absence of corroboration is adding insult to injury.

inconsistent with the rights to equality, dignity, self-determination, and privacy already contained in the 1990 Constitution of the Kingdom of Nepal as well as with several CEDAW provisions.[28] In Canada, sexual assault victims have used the Charter of Rights and Freedoms innovatively to sue a municipal police force in tort for injuries suffered when the police failed to warn women that they were investigating the activities of a serial rapist, arguing that failure to warn women violated section 7, pertaining to life, liberty, and security of the person, as well as section 15, related to equality rights.[29] The charter has also been recently used to combat technology-facilitated sexual violence.[30]

In various jurisdictions, constitutional justice has also shown to be a catalyzing force for legislative and executive action and has sometimes replaced glaring omissions or inaction. In Colombia, where the 1991 constitution was among the pioneer texts in including a provision foreseeing that "any form of violence in the family is considered destructive of its harmony and unity, and will be sanctioned according to law" (article 42), the Constitutional Court initially accepted writs of protection of constitutional rights (*tutelas*) for women subject to domestic violence by their husbands or companions, granting them relief.[31] The same court has more recently ordered the government to create programs to fill out

[28] See Advocate Meera Dhungana v. His Majesty's Government (Nepal), Writ No. 55 of the year 2058 BS (2001).

[29] See Jane Doe v. Board of Commissioners of Police for the Municipality of Metropolitan Toronto et al., [1998] 39 O.R. (3d) 487.

[30] See R. v. Jarvis, [2019] 1 S.C.R. 488, where the Supreme Court recognized the voyeurism provision in the Criminal Code as a violation of sexual integrity in the case of a male schoolteacher who used a camera pen to secretly film his female students' cleavages.

[31] This, at times, included both direct orders to their abusers to abstain from further violence against their partners and orders to local officials to provide appropriate protection relying on the rights to personal integrity (article 12), life (article 11), and protection of the family (article 42). See Corte Constitucional [C.C.] [Constitutional Court], septiembre 18, 1992, Sentencia T-523/92; agosto 31, 1994, Sentencia T-382/94; noviembre 2, 1994, Sentencia T-487/94; and diciembre 2, 1994, Sentencia T-552/94. After the Colombian Congress enacted legislation in 1992 providing a means of immediate judicial relief for victims of domestic violence, the Constitutional Court started rejecting *tutelas* in domestic violence, pointing to the fact that this alternative judicial procedure for immediate relief was now available (see also Corte Constitucional [C.C.] [Constitutional Court], septiembre 9, 1996, Sentencia T-420/96). By allowing these horizontal effects of fundamental rights to reach into family relations, the governing criterion has been whether one can identify a "clear asymmetry in the relations of power between individuals that denies, restricts, or eliminates personal autonomy and justifies state intervention to avoid the absolute instrumentalization or degradation of a human being." See Martha I. Morgan, "Emancipatory Equality: Gender Jurisprudence under the

public policy gaps concerning a gender-responsive treatment of forcefully displaced women.[32] In India and Nepal, on the other hand, courts have compelled the government to enact legislation to protect women from sexual harassment and even provided interim guidelines, relying to a significant extent on international norms.[33]

In terms of forms of reasoning, many of the constitutional decisions supporting women's claims show increasing awareness of the fact that violence against women actually affects all women and all of their fundamental rights and that it amounts to a sort of "gender disciplinary regime" affirming male dominance. This violence, it has been recognized, beyond affecting individual victims, erodes the very family structure that constitutions enshrine[34] and damages the sense of worth, self-esteem, and status of all women in society.[35] Similarly, concerning sexual violence, one can identify a positive, though by no means consistent,[36] evolution as regards courts questioning the terms under which women individually or collectively are said to give valid consent to sexual

Colombian Constitution," in Baines and Rubio-Marín, *Gender of Constitutional Jurisprudence*, 80.

32 See Corte Constitucional [C.C.] [Constitutional Court], enero 22, 2004, Sentencia T-025/04, including, among the disparate impact of forced displacement, the risk of sexual violence, sexual exploitation, or sexual abuse in the context of the armed conflict; and the risk of exploitation or enslavement by illegal armed actors to perform domestic chores and roles considered feminine in a society with patriarchal traits.

33 See, for India, the landmark case of Vishaka v. State of Rajasthan, AIR 1997 SC 3011; and, for Nepal, Prakash Mani Sharma v. Office of the Prime Minister, 2067, 52(9) NKP 1480 (2010).

34 See Corte Constitucional [C.C.] [Constitutional Court], diciembre 2, 1994, Sentencia T-552/94 (Colom.) regarding violence against women as affecting the public interest in the protection of the family as the constitutionally recognized basis of social organization.

35 In *Meera Dhungana*, the Nepalese court decided that rape "Not only . . . causes adverse impact on physical, mental, family and spiritual life of victim women, it also adversely affects on self-respect and existence of women. This offence is not only against victim women but also against the society as a whole. Murder destroys physical being of a person but the offence of rape destroys the physical, mental and spiritual position of victim women. . . . It violates all rights of a woman." See Advocate Meera Dhungana v. His Majesty's Government (Nepal), Writ No. 55 of the year 2058 BS (2001).

36 This positive evolution is, of course, not consistent. The Supreme Court of the Philippines, for instance, continues to base acquittals on the rape myth that nonresistance implies consent (see People v. Tionloc, G.R. No. 212193, 805 Phil. 907 [Feb. 15, 2017]) and has repeated this reasoning in overturning another rape conviction, arguing that "the mere presence of abrasions and contusions on her" did not "preclude the giving of her consent to the sexual intercourse" (see People v Mahinay, G.R. No. 199894, 808 Phil. 455 [Apr. 5, 2017]). See Bryan Dennis Gabito Tiojanco, "Gender and Constitutionalism in Philippines," in Chang et al., *Gender, Sexuality and Constitutionalism in Asia.*

practices, not only in general, but also within the family/interspousal framework – a domain that has traditionally been seen as protected by constitutional notions of privacy – or in the marketplace – a domain that has traditionally been seen as protected by the freedom of enterprise, expression, and choice of profession. Indeed, some courts are rightfully expressing concerns about background conditions for the exercise of free choice and about the ways in which even validly accepted individual actions can contribute to the structural subordination of women as a group. These structures of subordination are said to create an environment conducive to violence that defeats the egalitarian ethos that constitutions are said to strive for. In several countries, constitutional litigation concerning marital rape[37] and the restitution of conjugal rights,[38] as well

[37] See Advocate Meera Dhungana v. His Majesty's Government (Nepal), Writ No. 55 of the year 2058 BS (2001), striking down the rule that excluded a "wife" from the categories of women listed as potential victims of rape as breaching the constitutional right to equality and various international human rights instruments and rejecting the government lawyers' argument whereby "according to our Hindu traditions and values, a husband having sexual intercourse with his wife can never be considered rape." By the same court, see also Jit Kumari Pageni v. Office of the Prime Minister, 2065, 50(6) NKP 664 (2008), striking down statutory provisions differentiating the length of custodial sentences for the offenses of marital and nonmarital rape held on a similar basis (i.e., that the status of the woman is irrelevant to the offense of rape). See Sapana Pradhan Malla v. Ministry of Law, Justice and Parliamentary Affairs (Nepal), Writ No. 56 of the year 2058 (2001), striking down discrimination of prostitutes in the regulation of rape. These cases are cited in Mara Malagodi, "Gender, Sexuality and Constitutionalism in Nepal," in Chang et al., *Gender, Sexuality and Constitutionalism in Asia*, and basically question the assumption that, by consenting to marriage or to prostitution, one consents to unwanted instances of sexual encounters and conduct. In Turkey, a decision upholding the mitigation of the penalties for sexual assault and abduction if perpetrated against sex workers was hugely contested and "helped mobilize women's groups in the 1990s around a common agenda." See Anayasa Mahkemesi [AYM] [Constitutional Court], E.1988/4, K. 1989/9, Jan. 10, 1990. See also Emrah Oder, "Women and Constitution-Making in Turkey," in Rubio-Marín and Irving, *Women as Constitution-Makers*, 287.

[38] The right to the restitution of conjugal rights, which ensures a forcible return of the partner to the abandoned home, had been upheld by some courts on the basis that the intimate nature of marriage makes the application of constitutional principles inappropriate, as if "introducing a bull in a china shop. It will prove to be a ruthless destroyer of the marriage institution and all that it stands for" (see Harvinder Kaur v. Harmander Singh Choudhry, AIR 1984 Delhi 66, at 67 [India]). In 1984, in a different case, the Supreme Court of India sided with the Delhi court and held that conjugal rights are inherent in the very institution of marriage (Saroj Rani v. Sudarshan Kumar, AIR 1984 SC 1562 [India]). Both cases are cited in Nussbaum, "India, Sex Equality, and Constitutional Law," in Baines and Rubio-Marín, *Gender of Constitutional Jurisprudence*, 196. Recently, this understanding of privacy has been explicitly abandoned in *Justice K. S. Puttaswamy (Retd) v. Union of India*, AIR 2017 SC 4161 (India), a unanimous decision

as prostitution[39] or pornography,[40] have provided some of the scenarios for such debates and animated feminist (re)interpretations of privacy, market freedoms, and speech.

that argued for a more nuanced notion of privacy, respectful of individual autonomy, with a four-justice concurring opinion acknowledging feminist concerns and citing Catharine MacKinnon's groundbreaking book *Toward a Feminist Theory of the State* and its warning against privacy notions when used to cover up physical harm done to women. See concurring opinion drafted by Justice D. Y. Chandrachud. This judgment paved the way for further progressive decisions on individual autonomy and self-determination, such as adultery (Joseph Shine v. Union of India, AIR 2018 SC 4898 [India]) or LGBT rights (Navtej Singh Johar v. Union of India, AIR 2018 SC 4321 [India]).

39 For Taiwan, see Judicial Yuan [JY] [Constitutional Court], Interpretation No. 666 (Nov. 6, 2009), holding unconstitutional a law that fined only those engaging in sexual transactions for profit but not those purchasing sex; for South Korea, see Hunbeobjaepanso [Const. Ct.], Mar. 31, 2016, 2013Hun-Ka2, upholding a criminal law that penalized sex buyers as well as women who "voluntarily" become involved in commercial sex acts while protecting those "coerced" into prostitution. Despite admitting that the law indeed restricted sexual self-determination and the right to privacy of those involved in prostitution (both sellers and buyers) and the right of sex workers to choose their occupations, the court, by applying a proportionality test, upheld the law considering prostitution's harmful effect on society and underscored "that even voluntary sex work can undermine sex workers' personal autonomy by commercializing sex; that the sex industry can distort the regular flow of money and labor force in society; that sex work is by nature exploitative, given the inherent inequality between buyers and sex workers, most of whom are in economically disadvantaged positions; that commercializing sex harms sexual culture and sexual morality in society and is likely to contribute to increasing sexual violence crimes; and that punishing women in prostitution is necessary for suppressing the expansion of the commercial sex industry and the new inducement of young women or migrant women from less developed countries into the sex industry." See Shin, "Gender Equality, Individual Empowerment and Constitutional Rights Review." That said, there are still ongoing debates in Korean society with regard to criminally punishing sex workers (mostly women) and not only sex buyers, as many voices, including those of two dissenting justices, point out that it is difficult and normatively improper to distinguish women coerced into prostitution (who deserve protection) and voluntary sex workers (who deserve punishment) (see ibid.). Whatever its potential shortcomings, the reasoning of the South Korean Court certainly contrasts with the formalistic approach shown by other courts addressing the criminalization of prostitution. See, for instance, the South African case S. v. Jordan 2002 (6) SA 642 (CC), at para. 9, upholding a provision that criminalized only the activity of the prostitute and not that of the client, because it was couched in gender-neutral terms and covered both male and female prostitutes.

40 See, for instance, R. v. Butler, [1992] 1 S.C.R. 452 (Can.), upholding a Criminal Code provision prohibiting the making, distribution, and possession of pornography (defined not as just explicit sex but as sex with violence or explicit sex without violence that is degrading or dehumanizing). The regulation was acknowledged to curtail freedom of expression, but the court accepted that the limitation was justified as avoiding harm to society, given that the materials that portray women as objects for sexual exploitation and

As of recently, some groundbreaking decisions have also begun to foreground victims' broader needs and, borrowing from human rights standards, are expanding on the forms of remedies that should follow acts of violence, including measures of compensation, satisfaction, and guarantees of nonrepetition, in ways that rightly link the individual instances of violence presented before the courts to the wider structural phenomenon of gender violence in society.[41] This victim-centered approach and the ability to identify adequate remedies may in turn be facilitated by the growing inclination to identify certain phenomena as falling under the umbrella of gender violence, including instances of economic, reproductive, and obstetric violence, often with a disparate impact against minority women.[42]

abuse have a negative impact on the sense of self-worth and acceptance of individual women. On the legitimacy of curtailing forms of expression that eroticize women's coercion, violence, and subordination, see the seminal work of Catharine MacKinnon and Andrea Dworkin, *In Harm's Way: The Pornography Civil Rights Hearings* (Cambridge, MA: Harvard University Press, 1997). See also Cass Sunstein, *Democracy and the Problem of Free Speech* (New York: Free Press, 1995), 209. A large body of feminist literature supports the existence of a link between violent pornography and the normalization of violence, especially sexual violence, against women. For instance, see Susan Brison, "The Price We Pay? Pornography and Harm," in *Contemporary Debates in Applied Ethics*, eds. Andrew I. Cohen and Christopher Heath Wellman (Malden, MA: Wiley Blackwell, 2005). Other scholars, including feminist scholars, fear that these types of arguments reinforce sexist and conservative stereotypes of sexual behavior, especially female sexual behavior. For sources, see Katharine Gelber and Adrienne Stone, "Constitutions, Gender and Freedom of Expression: The Legal Regulation of Pornography," in *Constitutions and Gender*, ed. Helen Irving (Cheltenham, UK: Edward Elgar, 2017), 467.

41 See Amparo directo en revisión 5490/2016, Suprema Corte de Justicia de la Nación [SCJN], marzo 7, 2018, Semanario Judicial de la Federación y su Gaceta, Décima Época, Libro 63, febrero de 2019, Tomo I, Tesis 1a. XIV/2019 (10a.), página 724 (Mex.). On the right to economic compensation regardless of considerations of financial need, see Corte Constitucional [C.C.] [Constitutional Court], febrero 25, 2020, Sentencia SU080/20; and diciembre 11, 2019, Sentencia SU599/19 (Colom.), recognizing that women and girls who suffered forced contraception and forced abortions by their own armed groups should be recognized as "victims of armed conflict" in such a way as to guarantee their rights to integral reparations, including comprehensive, gender-sensitive, and specialized health care. For another sentence related to violence against women in armed conflict, see enero 15, 2020, Sentencia T-004/20 (Colom.).

42 See, for Mexico, Amparo directo en revisión 7134/2018, Suprema Corte de Justicia de la Nación [SCJN], Agosto 21, 2019, Semanario Judicial de la Federación y su Gaceta, Décima Época, Libro 77, agosto 2020, Tomo IV, Tesis 1a. XVIII/2020 (10a.), páginas 3057–58, stating that, in keeping with the principle of equality and the right of women to live a life free of violence, the effects of the conjugal partnership – including the sharing of income – must cease from the moment the husband unjustifiably fails to contribute either financially or through housework.

Finally, if the 1990s signaled the moment when women across the world began demanding human rights instruments and constitutions to explicitly express their rightful claim to a life free of violence, such claims have only gained in poignancy in the last decades, as feminist movements across the world have been pushing to expand the concern surrounding gender violence beyond domestic and intimate partner violence and have succeeded in having a greater impact on constitution-making processes. And, if the first constitutions making reference to gender violence included demands for the state to undertake actions to combat violence against women in the family domain,[43] more recent ones are referring to further forms of violence, thus showing a more sophisticated understanding of the manifold manifestations of violence against women.[44] Some of these provisions currently underscore the irrelevance of where the violence is perpetrated (in public or private spheres, or at the level of the general society) or make explicit reference to some common domains of violence beyond the family, such as the work site,[45] or enabling environments, such as the media.[46] They also render forms of state responsibility

[43] See, for instance, article 60 of the 1992 Constitution of Paraguay, compelling the state to "promote policies that aim at preventing violence within the family." See also article 226.8 of the 1988 Brazilian Constitution, referring to the suppression of violence in family relations. This trend continues to this day. Both Egypt and Tunisia have included a reference to the need to protect women from all forms of violence in their most recent constitutions for the first time. See, for instance, article 46 of the 2014 Tunisian Constitution and article 11 of the 2014 Egyptian Constitution.

[44] See article 35 of the 2016 Ivorian Constitution, endorsing the need for the state to take the necessary measures to eliminate "all forms of violence against women and girls," but also article 5 prohibiting "slavery, human trafficking, forced labor, physical or moral torture, cruel, inhumane, degrading and humiliating treatment, physical violence, female genital mutilation as well as all other forms of degradation of a human being"; article 7 of the 2016 Central African Republic Constitution, referring to the need to protect the woman and the child against "violence and insecurity, exploitation and moral, intellectual and physical neglect"; and articles 43 and 85 of the 2019 Cuban Constitution, mentioning the need for the state to protect women against gender violence but also condemning intrafamily violence as destructive of persons, families, and societies.

[45] See article 15 (II) of the 2009 Bolivian Constitution whereby women have a right not to be subjected to physical, sexual, or psychological violence both in the family and in society; article 331 of the 2008 Ecuadorian Constitution, sanctioning harassment and violence, both "direct and indirect," affecting women at work; article 25.b of the 2013 Zimbabwean Constitution, endorsing the need for the state to prevent domestic violence, but also article 52.a: "Every person has the right to bodily and psychological integrity, which includes the right to freedom from all forms of violence from public or private sources"; and a similar provision in article 29.c of the 2010 Kenyan Constitution.

[46] The 1996 South African Constitution protects freedom of expression, but in section 16 (2) (c) it expressly excludes "advocacy of hatred that is based on ... gender ... that

(including by omission or lack of due diligence) more explicit.[47] Some texts better reflect intersectional concerns by making reference to the variety of vulnerable groups that are often subject to violence and by mentioning the condition of "double vulnerability,"[48] while others refer to the need for special procedures and redress mechanisms for survivors,[49] or else express the inadmissibility of religion and custom-based practices that

constitutes incitement to cause harm." Article 46.7 of the 2008 Ecuadorian Constitution compels the state to protect against the influence of media promoting violence or gender and racial discrimination. Some courts have also underscored the impact that media can have in promoting discrimination, hatred, and violence against women. See, for instance, the Supreme Court of Nepal in Raju Chapagai v. Office of the Prime Minister, 2065, 50(7) NKP 823 (2008), issuing an order of mandamus to the Ministry of Information and Communication to implement a gender-sensitive advertising policy in response to the petitioner's argument that violence against women has an intimate relationship with advertisements objectifying women (see Chang et al., *Gender, Sexuality and Constitutionalism in Asia*). Some scholars deplore that, having demonstrated the powerful harms caused by pornography (including the silencing of women and the perpetuation of their inequality), "feminists have paid much less attention to other forms of hateful speech based on gender, even as such speech appears to be spreading and gaining greater influence through digital social media" and "the growth of misogynistic websites, blogs and forums" (known as the "manosphere") that "spread lurid vilification of women in general (and feminists in particular) and advocate rape and other violence." See Gelber and Stone, "Constitutions, Gender and Freedom of Expression," 476–77. These authors also notice the paucity of cases brought under these laws and point to some rare exceptions, including Sonke Gender Justice Network v. Malema 2010 7 BCLR 729 (EqC) (S. Afr.), and Human Rights Commission (Sask.) v. Engineering Students' Society, University of Saskatchewan (1989), 72 Sask. R. 161 (Can. Sask. C.A.). On feminist theory and freedom of speech, see Susan H. Williams, "Feminist Theory and Freedom of Speech," *Indiana Law Journal* 84, no. 3 (2009): 999–1013.

47 See article 15 (III) of the 2009 Bolivian Constitution, which specifies that the state shall adopt the necessary measures "to prevent, eliminate and punish sexual and generational violence, as well as any action or omission intended to be degrading to the human condition, to cause death, pain, and physical, sexual or psychological suffering, whether in public or private spheres," and article 46.4 of the 2008 Ecuadorian Constitution, ensuring "protection and care against all forms of violence, mistreatment, sexual exploitation of any other kind or against neglect leading to these situations."

48 See article 66.3 (b) of the 2008 Ecuadorian Constitution, which sanctions the right to "a life without violence in the public and private sectors" as well as the obligation of the state to adopt the necessary measures to "prevent, eliminate, and punish all forms of violence, especially violence against women, girls, children and adolescents, elderly persons, persons with disabilities and against all persons at a disadvantaged or in a vulnerable situation," and article 35 of the same constitution, making reference to the condition of "double vulnerability." See also section 71 of the 2017 Thai Constitution whereby the state should protect "children, youth, women, the elderly, persons with disabilities, indigent persons and underprivileged persons . . . from violence or unfair treatment."

49 See section 71 of the 2017 Thai Constitution, referring to the need to provide treatment, rehabilitation, and remedies to injured persons, and article 81 of the 2008 Ecuadorian

amount to or allow for such violence.[50] We are far from general trends on any of these fronts. As we will discuss, constitutional law has recently become a contested battlefield in the fight against gender-based violence, but these signs hold some promise that women will prevail.

4.2 New Abortion Constitutionalism and the Need for a Fuller Recognition of Women's Sexual and Reproductive Autonomy

Since the 1990s, an increasing number of constitutions have incorporated an explicit reference to the reproductive domain, going beyond the classic protection of motherhood, marriage, and the family (assumed heterosexual and reproductive) as essential to the structure of society. The protection of motherhood had an early appearance in constitutional law and, as we shall see, it has retained such centrality in contemporary constitutionalism by increasingly spelling out and expanding the protections for pregnant women and working mothers. Yet, while the protection of pregnancy and motherhood is something women have certainly fought for since the beginning of their emancipatory struggles, constitutionally speaking, it is difficult to separate such protections from a scheme sanctioning normative motherhood (i.e., the normalization of the expectation that women ought to be mothers) unless they are also accompanied by a firm recognition of both women's reproductive autonomy and a fair societal distribution of the costs around human reproduction, which also includes men. Until all these conditions are given, it is not surprising that some feminist scholars will remain suspicious of such "maternalist" constitutional provisions.

Constitution whereby "the law shall establish special and expeditious procedures for bringing to trial and punishing the crimes of domestic violence, sexual offenses."

50 See article 24.2.a of the 1994 Malawi Constitution, promising legislation to "eliminate customs and practices that discriminate against women, particularly practices such as sexual abuse, harassment and violence"; article 35.4 of the 1995 Ethiopian Constitution, which establishes that "Laws, customs and practices that oppress or cause bodily or mental harm to women are prohibited"; and article 38 (3) of the 2015 Nepalese Constitution, condemning "any physical, mental, sexual or psychological or any other kind of violence against women, or any kind of oppression based on religious, social and cultural tradition, and other practices." For an example of courts endorsing similar cautionary views, see Tribunal Constitucional [T.C.] [Constitutional Court], 29 de enero de 2021, Rol 8792-20 (Chile), declaring inapplicable a legislation for the protection of the Rapa Nui ethnic community in a case of rape perpetrated on Easter Island, which would result in a lower punishment than that foreseen in the Chilean Criminal Code.

Some of the reproduction-related constitutional provisions adopted in the new era of constitutionalism refer to family planning or the freedom to decide whether to bear children.[51] Others refer to some notions of bodily and reproductive autonomy,[52] whereas others foreground the notion of reproductive health, sometimes endorsing the state's obligation to explicitly provide for relevant services.[53] And while some constitutions now generically refer to sexual and reproductive rights (and even include human sexuality for the first time in the catalog of rights),[54] none of

[51] This is, for example, the case of several constitutions in former Yugoslav countries that have reproduced the model of the 1974 Yugoslav Constitution, which recognized family planning as a human right (article 191). See article 55 of the Slovenian Constitution (adopted in December 23, 1991), providing that "Everyone shall be free to decide whether to bear children" and that "The state shall guarantee the opportunities for exercising this freedom and shall create such conditions as will enable parents to decide to bear children." See also article 41 of the 1991 Republic of North Macedonia Constitution (as amended in 2019); article 63 in the 2006 Serbian Constitution (reproducing article 27 of the 1990 Serbian Constitution).

[52] Section 12 (2) of the 1996 South African Constitution provides that "Everyone has the right to bodily and psychological integrity, which includes the right a) to make decisions concerning reproduction; (b) to security in and control over their body." Section 27 (1) (a) also refers to the right to have access to reproductive health (as a right to be progressively realized). However, the extent to which such provisions covered a woman's right to choose when and whether to terminate a pregnancy was subject to debate. See Catherine Albertyn, "Women and Constitution-Making in South Africa," in Irving, *Constitutions and Gender*, 71.

[53] Article 38 of the 2015 Nepalese Constitution, an entire provision devoted to the rights of women, includes article 38.2 whereby "Every woman shall have the right to safe motherhood and reproductive health." Article 66.10 of the 2008 Ecuadorian Constitution refers to "the right to take free, responsible and informed decisions concerning one's health and reproductive life and to decide how many children to have"; and article 363.6 recognizes that the state is responsible for ensuring sexual and reproductive health services to protect the health and life of women, "especially during pregnancy, childbirth and postpartum."

[54] The 2009 Bolivian Constitution guarantees men's and women's sexual and reproductive rights (article 66), as does article 43 in the 2019 Cuban Constitution. Article 66.9 of the 2008 Ecuadorian Constitution refers to the right to make free, informed, and responsible decisions over sexuality and sexual orientation (with the state being obliged to ensure that these decisions are made under secure conditions). To this we must add the explicit incorporation of a ban on sexual orientation discrimination in some constitutions. Recent case law on the criminalization of forms and expressions of sexuality is also expressive of this, placing an emphasis on women's sexuality and the patriarchal orientation of old criminal law that protected women's sexuality in terms of "chastity" and male honor. See, for instance, Hunbeobjaepanso [Const. Ct.], Nov. 26, 2009, 2008Hun-Ba58 (S. Kor.), striking down a criminal provision penalizing a person who induces a woman who is not prone to an obscene act into sexual intercourse under pretense of marriage and reversing an earlier decision issued in 2002. See also Hunbeobjaepanso [Const. Ct.], Feb. 26, 2015, 2009Hun-Ba17 (S. Kor.), invalidating the crime of adultery.

them, however, make an express recognition of the right to interrupt an ongoing pregnancy or have an abortion. Clearly, all of these provisions lend themselves to a more or less expansive interpretation, but the fact is that only exceptionally have some of these newer clauses been judicially interpreted as grounding a right to abortion, as in South Africa.[55] The majority of them have not, including those in various Latin American constitutions that make a reference to the freedom to decide whether and how many children to bear.[56]

Moreover, as we have seen in Chapter 2, the existence of such provisions has not been considered the only decisive factor on the matter of abortion. In fact, in most countries, reproductive rights are regulated through ordinary nonconstitutional legal means. Also, in some constitutional regimes, the right to an abortion has been approached through "other rights provisions (such as those referring to liberty, privacy, bodily integrity and human dignity) although such norms have also been harnessed to qualify or limit reproductive autonomy."[57] Finally, there is the tradition of reading constitutions as also endorsing the necessary protection of unborn human life, not only when there are explicit provisions making reference to it, as there sometimes are,[58] but also in jurisdictions in which the constitutional text makes no reference to the

[55] In *Christian Lawyers' Association of South Africa v. Minister of Health (Reproductive Health Alliance as Amicus Curiae)*, 1998 (4) SA 1113 (T), the High Court of South Africa upheld the Choice on Termination of Pregnancy Act 1996 (Act no. 92 of 1996), allowing abortion on request in the first twelve weeks of pregnancy and affirming sections 12.2.a and 12.2.b as recognizing and protecting the right to abortion.

[56] Instead of grounding women's reproductive autonomy in ways that include the right to choose an abortion, these provisions reflected cynicism toward family planning. They have a certain tradition in the region, where they were constitutionally incorporated since the 1970s, alluding to a history of subjection to internationally sponsored population control programs that were designed not only to reduce the population but also to curb revolutionary movements in developing countries. See, for instance, the case of Nicaragua in Martha Morgan, "Founding Mothers: Women's Voices and Stories in the 1987 Nicaraguan Constitution," *Boston University Law Review* 70, no. 1 (1990): 52.

[57] See Rosalind Dixon and Jade Bond, "Constitutions and Reproductive Rights: Convergence and Non-Convergence," in Irving, *Constitutions and Gender*, 439.

[58] Constitutional references to human life prior to birth, the fetus, or life since conception can be found in a number of constitutions around the world, some of which have in fact been amended since the 1990s for this purpose. Some examples from Eastern Europe include the 1993 Slovak Constitution, which contains a provision (article 15 [1]) that reads, "Everyone has the right to life. Human life is worthy of protection already before birth." Also, Hungary's newly enacted constitution (2011) provides, in article II, that "foetal life shall be subject to protection from the moment of conception." See also n. 70 in this chapter.

fetus or human life since conception, but simply proclaims the right to life. For all these reasons, in this area of the law, jurisprudential interpretation continues to be as decisive as constitutional texts, if not more. This is especially the case because, in this domain, constitutional hermeneutics have often been shaped by metalegal considerations related to the value of human life, the understanding of the relationship between the pregnant woman and the fetus inside her, the role of motherhood in a woman's life, and the degree to which the cost of social reproduction should be collectively, and not just individually, borne.

In general, even in those countries with a tradition of deriving the duty to protect the fetus from the constitution, increasing degrees of autonomy have been constitutionally accorded to pregnant women over the last decades, with some worrisome expressions of stagnation or backlash, however, taking place after 2010 (discussed later in Chapter 5). In Western Europe, for instance, we observe how, since the turn of the century, more and more countries have departed from an indications model (criminalization plus exceptions) and have come to embrace a time-based model, allowing women to freely decide during a period of time whether or not to carry through with their pregnancies, with or without a mandatory reflection period, often after having gone through a counseling process. This counseling process is sometimes designed to dissuade women, while other times it is merely intended to ensure a woman makes informed decisions.

We have seen in Chapter 2 how the first attempts to move away from the primacy of the protection owed to the fetus in those countries where the abortion controversy was constitutionalized and the fetus was acknowledged to deserve constitutional protection were framed in purely instrumental ways, as exemplified in 1992 by the German Federal Constitutional Court's decision recognizing that punitive forms of protection of unborn life that translate into women's coercion are, for the most part, ineffective. Nevertheless, since the turn of the century, we observe a deeper paradigm shift pointing to an understanding whereby, even if we recognize the protection of the fetus to be constitutionally grounded, this does not imply its automatic constitutional prioritization, since a woman's reproductive autonomy, including her right to decide whether she wants to continue her pregnancy, must also be taken into account, especially if her right to sexuality is also to be duly acknowledged. Thus, both a woman's reproductive autonomy and the concern for the life of the unborn may deserve some form of constitutional protection. This, then, makes the act of balancing necessary and typically invites taking into account the developmental phase of the fetus when performing such an act. It also invites prioritizing forms of minimizing abortions that do not put the weight on pregnant women alone but distribute it on the community as a whole and that assist and enable – rather than punish, threaten, or coerce – pregnant women when making their reproductive choices. The latter point then underscores the collective assumption of the costs of human reproduction.

In recent years, this new understanding has allowed some European constitutional courts to enter the abortion debate and back periodic abortion models even while recognizing the constitutional obligation to grant some protection to unborn human life, as long as open counseling is provided to pregnant women. The best articulation of this paradigm shift can perhaps be found in a 2010 decision by the Portuguese Constitutional Court.[59] Here the court upheld legislation allowing women to have an abortion in the first ten weeks of pregnancy after undergoing nondissuasive counseling – in a process destined to provide women with the information needed to make a free, conscious, and responsible decision, with a three-day reflection period and the supplement of sexual education and state assistance to motherhood – as constitutionally sufficient protection of the unborn life in the early stages.[60] In the decision, the court rejected the claim that *dissuasive*

[59] Nevertheless, one must acknowledge that the seeds were planted sooner. In a dissent expressed by Mahrenholz and Sommer in the 1993 German abortion decision, they acknowledged that abortion regulation must take into account the state's duty to protect unborn life but also a woman's rights, respecting her dignity (article 1 [1] GG), physical integrity (article 2 [2] GG), and the free development of her personality (article 2 [1] GG). Proportionality analysis, their dissent recognized, had to apply, as the affirmation of a constitutional interest could not. The dissent recognized as a basic feature of the human condition that sexuality and the desire to have children do not necessarily coincide and that the consequences of such a divergence have thus far mostly fallen on women. This did not mean that the state does not have the constitutional duty (and not just the prerogative) to protect human life from the very beginning, but that, crucially, this is a duty that falls primarily on the state and cannot simply displace women as rights bearers (articles 1 and 2 GG).

[60] See Tribunal Constitucional (T.C.), Acórdão no. 75/2010, Diário da República n.° 60/2010, Série II de 2010-03-26. A decisive step in this direction was already taken by the 2007 decision of the Slovak Constitutional Court (PL. ÚS 12/01 No. 1/2007), validating its old system of abortion on request by reference to the duty of the state to protect both unborn human life – as an objective value that warrants constitutional protection of a lower intensity despite the constitution sanctioning that the principle that human life is worthy of protection even prior to birth (article 15.1) – and the right of women to reproductive self-determination as covered by their rights to dignity and the principles of freedom and privacy (explicitly referring to Roe v. Wade). For the court, the *Wesensgehalt* (essential content) of both these rights cover the right of a woman during a certain phase

counseling in those early stages was the minimum of constitutional protection owed to the fetus. In fact, the court considered dissuasive counseling to be a form of disrespect for women's autonomy. For the court, the autonomy and dignity recognized to pregnant women must have a bearing on the constitutional validation of the periodic model as well as on the nature and characteristics of the counseling process that is to accompany it, which cannot be infantilizing, paternalistic, or place women in a situation of emotional and psychological vulnerability.[61] This means that, in the early stages of pregnancy, the best protection of the unborn is the protection of the pregnant woman by enabling an informed decision-making process and providing relevant alternatives.[62] According to the Portuguese court, a sort of "soft law," more promotional than repressive in nature, is more conducive to altering a woman's motives and making her reconsider the decision in the few cases wherein the woman has not entirely made up her mind – that is, in the only cases where abortions can be stopped.[63] The primary responsibility to take actions that express respect for unborn life (and signal that abortion cannot simply be taken as another form of contraception) falls on the state, and not women. It is the responsibility of the state to undertake measures to avoid unwanted pregnancies (such as family planning and other forms of preventive measures) as well as pregnancy and motherhood-enabling measures.[64] Worthy of consideration among the latter are those measures that can ensure adequate living and working conditions for pregnant women and mothers and other social policies in favor of motherhood and family life.[65]

of her pregnancy to decide of her own accord whether to carry the fetus to term or have the pregnancy interrupted. On the other hand, the constitutional protection due to the unborn is considered satisfied by the gestational limit of twelve weeks, the procedural requirement that includes consulting a physician, who must inform about the potential health consequences of abortion, and paying an abortion fee, a requirement that the court interprets as inherently containing a dissuasive purpose. This is a rhetoric that, in the aftermath of the decision, was used by abortion opponents to reform the counseling procedure by enhancing its dissuasive force.

[61] See Tribunal Constitucional (T.C.), Acórdão no. 75/2010, Diário da República n.° 60/2010, Série II de 2010-03-26, § 11.4.16-18.

[62] See ibid., § 11.9.9.

[63] See ibid, § 11.4.10.

[64] Ibid.

[65] This balancing approach – which implies taking into account, on the one hand, women's right to privacy, freedom, and the free development of one's personality, and on the other, the constitutional value and public interest in the protection of unborn life derived from the right to life – was also followed by the Croatian Constitutional Court in a

Underlying this jurisprudential evolution is a shift in the vision of the aborting woman, who is constructed not as someone inclined to take the decision to proceed or discontinue her pregnancy lightly, or out of selfish or hedonistic reasons, but rather as influenced by the existence (or not) of adequate means of support and out of the conviction that she must avoid important harm to others. There is also the understanding that what is typically at stake for women when confronting this decision is not only the biological process of pregnancy and delivery but also the lifelong task of mothering and the long-term burdens on her existence that this form of care entails.[66] In sum, this new constitutional approach to abortion enables the embracing of a periodic model that allows women to decide, during the first weeks of pregnancy, out of principle and not just strategic reasons while also expecting some form of protection for the unborn. This requires foregrounding objective, rather than subjective, forms of protections – that is to say, seeking to avoid unwanted pregnancies and generate a reproduction-friendly society, rather than seeking "to rescue" each and every conceived fetus from the risk of being aborted. This approach thus "disestablishes" normative motherhood in ways European abortion constitutionalism had failed to do thus far. At the same time, unlike the US privacy-based model consolidated between the 1970s and the 1990s, it does not turn abortion into a purely private decision on the part of the woman, which society has no stake in – an approach that ends up circumventing the challenges that poor women and racialized minorities may have in accessing abortion services. Instead, it compels the state to undertake preventive and enabling measures to assist women in their reproductive choices by understanding motherhood and care as a service done for the benefit of the entire community, and it assists women by covering legal abortion procedures.

2017 decision validating its periodic model, established under socialism, which however suggests the possibility of reinforcing the protection of unborn life through noncoercive measures similar to those of other Western countries. See Ustavnog Suda [Constitutional Court], Feb. 21, 2017, U-I-60/1991, a decision on abortion.

66 See Tribunal Constitucional (T.C.), Acórdão no. 75/2010, Diário da República n.° 60/2010, Série II de 2010-03-26, § 14.9.10 (Port.). But see the dissent by Justice Rui Manuel Moura Ramos (§§ 2–3), for whom the protection of unborn life requires the protection of the existential reality of each individually conceived fetus through at least minimally effective means, including during the first ten weeks of pregnancy. Thus, nondissuasive counseling and the general existence of preventive and incentivizing measures cannot be said to satisfy the minimum protection owed to the existing fetus, since these measures fail to intervene directly in the mental decision-making process of a woman and discourage her from having an abortion.

This constitutional approach to abortion may have an impact in other areas of the world such as Latin America, where the constitutional protection of the unborn has a long history, and legislative proposals for abortion liberalization have systematically failed for years, encouraging activists, especially since the turn of the century, to seize the courts to fight against criminalization. Given the strong Catholic tradition of many Latin American countries, which generally accounts for the legislative impasse, together with the increasing resistance coming from sectors linked to the Evangelical Church, it is likely that the right to life and the value attached to unborn life will retain a crucial role in constitutional abortion debates in the region, impeding a US model from ever gaining hold. Yet the European "third way" may open new possibilities.[67] Certainly, this approach – acknowledging that, in the early stages of pregnancy, the protection of the unborn should be recognized but mostly thought of in terms of protection offered to the pregnant woman – could pave the way for the constitutional acceptance of the indications system in those countries where the total ban is still the norm or could even back a periodic model after it has been legislatively adopted, as has recently been the case in Argentina.[68] Something similar could happen in several other countries, including in the African and Asian continents, where some constitutions also protect unborn human life and some courts have nevertheless occasionally protected women's reproductive autonomy to support either a criminalization with exceptions or even a periodic model.[69] The explicit

[67] See Ruth Rubio-Marín, "Abortion in Portugal: New Trends in European Constitutionalism," in *Abortion Law in Transnational Perspective: Cases and Controversies*, eds. Rebecca Cook, Joanna N. Erdman, and Bernard M. Dickens (Philadelphia: University of Pennsylvania Press, 2014), 36–55.

[68] In this respect, the famous Colombian constitutional decision (C-355 of 2006) has been groundbreaking. It affirms the need to protect intrauterine life as an objective constitutional interest, as well as women's several affected rights in deciding that certain exceptions to the criminal ban are constitutionally mandatory (protection of physical and mental health and life of the woman; rape and serious malformations of the fetus) and require no prior judicial authorization. See Corte Constitucional [C.C.] [Constitutional Court], mayo 10, 2006, Sentencia C-355/06. Worth mentioning is also the 2008 decision by the Mexican Supreme Court upholding legislation passed in Mexico City, which allows abortions on demand as an expression of legislative discretion (see Acción de inconstitucionalidad 146/2007 y su acumulada 147/2007, Suprema Corte de Justicia de la Nación [SCJN], agosto 28, 2008, Semanario Judicial de la Federación y su Gaceta, Novena Época, marzo 2009, Tomo XXIX, página 1421).

[69] See the 2019 decision of the Constitutional Court of South Korea, overruling a 2012 precedent that stated that the government's interest in protecting the right to life of fetuses outweighed the restricted rights of pregnant women and holding that the blanket ban on

ban or regulation of abortion in some provisions of African constitutions[70] might, however, make this move more difficult in countries without prior constitutional amendments of the kind that could be triggered or facilitated by recent regional human rights milestones and might seem unlikely in a context of backlash against gender equality and human rights.[71]

In Latin America, the overall trend since the turn of the century has indeed been the adoption, expansion, and rightful implementation of the indications model, rather than the adoption of a periodic model, in a deliberately chosen gradualist strategy in contexts where the life of the unborn has often been awarded explicit constitutional protection.[72] This

abortion, especially before viability (and with the only statutory exceptions for rape or incest), infringes on the right to self-determination of women in violation of the proportionality principle. See Hunbeobjaepanso [Const. Ct.], Apr. 11, 2019, 2017Hun-Ba127, cited in Yoon Jin Shin, "Gender Equality, Individual Empowerment and Constitutional Rights Review."

70 Several constitutions in the African continent not only protect life since conception but also explicitly ban abortion, at least in principle, though sometimes they also allow for some exceptions and grant legislative discretion to decide the circumstances under which it can be legal. Article 22 of the 1994 Ugandan Constitution states that "No person has the right to terminate the life of an unborn child except as may be authorised by law," a provision that is replicated in article 12 of the 1991 Zambian Constitution. Article 26 of the 2010 Kenyan Constitution establishes that "Every person has the right to life. The life of a person begins at conception. . . . Abortion is not permitted unless, in the opinion of a trained health professional, there is a need for emergency treatment, or the life or health of the mother is in danger, or if permitted by any other written law." Other texts, however, besides a ban on abortion also list the only justifications under which it can go unpunished and would thus impede broader interpretive approaches based on balancing. Article 15 (5) of the 2012 Somali Provisional Constitution, for instance, provides an example of a more restrictive approach that would presumably fend off the expansion of exceptions (aside from those strictly listed), not to mention a periodic solution. It provides that "Abortion is contrary to Sharia'ah and is prohibited except in cases of necessity, especially to save the life of the mother."

71 The African Commission on Human and Peoples' Rights called in January 2016 and again in January 2017 for the decriminalization of abortion across Africa, in line with the Maputo Protocol, binding on the forty-nine states that have ratified it. The protocol calls for safe abortions to be authorized by states in cases of "sexual assault, rape, incest and where the continued pregnancy endangers the mental and physical health of the mother or the life of the mother or the foetus" (article 14.2).

72 Several constitutions in the region include provisions that protect life since conception but do not ban abortion explicitly, and so they would lend themselves to the balancing approach described in the text. See, for instance, article 37 of the 2015 Dominican Republic Constitution, "The right to life is inviolable from conception until death"; article 3 of 1985 Guatemalan Constitution, "The State guarantees and protects the human life from its conception, as well as the integrity and security of the person"; article 4 of the

framing of the abortion question whereby the fetus (either as a rights holder – as sustained by the courts in Costa Rica[73] and El Salvador[74] – or simply as the embodiment of a constitutional value deserving constitutional protection – as defended by the courts in Colombia[75] and Brazil[76]) is granted constitutional protection has triggered calls for a proportionality analysis, yet it does not entirely cancel out the fundamental rights position of pregnant women.[77] In the past, the rule in the region had been the absolute criminalization of abortion, and different courts had called on the explicit or implicit right to life of the fetus in their constitutions to justify this (as well as on article 4 of the American Convention of Human Rights and sometimes even on encyclicals from the popes!).[78] Since 2004, however, several courts in the region have

1992 Paraguayan Constitution, "The right to life is inherent to the human person. Its protection is guaranteed, in general, from [its] conception"; article 67 of the 1983 Honduran Constitution, "The unborn shall be considered as born for all rights accorded within the limits established by law"; article 1 of 1983 Salvadoran Constitution, "El Salvador recognizes as a human person every human being since the moment of conception." On abortion constitutionalism in Latin America, see Paola Bergallo and Agustina Ramón Michel, "Constitutional Developments in Latin American Abortion Law," *International Journal of Gynecology and Obstetrics* 135, no. 2 (2016): 228–31.

[73] See Constitutional Chamber of the Supreme Court, decision No. 02792-2004, Mar. 17, 2004.

[74] See Corte Suprema de Justicia de El Salvador [Supreme Court of Justice of El Salvador], Sentencia 18/98, Nov. 20, 2007.

[75] Corte Constitucional [C.C.] [Constitutional Court], mayo 10, 2006, Sentencia C-355/06.

[76] See Supremo Tribunal Federal (S.T.F.) [Federal Supreme Court], Arguição de Descumprimento de Preceito Fundamental (ADPF) [Claim of Noncompliance with Fundamental Precept] No. 54, Relator: Min. Marco Aurélio, 12.04.2012, Díario da Justiça Eletrônico [D.J.e], 20.04.2012, 43. This decision was in response to a claim promoted by the feminist organization ANIS – Instituto de Bioética. Here, the court declared unconstitutional the interpretation of the Criminal Code that included the interruption of pregnancy in cases of anencephaly among the crimes categorized as abortion and established the state's obligation to provide for the procedure without prior judicial authorization.

[77] The Colombian Constitutional Court decision (C-355/06), for instance, begins with the necessary protection of unborn life to then argue that the legislative prohibition of abortion in all circumstances is unconstitutional because it extinguishes a woman's fundamental rights by reducing her to the condition of a receptacle of the fetus. See Corte Constitucional [C.C.] [Constitutional Court], mayo 10, 2006, Sentencia C-355/06. On proportionality, see Verónica Undurraga, "Proportionality in the Constitutional Review of Abortion Law," in Cook, Erdman, and Dickens, *Abortion Law in Transnational Perspective*, 77–98.

[78] See, for instance, the decision of the Colombian Constitutional Court rejecting an unconstitutionality challenge of the Penal Code provision that enforces criminal penalties for abortion in cases of pregnancies resulting from rape or involuntary

abandoned their precedents and come to accept that the protection of the unborn must be balanced against the rights of women. This has led them to uphold legislation proposing an indications system to deflect the attack of those wanting to stick to the total ban model (Costa Rica);[79] to reject a narrow reading or framing of some of the indications (Argentina);[80] to support actions to exact an indications model in order to overcome the total ban (Colombia);[81] to validate an indications model that had been legislatively adopted from those defending the total ban (Chile);[82] or even to validate a periodic model that had previously been adopted by the legislator (Mexico).[83] Crucially, in a few jurisdictions where courts have interpreted the protection due to the unborn to be satisfied with objective forms of protection (considering unborn life as a constitutionally protected value and not as a fundamental rights holder),

insemination, citing sections of encyclicals by Pope Paul VI and Pope John Paul II. See Corte Constitucional [C.C.] [Constitutional Court], enero 23, 1997, Sentencia C-013/97.

79 See Constitutional Chamber of the Supreme Court, decision No. 02792–2004, Mar. 17, 2004, upholding the health exception in the law by relying on the understanding that the legal protection of the right to life is gradual according to the stages of development of human life.

80 See Corte Suprema de Justicia de la Nación [CSJN] [National Supreme Court of Justice] 12/3/2012, "F., A. L. s/medida autosatisfactiva," Fallos de la Corte Suprema de la Nación, t. 335, 197, upholding the rape exception for all women, and not only for those mentally challenged, and establishing detailed criteria for the implementation of access to abortion services. See also Corte Constitucional de Ecuador, Sentencia No. 34-19-IN/21 y acumuladas, 20 abril 2021 (striking down legislation limiting the rape exception to mentally challenged women).

81 See Corte Constitucional [C.C.] [Constitutional Court], mayo 10, 2006, Sentencia C-355/06, striking down the law criminalizing abortion in all circumstances and declaring that abortion should not be considered a crime under three circumstances: when the life or health (physical or mental) of the woman is in danger; when pregnancy is the result of rape, incest, or unconsented artificial insemination; or when grave fetal malformations make life outside the uterus unviable.

82 See Tribunal Constitucional [T.C.] [Constitutional Court], 28 de agosto 2017, Rol 3729-17, and 10 de agosto de 2017, Rol 3751-17, declaring constitutional a law decriminalizing the voluntary interruption of pregnancy under three exceptions (risk to the woman's life, fetal unviability, and rape). This was approved by Congress in 2017, before its promulgation.

83 See Acción de inconstitucionalidad 146/2007 y su acumulada 147/2007, Suprema Corte de Justicia de la Nación [SCJN], agosto 28, 2008, Semanario Judicial de la Federación y su Gaceta, Novena Época, marzo 2009, Tomo XXIX, página 1421. Currently, and since 2017, there is a case pending before the Brazilian Supreme Court aiming at the decriminalization of the voluntary interruption of pregnancy during the first twelve weeks.

this has enabled them to affirm the legislative option (Colombia)[84] or to validate the legislative adoption of a periodic model (Mexico).[85]

It is worth underscoring that, in some of these instances (as in Colombia,[86] Brazil,[87] El Salvador,[88] or Bolivia[89]), those triggering the relevant case have been women's groups involved in strategic litigation or proactive female litigants responding against legislative inaction in the context of a strong reaction of religious conservatism against the advancement of women's rights since the beginning of democratization processes.[90] Moreover, some of this litigation has promoted unprecedented levels of public deliberations by opening new institutional channels for the participation of social actors in their decisional processes.[91]

[84] Corte Constitucional [C.C.] [Constitutional Court], mayo 10, 2006, Sentencia C-355/06 (Colom.). In February 2022, the Colombian Constitutional Court decriminalized abortion during the first twenty-four weeks of pregnancy, relying on the right to health, the freedom of conscience, and the principle of equality. See Corte Constitucional [C.C.] [Constitutional Court], febrero 21, 2022, Sentencia C-055/22.

[85] See Acción de inconstitucionalidad 146/2007 y su acumulada 147/2007, Suprema Corte de Justicia de la Nación [SCJN], agosto 28, 2008, Semanario Judicial de la Federación y su Gaceta, Novena Época, marzo 2009, Tomo XXIX, página 1421, validating a law that legalizes first-trimester abortion. More recently, in September 2021, the court has also struck down the full criminalization of abortion in the state of Coahuila (Acción de Inconstitucionalidad 148/2017).

[86] Corte Constitucional [C.C.] [Constitutional Court], mayo 10, 2006, Sentencia C-355/06, responding to the strategic litigation led by a feminist lawyer, Mónica Roa, director of Women's Link Worldwide Colombia, among others.

[87] Supremo Tribunal Federal (S.T.F.) [Federal Supreme Court], Arguição de Descumprimento de Preceito Fundamental (ADPF) [Claim of Noncompliance with Fundamental Precept] No. 54, Relator: Min. Marco Aurélio, 12.04.2012, Díario da Justiça Eletrônico [D.J.e], 20.04.2012, 43.

[88] Corte Suprema de Justicia de El Salvador [Supreme Court of Justice of El Salvador], Sentencia 18/98, 20 de noviembre de 2007, denying the claim filed by two university students requesting the court to declare that the absence of exceptions to the criminalization of abortion in the 1997 Penal Code was unconstitutional by omission.

[89] See Tribunal Constitucional Plurinacional [T.C.P.] [Plurinational Constitutional Court], febrero 5, 2014, Sentencia 0206/2014 (Bol.), in response to a claim submitted by Patricia Mancilla Martínez, a progressive female deputy of the Plurinational Legislative Assembly and member of Evo Morales's MAS party, requesting the declaration of unconstitutionality of several articles of the Bolivian Penal Code related to the criminalization of abortion.

[90] See Debora Diniz and Ana González Vélez, "Aborto na Suprema Corte: o caso da anencefalia no Brasil," *Revista Estudos Feministas* 16, no. 2 (2008): 647–52. See also Isabel Cristina Jaramillo Sierra and Tatiana Alfonso Sierra, *Mujeres, cortes y medios: la reforma judicial del aborto* (Bogotá: Siglo del Hombre Editores and Universidad de los Andes, 2008); Alba Ruibal, "Using Constitutional Courts to Advance Abortion Rights in Latin America," *International Feminist Journal of Politics*, 23, no. 4 (2021): 579.

[91] In 2008, during its decision-making process on the legalization of abortion in Mexico City, the Mexican Supreme Court carried out a series of innovative actions with regard to its interaction with civil society. Among them, it created a special online forum on its

This represents an interesting contrast with European abortion constitutionalism, which has remained reactive in nature to this day and where constitutional courts have been seized overwhelmingly by political forces resisting progressive legislative changes.

In Latin America, the constitutional battle has so far better served the goal of overcoming the total criminalization of abortion (through the introduction, expansion, or validation of exceptions), making sure that the practical obstacles impeding legal abortions are removed, rather than affirming the autonomy of pregnant women to freely decide whether to carry through a pregnancy at its early stages. Yet, despite its relatively modest achievements, the region's abortion constitutionalism offers some of the most interesting examples of the difference that an equality-sensitive approach to abortion can make when it comes to constitutional reasoning. Although European abortion constitutionalism had already expressed the importance of assuming collective responsibility for a reproduction-friendly society, the Latin American case law best exemplifies an awareness of the challenges surrounding access to abortion in those instances, however limited, in which it is legal to do so but both attitudinal and institutional obstacles render it inaccessible – a concern that, in the context of Latin America, as in many other parts of the world, has obvious class, and often also racial, undertones.[92]

website for the publication of documents and comments on the abortion case and, for the first time in its institutional history, convened public hearings, which were broadcast through the Judicial Channel. In Brazil, when dealing with ADPF 54, on abortion in cases of anencephaly, the Federal Supreme Court convoked four public hearings, which took place in 2008. In 2018, during the process of ADPF 442 regarding the decriminalization of first-trimester abortion, the Supreme Court convoked once again two public hearings. See Supremo Tribunal Federal (S.T.F.) [Federal Supreme Court], Arguição de Descumprimento de Preceito Fundamental (ADPF) [Claim of Noncompliance with Fundamental Precept] No. 54, Relator: Min. Marco Aurélio, 12.04.2012, Díario da Justiça Eletrônico [D.J.e], 20.04.2012, 43; and Arguição de Descumprimento de Preceito Fundamental (ADPF) [Claim of Noncompliance with Fundamental Precept] No. 442, Relatora: Min. Rosa Weber, 27.03.2018.

92 Both Argentina and Colombia have rich case law on how their indications model is to be interpreted in ways that women can effectively access abortion. The case law in Argentina has referred to considerations such as the need to avoid time-consuming and unnecessary bureaucratic procedures; the need to undertake information campaigns to tackle misinformation about the requirements to access abortion (including the common mistake of asking for judicial authorizations when the law does not require them); or the need to tackle the illegal practice of health professionals when they refuse to practice abortions, even when the law allows abortions – all of which, the court has stated, could amount to expressions of institutional violence against women (see Paola Bergallo, "The Struggle Against Informal Rules on Abortion," in Cook, Erdman, and Dickens, *Abortion Law in Transnational Perspective*, 143–66). The case law in Colombia has also spelled out the

Ideally, concerns around access should also be relevant in the few instances in which the constitution is interpreted as sanctioning the right to abortion. Only this would ensure that abortion is recognized as both a liberty (from interference) and a right supporting positive obligations. Nepal, coming from a horrendous past of abortion criminalization, offers today one of the few constitutional experiences exemplifying this point and showing the importance of intersectional sensibilities. In 1997, Nepal adopted what was to be an interim constitution, with a specific section devoted to the Rights of Women (article 20 [2] of the Interim Constitution), recognizing that "Every woman shall have the right to reproductive health and other reproductive rights," a clause that the 2015 amended constitution has kept in a different provision (article 38 [2]). In 2009, the Supreme Court of Nepal decided on the landmark case *Lakshmi Dhikta v. Nepal* in response to a plaintiff, a poor woman, mother of six, who had not been able to cover the required USD 15 abortion fee. The court recognized article 20 (2) as covering a whole umbrella of reproductive rights, including the right to information about, and access to, family planning and to use such methods to prevent pregnancy; the right to decide whether to have children or not; and the right of a pregnant woman to discontinue pregnancy if she does not wish to bear children. As for the latter, the court determined that the state must not only formally recognize but also actively ensure access to abortion to all women, including poor, rural, and marginalized women who, traditionally, have been the ones risking their lives through informal abortion practices in a country that until 2002, had some of the most restrictive abortion legislations in the world. In doing this, the Nepalese Supreme Court relied on women's dignity, physical integrity, autonomy, self-determination, and equality. Explicitly endorsing the concept of transformative equality, the court argued for the need "to liberate women as moral agents equal to men and let them decide for themselves how to manage their sexuality and family life." For the court, "the fact that

conditions under which conscientious objection can be claimed and has specified that it constitutes an individual right that can only be exercised by the health staff directly involved in the procedure, and not collectively, by an institution, the judiciary, or civil servants. See Corte Constitucional [C.C.] [Constitutional Court], mayo 10, 2006, Sentencia C-355/06; febrero 28, 2008, Sentencia T-209/08; and mayo 28, 2009, Sentencia T-388/09. See also Tribunal Constitucional Plurinacional [T.C.P.] [Plurinational Constitutional Court], febrero 5, 2014, Sentencia 0206/2014 (Bol.), striking down or narrowly interpreting several of the problematic legal requirements to access abortion according to the exceptions in Bolivia.

women are by nature able to become pregnant does not mean that they must become pregnant." In fact, forcing women to continue with unwanted pregnancies means "transforming them into mere instruments" and imposing on them a "form of slavery."[93]

The Nepalese decision's appeal to equality, relevant to address the particular needs of poor women but also the specificity of women's reproductive biology in order to back a positive right to a publicly funded abortion, constitutes a rare exception in constitutional law. But over the last decades, other courts around the world have been joining in the adoption of equality lenses to discuss abortion even when they fall short of recognizing the right to freely have an abortion or the right to have the state cover its cost. In the past, such considerations were often triggered by the need to rebut the argument that men/spouses should have an equal say on abortion decisions.[94] In more recent times, equality considerations have gone beyond this in other interesting ways, including the articulation of multicultural concerns. Thus, despite its modest findings, one of the most striking examples of a constitutional narrative foregrounding a multicultural perspective when discussing abortion is probably contained in a 2009 decision by the Bolivian Constitutional Court, a decision that links certain forms of regulation of abortion to the joint effects of patriarchy and colonialism and offers alternative cultural lenses through which to understand the relationship between the woman and the fetus.[95] Interestingly,

[93] See Lakshmi Dhikta v. Government of Nepal, Writ Petition No. WO-0757 of the year 2067 BS (2009). For a discussion of the decision, see Melissa Upreti, "Toward Transformative Equality in Nepal: The *Lakshmi Dhikta* Decision," in Cook, Erdman, and Dickens, *Abortion Law in Transnational Perspective*, 279–303. Articulating a similar concern around the reproductive rights of marginalized groups, see Manju and Others v. Government of Nepal, Writ No. 070-WO-0194, S.C. Nepal (2013). The case was decided on Aug. 8, 2017, and the Nepalese Supreme Court ruled that the government is obliged to provide access to contraceptives information and services across the country, especially in remote areas and to marginalized groups.

[94] Courts in several countries around the world have rejected the claim that spousal authorization was required for a woman to have an abortion. Examples include France, Conseil d'État (Council of State) decision CE Ass., Oct. 31, 1980, 13028, Rec. Lebon; the United States, Planned Parenthood of Southeastern Pennsylvania v. Casey, 505 U.S. 833 (1992); Mexico, Acción de inconstitucionalidad 146/2007 y su acumulada 147/2007, Suprema Corte de Justicia de la Nación [SCJN], agosto 28, 2008, Semanario Judicial de la Federación y su Gaceta, Novena Época, marzo 2009, Tomo XXIX, página 1421; and Nepal, Achyut Prasad Kharel v. Office of the Prime Minister and Council of Ministers and Others, Writ No. 3352 of the year 2061 (2004), decided on Aug. 4, 2008 (2065 BS).

[95] See Tribunal Constitucional Plurinacional [T.C.P.] [Plurinational Constitutional Court], febrero 5, 2014, Sentencia 0206/2014. Bolivia's 2009 constitution recognizes that "women and men are guaranteed the exercise of sexual rights and their reproductive rights"

the argument to reject men's equal decision-making power in the courts' decisions has often relied on the obvious understanding that, physiologically speaking, men and women are differently situated when it comes to pregnancy and labor (and the specific demands and risks they entail for women) and on the fact that, when it comes to the duties and responsibilities that follow from parenting and that are not strictly biologically justified, they typically continue to fall disproportionately on women, something legal orders have thus far mostly failed to remedy.[96] We shall return to this at the end of this chapter.

4.3 A Positive Right to Motherhood and the Foregrounding of a Caring Citizenship

For the longest time, the normalization of motherhood that the new abortion constitutionalism aims to unsettle found constitutional expressions reinforcing its premise. After all, in many countries, the first and, sometimes, the only constitutional provisions making a specific reference to women were provisions mentioning the protection of motherhood or pregnancy.[97] Also, as we have seen in Chapter 1, in many jurisdictions, provisions concerning women's equality or the abolition of sex-based privileges made their first appearance along with such maternalist protections.

The fact that motherhood and, more generally, family protection clauses appeared quite soon in constitutional history shows that the family was expected to be the foundational unit of the modern political order and that women, within it, were expected to bear and raise children

(article 66). On the basis of it, the plaintiff, congresswoman Patricia Mancilla Martínez, challenged the criminalization of abortion in Bolivia (along an indications model) and asked for a periodic model that would recognize abortion on demand. She also underscored the need to eliminate some of the requirements in the criminal code for accessing abortion through the indications foreseen (such as the requirement of judicial authorization or the need to undertake legal proceedings against the perpetrator in case of abortion as a result of rape). Deriving the protection due to unborn life from the right to life and interpreting article 66 restrictively, the court dismissed the claim of abortion on demand but struck down or interpreted narrowly several of the problematic legal requirements to access abortion according to the exceptions already contained in the law.

96 See Acción de inconstitucionalidad 146/2007 y su acumulada 147/2007, Suprema Corte de Justicia de la Nación [SCJN], agosto 28, 2008, Semanario Judicial de la Federación y su Gaceta, Novena Época, marzo 2009, Tomo XXIX, página 1421 (Mex.).

97 The 1917 Mexican Constitution, for instance, did not grant women equal voting rights, nor did it prohibit discrimination on the grounds of sex. Its only mention of women was a mandate of protection of pregnant women in the workplace.

as their primary contribution to society. At the same time, women, both as dependent spouses and caretakers, were deemed in need of protection, a "protection" that in many ways justified measures that clearly limited rather than amplified their range of options in the marketplace. Even when the most blatant exclusions were overcome, women remained placed in the social assistance (rather than the social insurance) side of "two-tier" welfare systems, which continued to assume women's roles as mothers and caretakers as primordial and relied on the male-family provider paradigm, understanding women's employment as secondary at best to their motherhood roles.[98] However, until the late 1980s and 1990s, these constitutional motherhood protections were typically expressed in the form of a generic mandate or directive principle to state powers, in provisions that did not grant women enforceable rights, not even when their wording seemed to clearly indicate otherwise.[99]

As we have seen, to some extent, it is this lack of directly enforceable motherhood-related rights that has invited the prohibition of sex-based discrimination to become one possible venue to derive enforceable protections for pregnant women and working mothers in the maternalist accommodationist strand of inclusive constitutionalism. Yet, as noted in Chapter 2, this strategy – with various degrees of success in different constitutional traditions – relied on the possibility of embracing a notion of "sex" as covering both biological and *functional* distinctions between the sexes, thus

[98] See Ann Shola Orloff, "Gender and the Social Rights of Citizenship: The Comparative Analysis of Gender Relations and Welfare States," *American Sociological Review* 58, no. 3 (1993): 315.

[99] Perhaps the best exemplification of this is article 41.2.2 of the 1937 Irish Constitution (which makes reference to the obligation of the state to ensure that "mothers shall not be obliged by economic necessity to engage in labour to the neglect of their duties in the home"). Throughout Irish constitutional history, women litigants have unsuccessfully tried to call on this provision to exact protections as household caretakers. Often cited is the case of *L. v. L.*, [1992] 2 IR 77, in which the Irish Supreme Court rejected a claim by a married woman that was based specifically on article 41.2, holding that, even though the plaintiff had worked exclusively within the home throughout her marriage, she was not entitled to a 50 percent interest in the family home and that article 41.2 in the constitution could not support her claim. This, of course, is not to deny that, on some occasions, constitutional provisions (not directly relevant to motherhood) have been used to protect mothers. In Canada, for instance, arguments in reference to the "security of the person" provision in the Charter of Rights and Freedoms (article 7) have been used successfully to convince the court to extend state-funded legal aid to indigent parents (who are frequently single-parent mothers) requiring legal counsel to defend against state-initiated child protection proceedings. See New Brunswick (Minister of Health and Community Services) v. G. (J.), [1999] 3 S.C.R. 46.

inviting a further normalization of women's motherhood roles. Moreover, this constitutional antidiscrimination strategy had an inherently limited capacity because it was mostly to deploy its effects in the public sphere, especially in the employment domain – explicitly or implicitly relying on a male comparator – depriving women of meaningful options to constitutionally articulate claims around the needs and disadvantages they experience in relation to their reproductive capacity or, more generally speaking, their reproductive choices. The difficulty in advancing positive abortion rights as a matter of equality/nondiscrimination shows this to be the case.

Deep down, the need to rely on a male comparator to articulate motherhood-related protections is a testimony to the fact that women have simply not been the protagonists in constitution-making processes. Until very recently, this has translated into a general neglect of the sexual and reproductive domains in constitutions, as well as in the impossibility of foregrounding mothering, parenting, and, more generally speaking, caring, as an inherent and meaningful form of human capability and a citizenship-like contribution to the general well-being of society. If we look closely to the mostly unwritten history of women's unsuccessful constitutional engagements, we find reasons to believe that, had women been able to lead constitution-making processes, a rich and complex right to motherhood and parenting (with both positive and negative dimensions) might have seen the light of day in written constitutions early on and certainly after second-wave feminism politicized family dynamics. For instance, women's groups in Nicaragua, having been very active during the revolutionary struggle to overcome the Somoza dictatorship, remained equally active in the constitution-making process that followed and that led up to the 1987 constitution (still in force today). In its petition to the Special Constitutional Commission, the Asociación de Mujeres Nicaragüenses Luisa Amanda Espinoza (AMNLAE – Luisa Amanda Espinoza Association of Nicaraguan Women), the main organization for women, had a whole section devoted to what they called "right to motherhood," with a comprehensive vision that included:

a) The real exercise of women's right to responsibly and freely decide the children they want and the moment in their lives in which they want to have them.
b) The elimination of all forms of discrimination against pregnant women or mothers in access to, preservation of, and promotion in employment.
c) Guaranteeing special attention to the reproductive health of women.

d) Assuring the complement of the right to subsidies and benefits to all pregnant workers, putting emphasis on those women who historically have been left out of social benefits.
e) Aiding the organization of collective forms of caring for the children of the working family in order to permit the fullest integration of men and women into the tasks of production.[100]

In the end, only a fraction of this made it to the final text.[101] Thus, under a section devoted to the "rights of the family," the constitution recognizes the family as "the fundamental nucleus of society" with "the right to protection by society and the State" (article 70). The constitution also includes a provision that declares that the state is to award special protection to the process of human reproduction (article 74.1); that women must be especially protected during pregnancy and enjoy remunerated leave and social security benefits (article 74.2); and that nobody shall deny employment to women on the basis of their pregnancy or dismiss them during or after it, in accordance with the law (article 74.3).

In many ways, the Nicaraguan text is not a rarity in comparative contemporary constitutionalism, where we find clauses of the traditional type (making generic reference to the safeguarding of motherhood in the context of protecting family and marriage,[102] as well as to motherhood, conceptualized as a condition of vulnerability, sometimes

[100] Also, aware of the dangers of "protectionist" legislation, they warned that "this necessary protection for maternity must not implicate a) discrimination against pregnant women in access to employment or to certain jobs, or b) generalizations to all women of supposedly protectionist restrictions, as if all women were always pregnant or nursing." See Morgan, "Founding Mothers," 66.

[101] The abortion demand, which was thought to be encompassed by the right to responsibly and freely decide on the number of children and the moment in their lives in which women want to have them, was abandoned amid a lively opposition, mainly from religious groups.

[102] See article 6 of the 1949 German Constitution ("[1] Marriage and the family shall enjoy the special protection of the state" and "[4] Every mother shall be entitled to the protection and care of the community"); article 21.1 of the 1975 Greek Constitution ("The family, being the cornerstone of the preservation and the advancement of the Nation, as well as marriage, motherhood and childhood, shall be under the protection of the State"); article 18 of the 1997 Polish Constitution ("Marriage, being a union of a man and a woman, as well as the family, motherhood and parenthood, shall be placed under the protection and care of the Republic of Poland"); article 21 of the 2010 Nigerian Constitution ("Marriage and family constitute the natural and moral base of the human community. They are placed under the protection of the State. The State and public collectivities have the duty to see to the physical, mental and moral health of the family, particularly of the mother and of the child").

paternalistically assimilated to other vulnerable groups or conditions such as children, the youth, the sick, the elderly, or the disabled)[103] coexisting with other forms of provisions that have proliferated since the late 1980s. Such provisions usually refer to motherhood, pregnancy-related social security, and employment benefits, as well as to accommodation measures seeking to protect the health and employment prospects of the pregnant/working mother and the well-being of the child.[104] Only the latter would seem to ground enforceable rights for

[103] See article 51 of the 1949 Costa Rican Constitution ("The family, as [a] natural element and foundation of society, has the right to the special protection of the State. The mother, the child, the elder and the helplessly sick will equally have right to that protection"); article 203 of the 1988 Brazilian Constitution ("Social assistance shall be rendered to those who need it, regardless of contributions to social security," with one of its main objectives being the "protection of the family, maternity, childhood, adolescence and old age"); article 65.3 of the 2010 Croatian Constitution ("Young people, mothers, and disabled persons shall be entitled to special protection at work"); article 41.2 of the 2000 Swiss Constitution ("The Confederation and Cantons shall endeavour to ensure that every person is protected against the economic consequences of old-age, invalidity, illness, accident, unemployment, maternity, being orphaned and being widowed").

[104] For a precursor in this regard, see article 72 of the 1972 Panamenian Constitution ("Motherhood of the working woman is protected. The pregnant woman may not be separated from her public or private employment for this reason. For a minimum of six weeks prior to confinement and eight weeks thereafter, she is entitled to rest with the same remuneration that she was receiving, and her job shall be kept for her, as well as all the rights inherent to her contract. Upon returning to work, the mother may not be dismissed for one year, except in special cases prescribed by law, which shall in addition, regulate the special working conditions of the pregnant woman"). Similar clauses have proliferated around the world since the 1990s, with special force in postsocialist countries and Latin America, where these rights are also often spelled out in quite a level of detail. See article 14 of the 1991 Bulgarian Constitution, which recognizes that "the family, motherhood and children shall enjoy the protection of the State and society" and article 47.2 whereby "mothers shall be the object of special protection on the part of the State and shall be guaranteed prenatal and postnatal leave, free obstetric care, alleviated working conditions and other social assistance"; article 43 of the 1991 Colombian Constitution ("Women and men have equal rights and opportunities. Women cannot be subjected to any type of discrimination. During their periods of pregnancy and following delivery, women will benefit from the special assistance and protection of the State and will receive from the latter food subsidies if they should thereafter find themselves unemployed or abandoned"); article 35.5 of the 1994 Ethiopian Constitution ("a. Women have the right to maternity leave with full pay. The duration of maternity leave shall be determined by law taking into account the nature of the work, the health of the mother and the well-being of the child and family; b. Maternity leave may, in accordance with the provisions of law, include prenatal leave with full pay"); article 41 (2) of the 1992 Slovak Constitution ("A pregnant woman shall be guaranteed a special treatment, protection in employment, and adequate working conditions"); article 75.23 of the 1994 Argentine Constitution

the positive protection of mothers, although the extent to which this is the case depends on various factors, including the section of the constitution where these clauses appear (i.e., whether they are enforceable fundamental rights or non-directly enforceable guiding principles) and, more generally speaking, if and how constitutions are given normative force and interpreted. Often, it is labor codes that provide the main regulatory backbones to such protections, as these, for the most part, continue to address women in their double roles of mothers and workers rather than purely in the former.

In principle, there is nothing to object about, and much to be said for, the proliferation of entitlements, such as paid leaves, in constitutions seeking to protect pregnant women and working mothers – a process that only accompanies their gradual incorporation into the labor market. Courts around the world certainly continue to this day to rely on constitutions – some of which now incorporate an explicit ban on discrimination on the grounds of pregnancy[105] – to enrich the body of constitutional law that assists pregnant women and recent mothers on leave to counter the discrimination and lack of reasonable accommoda-

(stating that Congress is empowered "to enact a special and integral social security system that protects needy children, from gestation through the end of elementary schooling, and that protects the mother during pregnancy and nursing"); article 7. XVIII of the 1988 Brazilian Constitution recognizing among workers' rights the right to "paid maternity leave without loss of job for a period of one hundred-twenty days"; article 32.2 of the 1993 Czech Constitution ("Pregnant women are guaranteed special care, protection in labor relations, and suitable work conditions"); article 43 of the 2008 Ecuadorian Constitution ("The State shall guarantee the rights of pregnant and breast-feeding women to: 1. Not be discriminated for their pregnancy in education, social, and labor sectors; 2. Free maternal healthcare services; 3. Priority protection and care of their integral health and life during pregnancy, childbirth and postpartum; 4. The facilities needed for their recovery after pregnancy and during breast-feeding"); article 45.V of the 2009 Bolivian Constitution whereby "women have the right to a safe maternity, with an inter-cultural practice and vision; they shall enjoy the special assistance and protection of the State during pregnancy and birth and in the prenatal and postnatal periods" and then again in article 48.VI, "Women shall not be discriminated against or fired because of their civil status, because of pregnancy, because of their age or physical features, or because of the number of children they have. It is guaranteed that pregnant women and parents cannot be dismissed from employment until the child completes one year of age."

105 See, for instance, section 9.3 in the Constitution of South Africa and article 18 of the Constitution of Nepal. Other times, as we have seen, this is derived from the prohibition of sex-based discrimination.

tion they encounter in the employment market[106] as well as in the educational domain;[107] to expand their social security and parental protections;[108] and to remove discriminatory elements that they may

[106] In fact, several jurisdictions have replicated longstanding tools to ensure the job security of union activists in order to protect them against loss of employment for reasons related to pregnancy or other forms of discrimination linked to the enjoyment of rights and benefits, as well as the protection of motherhood. They have similarly crafted an ever-expanding notion of sex discrimination to heighten the protection of employed pregnant women and early mothers. See, for instance, the Spanish Constitutional Court decision S.T.C., Jan. 16, 2017 (No. 2/2017) and S.T.C., Oct. 4, 2004 (No. 161/2004), on the right to reasonable accommodations for pregnant women and women on maternity leave or leave because of a risky pregnancy. See also similar case law in Colombia (Corte Constitucional [C.C.] [Constitutional Court], septiembre 25, 1997, Sentencia C-470/97; octubre 28, 1996, Sentencia T-568/96; diciembre 9, 1996, Sentencia C-710/96; febrero 23, 2012, Sentencia T-126/12; febrero 13, 2013, Sentencia SU070/13); Peru (Tribunal Constitucional [T.C.] [Constitutional Court], Nov. 6, 2008, file No. 05652-2007-PA/TC); and Mexico (Amparo directo 29/2018, Segunda Sala de la Suprema Corte de Justicia de la Nación [SCJN], Ponente: Ministra Yasmín Esquivel Mossa, mayo 22, 2019; and Amparo directo en revisión 5139/2018, Segunda Sala de la Suprema Corte de Justicia de la Nación [SCJN], Ponente: Ministro Alberto Pérez Dayán, noviembre 14, 2018). See also Constitutional Chamber of the Supreme Court, decision No. 13502-2018, Aug. 17, 2018 (Costa Rica), striking down a norm impeding elected women in maternity leave to swear in their position, inadequately limiting their right to employment and to exercise political office, thus preventing them to duly balance their role as mothers and professionals. On reasonable accommodations of pregnant women in the employment domain, see also Corte Suprema de Justicia de la Nación [CSJN] [National Supreme Court of Justice], 04/06/2013, "Visone Gloria Beatriz c/ Hospital Vicente López y Planes – Unidad Hospitalaria de General Rodríguez – s/ Accidente de trabajo," V. 206. XLV. RHE (Arg.), successfully challenging insufficient compensation for moral damages due to the death of a child as a result of early labor and poor working conditions for a pregnant woman.

[107] For examples of constitutional litigation concerning pregnancy discrimination in the educational domain, see Colombia (Corte Constitucional [C.C.] [Constitutional Court], junio 17, 1992, Sentencia T-420/92; junio 22, 1994, Sentencia T-292/94; and noviembre 11, 1998, Sentencia T-656/98); Malaysia (Constitutional Court, Noorfadilla binti Ahmad Saikin v. Chayed Basirun and Ors [2012] 1 Malayan Law Journal 832), dismissal of pregnant local schoolteacher; Peru (Tribunal Constitucional [T.C.] [Constitutional Court], Dec. 9, 2015, file No. 01423-2013-PA/TC), destitution of a woman cadet because she entered the military school while pregnant.

[108] See Supremo Tribunal Federal (S.T.F.) [Federal Supreme Court], Ação Direta de Inconstitucionalidade (ADI) [Direct Action of Unconstitutionality] No. 1946, Relator: Min. Sydney Sanches, 03.04.2003, Díario da Justiça [D.J.], 10.04.2003 (Braz.), in regard to maternity leave pay not counting toward the constitutional cap introduced in 1998 on the amount of benefits to be paid to workers by the general social security system, leaving the rest to be paid by employers so as not to disincentivize the hiring of women. For the Netherlands, see Centrale Raad van Beroep (CRvB) (Central Council of Appeal), F.M.M. C., W.P.M. B. and A.J.C. A. v. Regional Health Insurance Foundation, AB 1996, 501, holding unconstitutional a provision requiring women to contribute financially to

contain,[109] in many cases filling out the gaps of existing legislative frames. Problematic is, however, the paternalistic undertone in the ways these protections are sometimes framed (when they convey women's weakness or fragility) and the coexistence of these protections with other norms still sanctioning, in glorifying terms, family and marriage (the latter often framed in explicitly heterosexual, procreative terms). Moreover, all of this is often combined with the insufficient recognition of women's negative "freedom from unwanted motherhood" (through duly recognized rights to contraception, family planning, and abortion) and of the centrality of other forms of care, beyond maternal care, in the same constitutions. It is this resulting combination that is problematic to the extent that, far from foregrounding women's full and equal autonomy, such combination still signals an insufficient departure from normative motherhood and the dominant "care/control paradigm" of the traditional welfare system.

For all these reasons, a truly emancipatory and intersectional agenda, of which we find scattered but growing expressions in constitutional litigation, would seem to require several additional items, including greater safeguards for women's reproductive health (broadly conceived and beyond those referred to in the employment context)[110] and the protection of one's reproductive capacity, of which minority and

their postnatal care, relying to a significant extent on international standards such as the International Labour Organization's conventions on maternity protection (no. 103) and social security (minimum standards) (no. 102), which were held to have direct effect.

109 See, for Germany, BVerfG, 1 BvL 2/10, 1–61, July 10, 2012, holding unconstitutional the exclusion of foreign nationals with residence permits issued on humanitarian grounds from the federal child-raising allowance and the federal parental allowance.

110 Irving celebrates the broad concept of reproductive health adopted at the International World Conference on Population and Development in Cairo in 1994 and the World Conference on Women in Beijing in 1995, a definition that highlights the need to have a satisfying and safe sex life; the capability to reproduce and the freedom to decide if and when to do so (by having access to safe, effective, affordable, and acceptable methods of family planning, as well as to appropriate health care services that will enable women to have a safe childbirth). At the same time, she notices that such definition should be extended to cover "women's needs before pregnancy, including during menstruation, and after childbirth, both with respect to the physical injuries produced by childbirth, and as caregivers of infants." It should also cover the needs of "nonreproductive women, those who are incapable of bearing children, either before or after menopause." In essence, she rightly claims that "women should not be subject to discriminatory treatment, socially, legally, or medically, because they are infertile or post fertile. Nor, in the converse, should infertility be required as a criterion for entitlements." See Helen Irving, *Gender and the Constitution: Equity and Agency in Comparative Constitutional Design* (Cambridge: Cambridge University Press, 2008), 196–97.

racialized women are often unduly deprived.[111] The agenda should also provide greater recognition of care forms besides mothering/parenting, such as taking care of the sick, disabled, and the elderly; greater recognition of mothering/parenting outside the context of the traditional marital family (think of nonmarital or de facto unions,[112] single parenting,[113] gay parenting,[114] trans parenting, or mothering/parenting outside of the family/household context);[115] and greater recognition/dignification of care both as productive labor – with its opportunity costs[116] – when

[111] "Women and girls need protection from coerced or forced sterilization, from environmental pollutants that compromise their fertility, from customary practices that render sexual intercourse difficult or painful or that damage the reproductive organs, and from ideologies that either coercively promote or discourage reproduction." See ibid., 212.

[112] For the potential relevance of such protection, see Quebec (Attorney General) v. A, [2013] S.C.C. 5, [2013] 1 S.C.R. 61, where the Canadian Supreme Court refused Charter protection to an unmarried immigrant mother of three children after the break-up of her relationship with their billionaire Quebecois father who had refused to marry her, validating Quebec Civil Code's restriction of support and property division dispositions to married couples and leaving unmarried couples in a law-free or private zone that is detrimental to mothers.

[113] For constitutional battles with great impact on single parenthood, see the right of single women to access medically assisted reproduction (decisions of the Slovenian Constitutional Court from Oct. 1, 2013, U-I-242/12; and Jan. 12, 2016, U-I-249/14-8, and of the Australian High Court, Re McBain; Ex parte Australian Catholic Bishops Conference [2002] HCA 16); the right of indigent parents, who frequently are single-parent mothers, to free legal aid to defend against state initiated child protection proceedings (Canadian Supreme Court, New Brunswick [Minister of Health and Community Services] v. G. (J.), [1999] 3 S.C.R. 46); the right not to suffer employment discrimination because of a pregnancy out of wedlock (Supreme Court of the Philippines, Capin-Cadiz v. Brent Hospital and Colleges, G.R. No. 187417, 781 Phil. 610 [Feb. 24, 2016], and Leus v. St. Scholastica's College Westgrove et al., G.R. No. 187226, 752 Phil. 186 [Jan. 28, 2015]); the right to reinforced protection in employment stability for women heads of households (Corte Constitucional [C.C.] [Constitutional Court], marzo 5, 2018, Sentencia T-084/2018 [Colom.]); the right for alimony and maintenance of the custodial parent, very often mothers (South Africa's Constitutional Court decision in *Bannatyne v. Bannatyne*, 2003 2 SA 363 [CC]).

[114] For examples from several jurisdictions covering child custody, single-parent and second-parent adoption, as well as joint adoption, see Angioletta Sperti, *Constitutional Courts*, 171–92.

[115] See Corte Suprema de Justicia de la Nación [CSJN] [National Supreme Court of Justice], 11/02/2020, "Internas de la Unidad N° 31 SPF y Otros s/Habeas corpus," Fallos de la Corte Suprema de la Nación, t. 343, 15 (Arg.), on benefits for pregnant women and mothers while in prison. See also article 5 L in the Brazilian Constitution, referring to the right of female prisoners to have access to their children while nursing.

[116] See, for Canada, Moge v. Moge, [1992] 3 S.C.R. 813, recognizing, for the purpose of determining the duration of spousal support, the negative employment effects caused by the household caretaking role adopted in the first marriage, which continued to operate even after entry into another relationship. See also, for Mexico, Amparo directo en

performed in the family "for free" and as a form of employment when performed as a commodity,[117] including setting limits to the forms and ways of its commodification.[118] Similarly, it would seem to require the redefinition and reevaluation of fatherhood around caretaking, a point we will return to, as well as broader ranges of measures for "defamilization" to better reflect the collective assumption of the costs of social reproduction and the necessary communal involvement and support of

revisión 2764/2013, Suprema Corte de Justicia de la Nación [SCJN], noviembre 6, 2013, Semanario Judicial de la Federación y su Gaceta, Décima Época, Libro 4, marzo de 2014, Tomo I, Tesis 1a. CI/2014 (10a.), páginas 539–40, upholding a rule mandating the sharing of goods acquired during marriage in favor of the partner who took care of the household as a measure to ensure women's equality; and Amparo directo en revisión 1754/2015, Primera Sala de la Suprema Corte de Justicia de la Nación [SCJN], Ponente: Ministro Arturo Zaldívar Lelo de Larrea, octubre 14, 2015, confirming the right to alimony payment to a sick divorced wife who had been the primary caretaker of the home, even though she had her own retirement pension, taking into account double shift and her health condition.

117 Often, the care of persons and the cleaning of domestic spaces are lumped together under the banner of "domestic" work, mirroring the unpaid work that women often perform within the household, which is devalued as a form of employment. See, for Colombia, Corte Constitucional [C.C.] [Constitutional Court], julio 21, 1998, Sentencia No. C-372/98, invalidating provisions in the Labor Code that contemplated lesser unemployment benefits for domestic workers, finding however that certain differences, such as maximum hours of work, are reasonable in light of the nature of the work; for Costa Rica, see Constitutional Chamber of the Supreme Court, decision No. 03150–94, June 28, 1994, upholding a provision in the Labor Code that established a 12-hour working day, with half a day of rest for domestic workers, contrary to the ordinary 8-hour daily work schedule, 48 hours weekly, and one day of rest after six consecutive days of work – as foreseen under articles 58 and 59 of the constitution as well as in the International Labour Organization's convention 111. The court thus argued that domestic service is an exceptional situation that cannot be equated with other forms of employment. Nevertheless, see, for Mexico, Amparo directo 9/2018, Segunda Sala de la Suprema Corte de Justicia de la Nación [SCJN], Ponente: Ministro Arturo Pérez Dayán, diciembre 5, 2018, striking down legislation redeeming employers from enrolling domestic workers in the social security registry as being discriminatory and violating the human right to social security, given the disparate impact of such legislation on women. The connection between cleaning and women has often entailed pay discrimination in feminized employment categories devoted to cleaning. See, for instance, the Spanish Constitutional Court's decisions S.T.C. May 7, 1991 (No. 145/1991) and May 20, 1998 (No. 147/1995), in which the court struck down this form of discrimination by calling on the notion of indirect discrimination.

118 See Corte Constitucional [C.C.] [Constitutional Court], diciembre 18, 2009, Sentencia T-968/09, (Colom.), arguing, on the basis of article 44's protection of children, that the fact that a mother is a surrogate does not entail that she has less of a right to retain her own right to the children she delivered, especially when, despite her poor economic condition – which the intended father had purposefully sought by looking for a destitute person to act as a surrogate – the children were properly being taken care of.

human interdependency along the lines of what some have called a "careful citizenship."[119]

Instead, what we find is that the marital family continues to be considered the natural repository of care duties and dispositions and that the general lack of work/life balance policies making full-time employment and caretaking compatible continues to deepen other forms of privilege. A "global care chain" has emerged whereby migrant women are primarily responsible for reproductive activities (meaning "labor activities needed to sustain the productive labor force, including cleaning, caretaking of the elderly, children, and other dependents").[120] Whether performed in the households or in the market, domestic work and childcare are done for free at home, and much of this paid work is seriously undervalued. As a result, wealthier individuals and families end up privately buying assistance, typically from other poorer, migrant, or racialized women. Otherwise, overstretched couples would still dominantly abide by a market rationality that compels women to take lower-paid, part-time, more flexible, and more precarious employment to be able to combine it with family obligations. None of these seem particularly egalitarian scenarios.

One of the main challenges of this scenario, therefore, has to do with how to advance in a coordinated manner on all fronts, as the increased valorization of care without the adequate subversion of care roles and some degree of "defamilization" may in fact contribute to entrenching existing gender roles. At the same time, any reform that looks to subvert gender roles but does not take into account long-existing gender patterns and their impact on people's lives risks treating the "generation in-between" unfairly. An example to illuminate such complexity may be useful. It refers to the difficulty of attaching economic value to care labor in the

[119] For a relational understanding of citizenship centered around care, see Joan Tronto, "Care as the Work of Citizens: A Modest Proposal," in *Women and Citizenship*, ed. Marilyn Friedman (Oxford: Oxford University Press, 2005), 131; Nancy Fraser, "Gender Equity and the Welfare State: A Postindustrial Thought Experiment," in *Democracy and Difference: Contesting the Boundaries of the Political*, ed. Seyla Benhabib (Princeton, NJ: Princeton University Press, 1996), 234. For an endorsement of the notion of "careful citizenship," see Ruth Lister, *Citizenship: Feminist Perspectives*, 2nd ed. (New York: New York University Press, 2003), 180. See also Blanca Rodríguez Ruiz, "Hacia un estado post-patriarcal: Feminismo y cuidadanía," *Revista de Estudios Políticos*, no. 149 (2010): 87–122.

[120] See Siobhán Mullally, "Migration, Gender, and the Limits of Rights," in *Human Rights and Immigration*, ed. Ruth Rubio-Marín (Oxford: Oxford University Press, 2014), 167. See also Helma Lutz, "Gender in the Migratory Profess," *Journal of Ethnic and Migration Studies* 36 (2001): 1647–63, at 1652.

family without entrenching gender stereotypes or gendered realities around the male breadwinner family model. In some decisions regarding spousal support or alimony after divorce, Germany's Federal Constitutional Court (FCC) has invalidated calculation systems that gave no monetary value to care work during marriage. Concretely, in 2002, the FCC abolished the method used to determine the amount of spousal support because, in calculating the achieved standard of living, it only took the breadwinner's income into account, splitting it into two. The alternative calculation method, endorsed by the court, used the wage of the caretaker spouse when reentering the labor market after divorce as a surrogate to monetize the value of the work of taking care of the family during marriage. It then added this amount to the breadwinner's income and divided it by two.[121] The new method, therefore, generally led to the breadwinner spouse having to pay a higher amount of spousal support after divorce, but it discouraged the reentry into the labor market of the primary caretaker, often, the wife. In 2008, there was a legislative reform adopting the principle of individual responsibility of the spouses to make a living after divorce. Fortunately, the new law was careful to retain the possibility of spousal support, though only for strictly enumerated grounds, including support for the raising of children, in case the dependent spouse does not find appropriate employment immediately after divorce or if the income from postdivorce employment is not sufficient to fully support living costs. Even so, it is questionable that the reform fully takes into account the many ways in which the breadwinner family model is still privileged and the impact it has on women postdivorce.[122]

In light of this, perhaps it is time to think of a new constitutional agenda – of which there are only scattered but promising expressions – with elements that could include options as varied as articulating strong protections for safe motherhood and reproductive health but also directive principles compelling state powers to assume collective and communal responsibility for assisting with the management of dependence and

[121] See BVerfGE 105, 1, Feb. 5, 2002, relying on the basis of the constitutional protection of family life (article 6 [1] GG) in conjunction with the principle of sex equality (article 3 [2] GG).

[122] Indeed, legal incentives for the breadwinner model are still in place (e.g., tax splitting, free health care for the spouse), which, coupled with the fact that often no social security is linked to part-time and often precarious "minijobs" that women overwhelmingly have (i.e., to combine motherhood, caring, and paid employment), lead housewives to continue to face challenges after a divorce, when they find that their standard of living is no longer guaranteed.

care,[123] as well as incorporating the necessary recognition and protection of the multiple and varied forms of loving and caring families that exist, including de facto unions and monoparental families.[124] We could also think of the need to craft a new fundamental right to care as an essential dimension of human flourishing or to reasonable accommodations for the purpose of work/family life balance.[125] To this, we could add the possibility of having those constitutions that refer to citizens' duties explicitly incorporate the duty to care.[126]

An example of how this can be done stems, once more, from new constitutionalism. Under chapter 9, devoted to responsibilities, the

[123] In its section related to directive principles, policies, and obligations of the state, the Constitution of Nepal underscores in article 51(j) the importance of 1) the employment of single women; 2) their self-reliance; 3) the need to secure reproductive services and facilities; and 4) the economic evaluation of their work and contribution with regard to childcare and care for the family.

[124] Many Latin American constitutions explicitly provide nonmarital unions with a degree of protection equal to that of formalized marriages, partly in recognition of the traditionally high degree of incidence of such unions in the region (see article 68 of the 2008 Ecuadorian Constitution and article 64 [I] of the 2009 Bolivian Constitution), or refer to family forms in an open and fluid manner (see article 6.D.2 of the 2017 Political Constitution of Mexico City: "All structures, manifestations, and forms of familial community are recognized as having equal rights, wholly sustained by law and supported in their care tasks"). Some constitutions also make explicit reference to the need to protect a healthy and safe familial household regardless of social and economic conditions, as well as those responsible for it (see, for instance, article 40 of the 2008 Ecuador Constitution and article 64 [II] of the 2009 Bolivian Constitution). See also article 43 of the 1991 Colombian Constitution, making explicit reference to the protection of women heads of family.

[125] We can indeed find some incipient doctrinal attempts in this direction. We could mention a case in Spain where, in responding to a male plaintiff, the Constitutional Court endorsed the need to interpret legislation aimed at facilitating work/family life balance rigorously and expansively on the basis that such legislation is to be read as an expression of a duty to reasonable accommodation deriving from the prohibition of discrimination on the grounds of family responsibilities (read out from article 14, an open-ended, nondiscrimination provision) and in connection with the duty of parents to assist their children (covered by article 39.3, which, in theory, is a nonenforceable directive principle). See S.T.C., Mar. 14, 2011 (No. 26/2011).

[126] In a way, this would be an expansion of the constitutional provisions and case law that already empower women and children to enforce the recognition of paternity against the father's will, doing so by placing emphasis on care rather than biological parenting and expanding the duty of care also beyond the confines of biological parenthood. For an example of the former, see the Spanish Constitutional Court's decision S.T.C., Jan. 15, 1994 (No. 7/1994), a landmark decision on the recognition of paternity against the father's will, which grants high evidentiary value to the unjustified refusal of a man to have a DNA paternity test done in those cases where no other conclusive proof of paternity exists.

2008 Ecuadorian Constitution contains a provision (article 83) that lists the duties and obligations of all Ecuadorians. Together with duties such as abiding by and enforcing the constitution and the law (83.1) or defending the territorial integrity of Ecuador and its natural resources (83.3), it recognizes (83.16) the duty to "help, feed, educate and raise one's children," acknowledging this duty to be "a *joint responsibility of mothers and fathers, in equal proportion.*"[127] In article 333, the constitution then considers "unpaid work of self-sustenance and *care-giving*, carried out in the home" to be "recognized as productive work." Consistently, it also acknowledges the need for the state

> to strive towards a labor system that works in harmony with the needs for human *care-giving*, and that facilitates suitable services, infrastructure and work schedules; it shall, in particular, provide *services for child care*, care for persons with disabilities, and other services as needed for workers to be able to perform their labor activities; it shall furthermore foster the *joint responsibility and reciprocity of men and women in domestic work and family obligations*. (Italics are ours)

It is further recognized that, in this system, "social service protection shall be progressively extended to persons who are responsible for unpaid family work at home."

Clearly, provisions such as these are framed in programmatic terms, but they are certainly reflective of a cultural shift, pointing to the need to both "degender" and "center" care. In doing so, they question the contours of spheres thus far defined as public and private and of the corresponding genders associated with them.[128] As a result, they disestablish gender as a constitutional endeavor. It is to the question of "degendering care" that we now turn to.

4.4 The New Constitutional Father?

We must celebrate when constitutions explicitly refer to positive motherhood rights as well as to fathers in their caring roles, as some have begun to do since the turn of the century. It is true that some older constitutional provisions already contained some undifferentiated mention to

[127] See also article 18 of the 2015 Rwandan Constitution, recognizing the fact that "both parents have the right and duty to bring up their children."

[128] See Ruth Rubio-Marín, "The (Dis)establishment of Gender: Care and Gender Roles in the Family as a Constitutional Matter," *International Journal of Constitutional Law* 13, no. 4 (2015): 787–818, at 817.

parenthood.[129] Yet, only in more recent times, constitutions have been drafted in ways that render men's expected involvement in caretaking more explicit by making a direct reference to fatherhood and sometimes even elaborating quite thoroughly on the vision of an egalitarian family structure.[130] Interesting is also the new language used to refer not only to equal rights but also to equal opportunities within marriage, endorsing a substantive equality rhetoric in the family domain.[131]

[129] See, for instance, article 6 (2) of the 1949 German Constitution ("The care and upbringing of children is the natural right of parents and a duty primarily incumbent upon them. The state shall watch over them in the performance of this duty") and article 47 (1) of the 1991 Bulgarian Constitution ("The raising and upbringing of children until they come of legal age shall be a right and obligation of their parents and shall be assisted by the State").

[130] See the 1999 Venezuelan Constitution's articles 75 ("The State shall protect families as a natural association in society, and as the fundamental space for the overall development of persons. Family relationships are based on equality of rights and duties, solidarity, common effort, mutual understanding and reciprocal respect among family members. The State guarantees protection to the mother, father or other person acting as head of a household") and 76 ("Motherhood and fatherhood are fully protected, whatever the marital status of the mother or father. Couples have the right to decide freely and responsibly how many children they wish to conceive and are entitled to access to the information and means necessary to guarantee the exercise of this right. The State guarantees overall assistance and protection for motherhood, in general, from the moment of conception, throughout pregnancy, delivery and the puerperal period, and guarantees full family planning services based on ethical and scientific values"). See also article 69 of the 1991 Colombian Constitution: (1) *Responsible motherhood and fatherhood* shall be fostered; and the mother and father shall be obliged to take care, raise, educate, feed, and provide for the integral development and protection of the rights of their children, especially when they are separated from them for any reason ... (5) The state shall promote the *joint responsibility of both mother and father* and shall monitor fulfillment of the *mutual duties and rights* between mothers, fathers, and children (italics are ours); article 64.1 of the 2009 Bolivian Constitution; and article 68 of the Portuguese Constitution as revised in 1992 ("1. In performing their irreplaceable role in relation to their children, particularly as regards the children's education, fathers and mothers have the right to protection by society and the state, together with the guarantee of their own professional fulfilment and participation in civic life. 2. Motherhood and fatherhood constitute eminent social values. 3. Women have the right to special protection during pregnancy and following childbirth, and working women also have the right to an adequate period of leave from work without loss of remuneration or any privileges. 4. The law shall regulate the attribution to mothers and fathers of rights to an adequate period of leave from work, in accordance with the interests of the child and the needs of the household").

[131] See article 62 in the 2009 Bolivian Constitution ("The State recognizes and protects the *family* as the fundamental nucleus of society, and guarantees the social and economic conditions necessary for its full development. Every member has *equal rights, obligations and opportunities*" [italics are ours]).

Constitutional conversations around the need to rethink caretaking and accommodate a new vision of fatherhood, however, have not been limited to new constitutionalism. In older constitutional democracies, these debates have also come to the fore at the turn of the century, hand in hand with the flourishing of claims and policies to ensure a more equal sharing of care obligations and a better work and family life balance for all. These measures, mostly expressed in legislative agendas, include paid family- and care-related leaves; paternity leaves; longer gender-neutral parental leaves; and specific mechanisms to encourage men to take such leaves, including by making them nontransferable. Progress has been slow in this regard, and, if we take the example of paternity/maternity leaves, we come to the realization that, where they do exist, paternity leaves are, for the most part, still optional or much shorter than maternity leaves. The idea that men's role in care and parenting, while increasingly important, is still subsidiary to women's, remains dominant. The conflation of pregnancy, labor, breastfeeding, and upbringing into one single and all-embracing concept – namely, that of motherhood – has generally made it difficult in most jurisdictions to disentangle the different tasks and functions involved, even though the proliferation of diverse forms of parenting (e.g., through adoption, but also via artificial reproductive technologies) and the gradual overcoming of gender codes are inevitably pushing in this direction. Needless to say, in some countries, policies seeking transformation are being gradually adopted without any constitutional involvement, including in many of the Northern European countries that have been at the vanguard in pushing the agenda of state and male involvement in the provision of care, countries that, for the most part, lack a strong rights-based constitutional tradition.[132] Nevertheless, in other countries, the agenda has indeed triggered constitutional contestation, often in the direction of supporting change but occasionally also to resist transformation.

In consolidated constitutional democracies, one can indeed identify some ongoing debates about the need to undertake constitutional amendments that would allow to duly recognize the centrality of care, the social relevance of reproductive work, and the need to overcome old

[132] Regarding parental leaves, Norway was the first country in the world to adopt a "daddy's quota" in 1993, and Iceland is famous for its equally shared parental leave, out of which an equal share is mandatory for men. For a quick overview, see Ingólfur V. Gíslason and Guðný Björk Eydal, eds., *Parental Leave, Childcare and Gender Equality in the Nordic Countries* (Copenhagen: Nordic Council of Ministers, 2011).

notions of women's citizenship built primarily around them. In Ireland, for instance, where a true constitutional gender revolution has taken place in recent years after two referenda – one in 2015 and another in 2018 – that introduced constitutional amendments to the old 1937 constitution to legalize same-sex marriage and abortion, there have also been fascinating debates about the future of article 41 of the constitution. Probably one of the most explicit remaining constitutional expressions of the old breadwinner family model in the Western world, the provision states that "the State recognises that by her life within the home, woman gives to the State a support without which the common good cannot be achieved" and shall therefore "endeavour to ensure that mothers shall not be obliged by economic necessity to engage in labour to the neglect of their duties in the home."[133] There have been fairly recent and, as of yet, unresolved discussions as to whether this provision should be entirely removed or, as was overwhelmingly supported by a participatory constitutional convention in 2013, kept but rendered gender neutral and include within it a reference to care beyond the home to underscore the central importance of care for social reproduction.[134]

More frequent than constitutional amendments (which would seem particularly challenging in federal systems in which family matters are often devolved to the subnational level)[135] are new constitutional interpretations that are being tried to challenge both the remaining gender-based and care-related explicit differentiations, as well as formally gender-neutral legal rules that still shape interpersonal relations and care

[133] Similar provisions are to be found elsewhere. See, for instance, article XIII, section 14 of the 1987 Philippine Constitution, referring to the need to "protect working women by providing safe and healthful working conditions, taking into account their maternal functions, and such facilities and opportunities that will enhance their welfare and enable them to realize their full potential in the service of the nation."

[134] See Silvia Suteu, "Women and Participatory Constitution-Making," in Irving, *Constitutions and Gender*, 31. But see Oran Doyle, *The Constitution of Ireland: A Contextual Analysis* (Oxford: Hart Publishing, 2018), 205, arguing that this provision has effectively fallen into desuetude.

[135] Although in some jurisdictions, including Australia (see section 51 [xxi] and [xxii]), it is the federal legislature that has been given power to regulate family law, it has been argued that federal arrangements often leave the traditional spheres of welfare, health, and family matters outside what is considered the "national" domain and that this taxonomy often places women "outside the discursive sphere of the constitutional community" and confines their interests and needs to the local. See Irving, *Gender and the Constitution*, 69, 74. See also Resnik, "Reconstructing Equality," 393; and Jill Vickers, "'Gendering' Federal Constitutions,'" in Irving, *Constitutions and Gender*, 188.

assumptions in ways that entrench traditional gender roles. Let us briefly examine both moves.

4.4.1 *Removing the Remaining Sex-Based, Care-Related Differentiations*

Since formal distinctions in parental access to care leaves are still found in most legal systems and can, arguably, no longer be considered indisputably "objectively justified" – at least to the extent that they go beyond the strictly necessary time for the mother's natural physical recovery after childbirth or to accommodate natural breastfeeding – they are providing fruitful battleground. By way of example, we can cite the case of Italy, where, despite its 1949 constitution's explicit sanctioning of the importance of motherhood duties within the family, we find a series of cases agreeing to the extension of legislative maternity leaves to fathers. This has been implemented since the late 1980s and early 1990s and has relied on a joint reading of the sex equality principle in article 3 and the recognition of spousal equality in marriage in article 29. This move has required abandoning the distinction between these articles, a distinction the Italian Constitutional Court had previously sustained to argue that, with respect to family matters, the relevant provision was article 29 rather than article 3. For the court, the first concerned women's equality *within the family entity* and had its own specific logic (a logic that sometimes justified giving preference to what were considered "family interests," such as the principle of family unity), while the second concerned women's equality as individuals *within society*.[136]

In recent years, this hermeneutic shift, abandoning family exceptionalism, has allowed the Italian Constitutional Court to move past an exclusive focus on motherhood and to consider the parent–child relationship beyond the rigid focus on traditional gender roles.[137] As a result,

[136] See Sentenza 126/1968 (Dec. 16, 1968) and Sentenza 147/1969 (Nov. 27, 1969), both dealing with regulations on adultery that allocated a distinctive treatment to the adulterous wife. This public/private separation, which hides the interrelationship between the societal and the familial spheres, persisted until the court started to address the issue of caring needs of working parents. It is at this point that we see that the boundaries between public and private begin to blur and that the court starts resolving cases by relying on articles 3 and 29 jointly (see Sentenza 341/1991 [July 11, 1991], Sentenza 179/1993 [Apr. 2, 1993], and Sentenza 385/2005 [Oct. 11, 2005]).

[137] See Sentenza 1/1987 (Jan. 14, 1987), establishing a right to paid paternity leave and paid daily rest for biological fathers employed as dependent workers in case of death or

fathers have increasingly benefited from the extended rights and obligations established by the constitution for parents in general.[138] Nevertheless, full equality between mothers and fathers has not yet been achieved: the legislator has not provided for it and the Italian Constitutional Court has not deemed this to be problematic so far.[139] Thus, although in almost every instance the court has agreed to the extension of maternity leaves to plaintiff fathers, sometimes even explicitly referring to changing perceptions around gender roles,[140] in all instances, fathers have been allowed to access work benefits related to childcare in case of adoption/foster parenthood or when natural working mothers either renounced or were unable to enjoy them. This is a distinction that the Constitutional Court has been willing to justify based on the need to protect the mother's health and her presence during the first year of the child (literally referring to "the call of nature"), and – in

serious illness of the dependent working mother, arguing that nonextension would amount to discrimination against working fathers and those minor children who can only rely on their fathers' care.

[138] Following the jurisprudential line of Sentenza 1/1987 (Jan. 14, 1987), see also Sentenza 341/1991 (July 11, 1991), which included foster fathers among those dependent workers who were allowed access to paid paternity leave; Sentenza 179/1993 (Apr. 2, 1993), extending the scope of the right to paid daily rest for biological fathers employed as dependent workers beyond the cases of widowhood or serious illness of the mother, as envisaged by Sentenza 1/1987, to include all situations where the mother or dependent worker had renounced to her own right to paid daily rest; and Sentenza 385/2005 (Oct. 11, 2005), recognizing fathers who are freelance workers the right to paid paternity leave as an alternative to freelance mothers, provided that the latter have renounced this right. See also Sentenza 105/2018 (Apr. 11, 2018), confirming this doctrine.

[139] Indeed, a close reading of the court's case law shows a narrative that foregrounds the principle of the best interest of the child much more than gender equality and interprets preferential access to the mother in the first months of life as justified by such interest. This is particularly visible in Sentenza 341/1991, Sentenza 179/1993, and Sentenza 385/2005. This is also true in jurisdictions like Colombia, where the right to a paternity leave has been recognized as part of the fundamental right to the child (article 44) to receive adequate care and love and to create a relation with both their parents, and as a manifestation of the fundamental right to create a family (article 42), yet without the need to fully equalize maternity and paternity leaves. See Corte Constitucional [C.C.] [Constitutional Court], marzo 14, 2019, Sentencia T-114/2019.

[140] See, for instance, Sentenza 179/1993 (Apr. 2, 1993), literally stating that "while not overlooking the social function of maternity, the prevailing interest of the child has acquired more and more importance and – moving past a rigid view on the different roles of parents and of the absolute priority of the mother – equal rights and obligations have been recognized to both spouses, together with their mutual integration in the care and psychophysical upbringing of their child" (§ 3) (our translation).

relation to the latter – on the best interest of the child.[141] The claim to simply allow partners to jointly decide who should enjoy the bulk of maternity leave in case of childbirth has not been accepted, not even on grounds of sex equality.[142]

Although, in recent years, many states have reformed their parental leaves system with the aim of increasing men's uses thereof (including by raising pay levels and adopting both mandatory paternity leaves and nontransferable periods of parental leave), full equalization between paternity and maternity leaves – with the narrow exception of what would be biologically justified – is a battle that has seldom been legislatively conquered and never constitutionally won so far, including in those jurisdictions that have embraced quite an articulate argumentative narrative supporting the idea of "the new father" in its case law. This is certainly the case of the Colombian Constitutional Court, which in 2003, when invalidating the terms of a newly established paternity leave (which the law had made conditional on the father either being married or able to demonstrate two years of cohabitation with the mother), made explicit reference to "the 'masculine revolution' of the end of the millennium"; "a new generation of fathers who have discovered that they can get involved in their children's upbringing, just as mothers do, without damage to their virility"; and an "emerging model of 'committed fatherhood' characterized by the elements of responsibility, emotional nurturing, physical accessibility and material support."[143] But the claims of caretaking – or, at least, intended caretaking – for fathers are certainly being pushed constitutionally in more and more jurisdictions. And, in countries such as Spain, with a long tradition of cases in which benefits and accommodations reserved for women had been justified as positive measures to assist women in the labor market along the maternalist

[141] See Sentenza 150/1994 (Apr. 14, 1994), upholding the exclusion of working fathers married to women business owners from six-months' maternity leave, which women business owners did not enjoy either, even though the husbands of women who were dependent workers, as well as women dependent workers themselves, were assigned such leave.

[142] See Sentenza 285/2010 (July 20, 2010).

[143] Corte Constitucional [C.C.] [Constitutional Court], abril 1, 2003, Sentencia C-273-03, (Colom.). Later related case law includes Corte Constitucional [C.C.] [Constitutional Court], marzo 18, 2009, Sentencia C-174/09; septiembre 22, 2009, Sentencia C-663/09; and mayo 24, 2012, Sentencia C-383/12.

accommodationist model,[144] dissenting voices on the bench supported the view that only strictly biological differences, and not traditional caretaking roles, deserved to be accommodated and endorsed egalitarian parental leaves that have since been legislatively adopted.[145]

Be that as it may, litigations pushing for an increased equalization of fathers' care rights raise the question as to who exactly the affected rights holders are. This is probably one of the reasons why courts so promptly appeal to the interests of the child as a relevant and undisputable parameter (although they can barely refrain from endorsing in a more or less explicit way one or another view on gender relations when interpreting what is actually in the best interest of a child). Arguably, in those regimes that have opted for the rule of strict gender neutrality and a perfectly symmetrical approach to the antidiscrimination ban, distinctions that disadvantage the father can more easily be said to amount to sex-based discrimination. Instead, those regimes that have

[144] See, for instance, the Spanish Constitutional Court's decisions S.T.C., Mar. 25, 1993 (No. 109/1993), and S.T.C., June 14, 1993 (No. 187/1993). In both cases, male workers claimed sex discrimination because the Labor Code (which was subsequently reformed to include men under the influence of European Court of Justice case law) only allowed women, and not men, to adjust their working schedule to feed a newborn, either naturally or artificially. And, in both cases, the court denied plaintiffs their claims on the grounds that the norm had been adopted to compensate for women's unfavorable situation in the labor market, in view of statistics that showed that women have more difficulty working after children are born than men do. The majority decision was not completely impervious to this but claimed that the statute dealt with employment relations and was not concerned with the organization of the family or the sharing of responsibilities between mother and father.

[145] See dissenting opinion by Judge María Luisa Balaguer Callejón in the Spanish Constitutional Court's decision S.T.C., Oct. 29, 2018 (No. 117/2018). The appellants included an organization explicitly devoted to the cause of fathers' rights. In the decision, Balaguer Callejón, a feminist constitutional scholar, argued that a system of 16 weeks' permit for the mother and 13 days' permit for the father, valid at the time, had a discriminatory impact on women's employment opportunities as well as on the need to protect the bond between fathers and their descendants. See also S.T.C., May 19, 2011 (No. 75/2011), distinguishing between, on the one hand, maternity leaves – which the court sees as affirmative action-types of measures to protect female workers giving birth by enabling them to reconcile family life and employment without risk to health or of being subject to discrimination (and thus grounded on the Spanish Constitution's article 14, equality provision) – and, on the other, parental leaves in the case of adoption, which the court links to the duty of state powers to protect the family (article 39.1), failing to consider a father's parenthood rights, either under article 14 or 39, even though the questioned norm foresaw the possibility of the mother delegating the leave to the father, except for the mandatory period of leave (arguably the only distinction that can be justified on the grounds of ensuring the biological recovery of the mother).

opted for an asymmetrical/antisubordination approach have greater difficulty in accepting men's sex-based discrimination claims (given that men are not recognized to be a historically disadvantaged group). Thus, such regimes have been more prone to uphold the remaining distinctions as a way of validly compensating women for the enduring societal discrimination (since, statistically, women continue to devote more time to care and take available voluntary care leaves more often). In due course, however, unless distinctions are narrowly crafted, it is likely that these regimes will also start to strike them down for invalidly perpetuating care-related gender stereotypes that add to the disadvantages women encounter in accessing equal opportunities in the employment domain and beyond. And yet it would be possible to stick to an antisubordination/asymmetrical logic and still claim that men's deprivation of equal opportunities to care in fact represents one of the few possible genuine cases of sex/gender-based discrimination against men. This would need to be accompanied by the prior reevaluation of care and nurturing we discussed, as activities from which traditional and hegemonic models of masculinity have deprived men and that have, at best, so far been primarily conceptualized and treated, if not totally ignored, as burdens and employment-related impediments. Instead, the idea is that they would now be valued as an important dimension of human flourishing that both men and women should be able to enjoy. This interpretive shift will be facilitated if discrimination on the basis of family responsibilities or caretaking comes to be understood or even crafted as a constitutionally banned form of discrimination that can equally protect caretaking men and women.

4.4.2 Gender-Neutral Legal Orders Shaping Interpersonal Relations and Implicit Gender Role Assumptions

Removing the remaining sex-based differentiations that to this day survive in relation to care roles in legal systems, along with the help of a new constitutional doctrine willing to apply sex equality notions in new domains and ways, would only be the beginning of the endeavor of disestablishing care-related gender roles in the private sphere. In fact, no subversion of established gender roles will be complete unless it is accompanied by the recognition that even a formally gender-neutral legal order that no longer differentiates between men and women as mothers and fathers is insufficient to overcome the many gendered ways in which our legal systems shape interpersonal relations and the care assumptions on which they rest. What is also necessary is to go beyond formal equality in the so-called private sphere by abandoning the myth of state neutrality and piercing the veil of family privacy in order to craft sex egalitarian default presuppositions, free from normative motherhood and care stereotypes. Furthermore – and this too cannot be the task of constitutional law alone – it is also necessary to take into account that reproductive work must be given a higher consideration and that the rigid divide between productive and reproductive labor must be overcome.

In constitutional litigation, courts around the world have, for the longest time, resisted equality interpretations that required looking into the impact of formally gender-neutral rules in terms of the valuation and distribution patterns of care work they encouraged. Yet it is clear that such rules can be found in the most varied domains and include not only employment and social security norms but also norms on taxation, divorce, and alimony, just to name a few. The problem is that their joint effect in entrenching traditional gender norms can no longer be ignored, and whereas the notion of gender mainstreaming to which many contemporary democracies are committed to should render such effects visible and invite law reform, the question of whether there are any constitutional remedies to trigger such reform in case of inaction remains compelling. So far, the explicit or implicit reasoning to counter such attempts has too often been that it was not for the state to interfere in "freely negotiated" family arrangements, ignoring that in fact the formally neutral rules were de facto, not neutral, and rather favored certain family and care arrangements over others. More recently, we find examples of constitutional courts departing from prior precedent, if not to allow plaintiffs to produce the necessary changes, at least to avoid getting in the way of legislative reforms pushing in the right direction.

The evolution of the case law of the Federal Constitutional Court (FCC) in Germany in this respect is revealing. Since the beginning, the FCC had systematically defended the need for state neutrality in family affairs, a neutrality that, in fact, had overwhelmingly supported the breadwinner family model as a valid option. Take taxation law as an example.[146] Germany had traditionally had a cumulative taxing system for married couples bringing the income of both spouses together for taxation purposes. Due to Germany's progressive taxation, this system

[146] See Maria Wersig, "Overcoming the Gender Inequalities of Joint Taxation and Income Splitting: The Case of Germany," in *Challenging Gender Inequality in Tax Policy Making: Comparative Perspectives*, eds. Kim Brooks, Åsa Gunnarsson, Lisa Philipps, and Maria Wersig (Oxford: Hart Publishing, 2011), 213–34.

had disadvantaged both married couples and two-income earner families, which led the FCC to strike it down.[147] In its place, a "splitting" system was adopted, allowing the total earnings of the couple to be divided into two and the tax to be calculated by doubling the amount of tax due on half their joint income. This system made it unprofitable for both spouses to keep working unless they had similarly high incomes and, therefore, encouraged traditional family arrangements, with its "neutrality" being no more than an illusion.[148]

Although the German court has never rhetorically abandoned its commitment to state neutrality and the preservation of a couple's autonomy when it comes to internal family arrangements, its jurisprudence in the new millennium shows a greater awareness of the impossibility of strict neutrality and a greater willingness to foreground the constitutional mandate of gender equality within the family. As in Italy, this jurisprudential shift has been accompanied by the court building on the equality provisions (article 3 [2] and 3 [3]) and the antidiscrimination doctrine built around them, instead of relying, as before, on the family provision (article 6).[149] Interestingly, some of this new jurisprudence was triggered

[147] See BVerfGE 6, 55, Jan. 17, 1957. In fact, the explicit purpose of cumulative taxation dating back to the times of National Socialism had been to discourage wives from entering the labor market. See Blanca Rodríguez Ruíz and Ute Sacksofsky, "Gender in the German Constitution," in Baines and Rubio-Marín, *Gender of Constitutional Jurisprudence*, 163. A similar taxation system was also successfully challenged in Spain, see the Constitutional Court's decision S.T.C., Feb. 20, 1989 (No. 45/1989).

[148] Other formally neutral tax regulations with a disparate gender impact have been challenged in Germany as well as in many other jurisdictions, often with rather limited success. See, for instance, BVerfGE 47, 1, Oct. 11, 1977, denying income-earning mothers the right to tax deduction for childcare costs; Symes v. Canada, [1993] 4 S.C.R. 695 (Can.), an unsuccessful challenge of the denial to a business woman of the option of deducting childcare costs at the higher business expense rate rather than the ordinary rate; and Thibaudeau v. Canada, [1995] 2 S.C.R. 513 (Can.), an unsuccessful challenge of income-splitting provisions requiring the custodial mother to add child support payments to her taxable income while letting the divorced father treat them as deduction.

[149] This new jurisprudence builds heavily on gender discrimination cases, including on pension schemes because of child-raising periods and part-time work. See, for instance, BVerfGE 113, 1, Apr. 5, 2005 (occupational pension provision and statutory child-raising period); BVerfGE 121, 241, June 18, 2008 (pension for part-time civil servants); BVerfG, 1 BvR 1409/10, Apr. 28, 2011 (occupational pension scheme and omission of maternity protection). In these cases, the FCC looks at the roots of gender inequality and, relying on a contextual and substantive interpretation method, remarks on the gendered division of work and the lack of childcare facilities, among others, to explain why women often take a childcare break from work or work part-time and how rules that do not take this into account directly or indirectly disadvantage women. See Cara Röhner, *Ungleichheit und Verfassung. Vorschlag für eine relationale Rechtsanalyse*

by challenges to legislative measures that have been passed with the explicit purpose of subverting traditional family arrangements and encouraging fatherhood and parenting as care, and not just income earning. An illustrative example is a series of cases dealing with parental leave reform legislation adopted in 2006, altering the method for calculating the amount of parental allowance so as to encourage rotation between spouses in the taking of the leave. The new system came to be attacked by parents wanting to defend traditional gender roles by relying precisely on family privacy and state neutrality notions that the FCC had previously coined to the support of the breadwinner family model. Yet, this time, the court supported the validity of the legislation and interpreted the aim of overcoming traditional care roles as best serving the gender equality principle enshrined in the German Basic Law.[150]

It is not surprising that this doctrinal evolution challenging the hegemony of the breadwinner family model has come along with both a renewed commitment to gender equality, as applying also to family relations, and a reevaluation of the father figure in terms of care expectations. Until the 1980s, the court had validated assumptions about men playing only a secondary role in child-rearing in a series of decisions concerning the rights of fathers in relation to their natural children, which seemed to rest on the idea that the father's connection to the children was built only indirectly through his relationship to the children's mother.[151] But this, too, began to gradually change in the 1990s,[152]

(Weilerswist: Velbrück Wissenschaft, 2019), 161ff, on gender equality in German constitutional law, and especially 210ff, on indirect sex discrimination, pension schemes, and family work.

150 See BVerfG, 1 BvR 2712/09, June 6, 2011. See also BVerfG, 1 BvR 1853/11, Nov. 9, 2011; and BVerfG, 1 BvL 15/11, Aug. 19, 2011.

151 See, for all, BVerfGE 56, 363, Mar. 24, 1981. In these cases, the FCC had upheld the then existing legislation granting mothers exclusive custody of children born out of wedlock, even when the mother and father lived together and wished to share their children's custody. In doing so, the court had underscored the importance of the tie that is formed between mother and child from birth and the need to avoid disharmony by granting fathers entitlements that they can exercise against the mothers' wishes. At the time, none of this was seen as contrary to the gender equality provision (article 3 [2] GG), even though the underlying assumption seemed to be that a father's attachment to his children was built only indirectly through his relationship with the children's mother. The FCC repeated its opinion in 2003 (see BVerfGE 107, 150; and BVerfG, 1 BvL 20/99, Jan. 29, 2003) overruled by the European Court of Human Rights's decisión in Zaunegger v. Germany, App. No. 22028/04, 50 Eur. Ct. H.R. Rep. 38 (2010).

152 See, for instance, BVerfGE 84, 168, May 7, 1991, when the FCC confirmed that, as a general rule, single mothers must be granted the exclusive custody of their children, but

when the central role of fatherhood – both for the individual man and for the welfare of the child – came to be acknowledged.[153]

Overall, while the described transformations are to be welcomed as having a clear emancipatory potential for both men and women, some important caveats should be added in line with the insights discussed in Section 2.2 of Chapter 2 concerning the need to adequately share the costs of transitions toward more egalitarian systems so as to not further curtail the life project of those who were already most disadvantaged under the discriminatory regime that is being left behind. More concretely, this truly transformative project relies both on the reassessment of caring and being cared for as a universal primary good and of the greater collective assumption of care needs. However, given the current gender-biased caring patterns and the insufficient public involvement in social reproduction, which entail serious socioeconomic disadvantages for women, it is important that changes be introduced in such a way that men who have not opted for a care-centered approach to fatherhood so far are not unduly rewarded through forward-looking norms that encourage new understandings of fatherhood to the detriment of those

that joint custody between mother and father should be allowed when both mother and father wished to embrace this solution.

153 See, for instance, BVerfGE 114, 357, Oct. 25, 2005. See also Fraser v. Children's Court, Pretoria North and Others 1997 (2) SA 261 (CC) (S. Afr.), striking down the constitutionality of a provision of a childcare act that did not require the consent of the father to give up a child for adoption when the child was born outside of marriage and without taking into account any other circumstances, such as the age of the child or the relationship developed between the father and the child. It has also been observed that a limited fatherly responsibility for children born out of wedlock can also overburden the mother with care and financial responsibilities. See, for instance, the Indonesian Constitutional Court decision 46/PUU-VIII/2010, para. 3.13, providing constitutionally conform interpretation of article 43 (1) of Indonesia's 1974 Marriage Law, which foresaw that children born out of wedlock only had a civil legal relationship with their mother and her family, to include also the father and his family by considering such provision unjust, given that both parents are responsible for the care of the child and that children born out of wedlock should not be denied support from their biological fathers. See also Trociuk v. British Columbia (Attorney General), [2003] 1 S.C.R. 835 (Can.), in which a man successfully invoked section 15 of the Canadian Charter (sex equality rights) to challenge legislation that protected a birth mother from being forced to acknowledge a biological father on the birth registration form and to include his surname in the child's surname. This decision was, however, constructed on the basis of men's discrimination on the grounds of sex and was controversial because many saw it as disadvantaging the many mothers and would-be mothers who deliberately choose to be single mothers – something that suggests that it is important to place all of these decisions in their adequate sociocultural contexts.

women who have so far primarily devoted themselves to caretaking, often at the expense of forgoing or severely limiting their already scarce employment opportunities. Cultural transformations, as we have seen, create transition dilemmas and invite necessary reflections about the role of constitutional actors and the societal conditions that must be observed for them to reflect or propel emancipatory change in fair processes. This, in turn, might require a dialogue between courts and legislators as to how to best live up to updated readings of gender equality norms but also for courts to think of the risks that the possibility of leveling down may entail, especially when idealized notions of fatherhood are not sufficiently backed by empirically contrasted social evolutions.[154] It may also require that both courts and legislators think of the need for transitional or compensatory mechanisms to ensure the overall fairness of the transformation process. It certainly demands that the new concept of fatherhood that courts and legislators embrace is one that does not only foreground biological features but also caring functions[155] and that,

154 Raising these kinds of concerns, see, for instance, in Argentina, Corte Suprema de Justicia de la Nación [CSJN] [National Supreme Court of Justice], 24/09/2020, "Puig. Fernando Rodolfo c/Minera Santa Cruz S.A. s/ Despido," Fallos de la Corte Suprema de la Nación, t. 343, 1037 (Arg.), holding that a legal provision establishing the presumption that dismissing women without justification within six months of contracting marriage should be interpreted equally for newly-wed men. This decision recognized that – although this special protection was historically connected to women because they were expected to take care of children and the household, in a context in which new sociocultural paradigms push in the direction of equal assumptions of family responsibilities by husband and wife – this legal provision must now be interpreted as also encompassing men in order to duly protect the institutions of family and marriage. Note that an emphasis on discrimination, rather than an updated reading of what the protection of modern families and marriages require, could instead have led to striking such provision altogether.

155 See, for Mexico, Amparo directo en revisión 2252/2013, Suprema Corte de Justicia de la Nación [SCJN], diciembre 4, 2013, Semanario Judicial de la Federación y su Gaceta, Décima Época, Libro 3, febrero 2014, Tomo I, Tesis 1a. LXIV/2014 (10a.), 1a. LXVI/2014 (10a.), and 1a. LXV/2014 (10a.), páginas 654–55, 657–58, 659–60, respectively, where the court endorses the need to interpret the Civil Code norms on custody free of gender stereotypes and grants custody to the father, who had been the primary caretaker. Similarly, on granting custody to the mother by default as being discriminatory, see Amparo en revisión 331/2019, Suprema Corte de Justicia de la Nación [SCJN], 21 de noviembre de 2019, Semanario Judicial de la Federación y su Gaceta, Décima Época, Libro 77, agosto 2020, Tomo IV, Tesis 1a. XV/2020 (10A.), páginas 3051–53. See, for Colombia, Corte Constitucional [C.C.] [Constitutional Court], abril 13, 2005, Sentencia SU389/05, and noviembre 5, 2003, Sentencia C-1039/03, striking down legislation to protect mothers, but not fathers, in single-headed households with no other source of income from being fired from their employment.

therefore, is flexible enough to accommodate varying and fluid family formations and the more gender stereotype–free and fragmented fatherhood and parenting roles that the high divorce rates, the reliance on artificial reproductive technologies, and the parenting claims of homosexual and transsexual citizens are bringing about.[156] No better context than the one provided by the COVID-19 pandemic to show the urgency of unearthing the importance of care in contemporary societies but also the ways in which it mostly rests on women and other marginalized groups. Unfortunately, whereas some data show fathers' greater involvement in caretaking during lockdown and pandemic times raising hopeful prospects for transformation, they do not seem to outweigh the data pointing to a massive loss of female employment and a threatening return of women in many societies to their traditional roles as mothers and caretakers.[157]

[156] See Richard Collier and Sally Sheldon, *Fragmenting Fatherhood: A Socio-Legal Study* (Oxford: Hart Publishing, 2008); Nancy E. Dowd, *Redefining Fatherhood* (New York: New York University Press, 2000); Alice Margaria, *The Construction of Fatherhood: The Jurisprudence of the European Court of Human Rights* (New York, NY: Cambridge University Press, 2019). For a decision affirming the figure of the "social father" over narrow conceptions of biological fatherhood, see Tribunal Constitucional [T.C.] [Constitutional Court], Nov. 30, 2007, file no. 09332-2006-PA/TC (Peru), upholding the claims of a man who had been denied a club's membership card for "his daughter" (actually, his wife's biological daughter) because the club considered that she was not a consanguineous daughter and explicitly recognizing that families are institutions that are subject to new social contexts, can adopt different forms, and should be respected for their differences.

[157] See Alice Margaria, "Fathers, Childcare and COVID-19," *Feminist Legal Studies* 29, no. 1 (2021): 133–44, https://doi.org/10.1007/s10691-021-09454-6.

5

Toward a Constitutional Gender Erasure or a Constitutional Gender Reaffirmation?

5.1 Gender Constitutionalism in the New Millennium

During the last decade, we have been witnessing a true "gender war," with thousands of citizens around the world taking to the streets to either celebrate or protest against newly sought or achieved milestones in the conquest of rights for women and sexual minorities. Examples from various geographies abound. On December 30, 2020, thousands of women flooded the streets of Buenos Aires to celebrate abortion legalization in the country, just a few weeks before the passing of a constitutional reform in Honduras on January 27, 2021, which amended its constitution to ban abortion and same-sex marriage. At the same time, since October 2020 and up to the time of writing, the Women's Strikes movement – a movement that took inspiration from the 1975 women's strike in Iceland, which encouraged women to stop cooking, cleaning, and caretaking for one full day – is inviting women in Poland, who have been joined by other workers' groups as varied as taxi drivers, farmers, and coal miners, to massively take to the streets and protest against a Constitutional Court decision banning abortion in the case of severe malformation of the fetus (the main reason for abortion in an overwhelmingly Catholic country). The decision, now under challenge before the European Court of Human Rights, understandably infuriated many Polish women, including those who, on the Black Monday of October 3, 2016, had successfully mobilized to strike against abortion bans that were being considered by the right-wing governing party at the time and that now seem to have been achieved via the intervention of a court with doubtful judicial independence. This was not the only battle on gender politics fiercely fought for on the ground. Less than three years before the Polish Black Monday, on January 13, 2013, hundreds of thousands had taken to the streets of Paris in a call by La Manif Pour Tous against the legalization of same-sex marriage (*marriage pour tous*), a legalization that finally took place on May 18, 2013, when France became the thirteenth country worldwide to allow same-sex couples to marry. And, on March 22, 2015, the Republic of Ireland voted overwhelmingly to legalize same-sex marriage in a historic referendum, with more than 62 percent of the population (with majorities in every constituency but one) voting in favor of amending the country's constitution to allow gay and lesbian couples to marry. This vote foreshadowed, by an even larger majority, another referendum that took place on May 25, 2018, when 66.4 percent of the population decided to overturn the abortion ban in the country by repealing the Eighth Amendment of the Constitution granting an equal right to the life of the mother and the unborn. Both of these processes were preceded by deliberative democracy initiatives.

The expansion at the turn of the century of family and marital forms, as well as marriage beyond heterosexual unions, seems to lie at the heart of an increasing politicization and social polarization around gender politics in the new millennium. Many mostly right-wing, religiously imbued, and conservative forces deplore the changes and see in them the paramount expression of the dissolution of the "traditional" family, whereas others celebrate them as a key tenet of the democratization of the family. Strictly speaking, the expansion of the right to marriage and parenthood of gay and lesbian persons can be considered belated key achievements of inclusive gender constitutionalism crucial for the equal citizenship of sexual minorities. Undeniably, it is also connected to the transformation of the family ethos and the traditional gender order within the family, and thus to transformative gender constitutionalism.

In historical terms, the first equality claims of LGBT+ were, in fact, expressed at the same time as second-wave feminism was triggering women's inclusive constitutionalism, both feeding off the sexual revolution of the 1960s. Rising out of the Stonewall Riots of June 1969, the contemporary LGBTQI+ movement was born as a spontaneous and bottom-up initiative that, besides reappropriating the image of LGBT+ people, sought tolerance, decriminalization, and protection in a plurality of areas, spanning from protection from discrimination to the depathologization of homosexuality (which was eventually removed from the list of mental illnesses by the American Psychiatric Association in 1973). As of the 1980s, the radical and sexual liberation demands that were so central in the first phase of the movement began to tone down, and social integration and participation in society at large began to be encouraged.[1]

[1] See Omar Encarnación, *Out in the Periphery: Latin America's Gay Rights Revolution* (Oxford: Oxford University Press, 2016), 18–28.

This approach soon led to demands for marriage equality, which can be traced back to the late 1980s and early 1990s. Originally emerging in Northern Europe, they quickly spread to the rest of the continent and to North America, and from there, to selected areas of the Global South. Clear and concrete results began to appear after the turn of the century.

The demand for same-sex marriage is inextricably linked to the previous revolution in the understanding of heterosexual marriage and the gender order established around it. As Stephanie Coontz explains, several factors account for this, some going way back in time. For one thing, the availability of birth control mechanisms since the late 1960s produced a growing number of childless marriages. This, in turn, weakened the link between marriage and parenthood and challenged some of the old justifications for both privileging marriage over all other relationships and limiting it to heterosexual couples.[2] At the same time, the expansion of the rights of nonmarital children and unwed mothers in the 1960s and 1970s also "stripped marriage of a role it had played for thousands of years and weakened its hold on people's political and economic rights and obligations."[3] All in all, by the late 1970s, these trends, together with women's growing presence in the labor market and the increase in the number of dual-earner marriages, translated into a fundamental transformation of people's ways of conceiving personal relationships. Love, self-fulfillment, intimacy, support, and emotional gratification came to be foregrounded when thinking of stable, potentially lifelong partnerships, and it did so at the expense of conformity to social roles. In this context of enhanced personal autonomy, the acceptance of singlehood, unmarried cohabitation, childlessness, divorce, and out-of-wedlock childbearing increased in the Western world and elsewhere,[4] making marriage "lose its power to organize sexual behavior, living arrangements, and child rearing."[5]

The link between the radical transformation in the understanding of heterosexual marriage and the appearance of the demand for same-sex marriage helps explain why those opposing gay marriage to this very day include not only religious sectors of society but, more generally, cultural traditionalists simply regretting the loss of the nuclear, heterosexual,

[2] Stephanie Coontz, *Marriage, a History: How Love Conquered Marriage* (New York: Penguin Books, 2006), 255.

[3] Ibid., 257.

[4] Ibid., 258.

[5] Ibid., 262.

marital family.[6] After all, it was heterosexuals who, by creating many competing structures for organizing intimacy, sexuality, and the upbringing of children, eroded the cultural hegemony of the breadwinner family model and the strict division of labor between men and women on which it rested.[7] And if divorce, single parenthood, and cohabitation among heterosexuals had already stirred the foundations of the marital institution, it was the reproductive revolution linked to artificial reproduction technology that ended up "shak[ing] up all the relationships once taken for granted between sex, marriage, conception, childbirth, and parenting."[8] "People who could not become parents before can now do so in such bewildering combinations that a child can potentially have five different parents: a sperm donor, an egg donor, a birth mother, and the social father and mother who raise the child."[9] New technologies are also currently available for married people who want to avoid having children altogether while we also witness an ongoing explosion of solitary living in all industrial countries.[10] This is the context in which the global trend toward the adoption of laws recognizing civil partnerships and same-sex unions in the form of marriages and domestic partnerships have taken place, granting same-sex couples many of the same legal rights married heterosexuals have enjoyed so far (including insurance benefits, inheritances, and other legal privileges).

Parallel to the gradual erosion of the heteronormative construction of the institutions of marriage and the family, the turn of the century has also witnessed the proliferation and deepening of the claims of trans and intersex persons. If the older claims of trans activists were first articulated in the 1950s and 1960s and concerned their ability to have their legally assigned sex/gender at birth changed so as to match their felt sex/gender, with the end of the century came the gradual problematization of the different conditions commonly set for the transition, including automatic divorce, prior sterilization or surgery of primary sexual characteristics,

[6] Ibid., 274. At the same time, there is a risk of foregrounding recognition politics to the detriment of redistributive agendas and, in particular, of economic right-wing politicians embracing a progressive social agenda while pursuing regressive economic policies. An example of this might be the United Kingdom, where the Conservative-led government introduced same-sex marriage in 2013 but at the same time has been pursuing a policy of economic austerity that has disproportionately harmed women.

[7] Ibid.

[8] Coontz, *Marriage, a History*, 275.

[9] Ibid., 277.

[10] Ibid.

hormone treatment, and certification of gender dysphoria. Since the 1990s, we have also observed the rejection of sex normalization surgeries of intersex children.[11] The new millennium is seeing additional claims come to the fore, such as the aspiration to be protected from all forms of discrimination (related to gender identity or sexual orientation), which recent constitutional texts explicitly grant for the first time.[12] Other claims include the right to have self-determination be the only legitimate guiding principle for gender/sex ascription as well as the challenge to binary and rigid sexual categories, all of which, some have started to predict, are possibly laying the ground for demands to be free from all forms of sex/gender categorizations[13] – or, in other words, the complete challenge of sex/gender as legal institutions. In sum, the turn of the century has seen the spark of a still incipient gender/sexual revolution that has come to question the very categories the gender apparatus has relied on, thus expanding in significant ways a gender agenda that has so far focused on challenging traditional gender roles, separate gendered spheres, and gender subordination.

The extent to which women's sexual and reproductive rights, but also same-sex marriage and the affirmation of the right of gender nonconforming individuals to define their own identity, have come to be perceived as a challenge to the traditional gender order – arguably a structural feature of society and the political community – accounts for the backlash and neoconservative reactions of the antigender movements across the world. The targets of antigender movements have indeed included LGBTQI+ and reproductive rights (such as contraception, abortion, and reproductive technologies) but also sex and gender education in schools, gender studies as an academic discipline, and the very concept of gender to explain the power dynamics behind violence against women. More recently, trans rights have also become the object

[11] See Morgan Carpenter, "The Human Rights of Intersex People: Addressing Harmful Practices and Rhetoric of Change," *Reproductive Health Matters* 24, no. 47 (2016): 74, 79. See also Markus Bauer, Daniela Truffer, and Daniela Crocetti, "Intersex Human Rights," *International Journal of Human Rights* 24, no. 6 (2019): 724–49.

[12] See, for instance, article 42 of the 2019 Constitution of Cuba; article. 4.C.2 of the 2017 Political Constitution of Mexico City; article 11.2 of the 2008 Constitution of Ecuador; and article 14.II of the 2009 Constitution of Bolivia.

[13] See Stefano Osella and Ruth Rubio-Marín, "The Right to Gender Recognition before the Colombian Constitutional Court: A Queer and *Travesti* Theory Analysis," *Bulletin of Latin American Research* 40, no. 5 (2021): 650–64; Stefano Osella, "'De-gendering' the Civil Status?: A Public Law Problem," *International Journal of Constitutional Law* 18, no. 2 (2020): 471–75.

of attacks, even in the context of opposition against other agendas that are seen as deeply interconnected.[14] These antigender movements are part of an "organized transnational – and increasingly global – phenomenon"[15] that appeared in the late 1990s in several European countries and elsewhere, particularly in Latin America, building on the preexisting infrastructure of earlier antiabortion groups in the United States and other countries. Yet its permeation into civil society is a phenomenon of the last decade. There has been an increasingly sophisticated opposition across the globe manifested in particularly efficient virulent fights and resistance by an alliance of far-right and religious actors joining forces and mobilizing in a struggle against what has come to be coined as "gender ideology" – a short term for everything that, since the 1990s, has challenged the traditional family and the gender order, fostering a populist wave of moral panic around the trope "Save Our Children." Let us take it in steps.

5.2 Constitutional Challenges to the Hegemony of the Heterosexual Marital Family

In 1993, the Supreme Court of Hawaii released its groundbreaking judgment, *Baehr v. Lewin*,[16] holding for the first time in the world that the denial of a marriage license to a same-sex couple amounted to a violation of equal protection under the state constitution. "The case was the result of a long-term legal, political and cultural battle for sexual orientation equality starting in the United States as early as the 1950s."[17] Although building on "piecemeal victories of LGBT movements, ranging

[14] Thus, in the 2015 Slovenian referendum campaign to entrench heterosexual marriage in the constitution, transgender people were objectified as the ultimate goal of gender ideologies. See David Paternotte and Roman Kuhar, "The Anti-gender Movement in Comparative Perspective," in *Anti-gender Campaigns in Europe: Mobilizing Against Equality*, eds. Roman Kuhar and David Patternote (London: Rowman and Littlefield International Ltd., 2017), 256. In Poland, the Church also claimed that gender-based protections, which were increasing in importance after the ratification of the Istanbul Convention, would have led to homosexuality and transsexuality. See Andrea Krizsán and Raluca Maria Popa, "Contesting Gender Equality in Domestic-Violence Policy Debates: Comparing Three Countries in Central and Eastern Europe," in *Varieties of Opposition to Gender Equality*, ed. Mieke Verloo (New York: Routledge, 2018), 98.

[15] See Kuhar and Paternotte, *Anti-gender Campaigns in Europe*, 253.

[16] Baehr v. Lewin, 74 Haw. 530, 852 P.2d 44 (1993).

[17] See Angioletta Sperti, *Constitutional Courts, Gay Rights and Sexual Orientation Equality* (Oxford: Hart Publishing, 2017), 1.

from decriminalisation of sexual acts, to family and parental rights, to the right to have relationships legalised, to social and workplace benefits,"[18] the decision still provoked an important backlash, "set[ting] off a firestorm of anti-gay legislation in other states and at the national level."[19] It would take more than a decade before other courts followed its guidelines in recognizing same-sex marriage as constitutionally required.

Given that most constitutions in the world contain provisions that refer to marriage and family life, whether in the form of a fundamental right to marry or by recognizing marriage and the family as institutions that the state is bound to protect, it is not surprising that the flourishing of nonmarital familial forms and the spread of claims by gays and lesbians to access the rights attached to marriage would become the source of significant constitutional controversy around the globe. Yet constitutional, supreme, or for that matter, human rights courts have, for the most part, not led the way in the recognition of equal marriage, despite having "played a key role in forging the legal debate over sexual equality," with every single achievement leading to "a further advancement towards sexual orientation equality."[20] Indeed, constitutional and supreme courts have often been called upon to react against, rather than to trigger, legislative agendas advanced by social and political forces seeking to disestablish family and marital heteronormativity. Initially, these agendas have been carried out through the recognition of same-sex partnerships but, since the turn of the century, they have also targeted the increasing recognition of same-sex marriage.[21]

[18] Ibid.

[19] See William N. Eskridge, Jr., "Backlash Politics: How Constitutional Litigation Has Advanced Marriage Equality in the United States," *Boston University Law Review* 93, no. 2 (2003): 275–323, at 284. See also Michael J. Klarman, *From the Closet to the Altar: Courts, Backlash, and the Struggle for Same-Sex Marriage* (Oxford: Oxford University Press, 2012).

[20] Sperti, *Constitutional Courts*, 1. Emblematic in this respect is the ECHR's gender jurisprudence: while it has been relatively proactive and leading the way in terms of trans rights, it stopped short of subverting the heteronormative framework of human rights it operates under, as epitomized by its enduring refusal to rule that the lack of same-sex marriage amounts to a violation of the European convention.

[21] As of Jan. 29, 2021, these include Argentina, Australia, Austria, Belgium, Brazil, Canada, Colombia, Costa Rica, Denmark, Ecuador, Finland, France, Germany, Iceland, Ireland, Luxembourg, Malta, the Netherlands, New Zealand, Norway, Portugal, South Africa, Spain, Sweden, Taiwan, the United Kingdom, the United States, and Uruguay. In Mexico, same-sex marriage is legal in only some state jurisdictions. See Pew Research Center, "Same-Sex Marriage Around the World," http://www.pewforum.org/2015/06/26/gay-marriage-around-the-world-2013/.

In the struggle around same-sex marriage recognition, constitutions have often been seized as reactionary tools in accordance with the central role played by the traditional gender order enshrined in them since the inception of constitutionalism. And, although the positions of constitutional and supreme courts around the world when confronting the question of gay marriage have varied, it is interesting to note that many have not necessarily taken the constitutional text as a decisive factor,[22] and only a few have deemed same-sex marriage to be constitutionally required. More often, high courts have been willing to require or at least accept that, under other more or less generic constitutional principles or provisions (including the right to free development of one's personality or the right to family life), same-sex unions be recognized as family and be awarded some form of legal status and that same-sex partners enjoy a more or less similar set of rights as persons in different heterosexual unions.[23] In so doing, however, some constitutional courts have been complacent with the legislative choice to consider that heterosexual couples and homosexual couples constitute two different classes and that therefore, constitutional equality does not mandate their equal access to marriage.

As we have seen, only some courts were willing to have their constitutions lead the way forward. After *Baehr v. Lewin* in 1993, it would be a decade before another US state supreme court endorsed a similar position.[24] At a national level, a clear landmark was the 2004 Canadian Supreme Court decision, *Reference re Same-Sex Marriage*,[25] affirming the legislative authority of the Parliament of Canada to regulate same-sex

[22] After all, most constitutions neither explicitly defined marriage nor explicitly mentioned sex or gender difference as a prerequisite for marriage, since the definition of marriage was usually found in civil codes, statutes, and judicial precedents. Some constitutions only referred to the institution of marriage emphasizing its narrow connection with the family, and as deserving constitutional protection. Other constitutional texts did not explicitly include the right to marriage and let courts derive it from other privacy or autonomy-related provisions. Yet other constitutions, following the text of international documents, stated that men and women have the right to marry and to found a family.

[23] See Sperti, *Constitutional Courts*, 49–76.

[24] In the United States, several state courts defended the option of same-sex marriage as constitutionally required, including those in Massachusetts [Goodridge v. Department of Public Health, 798 N.E.2d 941 (2003)], Iowa [Varnum v. Brien, 763 N.W.2d 862 (2009)], Connecticut [Kerrigan v. Commissioner of Public Health, 289 Conn. 135 (2008)], and California [In re Marriage Cases, 183 P.3d 384 (2008)].

[25] Reference re Same-Sex Marriage, [2004] S.C.C. 79, [2004] 3 S.C.R. 698.

marriage.[26] But only in 2005 do we find the first constitutional case at a national level recognizing a constitutionally grounded right to marriage in favor of same-sex couples. This was the Constitutional Court of South Africa's *Fourie* decision,[27] in which the court deemed the exclusion of same-sex stable relations from the institution of marriage an unfair discrimination act based on the sexual orientation of the type explicitly banned under section 9 (3) of the constitution, as well as a violation of the right to dignity (section 10). In doing so, the court essentially relied, among other considerations, on the fact that South Africa has a multitude of family formations that evolve in tandem with society and that it is therefore inappropriate to entrench any particular form of family as the only socially and legally acceptable one or else to rely on religious doctrine as a valid source for interpreting the constitution. Similarly, the court underscored the need to acknowledge the long history of marginalization and persecution of gays and lesbians and the country's constitutional commitment to radically breaking away from a past based on intolerance and exclusion. Marriage, the court considered, was a complex social institution that entailed a unique set of rights and responsibilities with material repercussions, but also an institution with intangible benefits that affected the right to self-definition in a most profound way.[28]

It would be another decade before the US Supreme Court delivered its landmark *Obergefell* decision on same-sex marriage on June 26, 2015,[29] granting certiorari against those states that refused to recognize marriage celebrated in other states of the Union and to include same-sex couples within the scope of marriage. This took place amid much preceding controversy among the LGBT community as to whether the time was ripe for strategic same-sex marriage litigation, which could otherwise backfire. Combining liberty and equality interests in a dignity-framed

[26] Although remaining silent as to same-sex marriage was required by section 15 (1) of the Canadian Charter of Rights and Freedoms, the decision has been acknowledged to have helped generate momentum for national legislative action to legalize same-sex marriage. See Kenji Yoshino and Michael Kavey, "Immodest Claims and Modest Contributions: Sexual Orientation in Comparative Constitutional Law," in *The Oxford Handbook of Comparative Constitutional Law*, eds. Michel Rosenfeld and András Sajó (Oxford: Oxford University Press, 2012), 1091.

[27] See Minister of Home Affairs and Another v. Fourie and Another 2006 (1) SA 524 (CC).

[28] Ibid., at par. 59, 65, 67, 68, 71, 72, and 98.

[29] Obergefell v. Hodges, 576 U.S. 644 (2015).

decision, *Obergefell* relied on a plurality of constitutional principles, including the due process clause and the equality clause enshrined in the Fourteenth Amendment of the US Constitution. In affirming same-sex marriage, the Supreme Court referred to marriage as an institution deeply connected to individual autonomy, one that uniquely dignifies individuals, safeguards children, and represents a keystone of the national legal order.[30] Marriage, the majority opinion delivered by Justice Kennedy held, was "the foundation of the family and society, without which there would be neither civilization nor progress."[31] And whereas "the stability which marriage gives is beneficial to society as a whole, such a stability does not know the difference between same-sex and different-sex couples."[32]

The words of the US Supreme Court would of course invite mixed reactions, including by many who celebrated the egalitarian outcome but regretted the romanticized and rather conservative picture of marriage endorsed by the court, which could be read as symbolically relegating nonmarital families as well as alternative forms of caregiving and resource-pooling relationships that do not try to replicate the traditional marital/sexual scheme.[33] Yet the trend began to spread across the continent, and, a year later, the Colombian Constitutional Court was one of the first courts in Latin America, along with Ecuador, to fully recognize – on the basis of dignity, liberty, and equality – the right to marry a person of one's choice, regardless of sex.[34] In 2017, in Asia, a continent where much of the constitutional litigation is still concerned with sodomy laws, Taiwan's Constitutional Court gave the legislator a two-year deadline to provide a legal basis to recognize same-sex marriage, something it finally did in 2019.[35]

[30] Ibid.

[31] Obergefell v. Hodges, 576 U.S. 669 (2015).

[32] Ibid.

[33] See Melissa Murray, "*Obergefell v. Hodges* and Nonmarriage Inequality," *California Law Review* 104, no. 5 (2016): 1207–58. In this regard, the Constitutional Court of South Africa's ruling has been praised for its critical approach to permit same-sex marriage without overglorifying marriage. See Holning Lau, "Marriage Equality and Family Diversity: Comparative Perspectives from the United States and South Africa," *Fordham Law Review* 85, no. 6 (2017): 2615–28.

[34] See Corte Constitucional [C.C.] [Constitutional Court], abril 28, 2016, Sentencia SU214/16.

[35] See Judicial Yuan [JY] [Constitutional Court], Interpretation No. 748 (May 24, 2017), decided on the basis of autonomy (article 22 of the constitution) and equality (article 7 of the constitution).

Courts relying on the constitution have very often relied on the premise that, if not marriage, same-sex couples deserved – or, short of that, could at least be awarded – a more or less equivalent and legally recognized status, as the examples of Brazil, Hungary, Germany, and Slovenia show.[36] Beyond this, some courts, including those in Belgium, Portugal, Mexico, Spain, and France, have validated same-sex legislation ex post[37] – sometimes, as in Portugal[38] and France,[39] after having previously rejected constitutionally grounded claims to be the first in

[36] See court decisions of Brazil, Supremo Tribunal Federal (S.T.F.) [Federal Supreme Court], Ação Direta de Inconstitucionalidade (ADI) [Direct Action of Unconstitutionality] No. 4277, Relator: Min. Ayres Britto, 05.05.2011, R.T.J. 219/212, recognizing that same-sex and heterosexual stable unions deserve the same treatment and thus opening the door to same-sex marriage, since the legal order allowed for stable unions to be transformed into marriage; Hungary, Alkotmánybíróság [AB] [Constitutional Court], 32/2010. (III. 25.), Alkotmánybíróság Határozatai (AK) [Official Gazette of the Constitutional Court], Mar. 2010, vol. XVIII, no. 3, holding that the introduction of an institution similar to marriage for same-sex couples is a duty of the state imposed by the constitution; Germany, BVerfGE 105, 313, July 17, 2002, arguing that the specific protection due to marriage under article 6 (1) of the German Basic Law does not prevent the legislature from providing rights and duties for same-sex civil partnerships that are equal or similar to those of marriage, later modified by BVerfGE 124, 199, July 7, 2009, implying in fact that the same treatment is required; and Slovenia, Constitutional Court decision U-I-425/06-10 from July 2, 2009 (Blažič and Kern v. Slovenia), striking down the differential treatment in inheritance law to the detriment of same-sex couples (translated text available at https://www.equalrightstrust.org/ertdocumentbank/Blazic%20and%20Kern%20v%20Slovenia.pdf).

[37] The Belgian, Portuguese, Mexican, Spanish, and French constitutional courts all struck down constitutional challenges against same-sex marriage after it had been legislatively enacted. See Belgian Cour Constitutionnelle [Constitutional Court], Oct. 20, 2004, n ° 159/2004, M.B., Oct. 29, 2004, p. 74279; Portuguese Tribunal Constitucional (TC) [Constitutional Court], Acórdão No. 121/2010, Diário da República n.° 82/2010, Série II de 2010-04-28; Mexican Suprema Corte de Justicia de la Nación [Supreme Court of Justice of the Nation], Acción de inconstitucionalidad 2/2010, Pleno de la Suprema Corte de Justicia [SCJN] Semanario Judicial de la Federación y su Gaceta, Novena Época, diciembre de 2010, Tomo XXXII, página 991; Spanish Constitutional Court, S.T.C. Nov. 6, 2012 (No. 198/2012); and French Conseil constitutionnel [CC] [Constitutional Council] decision No. 2013-669DC, May 17, 2013, J.O. 0114. This was also effectively the case in Northern Ireland (see Close [Grainne] and Shannon Sickles and Christopher Flanagan-Kane and Henry Flanagan-Kane's Application [2020] NICA [Civ] 20).

[38] See Tribunal Constitucional [TC] [Constitutional Court], Acórdão No. 359/2009, Diário da República n.° 214/2019, Série II de 2009-11-04.

[39] See Conseil constitutionnel [CC] [Constitutional Council] decision No. 2010-92QPC, Jan. 28, 2011, J.O. 004 (Fr.), holding that the legislator had the discretion to distinguish between homosexual and heterosexual couples or open the institution of marriage to same-sex couples because the constitution did not prohibit equal marriage, but also that same-sex marriage could not be introduced by means of judicial review of legislation.

granting same-sex rights absent legislative action. Others, like the Italian Constitutional Court, have arguably defended legislative discretion, even in the absence of legislation.[40] Only in exceptional cases, which include those of Germany,[41] Ireland (before the constitution was amended

[40] See Sentenza 138/2010 (Apr. 14, 2010), recognizing the right of persons to live freely in same-sex unions, understood as stable cohabitation between persons of the same sex, but leaving it to the discretion of the legislator to decide the time, modality, and limits of legal recognition and excluding the view that such recognition may be achieved only through same-sex marriage. That said, and especially in light of a later decision (Sentenza 170/2014, June 11, 2014), some authors have argued that, through an originalist interpretation of the constitution, the court tied heterosexuality and marriage together, foreclosing marriage for same-sex couples and leaving constitutional amendment as the only recourse for same-sex marriage to be legalized. For a glimpse of the debate, see Andrea Pugiotto, "Una lettura non reticente della sent. n. 138/2010: il monopolio eterosessuale del matrimonio," Forum di Quaderni Costituzionali (2011), http://www.forumcostituzionale.it/wordpress/images/stories/pdf/documenti_forum/paper/0226_pugiotto.pdf, or Marta Cartabia, "Le avventure giuridiche della differenza sessuale," in *Identità sessuale e identità di genere*, ed. Francesco D'Agostino (Palermo, It.: Giuffré Editore, 2012). See also, in contrast, Barbara Pezzini, "Il matrimonio same sex si potrà fare. La qualificazione della discrezionalità del legislatore nella sentenza n. 138/2010 della Corte costituzionale," *Rivista AIC – Associazione dei Constituzionalisti*, no 4 (2010), https://www.rivistaaic.it/it/rivista/ultimi-contributi-pubblicati/barbara-pezzini/il-matrimonio-same-sex-si-potr-fare-la-qualificazione-della-discrezionalit-del-legislatore-nella-sentenza-n-138-2010-della-corte-costituzionale. See also, for Costa Rica, Constitutional Chamber of the Supreme Court, decision No. 12782–2018, Aug. 8, 2018, upholding legislation that only provided for heterosexual marriage against discrimination claims, arguing that only the legislator had the democratic legitimacy required to introduce same-sex marriage.

[41] See BVerfGE 10, 59 (66), July 29, 1959; BVerfGE 105, 313 (342–43), July 17, 2002, and BVerfGE 137, 273 (342), Oct. 22, 2014, all reaffirming "heterosexuality" as an inherent and constituting characteristic of marriage on the basis of the procreative specificity of the heterosexual couple. In accordance with this case law, Germany opted for the separate tracks option and established the possibility of registered partnerships for same-sex couples. According to BVerfGE 105, 313–65, the option of civil partnership for same-sex couples expresses the legislator's embodiment of the constitutional principles of free development of one's personality (article 2 GG) and equality (article 3 GG) without deriving a subjective right to protection from such provisions (Rn. 88). The decision states that the special protection of marriage under article 6 (1) prohibits placing marriage in a worse position compared to any other form of living (Rn. 92), something that cannot be said to happen simply because same-sex partnerships are recognized (Rn. 93) but does not require the legislator to actively disadvantage different forms of living arrangements compared to marriage either (Rn. 98). In other words, the constitutional sanctioning of the institution of (heterosexual) marriage does not prohibit the legislature from offering legal forms for permanent cohabitation to other constellations of persons beyond the union of man and woman (Rn. 103).

following the famous 2015 referendum),[42] Poland,[43] or Hungary,[44] have constitutions been read by constitutional courts as *necessarily* reserving marriage for heterosexual couples, thus ruling out the option of same-sex marriage. Some courts, like the Polish Constitutional Court, have furthermore interpreted this thesis as also limiting the kinds of rights and recognition forms that can be granted to same-sex unions or single parents, in the understanding that the marital institution could otherwise be unduly devalued. Yet other courts have interpreted the constitutional monopoly granted to heterosexual marriage as compatible with either requiring (as in Hungary)[45] or allowing (as in Germany) the legislator to open other channels for the recognition of same-sex unions, or else granting same-sex couples more or less the same rights as married couples[46] – an interpretation that has, however, not ultimately precluded

[42] See Zappone and Gilligan v. Revenue Commissioners & Ors [2006] 2 IR 417 (H. Ct.), concluding that, under article 41 of the 1937 constitution, marriage was understood to be confined to persons of the opposite sex. The referendum on May 22, 2015, amended the Irish Constitution to provide (article 41.4) that "marriage may be contracted in accordance with law by two persons without distinction as to their sex," giving way to same-sex legislation being passed (Thirty-Fourth Amendment to the Constitution, Marriage Equality Act, Aug. 26, 2015).

[43] Judgment of the Polish Constitutional Tribunal of May 11, 2005, K 18/04 (the Accession Treaty).

[44] See Alkotmánybíróság (AB) [Constitutional Court], 14/1995. (III. 13), Magyar Közlöny (MK) [Official Gazette of Hungary], 1995/20, holding that the exclusion of same-sex couples from common law civil unions contravened the principle of equal treatment and human dignity.

[45] Ibid. See also Alkotmánybíróság (AB) [Constitutional Court], 154/2008. (XII. 17.), Alkotmánybíróság Határozatai (AK) [Official Gazette of the Constitutional Court], available at https://hunconcourt.hu/uploads/sites/3/2017/11/en_0154_2008.pdf, holding that same-sex partnerships should be recognized by the legislator but striking down a statute that allowed heterosexual couples to enter into registered partnerships. For the court, this option did not sufficiently differentiate between marriage and partnership, thus arguably curbing the value of marriage under the constitution.

[46] In fact, in Germany, the court gradually came to equalize the rights and prerogatives attached to marriage and same-sex partnerships through a case law affirming that there is no convincing reason for a different treatment of gay/lesbian couples and married couples and that a different treatment can in fact constitute discrimination because of sexual orientation (article 3 [1] GG). On the topic, see Anna Katharina Mangold, "Ehe für alle: Der Kampf um die Gleichberechtigung," *Blätter für deutsche und internationale Politik* (October 2015), 111–20. The case law includes BVerfGE 124, 199, July 7, 2009 (on survivors' pensions); BVerfGE 126, 400, July 21, 2010 (on inheritance tax); BVerfGE 133, 377, May 7, 2013 (on taxation systems); and BVerfGE 133, 59, Feb. 19, 2013 (on successive adoption by registered civil partners on the basis of children's rights but also by explicit reference to the protection of queer families under article 6 [1] GG). After same-sex marriage legislation was passed in 2017, it has been argued that this represents a

same-sex marriage from being legislatively embraced in Germany in 2017, even without a constitutional reform.

Interesting is the fact that, despite the clear link between the heterosexual traditional marriage and patriarchy, almost none of these cases have attached any significance to the constitutional commitment to gender/sex equality in their reasoning. This is an argument that even plaintiffs have mostly ignored, foregoing both the possibility of a formalistic reading of equality that could have gone to their advantage (after all, it is the "sex" of a person that prevents that person from marrying another person of their same "sex" when same-sex marriage is not allowed) and, more importantly, that of the need to combat gender roles stereotypes entrenched in marriage when understood as heterosexual in essence. Yet this did not have to be the case. In fact, the first same-sex couple whose quest for a marriage license reached the US Supreme Court in 1971 did include in their case a claim of sex discrimination along with other federal claims,[47] and in 1999, *Baehr v. Lewin* was decided by the Supreme Court of Hawaii on the basis of an equal protection clause, read as banning sex-based discrimination. Instead, the few court decisions that have derived a constitutional right to same-sex marriage have typically grounded their reasoning in an updated egalitarian reading of the institution of marriage that explicitly departs from tradition, combined sometimes with an expansive reading of the principle of nondiscrimination to include the ban on sexual orientation – about which older constitutional texts remain silent[48] – and often supported by an appeal to dignity as a synthesis between equality and liberty values.[49]

case of a *Verfassungswandel*, where a change in fundamental societal convictions justifies constitutional change without the need of a formal amendment of article 6 (1) GG.

47 See Baker v. Nelson, 191 N.W.2d 185, 187 (Minn. 1971), appeal dismissed, 409 U.S. 810 (1972), holding that a state's denial of a marriage license to a male couple did not violate the US Constitution. Notice that the appeal was dismissed by the US Supreme Court at a time when the court had not yet held any sex-respecting rule to be constitutionally problematic. See also Baehr v. Lewin, 74 Haw. 852 P.2d 44, 63–64 (1993), decided by the Supreme Court of Hawaii on the basis of sex equality.

48 An explicit mention to sexual orientation discrimination was only introduced in more recent constitutions. See, for instance, section 9 (3) of the 1996 Constitution of South Africa; article 13.2 of the 1976 Constitution of Portugal (as amended in 2005); article 12 (chap. 2, pt. 4) of the 1974 Constitution of Sweden (as amended in 2012); and article 1 of the Constitution of Mexico of 1917 (as amended in 2015). In other instances, the banning of sexual orientation discrimination has been judicially derived. See, for example, Egan v. Canada, [1995] 2 S.C.R. 513 (Can.), considering it an illegitimate ground of discrimination under section 15 of the 1982 Canadian Charter of Rights and Freedoms.

49 See Sperti, *Constitutional Courts*, 115ff., 140–70.

Surely, some old constitutional texts as well as most human rights instruments of the post–World War II rights revolution recognize the right to marriage explicitly to "men" and "women," reflecting common assumptions of the time.[50] This, therefore, may be one of the reasons why the sex equality provisions contained in those constitutions and human rights instruments could not be read as endorsing the option of same-sex marriage[51] and why even legislative attempts to move in such direction could be expected to trigger constitutional resistance. Nevertheless, what's interesting is that such litigation has expanded worldwide regardless of whether the institution of marriage itself had or lacked explicit constitutional sanction (as in the United States, where the right to marry has only been jurisprudentially derived)[52] or whether the constitutional provision establishing the right to, and the institution of, marriage did so in terms that rendered its heterosexual nature explicit. In fact, this aspect has not even been considered the most decisive in much of the litigation, since it has been generally assumed that the heterosexual gender order was simply the norm at the time many of the constitutions and human rights instruments were drafted. Instead, what, to a large extent, seems to have prevailed in the positions taken by the different constitutional courts around the world has been their understanding of the essential function expected from the marital institution (both when the constitution was drafted but also in present times) and their views on

[50] See, for instance, article 16 of the 1948 Universal Declaration of Human Rights; article 23 of the International Covenant on Civil and Political Rights; article 10 of the International Covenant on Economic, Social and Cultural Rights; and article 12 of the European Convention on Human Rights.

[51] For this reason, the European Court of Human Rights has so far refused to recognize a right to same-sex marriage, leaving this within the states' margin of appreciation. See Schalk and Kopf v. Austria, App. No. 30141/04, 218 Eur. H.R. Rep. (2010). The Charter of Fundamental Rights of the European Union is notably gender neutral in the guarantees related to the right to marry (article 9).

[52] The right to marry has so far been protected by the Supreme Court for over forty years, with a jurisprudential trend that began in *Loving v. Virginia*, 388 U.S. 1 (1967). See also Zablocki v. Redhail, 434 U.S. 374, 384 (1978), and Turner v. Safley, 482 U.S. 78, 95 (1987). For a more recent and specific reference to same-sex couples, see The United States v. Windsor, 570 U.S. 744 (2013), where the opinion of the court placed considerable emphasis on the absence of a definition of marriage in the US Constitution, something that was seen as leaving the matter to the states, which since 1972 had already been recognized the power to reserve the marital status to opposite-sex couples (see Baker v. Nelson, 409 U.S. 810 [1972]). That said, one can find case law from as early as the end of the nineteenth century, when the Supreme Court acknowledged the heterosexual and monogamous nature of marriage (Reynolds v. United States, 98 U.S. 145 [1878]).

their institutional competence when it came to updating the meaning of the institution of marriage, mostly vis-à-vis that of the democratically elected legislator. We therefore find jurisdictions, such as Spain or Colombia, in which, despite the relevant constitutional provisions containing explicit traces of the heterosexual nature of marriage, courts have refrained from leaving behind traditional understandings of the institution to accommodate modern-day meanings, even when this required twisting some basic hermeneutic rules.[53] Similarly, we have examples of constitutions that are silent about this feature and courts that have nevertheless been willing to define the heterosexual nature of marriage as a tradition-based, intrinsic, essential, or inherent element of the institution, which, as we have seen, was the case in Italy and Germany.

Instead, the courts that have supported the need or possibility of same-sex marriage – but also those that have argued for the need to ensure that, when marriage and legal partnerships are recognized side by side, they come attached with a similar set of rights and obligations – have all underscored the need to depart from traditional understandings and capture the new essence of marriage (or legal partnerships) by referring to the importance of lasting commitment, support, love, affection, trust, respect, and mutual responsibility while also highlighting the relevance of these unions for the stability of individuals and society in general. Thus, in 2009, striking down the lesser rights to inheritance recognized to same-sex partners as opposed to married couples, the Slovenian Constitutional Court referred to registered partnerships in the following terms: "Registered partnership is a relationship which is in content similar to marriage or civil partnership. The stable connection between two persons, who are close to each other, who help and support each other is the key element of both. The ethical and emotional essence of a registered partnership … in which partners have to respect, trust and

[53] In Spain, where article 32 recognizes "man" and "woman" the right to marriage, the Constitutional Court was willing to interpret the institution of marriage in view of its contemporary understanding and validate a reform of the Civil Code introducing same-sex marriage, arguing, among other things, that although the constitution refers to a "man" and a "woman," it does not specify *with whom* such man and woman are entitled to marry (see S.T.C., Nov. 6, 2012 [No. 198/2012]). Much the same can be said about article 42 of the Constitution of Colombia, which expressly states that marriage can be celebrated between a man and a woman. The Colombian Constitutional Court simply states that, even if such a provision enshrines a right for heterosexual people, it does not allow to read from it the exclusion of other forms of marriage, grounding on changed societal conceptions the obligation to recognize same-sex marriage (Corte Constitucional [C.C.] [Constitutional Court], abril 28, 2016, Sentencia SU214/16, § 10).

help each other, is similar to the union between a man and a woman."[54] Similarly, these decisions have underlined a departure from a type of marriage that is exclusively focused on reproduction or even on sexuality[55] – sometimes even noting that the ability, desire, or promise to procreate in fact had not traditionally been a prerequisite for a valid

[54] See Constitutional Court decision U-I-425/06-10 (Blažič and Kern v. Slovenia) (translated text available at https://www.equalrightstrust.org/ertdocumentbank/Blazic%20and%20Kern%20v%20Slovenia.pdf). In upholding same-sex marriage, the Spanish Constitutional Court (S.T.C., Nov. 6, 2012 [No. 198/2012], p. 9) argued that, after the reforms introduced in the Civil Code allowing for same-sex marriage, the institution of marriage had been "preserved in terms that are perfectly recognizable by Spanish society as an affective community generating a tie, a society of reciprocal help between two persons sharing the same status within this institution, who voluntarily decide to unite in a joint family life project, freely accepting the rights and duties that pertain to the institution, explicitly manifesting their will through the formalities contemplated to that effect by the legal order. Equality between the spouses, free will and free choices of spouse, and the explicit manifestation of such will constitute the essential features of the institution of marriage." Similar references to reciprocal care, support, loyalty, and personal and communal stability are to be found in all other decisions validating or mandating same-sex marriage. For instance, in Obergefell v. Hodges, the Supreme Court stated (citing *Griswold*) that "Marriage is a coming together for better or for worse, hopefully enduring, and intimate to the degree of being sacred. It is an association that promotes a way of life, not causes; a harmony in living, not political faiths; a bilateral loyalty, not commercial or social projects. Yet it is an association for as noble a purpose as any involved in our prior decisions." It also argued that marriage "offers the hope of companionship and understanding and assurance that while both still live there will be someone to care for the other" (Obergefell v. Hodges, 576 U.S. 667 [2015]).

[55] See, most explicitly, Suprema Corte de Justicia de la Nación [Supreme Court of Justice of the Nation], Acción de inconstitucionalidad 2/2010, Pleno de la Suprema Corte de Justicia [SCJN] Semanario Judicial de la Federación y su Gaceta, Novena Época, diciembre de 2010, Tomo XXXII, página 991, noting that the concept of marriage had evolved and its traditional conception had been surpassed – the reproductive function having stopped being the most important element – and that, in view of the general protection afforded to the family by article 4 of the constitution, it was the legislator's duty to adapt normativity to social reality so as to provide due safeguard to all types of families, with sexual orientation constituting but one form of expression of human nature, and not something that necessarily affects the quality of a person (and, thus, their capacity to be a parent). See also Colombia's Sentencia SU214/16, § 7, in which the Constitutional Court argued that "The purpose of marriage is not only the development of sexuality and procreation, but also the consolidation of the interpersonal bonds which consent to create a family. On the contrary, if this was the case, the heterosexual couples who freely decide not to procreate, or those people who may be physically impaired to procreate, could not marry. Similarly, those who cannot develop a full sexual life would not be able to marry." See also the Constitutional Court of South Africa's *Fourie* (§ 70) decision cited above (n. 27), noting that "Marriage law thus goes well beyond its earlier purpose in the common law of legitimizing sexual relations and securing succession of legitimate heirs to family property."

marriage[56] and that the ability to properly care and raise children does not depend on the sexual orientation of the parents.[57] In contrast, those courts that have defended the traditional (explicit or implicit) understanding of marriage as a heterosexual institution or validated important differences between the treatment of marriages and other forms of unions have continued to place the emphasis on the procreative difference of same-sex, as opposed to different-sex, unions. These alleged procreative differences have sometimes been understood in strictly biological and functional terms, but they have also generally referred to the better ability of heterosexual unions to reproduce and parent, underscoring the need for marriage to remain centered on reproduction rather than the pursuit of happiness, companionship, or emotional gratification.[58]

[56] See Obergefell v. Hodges, at 15–16: "In light of precedent protecting the right of a married couple not to procreate, it cannot be said the Court or the States have conditioned the right to marry on the capacity or commitment to procreate. The constitutional marriage right has many aspects, of which childbearing is only one."

[57] See the Constitutional Court of South Africa's *Fourie* decision (§ 67), noting that both "parents have an ineluctable duty to support their children and that this duty to support children arises whether the children are born of parents who are married or not." See also the US Supreme Court's decision in *Obergefell*, at 15: "As all parties agree, many same-sex couples provide loving and nurturing homes to their children, whether biological or adopted. And hundreds of thousands of children are presently being raised by such couples." In this respect, *Fourie* built on National Coalition for Gay and Lesbian Equality v. Minister for Home Affairs, requesting the Constitutional Court of South Africa to decide whether it was unconstitutional for immigration law to facilitate immigration into South Africa of the spouses of permanent South African residents but not to afford the same benefits to gays and lesbians in stable same-sex life relationships with South African residents. Writing for the court, Justice Ackermann defined marriage as a "consortium omnis vitae" that "creates a physical, moral and spiritual community of life" and concluded that "gays and lesbians in same-sex life partnerships are as capable as heterosexual spouses of expressing and sharing love in its manifold forms including affection, friendship, eros and charity." Also, "they are likewise as capable of performing intimate, permanent, committed, monogamous, loyal and enduring relationships; of furnishing emotional and spiritual support; and of providing physical care, financial support and assistance in running the common household." See National Coalition for Gay and Lesbian Equality v. Minister for Home Affairs 2000 (2) SA 1, at 53 (a) (iv) and (v).

[58] For Germany, see BVerfGE 105, 313, July 17, 2002, justifying the two-tracks approach (in force at the time) on the basis that children of both spouses can be born to a permanent two-person relationship between a man and woman but not to a same-sex partnership. An understanding of marriage focused on procreation can also be found in the dissenting opinions of Justices Roberts and Alito in the *Obergefell* decision. Justice Roberts argues, at 5, that "for the good of children and society, sexual relations that can lead to procreation should occur only between a man and a woman committed to a lasting bond. Society has recognized that bond as marriage." On the other hand, Justice Alito claims, at 4, that "this

In terms of the gender order, then, the constitutional milestones around same-sex relations point to the gradual disestablishment of heterosexual marriage as the foundation of family and society by allowing for same-sex marriage to compete with other forms of legally recognized family formations, which in fact lack the history and connotation of gender differentiation and subordination that heterosexual marriage has. This potentially contributes to the disestablishment of gender roles and to the victory of the modern invention of the love-based marriage to the detriment of the more traditional procreation-oriented, complementarity-based, gender roles-defining marriage.

In this new order, sex equality has been said to require both the opening of the marital institution to same-sex couples and the recognition of alternative nonmarital forms of cohabitation, which are open to all and are inspired by the same solidarity, support, and reciprocal care logic.[59] The "separate but equal" track, reserving civil unions or registered partnerships for same-sex couples while according them similar or equivalent benefits, protections, and responsibilities, has been said to fail to live up to equality, sending a message of subordination to both gays and lesbians, on the one hand, and heterosexual women, on the other. As Case rightly argues, "Withholding from same-sex couples the opportunity to marry devalues their unions both symbolically and practically, while restricting marriage to male-female couples and male-female couples to marriage forces women who wish to unite themselves to men under state law to do so in an institution whose all too recent legal history is one of subordinating wives both practically and symbolically,

understanding of marriage, which focuses almost entirely on the happiness of persons who choose to marry, is shared by many people today, but it is not the traditional one. For millennia, marriage was inextricably linked to the one thing that only an opposite-sex couple can do: procreate." See Obergefell v. Hodges, 576 U.S. 644 (2015).

[59] In the United Kingdom, the Supreme Court has ruled that the nonavailability of civil partnerships for heterosexual couples is a breach of the European Convention on Human Rights. See R. (Steinfeld and Keidan) v. Secretary of State for International Development, [2017] EWCA (Civ) 81, [2018] UKSC 32. Since 2013, both opposite-sex and same-sex couples could marry, but only same-sex couples could enter civil partnerships. As a result, since 2019, opposite-sex couples can enter civil partnerships. The *Steinfeld* case was taken by a couple who objected to the patriarchal nature of the traditional marriage and wanted to enter a union based on more modern notions of equality. However, the Supreme Court's reasoning was based on traditional equality logic rather than a critique of the institution of marriage. In any event, the Supreme Court judgment goes beyond the ECHR on this question. See Ratzenböck and Seydl v. Austria, App No. 28475/12 (Oct. 26, 2017), http://hudoc.echr.coe.int/eng?i=001-177916.

an institution reserved for them alone because of and not in spite of its 'traditional' (that is to say, patriarchal) significance."[60]

To this day, same-sex marriage still remains an object of contestation. Despite its undeniable symbolic importance, many progressive women have only lukewarmly celebrated the opening of the marital institution to gays and lesbians, as opposed to the altogether extinction of what they see as the patriarchal institution of marriage and its replacement by other new arrangements without a history of gender subordination. The latter is a solution that, it is argued, might have been more radically transformative, rather than simply inclusive or assimilationist.[61] Many others have also criticized how marriage equality can and has traveled with marital supremacy, questioning whether the opening of the marital institution to gays and lesbians in fact perpetuates the marital/sexual family to the detriment, or even the discrimination, of nonsexual forms of cohabitation and solidarity, single-headed households, or solo living, all of which should be valid options for all, but particularly for those who have traditionally been oppressed by the institution of marriage.[62] Yet others fear marriage equality advocacy risks "denigrating or shrinking an affective sexual liberty outside of marriage" and argue that the legal recognition of same-sex marriage threatens to bring same-sex relationships within the constraints of heterosexual relationships, further marginalizing a conception of intimacy and desire not based on marriage.[63]

[60] See Mary Anne Case, "What Feminists Have to Lose in Same-Sex Marriage Litigation," *UCLA Law Review* 57, no. 5 (2010): 1199–236, at 1223. See also Martha C. Nussbaum, *From Disgust to Humanity: Sexual Orientation & Constitutional Law* (Oxford: Oxford University Press, 2010), 129, supporting that same-sex couples should be allowed to marry in equal terms to different-sex couples because of the social and expressive value attached to marriage.

[61] See J. Jack Halberstam, *Gaga Feminism: Sex, Gender, and the End of Normal* (Boston: Beacon Press, 2012). For a more general view on the opposition to same-sex marriage from the left, see Nancy D. Polikoff, *Beyond (Straight and Gay) Marriage: Valuing All Families under the Law* (Boston: Beacon Press, 2009); Katherine Franke, *Wedlocked. The Perils of Marriage Equality* (New York: New York University Press, 2016).

[62] See Gregg Strauss, "What's Wrong with *Obergefell*," *Cardozo Law Review* 40, no. 2 (2018): 631–85; Courtney G. Joslin, "Discrimination In and Out of Marriage," *Boston University Law Review* 98, no. 1 (2018): 1–54; Chao-ju Chen, "Single Equality in the Age of Marriage Equality," *International Journal of Constitutional Law* 18, no. 2 (2020): 461–65, arguing that "single inequality is a product of patriarchy" and that "beyond marriage equality, a feminist agenda of single equality envisions a future of women's equal citizenship unmediated by the institutions of marriage, partnership, and parenthood."

[63] See Katherine M. Franke, "Longing for Loving," *Fordham Law Review* 76, no. 6 (2008): 2685–708, at 2685, 2688–89.

Constitutionally speaking, the overall abandoning of the institution of marriage seems much more unlikely, given its high prevalence, than its reinterpretation in parallel to the reinterpretation of the family concept in ever more inclusive terms. In fact, it could be reasonably argued that, as long as different institutions are allowed to exist and are open to all, and a comprehensively interpreted ban against discrimination on the grounds of marital and parental status that also protects single persons without children is put into place, it could be both unconstitutional (in most countries) and generally unwise to call on the entire abolition of the public institution of marriage and its reduction, at best, to one more form of private civil contract in the belief that this scenario would ensure women's equal status or, for that matter, represent greater freedom for all individuals.[64] Rather, care-centered feminist constitutionalism might want to retain an interest in preserving interpersonal solidarity, affection, care, and intimacy by protecting institutions, which, if properly conceived, can enhance autonomy and serve both individual and societal interests, given our shared interdependent nature. None of this, of course, is to deny the risks that come with an excessive "familization of care or dependence,"[65] some of which I addressed in Chapter 4.

Yet, as we shall see at the end of this chapter, the greatest contestation against same-sex marriage has come from the conservative front, which is engaging in much constitutional warfare. Conservative forces basically see equal marriage as a threat to the traditional family as a heterosexual and procreative institution and sometimes even as an existential threat linked to demographic concerns.[66] This conservative opposition, deeply connected to religious fundamentalism, has learned to use the language of rights and has endorsed a narrative of victimization to resist social innovation and preserve the majoritarian agenda that has always discriminated against gender and sexual minorities. It is precisely this

[64] For the defense of the abolition of marriage as a privileged legal category, see Martha Albertson Fineman, *The Neutered Mother, the Sexual Family and Other Twentieth Century Tragedies* (New York: Routledge, 1995), 228–30.

[65] See Nicola Barker, *Not the Marrying Kind: A Feminist Critique of Same-Sex Marriage* (London: Palgrave Macmillan, 2012), 158–62.

[66] See, for instance, Sara Garbagnoli and Massimo Prearo, *La croisade "anti-genre": du Vatican aux manif pour tous* (Paris: Textuels, 2017); Kuhar and Paternotte, *Anti-gender Campaigns in Europe*; David Paternotte, "Global Times, Global Debates? Same-Sex Marriage Worldwide," in "Social Politics 20 Years On," eds. Mary Daly and Barbara Hobson, special issue, *Social Politics: International Studies in Gender, State & Society* 22, no. 4 (2015): 653–74.

narrative and strategic turn that invites constitutional politics to become a preferred domain for lawfare in many jurisdictions.[67]

5.3 The Gender/Sex Categorization System under Constitutional Scrutiny: Toward the Affirmation of a Right to Gender Identity[68]

Over the last years, we have seen lawfare expanding in reaction to the increasing affirmation of the rights of trans persons challenging what some deem to be too narrow and others increasingly irrelevant notions of sex and gender around which legal orders have traditionally been – and, to a large extent, continue to be – organized. Thus, despite the irruption of same-sex marriage and the contestation it has triggered, marriage continues to be a central organizing institution that most constitutions around the world still refer to, sometimes in explicitly heterosexual terms. Moreover, most legal systems continue to rely on sex/gender-based distinctions for a variety of additional purposes including, among others, the administration of facilities, the identification of persons, the organization of sports, social security schemes, and affirmative action programs. In spite of this, and no doubt facilitated by the gradual erosion of traditional gender roles, the acceptance of same-sex marriage, and increasingly vocal and globally organized trans and intersex movements, we currently experience a multiplication of ways in which the legal categories and treatment of sex/gender have come to be problematized.

Not unlike the rest of the gender transformations we have been discussing, here too, many of the battles have been fueled by transnational activism but have eventually been won in national political battlefields. Therefore, although still very much the exception, we find that an increasing number of countries have passed laws admitting gender identity self-determination without external assessments or validation, a claim that has become central in trans identity rights vindications since at least the mid-1990s[69] and is now articulated in the

[67] For a feminist analysis, see Douglas Nejaime and Reva B. Siegel, "Conscience Wars Complicity-Based Conscience Claims in Religion and Politics," *Yale Law Journal* 124, no. 7 (2013): 2516–91.

[68] Much of this section is indebted to Ruth Rubio Marín and Stefano Osella, "El nuevo derecho constitucional a la identidad de género: entre la libertad de elección, el incremento de categorías y la subjetividad y fluidez de sus contenidos. Un análisis desde el derecho comparado," *Revista Española de Derecho Constitucional*, no. 118 (2020): 45–75.

[69] See Phyllis Randolph Frye, preface to "Appendix: The International Bill of Gender Rights," in *Transgender Rights*, eds. Paisley Currah, Richard M. Juang, and Shannon

widely traveled LGBTQI+ advocacy document known as the *Yogyakarta Principles* in its 2017 iteration: *Yogyakarta Principles Plus 10.*[70] Countries with legislation embracing self-determination or self-ascription rules include Argentina (since 2012), Belgium (2017), Bolivia (2017), Chile (2018), Denmark (2014), Ecuador (2016), Ireland (2015), Malta (2015), Norway (2016), Portugal (2018), and Uruguay (2018).

Although much of the agenda has proceeded legislatively, we observe a growing constitutionalism around the claims of trans and intersex persons with constitutional principles being called upon to either resist progressive changes or to advance them. Consequently, relying on a wide variety of rights provisions – among others, the right to dignity, health, free development of one's personality, privacy, equality, and freedom of expression – several courts worldwide have come to question gender normalization procedures supporting an increasingly unconditional right to gender identity, eventually reaching self-ascription as well as nonbinary and fluid understandings of gender.[71] In this journey, as in many others, the incorporation of more or less binding regional human rights standards has also proved particularly useful.[72]

Price Minter (Minneapolis, MN: University of Minnesota Press, 2006); Jessica A. Clarke, "Identity and Form," *California Law Review* 103, no. 4 (2015): 747–839.

[70] In 2006, in response to well-documented patterns of abuse, a distinguished group of international human rights experts met in Yogyakarta, Indonesia, to outline a set of international principles relating to sexual orientation and gender identity. Principle 31 of the *Yogyakarta Principles Plus 10* demands the right "to change gendered information in such documents while gendered information is included in them." Consistently, they call on states to "ensure access to a quick, transparent, and accessible mechanism that legally recognises and affirms each person's self-defined gender identity."

[71] See, in this regard, Ruth Rubio-Marín and Stefano Osella, "The New Constitutional Right to Gender Identity: Adding Choice or Categories? A Comparative Enquiry" (unpublished manuscript); Marie-Xavière Catto and Stefano Osella, "The Sexed Subject," in *The Cambridge Companion for Law and Gender*, eds. Ruth Rubio-Marín and Stéphanie Hennette-Vauchez (Cambridge: Cambridge University Press, forthcoming).

[72] European Parliament, Resolution on the rights of intersex people (2018/2878[RSP]), Feb. 14, 2019, http://www.europarl.europa.eu/doceo/document/TA-8-2019-0128_EN.html; Inter-American Court of Human Rights, Advisory Opinion on Gender Identity, and Equality and Non-Discrimination of Same-sex Couples, OC-24/17, Inter-Am. Ct. H.R. (ser. A), https://corteidh.or.cr/docs/opiniones/seriea_24_eng.pdf; Council of Europe, Parliamentary Assembly, Resolution 2048 (2015) on Discrimination against Transgender People in Europe, Apr. 22, 2015, https://assembly.coe.int/nw/xml/XRef/Xref-XML2HTML-EN.asp?fileid=21736. For relevant case law under the ECHR, see Christine Goodwin v. United Kingdom, App No. 28957/95, 35 Eur. H.R. Rep. 18 (2002); I. v. United Kingdom, App No. 25680/94, 36 Eur. Ct. H.R. 967 (2003); Y. Y. v. Turkey, App. No. 14793/08 (Mar. 10, 2015), http://hudoc.echr.coe.int/eng?i=001-153134; and Garçon et Nicot v. France, Apps. No 79885/12, 52471/13, and 56596/13,

First in time – starting in the 1960s and with initial victories in the 1970s in Sweden and Germany[73] – was the struggle for gender reclassification in countries where the procedure was altogether denied, often with the reasoning that it would affect legal certainty about marital unions, which at the time were almost exclusively heterosexual. Italy is a case in point and offers an example of a country – which still limits marriage to heterosexual couples – where the Constitutional Court was asked to intervene to support legislation allowing transitions under vague conditions.[74] Although the court ultimately validated such legislation by calling on the right to the free development of one's personality and the fundamental right to health (articles 2 and 32 of the Italian Constitution), it interpreted it narrowly, arguing that the transformation of primary and secondary sexual characteristics (sterilization and body shape, respectively) lay at the very core of trans people's desires.[75]

The last decade has witnessed the gradual challenge of some of the common preconditions, legal effects, and procedural hurdles of

Eur. Ct. H.R. (Apr. 6, 2017), http://hudoc.echr.coe.int/spa?i=001-172913. See also Damian A. Gonzalez-Salzburg, Sexuality and Transexuality under the European Convention of Human Rights: A Queer Reading of Human Rights Law (Oxford: Hart Publishing, 2019).

[73] In Germany, an early transgender constitutional case (BVerfGE 49, 286, Oct. 11, 1978) forced the German legislator to approve a law on transsexuality in 1980. A rich and progressive case law has followed since. See BVerfGE 60, 123, Mar. 16, 1982 (on age requirements); BVerfGE 88, 87, Jan. 16, 1993 (on age requirements); BVerfGE 115, 1, Dec. 6, 2005 (on name change); BVerfGE 116, 243, July 18, 2006 (on the rights of transsexuals of foreign nationality); BVerfGE 121, 175, May 27, 2008 (on mandatory divorce); and BVerfGE 128, 109, Jan. 11, 2011 (on surgery/sterilization requirements). See Laura Adamietz, *Geschlecht als Erwartung. Das Geschlechtsdiskriminierungsverbot als Recht gegen Diskriminierung wegen der sexuellen Orientierung und der Geschlechtsidentität* (Baden-Baden: Nomos, 2011). For an overview of the rights of trans and intersex people in German, see also Cara Röhner, *Geschlechtliche Vielfalt im Recht*, in *Trans*, inter*, nicht-binäre Geschlechtlichkeiten*, eds. Christel Baltes-Löhr and René_Rain Hornstein (Stuttgart: UTB, 2021).

[74] Legge 14 aprile 1982, no. 164, art. 1.

[75] See Corte cost., 6 maggio 1985, n. 161, G.U. June 5, 1985, no. 131 bis, defending the constitutionality of Law 164 of 1982. In Spain, the provision referring to the free development of one's personality and the right to privacy (articles 10.1 and 18 of the Spanish Constitution) have also been relied on by the Spanish Constitutional Court to affirm the right to reclassification of children under a legislation requiring gender dysphoria diagnosis and two years of hormonal treatment, as long as they are sufficiently mature and stable in their identity affirmation. See S.T.C. July 18, 2019 [No. 99/2019]. See also Ruth Rubio-Marín and Stefano Osella, "Le precondizioni per il riconoscimento dell'identità sessuale," *Quaderni Costituzionali* 36, no.1 (2016): 61–88. Currently, the Spanish government is proposing a legislative change to adopt a pure self-determination model.

transitions relying on political battles and constitutional means. Both the Italian Constitutional Court[76] and the German Federal Constitutional Court,[77] for instance, were approached. These courts found that the automatic divorce imposed on a reclassified transsexual person constituted a violation of their fundamental rights, even though same-sex marriage was still not allowed in Germany at the time and still isn't in Italy. Under the influence of the European Court of Human Rights' case law, the Italian Constitutional Court would eventually come to terms with the fact that surgery on primary sexual characteristics could no longer be legitimately required as a precondition for gender reclassification,[78] even while validating a system that still expects a complete and judicially certified transformation of the behavioral, psychological, and physical characteristics, in the understanding that the corporeal gender must correspond to the legal gender.[79]

Departing from the conception of a person's sex as an objective and measurable fact, and especially as a characteristic that is and ought to remain outside the reach of individual will, we find that, over the last few years, some courts, like the Colombian Constitutional Court in a 2015 decision,[80] have abandoned their precedent and embraced individual self-ascription without the need for judicial involvement.[81]

76 Corte cost., 11 giugno 2014, n. 170, G.U., June 18, 2014, n. 26.

77 See BVerfGE 121, 175, May 27, 2008.

78 Corte cost., 21 ottobre 2015, n. 221, G.U., Nov. 11, 2015, n. 45, rejecting the need for surgery on primary sexual characteristics as a precondition for changing one's sex and name in the civil registry. See also, for Brazil, Supremo Tribunal Federal (S.T.F.) [Federal Supreme Court], Ação Direta de Inconstitucionalidade (ADI) [Direct Action of Unconstitutionality] No. 4275, Relator: Min. Marco Aurélio, 01.03.2018, Díario da Justiça Eletrônico [D.J.e], 09.03.2018, 23.

79 Such findings have been confirmed in more recent case law in which the Italian Constitutional Court has again ruled out self-definition and supported the fulfillment of medical and judicial preconditions. See Stefano Osella, "Reinforcing the Binary and Disciplining the Subject: The Constitutional Right to Gender Recognition in the Italian Case-Law" (unpublished paper). See Corte cost., 21 ottobre 2015, n. 221 (this decision was confirmed with Corte Cost., 20 giugno 2017, n. 180, [5.1.] and [5.2.] [legal grounds], G.U. July 19, 2017, n. 29); Corte Cost., 21 giugno 2017, n. 185, G.U., July 19, 2017, n. 29.

80 Corte Constitucional [C.C.] [Constitutional Court], agosto 3, 1994, Sentencia T-504/94, (4).

81 Corte Constitucional [C.C.] [Constitutional Court], febrero 13, 2015, Sentencia T-063/15. Although not fully or explicitly embracing the principle of self-determination, a similar evolution from a biologicist understanding of sex and the immutability to a conception that underscores the dynamic, mutable, and socially contingent dimension of peoples' gender identity can be found in the Peruvian Constitutional Court's case law. In this regard, note the contrast in these decisions: Tribunal Constitucional [T.C.]

Interestingly, this move has been facilitated by the Colombian Constitutional Court's understanding of sex/gender as a socially constructed category with an explicit reference to feminist and queer theory, first developed in case law, rejecting early gender reassignment and normalization treatments practiced on intersex children.[82] Highlighting the drawbacks of the judicial procedure for gender reclassification, including its length, costs, and indeterminacy, this landmark 2015 decision relied on the fact that any external assessment of a person's gender "would typically require a degree of physical or psychological examination, as well as the evaluation of stereotyped features usually associated with one gender or the other, in ways that entail the unnecessary restriction of individual identity."[83] In the court's words, "these inquiries often force transgender persons to self-locate in a heteronormative extreme, so they can obtain a positive result which may permit their recognition. In many instances, this means that they will have to lie about their life, tastes and preferences and many aspects of their personality."[84] Additional jurisprudence has confirmed that the court does not intend for the right to gender identity to remain the privilege of a few, affirming also the claim to public funding of gender reassignment treatments.[85]

[Constitutional Court], Mar. 18, 2014, file No. 139-2013-PA/TC, caso *Pamela Estela Mendoza Moreno*); and Oct. 21, 2016, file No. 6040-2015-PA/TC, caso *Ana Romero Saldarriaga*.

82 In 1995, the Colombian Constitutional Court decided its first intersexuality case, rejecting early gender reassignment treatments practiced on intersex children in order to make them conform to the gendered physical expectations of one of the sexes. See Corte Constitucional [C.C.] [Constitutional Court], octubre 23, 1995, Sentencia T-477/95. Again, in 1999, see Constitutional Court (Corte Constitucional [C.C.] [Constitutional Court], mayo 12, 1999, Sentencia SU337/99), which underlined the need to protect intersex children from normalizing treatments that could be extremely dangerous for their psychological and physical health. Celebrating gender diversity and citing critical gender literature, the court insisted on the cultural origin of gender and denounced the foundation of intersex treatments to be in the "idea" that only two genders exist. See Ruth Rubio-Marín and Stefano Osella, "Between Rights and Pragmatism: Intersexuality before the Colombian Constitutional Court," in *The Legal Status of Intersex Persons*, eds. Jens M. Scherpe, Anatol Dutta, and Tobias Helms (Cambridge, UK: Intersentia, 2018).

83 Corte Constitucional [C.C.] [Constitutional Court], febrero 13, 2015, Sentencia T-063/15, II.7.2.5–7. See also Osella and Rubio-Marín, "The Right to Gender Recognition before the Colombian Constitutional Court."

84 See Corte Constitucional [C.C.] [Constitutional Court], febrero 13, 2015, Sentencia T-063/15, II.7.2.5–7.

85 See Corte Constitucional [C.C.] [Constitutional Court], noviembre 8, 2012, Sentencia T-918/12.

While self-ascription is likely to become more widely accepted in the Latin American region, especially since the Inter-American Court of Human Rights has adopted an advisory opinion endorsing it,[86] constitutional contribution is not likely to remain a regionally confined phenomenon. In fact, courts in other regions are also leading the way with respect to other important challenges to the traditional sex/gender-based classification system, including the challenge to the gender binary, a claim that has gained centrality in trans and parts of intersex advocacy. This view argues that the gender binary is a cultural construction and that nonbinary identities and bodies do exist, which is reflected in principle 31 of the *Yogyakarta Principles Plus 10*, demanding lawmakers to "make available a multiplicity of gender marker options."

The affirmation of the right to go beyond the binary has been first recognized in relation to nonconforming identities in South Asia.[87] Trans persons, commonly known as *hijras*,[88] have been present in the Indian subcontinent for centuries, legitimized by the gender-fluid figures described in ancient Hindu and Buddhist books[89] and by their highly positioned predecessors during the Islamic rule.[90] Hijras have played a sacred role in the subcontinental society, connected with the Hindu

[86] Inter-American Court of Human Rights, Advisory Opinion on Gender Identity, and Equality and Non-Discrimination of Same-sex Couples, OC-24/17, Inter-Am. Ct. H.R. (ser. A), https://corteidh.or.cr/docs/opiniones/seriea_24_eng.pdf.

[87] See Vanja Hamzić, *Sexual and Gender Diversity in the Muslim World: History, Law and Vernacular Knowledge* (London: I. B. Tauris, 2016).

[88] Transgender persons in the subcontinent are generally known as *hijras*, although there is a wide variety of names according to the multiplicity of linguistic and territorial singularities, for instance, the *kinnar*, in North India; the *aravani*, in South India; and the *khwaja sira*, in Pakistan. Hijras are transgender people that are born phenotypic males, although few are born intersexed. They do not identify themselves within the framework of binary genders, however. Hijras are supposed to have extraordinary fertility powers and have traditionally earned their living through fertility blessings at birth and wedding ceremonies, and since their colonial and postcolonial stigmatization, as sex workers and beggars. See Serena Nanda, *Neither Man nor Woman: The Hijras of India*, 2nd ed. (Belmont: Wadsworth Publishing Company, 1999); Gayatri Reddy, *With Respect to Sex: Negotiating Hijra Identity in South India* (Chicago: The University of Chicago Press, 2005).

[89] See Ruth Vanita and Saleem Kidwai, eds., *Same-Sex Love in India: Readings from Literature and History* (London: Palgrave Macmillan, 2001), 1–30.

[90] See Jessica Hinchy, "The Sexual Politics of Imperial Expansion: Eunuchs and Indirect Colonial Rule in Mid-Nineteenth-Century North India," in "Gender, Imperialism and Global Exchanges," special issue, *Gender & History* 26, no. 3 (2014): 414–37, at 414–19.

goddess of fertility[91] and Islamic Sufi practices.[92] Their blessed condition and religious status have favored their historical acceptance and continuity within their societies. The British rule, however, brought an anti-hijra campaign, criminalizing and marginalizing them under the Criminal Tribes Act of 1871, an act that mandated their registration and control, imposing severe limitations on their legal capacity.[93] With the arrival of independence, hijras reemerged in the context of a postcolonial discourse in the Indian subcontinent, challenging colonial values and norms, while the "indigeneity" of other sexual identities was contested owing to their "Western influence."[94] Thus, the construction of this hijra identity has developed in opposition to the *ex novo* uniformity of the Western LGBTQI+ movement, which explains why cutting edge case law on gender identity in the region coexists with oppressive practices targeting sexual minorities, such as the criminalization of sodomy.[95]

At the constitutional level, it was the Supreme Court of Nepal that in 2007 paved the way with its landmark case *Sunil Babu Pant*,[96] in which, citing international human rights standards while also referring to the autochthonous South Asian culture and the accommodation of *hijras* throughout the Indian subcontinent, the court recognized that the sexually and gender-diverse people have historically faced discrimination on account of their identity and ordered the government to introduce legislation respecting the fundamental rights of third-gender

[91] Reddy, *With Respect to Sex*, 96–98.

[92] Amen Jaffer. "Spiritualising Marginality: Sufi Concepts and the Politics of Identity in Pakistan," *Society and Culture in South Asia* 3, no. 2 (2017): 175–79.

[93] See Jessica Hinchy, *Governing Gender and Sexuality in Colonial India: The Hijra, c. 1850–1900* (Cambridge, UK: Cambridge University Press, 2019), 93–109.

[94] Aniruddha Dutta, "An Epistemology of Collusion: *Hijras*, *Kothis* and the Historical (Dis) continuity of Gender/Sexual Identities in Eastern India," in "Gender History Across Epistemologies," eds. Donna R. Gabaccia and Mary Jo Maynes, special issue, *Gender & History* 24, no. 3 (2012): 825–26.

[95] After the repealing of the Criminal Tribes Act in 1949, hijra activists highlighted that persecution did not entirely subside, given the persisting criminalization of anal sexual intercourse under section 377 of the Indian Code of Criminal Procedure. See Gee Imaan Semmalar, "Gender Outlawed: The Supreme Court Judgment on Third Gender and its Implications," Round Table India, http://roundtableindia.co.in/index.php?option=com_content&view=article&id=7377:because-we-have-a-voice-too-the-supreme-court-judgment-on-third-gender-and-its-implications&catid=120&Itemid=133. Section 377 was deemed unconstitutional in the 2018 decision of the Supreme Court in *Navtej Singh Johar v. Union of India*, AIR 2018 SC 4321, declaring consenting sex among adults legal.

[96] See Sunil Babu Pant v. Government of Nepal, Writ No. 914 of the year 2064 BS (2007).

individuals.[97] Soon after, in 2009, it was the Pakistani Supreme Court's turn to adopt a series of decisions aimed at granting legal recognition to the *khawaja sira* – transgender – people.[98] But, perhaps, the most famous decision in this regard has been the Indian Supreme Court's ruling in the landmark 2014 *Nalsa* case, in which it decided that "third gender" persons have a right to gender recognition under the Constitution of India (including self-identified gender identity as male, female, or third gender).[99] Going beyond the set of health and autonomy-based constitutional principles that other courts had primarily relied on thus far, the Indian Supreme Court decided to foreground equality concerns and explicitly made reference to the marginalization and destitution of these sexual minorities, largely blaming the legacy of English colonialism.

Yet, while South Asian courts have led the way combining fundamental rights and national/regional pride parlance, some European courts, too, are making inroads in challenging the gender binary, while others have clearly been less prone to do so.[100] Of those moving in this expansive direction, some courts seem to be doing so mostly out of a concern

[97] In 2017, Sunil Babu Pant obtained another favorable decision in which the court ordered the government to develop a policy enabling transgender people to change their name. See United Nations Development Programme and Asia Pacific Transgender Network, *Legal Recognition: A Multi-Country Legal and Policy Review in Asia* (Bangkok: UNDP, 2017), 32, 39. See also Maria Federica Moscati and Hari Phuyal, "The Third Gender Case Decision of the Supreme Court of Nepal on the Rights of Lesbian, Gay, Bisexual, Transsexual and Intersex People," *Journal of Comparative Law* 4, no. 2 (2009): 291–97; Kyle Knight, "Outliers: Sunil Babu Pant, the Blue Diamond Society, and Queer Organizing in Nepal," in *Studies in Nepali History and Society* 19, no. 1 (2014): 113–76. In a later case, the Supreme Court ordered that a transgender person be given a passport that matched their citizenship certificate. See United Nations Development Programme and Asia Pacific Transgender Network, *Legal Recognition*, 34.

[98] See the Supreme Court of Pakistan's various decisions on the Muhammad Aslam Khaki v. S. S. P. (Operations) Rawalpindi case, Constitutional Petition No. 43 of 2009, starting with the first hearing on June 16, 2009, being the case successfully disposed of on Sept. 25, 2012 (PLD 2013 SC 188). See also Shahnaz Khan, "What Is in a Name? *Khwaja Sara, Hijra* and Eunuchs in Pakistan," *Indian Journal of Gender Studies* 23, no. 2 (2016): 218–42.

[99] See National Legal Service Authority v. Union of India, AIR 2014 SC 1863. See Aniruddha Dutta, "Contradictory Tendencies: The Supreme Court's NALSA Judgment on Transgender Recognition and Rights," *Journal of Indian Law and Society* 5 (2014): 225–36.

[100] See, for instance, French Cour de cassation [Cass.] [Cassation Court] 1e. civ., May 4, 2017, Bull. Civ. I, No. 531, still affirming the sexual binary as foundational to law and social order. Even though the court acknowledged the existence of a right to gender identity under article 8 ECHR, it still rejected the possibility of a third gender.

for intersex individuals, some of whom, though clearly not all, have made the challenge of the sexual binary an important part of their contestation. Thus, a constitutional right to recognition of a nonbinary gender identity has been protected by the national constitutional courts in Germany and Austria, responding to the claims of intersex persons. In Germany, a challenged statute on a person's civil law status was found in violation of the general right to free development of one's personality (article 2 [1] GG) in conjunction with human dignity (article 1 [1] GG). Similarly, for the first time ever, it was found that the ban on sex discrimination also applies to people who do not identify as men or women and that article 3 (3) GG protects vulnerable groups in a gendered society.[101] The challenged statute allowed to leave the gender marker blank in the registration of intersex children but did not allow for the requested "third option." Similarly, in Austria, the Constitutional Court deemed the preclusion of a third-gender entry for intersex people an unjustifiable violation of the right to free development of one's personality under article 8 of the European Convention of Human Rights (ECHR).[102]

Most radical of all so far has been the Belgian Constitutional Court's 2019 decision, in which it has come to embrace the departure from the binary as a natural consequence of the right to gender identity, hence not limited to intersexual persons.[103] Its ruling struck down a 2017 law on gender recognition that allowed for gender self-determination but only within the binary, on the basis that it unjustifiably excluded the possibility of a nonbinary gender by violating the principle of equality (articles 10 and 11 of the Belgian Constitution) in combination with that of self-determination (article 22), read in light of article 8 of the ECHR. For the Belgian Constitutional Court, once gender identity is self-determined, the right to go beyond the binary naturally follows. And, although the court acknowledged that the constitution referred to the categories of "men"

[101] BVerfGE 147, 1, Oct. 10, 2017.

[102] Verfassungsgerichtshof [VfGH] (Constitutional Court), June 19, 2018, G-77/2018, https://www.ris.bka.gv.at/Dokument.wxe?Abfrage=Vfgh&Dokumentnummer=JFT_20180615_18G00077_00. See Elisabeth Holzleithner, "Geschlecht als Anerkennungsverhältnis. Perspektiven einer Öffnung der rechtlichen Kategorie im Zeichen des Prinzips gleicher Freiheit," *Jahrbuch des öffentlichen Rechts der Gegenwart. Neue Folge* 67, no. 1 (2019): 457–85.

[103] See CC [Constitutional Court], June 19, 2019, n °99/2019, M.B., Jan. 21, 2020, p. 2338, holding that the legislator could protect the identity right of nonbinary people by creating new legal identities or by abandoning the registration of either sex or gender identity.

and "women" – as when it sanctions the equality between them (articles 10 and 11 bis) – it was unwilling to derive from this fact the impossibility to recognize gender identities beyond the binary. Moreover, the Belgian decision recognized that the right to gender self-determination also entailed the right to a fluid gender identity.[104] Individuals who do not permanently identify with one gender are also the ultimate authority on their own definition, the court reasoned. They should, in principle, be able to redefine their legal identity when needed. This position challenges the dominant stance in those jurisdictions where gender is decided through self-determination, which tends to limit gender fluidity by including restrictions in the form of particularly stringent external controls, time lapses, or the total number of possible gender identity changes.

What no court has done to this day is to affirm the right to be free from all gender categorizations, deriving a negative freedom, so to speak, from the right to gender identity, and in no jurisdiction has gender registration been entirely abolished.[105] So far, this "freedom from gender classifications" seems to have reflected primarily the concern with individuals who, at birth, cannot be easily classified as falling within one of the categories. A 2013 legal reform in Germany allowed for parents of intersex children, with adequate medical certification, not to have their gender registered and to leave the gender marker open until later assignment, making them effectively "genderless."[106] That same year, the Colombian Constitutional Court specified that intersex children have a right to be temporarily inscribed in civil registries by leaving the gender marker blank, expressing a concern for their ability to access all public services in the meantime.[107] Beyond these exceptions motivated by the medical conditions of intersex children, the Austrian,[108]

[104] Ibid., ¶ B.8.8.

[105] See Osella, "'De-gendering' the Civil Status?," 471–75. There is currently a pending constitutional complaint brought by the German scholar Lann Hornscheidt against the legal obligation to register a gender.

[106] See Susanne Lilian Gössl and Berit Völzmann, "Legal Gender Beyond the Binary," *International Journal of Law, Policy and the Family* 33, no. 3 (2019): 403–29; Tobias Helms, "The 2013 German Law: Analysis and Criticism," in Scherpe, Dutta, and Helms, *The Legal Status of Intersex Persons.*

[107] Corte Constitucional [C.C.] [Constitutional Court], Julio 16, 2013, Sentencia T-450A/13.

[108] Verfassungsgerichtshof [VfGH] [Constitutional Court], June 19, 2018, G-77/2018, ¶ 6.2, https://www.ris.bka.gv.at/Dokument.wxe?Abfrage=Vfgh&Dokumentnummer=JFT_20180615_18G00077_00.

German,[109] and Belgian Constitutional Courts[110] have, in passing obiter dicta, questioned the necessity for gender to be incorporated as a defining feature into a person's civil status, deferring a decision to the legislators. In the meantime, some scholars are engaging in a search for a middle way between the total elimination of the legal sex category (which might be seen as sacrificing some legitimate goals) and the pervasive enforcement of rigid gender categories to the disadvantage of trans, intersex, and nonbinary persons.[111]

In sum, what we see is that the increasing – yet by no means unequivocal or consolidated – demise of the patriarchal structures of society, prompted by the challenge to traditional roles and the questioning of heterosexual marriage at its base, has brought about a challenge to a system of gender categorization and the presupposed consistency between individual corporeality – in particular, genitalia – and social appearance, and, in turn, legal identification.[112] Once such structures are questioned and, if gender continues to be recognized as a valid source of individual identity affirmation for many, the very presence of gender categories in the law, however defined, may be seen as arguably limiting the rights of sex/gender nonconforming people. This is why the contestation of gender categories is now to be found in the 2017 *Yogyakarta Principles Plus 10*.[113] And, whereas one can certainly argue that the use of sex/gender categories in the law may still serve other valid purposes related to security, fairness, or administrative expediency, once sex/

[109] See BVerfGE 147, 1 (24), Oct. 10, 2017, holding that, in accommodating the gender identity of nonbinary people, the legislator should have the option to add gender categories to the civil status or, alternatively, eliminate gender from it altogether.

[110] See CC [Constitutional Court], June 19, 2019, n °99/2019, M.B., Jan. 21, 2020, p. 2338. Along similar lines, see European Parliament resolution of Feb. 14, 2019 on the rights of intersex people (2018/2878 [RSP]).

[111] See Davina Cooper and Robyn Emerton, "Pulling the Thread of Decertification: What Challenges Are Raised by the Proposal to Reform Legal Gender Status?," feminists@law 10, no. 2 (2020), available at https://journals.kent.ac.uk/index.php/feministsatlaw/issue/view/45.

[112] Paisley Currah and Lisa Jean Moore, "'We Won't Know Who You Are': Contesting Sex Designations in New York City Birth Certificates," in "Transgender Studies and Feminism: Theory, Politics, and Gendered Realities," eds. Talia Bettcher and Ann Garry, special issue, *Hypatia* 24, no. 3 (2009): 113–18.

[113] Principle 31 demands states to "ensure that official identity documents only include personal information that is relevant, reasonable and necessary as required by the law for a legitimate purpose" and to "end the registration of the sex and gender of the person in identity documents such as birth certificates, identification cards, passports and driver licences, and as part of their legal personality."

gender categorization is itself treated as suspect, a proportionality analysis raises the question as to whether those purposes should not be achieved by less restrictive means.[114] After, all, we do need to ask ourselves, as Stefano Osella does, "what might be left of the justification of a system of gender categories when we reach the point in which a multiplicity of gender categories is available, the sexual binary increasingly contested, and sex is defined as a continuum with individuals [free] to determine their own gender without external assessment and validation?"[115] Now, more than ever before, the words of Judith Butler resonate strongly when she claims gender to be the "apparatus by which the production and normalization of masculine and feminine take place . . . a mechanism by which notions of masculine and feminine are produced and naturalized."[116] Is it not this very apparatus that we should free ourselves from?

As with same-sex marriage, these evolutions in the law have given rise to controversy both from left and right. Particularly significant in the public and online debate has been the opposition mustered by gender-critical feminists.[117] Gender-critical feminists reclaim the focus on "sex" – with a physical dimension – as the main cause and place of women's oppression. At times sheerly denying that trans women are women, some trans exclusionary feminists seem to suggest that "men who transgender" will behave "as other male persons" and be abusive in desegregated spaces.[118] In a seemingly more "moderate" – yet arguably

[114] See Heath Fogg Davis, *Beyond Trans: Does Gender Matter?* (New York: New York University Press, 2017. Currently, the US Congress is considering the Pregnant Workers Fairness Act (H.R. 2694, 116th Cong. [2019]), mandating pregnancy-specific accommodations, yet the proposed pregnancy accommodation statute is itself couched in gender-neutral, not sex-specific, terms and so could accommodate transgender men who are pregnant as well as cisgender women. See Jessica Clarke, "Pregnant People?," *Columbia Law Review* 119, no. 6 (2019): 173–99, at 179, observing that "not just women, but also transgender men and nonbinary people, become pregnant. While some transgender men and nonbinary people may seek surgical treatments that leave them incapable of pregnancy, not all do."

[115] See Osella, "'De-gendering' the Civil Status?," 474.

[116] See Judith Butler, *Undoing Gender* (New York, NY: Routledge, 2014), 42.

[117] See Sally Hines, "The Feminist Frontier: On Trans and Feminism," in *The Routledge Handbook of Contemporary Feminism*, eds. Tasha Oren and Andrea L. Press (New York: Routledge, 2019), 94–109.

[118] See Sheila Jeffreys, "The Politics of the Toilet: A feminist Response to the Campaign to 'Degender' a Women's Space," *Women's Studies International Forum* 45 (2004): 42, 46. For ongoing constitutional litigation on the use of public restrooms by transgender persons, see, for instance, Brazil, RE 845779 – Recurso Extraordinário, Relator: Min. Roberto Barroso, ongoing proceedings (22.10.2014). On the use of gender criteria in the context of rape crisis centers, see Kimberley Nixon v. Vancouver Rape Relief Society and

equally problematic – version, they claim that gender self-determination may create a legal loophole, challenging legibility according to gender standards and "embolden[ing] male opportunists to enter single sex spaces."[119] Some gender-critical feminists also fear a threat to women's substantive equality, with the not-too-well specified risk of trans women or opportunist men taking advantage of affirmative equality measures.[120] Some constitutional rulings have begun to echo this concern, like the Bolivian Constitutional Court in its 2017 decision.[121] Scholars and feminists supporting trans rights have in turn reacted by disputing such arguments, highlighting their conceptual and empirical flaws.[122] Furthermore, we have argued, denying gender self-determination to

British Columbia Human Rights Tribunal, 2007 CanLII 2772 (Can. S.C.), leave to appeal to the Supreme Court of Canada dismissed in 2007 after lower courts found no sex discrimination under the British Columbia Human Rights Act, https://www.scc-csc.ca/case-dossier/info/sum-som-eng.aspx?cas=31633.

119 See Alessandra Asteriti and Rebecca Bull, "Gender Self-Declaration and Women's Rights: How Self Identification Undermines Women's Rights and Will Lead to an Increase in Harms: A Reply to Alex Sharpe, 'Will Gender Self-Declaration Undermine Women's Rights and Lead to an Increase in Harms?' (2020) 83(3) *MLR* 539," *Modern Law Review Forum 003* (2020), https://www.modernlawreview.co.uk/asteriti-bull-sharpe/.

120 See "Labour: Row Over Inclusion of Trans Women in All-Women Shortlists," BBC, May 1, 2018, reporting on the – apparently – three hundred women who left the British Labour Party in protest against the inclusion of trans women within women-only electoral lists, https://www.bbc.com/news/uk-politics-43962349.

121 See Tribunal Constitucional Plurinacional [T.C.P.] [Plurinational Constitutional Court], noviembre 6, 2017, Sentencia 0076/2017, partially upholding an abstract review against Ley No. 807 de Identidad de Género of May 2016 (Gender Identity Statute), presented by some members of parliament. The decision upholds gender self-determination on the basis of dignity and free development of one's personality against a challenge framed around the alleged harms of "gender ideology." At the same time, it limits its scope to that of the individual identity/internally lived sphere, thus striking down a provision of the statute referring to the enjoyment of transitioned persons of "all other fundamental, political, employment, civil, economic and social rights." Such a provision would naturally enable trans persons to marry, adopt a child, or access gender quotas. For the court, since the rights of third parties are potentially affected, these aspects deserve to be subject to further democratic debate involving all actors of society, including parliament and civil society organizations. But see also Tribunal Supremo de Elecciones [Supreme Electoral Tribunal], resolution No. 8764-E3–2019 (Costa Rica), validating self-definition in interpreting a placement mandate imposing alternance in candidate lists for the purpose of gender parity and calling on the Inter-American Court of Human Rights Advisory Opinion on Gender Identity, and Equality and Non-Discrimination of Same-sex Couples, OC-24/17, Inter-Am. Ct. H.R. (ser. A) No. 24 (Nov. 24, 2017), https://corteidh.or.cr/docs/opiniones/seriea_24_eng.pdf.

122 See Aleardo Zanghellini, "Philosophical Problems with the Gender-Critical Feminist Argument Against Trans Inclusion," *SAGE Open* 10, no. 2 (2020); Alex Sharpe, "Will

preserve the legitimate objectives pursued by gender-critical feminists – namely, women's safety and equality – would be a disproportionate, even irrational, measure, failing to live up to a proportionality analysis, as long as better suited means that are less invasive of trans persons' rights are available. Many of these alternatives have barely begun to be explored.[123]

Yet the greatest opposition to gender fluidity has come from conservative venues. One telling example is Hungary, which has redefined legal sex as that assigned at birth on the basis of physical characteristics, nullifying the possibility of gender recognition.[124] Another example is the spread of conservative "bathroom bills," aimed to bar trans women from gender-segregated spaces reserved for cis women, allegedly for the sake of the latter's integrity and safety.[125] Such tensions are starting to reflect also in constitutional struggles, as some courts around the world, as we shall see, are accepting the invitation to react against the process of gender erasure that they see represented in the cause of the trans and intersex movement by attacking the theory of the social construction of sex/gender (what they call "gender ideology"), even if (or perhaps because) important women's rights causes are sacrificed in the process. In my view, this is the cautionary tale that feminists should have learned by now – namely, one about the risks of bitter internal divisions, especially when opposition to what we jointly defend and represent threatens all of us to a much greater extent than whatever it is we are fighting over, especially when this fight between feminisms, once blown out of

Gender Self-Declaration Undermine Women's Rights and Lead to an Increase in Harms?," *Modern Law Review* 83, no. 3 (2020): 539–57.

123 Ruth Rubio Marín and Stefano Osella, "La Autodeterminación de Género: *Gender Critical Radfems* a la Prueba de la Proporcionalidad," *IberICONnect* (blog), February 1, 2021, https://www.ibericonnect.blog/2021/02/la-autodeterminacion-de-genero-gender-critical-radfems-a-la-prueba-de-la-proporcionalidad/.

124 See article 3 of Hungary's omnibus Bill T/9943 (May 19, 2020, passed on May 28, 2020). The "birth sex" law means that transgender and intersex Hungarian citizens have lost all avenues for pursuing legal recognition. The law defines "birth sex" as "biological sex determined by primary sex characteristics and chromosomes." "Birth sex," as per the legislation, may only be medically determined and is unchangeable. A person is only permitted to have the legal name that is listed on the corresponding recognized male or female names registered. The law is currently under constitutional review. See "Hungary Rolls Back Legal Protections, Puts Trans and Intersex People at Risk," ILGA Europe, May 19, 2020, https://ilga-europe.org/resources/news/latest-news/hungary-rolls-back-legal-protections-puts-trans-and-intersex-people-risk.

125 See Laura Portuondo, "The Overdue Case against Sex-Segregated Bathrooms," *Yale Journal of Law and Feminism* 29, no. 2 (2018): 465–526.

proportion, can weaken us collectively, much to the joy of those disdaining feminism altogether.

5.4 Preemptive Action, Gender Equality Backlash, or the Reassertion of the Traditional Family Order

The described tensions have generated constitutional struggles, with some actors (both bottom-up and top-down) seizing the constitutional framework of rights and constitutional identity as battlefields and some courts accepting and others resisting the invitation to react against the gradual disestablishment of gender roles triggered by the advances of women's and sexual minorities' rights since the mid-1990s. The common thread bringing together resistance against anticipated changes and backlash against new milestones achieved seems to be the threat to the traditional family, for which various anti–gender equality actors blame an alleged common enemy they have identified as "gender ideology." This so-called gender ideology – a rather vague notion that includes movements for LGBTQI+ rights and women's equality, as well as various strands of scholarship deconstructing essentialist and naturalistic assumptions about gender and sexuality[126] – is presented as a threat to the natural law of creation,[127] grounded on the binary of the sexes by many who argue complementarity should be retained as the main framing concept of gender relations articulated in institutions such as marriage and family.[128] Their opponents, therefore, target the social construction of gender and the various agendas they perceive as deriving

[126] The criticized scholars belong to different and sometimes even contradictory schools of thought. Most of the criticism has been addressed to Simone de Beauvoir, Shulamith Firestone, Adrienne Rich, Monica (sic) Wittig, and especially Judith Butler. See Sara Garbagnoli, "Contra la herejía de la inmanencia: el 'género' según el Vaticano como nuevo recurso retórico contra la desnaturalización del orden sexual," in *¡Habemus género! La Iglesia Católica y la ideología de género: textos seleccionados*, eds. Sara Bracke and David Paternotte (Rio de Janeiro: Sexuality Policy Watch, 2018), 54, citing Benedict XVI's address to the members of the Roman Curia from Dec. 22, 2008, https://sxpolitics.org/GPAL/uploads/ebook-2018-17122018.pdf.

[127] Garbagnoli, "Contra la herejía de la inmanencia," 60.

[128] Since Pope Pius XII (1939–1958), and especially since John Paul II (1978–2005), the Vatican has renewed its discourse on the nature of women in response to feminist movements and social, political, and legal changes, substituting old visions of the gender order that had been challenged by arguments of transcendental nature. Departing from the perception of women as subordinated to men, this new outlook presents men and women as "equal in dignity" but different and complementary in nature. It sometimes serves to oppose a "bad" gender feminism to a new "good" feminism celebrating

from it in particularly aggressive ways. In many contexts, propping up male authority and promoting a nuclear family that sticks to the gender binary are seen as central tenets of broader nationalist projects and anti-imperialist agendas.

In Europe, for instance, the Council of Europe's Convention on Preventing and Combating Violence against Women and Domestic Violence, also known as the Istanbul Convention, has become the object of attacks amid wider conservative opposition to gender violence legislation, especially in Central and Eastern European (CEE) countries.[129] Much of the criticism has focused on the social understanding of the concept of "gender" that the convention endorses under its article 3.c,[130] and the scope of the phenomenon of violence against women in many countries is denied, as paternalistic or symmetrical approaches to combat it are offered in exchange of criticized international standards under the nationalist banner of the type of "we know best how to protect our women" or in the name of the traditional family.[131] In view of this, several constitutional courts, including those in Bulgaria and Poland, have been asked to declare the Istanbul Convention unconstitutional, under allegations that it violates the word and spirit of national constitutions that support a binary and biological understanding of the sexes. In the case of Bulgaria, the petition of the governing party leader prevailed, and the Constitutional Court's decision has decisively contributed

motherhood as women's ultimate vocation and mission. See Garbagnoli, "Contra la herejía de la inmanencia," 57, 62.

[129] See Krizsán and Popa, "Contesting Gender Equality in Domestic-Violence Policy Debates," 101–3, describing some of the common features of conservative opposition to gender violence legislation and actions, especially when framed in terms of gender equality. They include several claims of constitutional dimension, such as the alleged interference with family privacy, sex-based discrimination against men who are said to be victims of domestic violence just as often as women, the various due process rights of male defendants that might be undermined, and religious freedom. The authors explain how some of these claims find a particularly strong resonance in previous communist regimes, given their known interferences with family privacy and religious sentiments. Beyond these specific arguments, there is often the general claim that the convention violates something more generic and at the same time more fundamental, such as the country's constitutional identity, spirit, or axiology.

[130] Under article 3.c of the convention, "gender" shall mean the socially constructed roles, behaviors, activities, and attributes that a given society considers appropriate for women and men.

[131] See Andrea Krizsán and Conny Roggeband, *Politicizing Gender and Democracy in the Context of the Istanbul Convention* (Basingstoke: Palgrave MacMillan, 2021).

to stopping the ongoing ratification process.[132] However, in the case of Poland, which ratified the convention on April 27, 2015, and where the decision regarding its constitutionality is now pending, it has left the question wide open as to what the legal consequences would be were the convention to be declared unconstitutional ex-post.[133] In other countries, such as Hungary, similar arguments focused on the constitution and the constitutional identity of the nation have been at the core of the governing Fidesz party's refusal to ratify a convention that is said

132 In Bulgaria, the polemic was so fierce that in February 2018, the country's prime minister and leader of the GERB party, which governs in coalition with three far-right parties, withdrew a motion for ratification from Bulgaria's parliament. Moreover, seventy-five members of parliament from his party submitted a request before Bulgaria's Constitutional Court to establish if the Istanbul Convention contravened the spirit of Bulgaria's constitution, including its article 46 (1), which defines marriage as "a free union between a man and a woman." A decision was adopted on July 27, 2018, in which eight judges (four dissented) held that the convention indeed contradicted Bulgaria's constitution, on the basis that the social understanding of the concept of "gender" that the convention endorses under its article 3.c is not compatible with the constitutional reference to women as mothers and birth givers contained in the Bulgarian Constitution. In particular, the court relied on article 6 (2) of Bulgaria's constitution, banning sex-based discrimination, as well as article 47 (2), endorsing state protection for mothers, including prenatal and postnatal leave, obstetric care, and alleviated working conditions – a provision interpreted as enshrining a biological understanding of sex, with the court generalizing that "[t]raditionally, human society is built on binarism, or the existence of two opposite sexes, each of which has specific biological and social functions and responsibilities." See Radosveta Vassileva, "Bulgaria's Constitutional Troubles with the Istanbul Convention," *VerfBlog* (blog), Aug. 2, 2018, https://verfassungsblog.de/bulgarias-constitutional-troubles-with-the-istanbul-convention/. Most recently, the Bulgarian Constitutional Court was asked for an advisory opinion on whether "sex" and "gender" are different concepts, in the context of a trans rights case pending before the Bulgarian Supreme Court.

133 In December 2020, the government proposed a draft law that would change the binding scope of the Istanbul Convention. But, shortly before that, in July 2020, the Polish Prime Minister brought a petition before the Constitutional Court to review the compatibility of the Istanbul Convention with the constitution. The petition by the Polish government calls for a rejection of the convention's "ideological background," "ideological content," and "promoted specific world view." According to the petitioner, implementation of the convention may lead to "undermining the European legal tradition that – from the beginning – is aware of the distinction between men and women." Also, the tenet that gender is a sociocultural phenomenon enshrined in the convention, rather than a purely biological one, is characterized by the petitioner as "incompatible with the Constitution's axiology." As a result of the Istanbul Convention's application, "society may lose the ability to distinguish women from men." See Julia Kapelańska-Pręgowska, "Istanbul Convention in Poland – From Ratification to Unconstitutionality?," *IACL-AIDC Blog*, February 11, 2021, https://blog-iacl-aidc.org/gender/2021/2/11/istanbul-convention-in-poland-from-ratification-to-unconstitutionality.

to introduce "the category of 'gender' as a 'socially constructed role,' additionally to the procreative, biological sexes." Similar debates have taken place in Slovenia, where it has been argued that the convention would turn "gender ideology" into the official ideology of the state,[134] and in Croatia, where the government was forced to respond to conservative dissatisfaction by issuing an "interpretive statement," noting that ratification of the Istanbul Convention cannot be construed as meaning that Croatia accepts any element of the gender ideology, a disclaimer that arguably does nothing to detract from Croatia's obligations under the convention. The latest uproar comes from Turkey, however, after President Erdoğan announced Turkey's withdrawal from the Istanbul Convention by an overnight decree that is arguably unconstitutional, making explicit reference to Poland and to similar hesitant stances of other European countries vis-à-vis the convention.[135]

The transnational antigender movements feed off discussions on "gender ideology" that started globally at the time of the International Conference on Population and Development (Cairo, 1994) and the Fourth World Conference on Women (Beijing, 1995), foregrounding women's empowerment, sexual and reproductive rights, and gender as a relevant category of analysis for the purpose of understanding the proper nature of violence against women as a form of gender subordination.[136] These major international conferences gained relevance on the agenda of international and regional organizations, such as the United Nations System, the European Union, or the Organization of American States. The consolidation of feminist struggles and struggles for sexual diversity in the international arena triggered, in turn, a defensive affirmation, already expressed during these international conferences, by the Vatican, the Christian American right, as well as various other states from Christian and Muslim traditions.[137] Vindicating traditional

[134] See Agnieszka Graff, "Report form the Gender Trenches: War against 'Genderism' in Poland," in "The New Europe: 25 Years after the Fall of the Wall," eds. Barbara Einhorn and Kornelia Slavova, special issue, *European Journal of Women's Studies* 21, no. 4 (2014): 431–42.

[135] See Özlem Altan-Olcay and Bertil Emrah Oder, "Why Turkey's Withdrawal from the Istanbul Convention Is a Global Problem," OpenDemocracy, June 2, 2021, https://www.opendemocracy.net/en/can-europe-make-it/why-turkeys-withdrawal-from-the-istanbul-convention-is-a-global-problem/.

[136] See Mary Anne Case, "After Gender the Destruction of Man – The Vatican's Nightmare Vision of the 'Gender Agenda' for Law," *Pace Law Review* 31, no. 3 (2011): 802–17.

[137] See Joe Swiebel, "Gender and Sexualities at the United Nations," *Sextant*, no. 32 (2015): 25–41.

understandings of family and marriage, the narrative presented by the Catholic Church and its allies crafted the notions of "culture of death" and "gender ideology" as two different but complementary strategies arguably operated by feminism and activists for sexual diversity since the 1990s.[138] Whereas the first was linked to abortion and euthanasia and spread from the Vatican through its hierarchies across Latin American countries, the second – the concept of gender ideology – was the product of the analysis of American Catholic activists and intellectuals who managed to affect Catholic guidelines through their activist practices and came to play a key role in several European and Latin American countries in public and legislative debates on the decriminalization of abortion, the rights of same-sex couples, and the formulation of inclusive school curricula.

In terms of actors, the antigender movement currently encompasses a complex constellation in each country. It typically includes family associations, antiabortion groups, religious conservatives, nationalists and populists (mostly, though not exclusively, right wing), far-right groups, and Catholic dignitaries, even though the Catholic Church is not the only religious organization behind it. In fact, coalitions between Catholics and Evangelicals, Pentecostals, and other Protestants, but also Muslims, Jews, and other religious groups, have been documented in different countries around the world.[139] The various discourses against "gender ideology" that these actors display resonate strongly with several ongoing debates in Western societies, including "national and racial anxieties and resistance to globalization."[140] National and racial concerns are sometimes connected to demographic anxieties, particularly strong in Russia and parts of Eastern Europe,[141] which have also gained traction in the United States among white supremacists' demographic fears, as they see a white and Christian civilization under threat. They clearly resonate with the Church's foretelling of an "anthropological" revolution leading to the "self-destruction of humanity" unless a new human ecology comes to its rescue.[142] Resistance to globalization fuels the return of the national

138 See Mara Viveros Vigoya and Manuel Alejandro Rodríguez Rondón, "Hacer y deshacer la ideología de género," *Sexualidad, Salud y Sociedad – Revista Latinoamericana*, no. 27 (2017): 119.

139 See Paternotte and Kuhar, "The Anti-gender Movement in Comparative Perspective," 259, 293.

140 Ibid., 269.

141 Ibid.

142 Garbagnoli, "Contra la herejía de la inmanencia," 54, citing Benedict XVI's address to the members of the Roman Curia from Dec. 22, 2008.

in many European societies where several populist and far-right forces – often with an explicit antigender, antifeminist, antimigration, and homo/transphobic component – are agitating in a context in which claims to sovereignty, authenticity, and tradition are raised against "supranational diktats and the uniformization resulting from globalization,"[143] which international organizations led by cosmopolitan elites are said to be imposing in a new form of totalitarian indoctrination. A certain narrative of postcolonialism is especially dominant in the African continent, where, in spite of some celebrated progressive milestones (such as the early legalization of same-sex marriage in South Africa), the criminalization of abortion and homosexuality remains the norm and where Christianity is fast expanding thanks in part to American support and funding. The Catholic Church has at times accused "gender movements" and the agencies promoting gender awareness of coercively imposing, via funding, a "gender ideology" in the Global South.[144] Islamic conservative forces, including but not limited to those backing political Islam, also react against the supposed imposition of Western values, which they see as contrary to the traditional Shari'a-inspired Muslim family, foregrounding the complementarity of gender roles.

The "antigender discourse," fostered by the Vatican between the mid-1990s and the mid-2000s,[145] was later socialized for the purpose of mobilizing a wider constituency that has become particularly active since

143 Kuhar and Paternotte, *Anti-gender Campaigns in Europe*, 269.

144 David Paternotte and Roman Kuhar, "Disentangling and Locating the 'Global Right': Anti-gender Campaigns in Europe," in "The Feminist Project under Threat in Europe," eds. Miecke Verloo and David Paternotte, special issue, *Politics and Governance* 6, no. 3 (2018): 6–19, at 9. See also Kapya Kaoma, "La teoría antigénero del Vaticano y la política sexual: una respuesta africana," in Bracke and Paternotte, *¡Habemus género!*, 108–25. In Africa, homosexuality and even abortion are often "externalized" as something foreign to African culture, despite extensive evidence to the contrary, with a growing belief among the population that the United Nations, Europe, the United States, and human rights civil society organizations are trying to impose an agenda that is radically contrary to African culture, which is said to include a complementarity-based understanding of the sexes. Besides ensuring that life since conception remains anchored in African constitutions – 11 African countries still ban abortion in all cases, whereas 36 permit it only under certain circumstances, with only Cape Verde, South Africa, Mozambique, and Tunisia allowing it without restrictions – and homosexuality widely criminalized, the sudden growth of evangelical Christianity has translated into a rising rejection, not so much of gender ideology specifically, but of secularism and human rights more broadly speaking, as the latter are said to bring with it sexual permissiveness.

145 The process of building a counter-narrative is said to have culminated with the publication of the *Lexicon of Ambiguous and Debatable Terms Regarding Family Life and Ethical Questions* in 2003, consisting of about a hundred articles on sexuality and

the 2010s, relying on increasingly sophisticated funding schemes.[146] Thus, it is only over the last decade that we find its manifestations across different but shared tactics, including rallies and colorful events, sit-ins, protests, and narratives of self-victimization that support the depiction of "dissidents of gender ideology" as a threatened minority, displaying also an imagery of childhood that underscores children as paradigmatic vulnerable victims.[147] This form of mobilization has been seen to take place in reaction against various concrete policies, as exemplified by the "Family Day" demonstration in Rome in 2007 against a proposed law providing limited protection to same-sex couples[148] or that of the French La Manif Pour Tous[149] in 2013, fighting against the introduction of same-sex marriage under banners that included "We Want Sex, Not Gender" and "Do Not Touch Our Gender Stereotypes." Moreover, it has affected not only legislative agendas but also presidential campaigns and even the signing of peace treaties in some Latin American countries like Colombia.[150] The mobilizations have also operated preemptively, as a way of resisting the spread of developments taking place internationally, often through constitutional politics, as in Slovakia, Croatia, and Romania, where referenda for constitutional amendments to restrict marriage to heterosexual couples were organized to prevent the possibility of the legalization of same-sex marriage in the near future under foreign, regional, or international influences.[151]

As regards constitutional politics, the antigender equality movements have been articulated through a variety of tactics. These various tactics

bioethics written by over seventy different authors. See Kuhar and Paternotte, *Anti-gender Campaigns in Europe*, 255.

146 See the report by Neil Datta, Secretary of the European Parliamentary Forum for Sexual and Reproductive Rights, *Tip of the Iceberg: Religious Extremist Funders against Human Rights for Sexuality and Reproductive Health in Europe 2009–2018* (Brussels: European Parliamentary Forum for Sexual and Reproductive Rights, 2021), https://www.epfweb.org/sites/default/files/2021-06/Tip%20of%20the%20Iceberg%20June%202021%20Final.pdf.

147 Paternotte and Kuhar, "Disentangling and Locating the 'Global Right,'" 9–10.

148 See Garbagnoli, "Contra la herejía de la inmanencia," 64.

149 See Camille Robics, "Catholics, the 'Theory of Gender' and the Turn to the Human in France: A New Dreyfuss Affair?," *Journal of Moderns History* 87, no. 4 (2015): 892–923.

150 See Viveros Vigoya and Rodríguez Rondón, "Hacer y deshacer la ideología de género," 122.

151 See Kuhar and Paternotte, *Anti-gender Campaigns in Europe*, 256. More generally, on Europe, see also Mieke Verloo, *Varieties of Opposition to Gender Equality in Europe* (London: Routledge, 2018); Paternotte and Kuhar, "Disentangling and Locating the 'Global Right,'" 1–5.

have been supported by a change in discourse grammar and activism that now escapes the traditional opposition between the religious and the secular, insofar as it takes advantage of democratic mechanisms and sometimes also secular arguments to position its demands. Besides the tactic of *constitutional preemption*, which affirms the priority of the constitution against international human rights law (exemplified with the debates around the constitutional validity of the Istanbul Convention in CEE), other constitutional tactics displayed include *constitutional entrenchment*, meaning outright attempts to amend the constitution to (re)inscribe a traditional gender and family order that is presented as threatened. Constitutional contestation has also sought the overturning or narrowing down of precedents through judicial interpretations that would limit previously recognized rights in favor of women and sexual/gender minorities, a tactic that we could think of as a form of *constitutional erosion*. Finally, in addition to constitutional preemption, entrenchment, and erosion, we identify a tactic that we could name *constitutional co-option*. This tactic targets constitutional interpretation, yet, instead of seeking erosion by abolishing or altering the contours of rights in favor of disempowered groups, it relies on a broader "gestalt shift" and appropriation of the constitutional rights discourse, which calls on rights provisions to protect majority values against their perceived erosion as a result of the newly conquered equality and autonomy rights granted to women and gender dissidents.

The earliest expression of constitutional erosion is probably provided by the warfare against women's abortion rights in the United States, which in fact created much of the infrastructure that would then be picked up for the battles that, since the 1990s, began targeting the wider agenda supposedly advanced by "gender ideology." In fact, this constitutional warfare is quite old, given that, already in the years after *Roe v. Wade*, pro-life advocates organized against its doctrine – including at times through clinic violence and deadly attacks on abortion providers. And, while in the 1970s and early 1980s, many focused their energies on the passage of a human life amendment that would have also overturned the Supreme Court's decision, at the turn of the century, a more incremental strategy gained favor, aiming not to ban abortion but to gradually erode it through increasing regulation. This regulation, which came to focus less on the protection of the fetus and more on the supposed protection of women from the "harms of abortion" and "the greed of abortion providers," was in fact intended to hollow out the constitutionally granted right to abortion even without the court overturning it.[152]

This trend toward tighter restrictions on abortion accelerated dramatically in the wake of the 2010 midterm elections, which brought the Tea Party and other conservative candidates into office, for whom ending abortion was a key priority. States all over the country began to pass more laws regulating abortion in 2011 than in any other year in American history,[153] including some directly seeking the overturning of constitutional precedents, such as laws with abortion bans and laws prohibiting the termination of pregnancy once a fetal heartbeat was medically detectable, usually six weeks from conception. Supporting this legislative frenzy was the influential pro-life advocacy group Americans United for Life (AUL), founded in 1971 in response to the liberalization of abortion laws at state level, which has also supported antiabortion struggles in many other parts of the world.[154] Its activities include drafting model legislation such as those known as TRAP laws (Targeted Regulation of Abortion Providers), singling out abortion providers and imposing burdens on them different from, and far more severe than, those imposed on providers of health care services of comparable risk, with the intention of driving abortion providers out of business under the pretense of "protecting women,"[155] precisely in places where women are most vulnerable – not because abortion providers are rapacious, but rather because "health insurance rates are low, contraceptive needs of poor women poorly met and family planning services and sex education programs severely undermined."[156] So far,

152 See Cary Franklin, "The Story of Whole Woman's Health v. Hellerstedt and What it Means to Protect Women," in *Reproductive Rights and Justice Stories*, eds. Melissa Murray, Katherine Shaw, and Reva B. Siegel (New York: Foundation Press, 2019), 223–25.

153 Ibid., 227.

154 Ibid., 226.

155 Ibid., 227–28.

156 Ibid., 234. Another strategy used by pro-life groups has been to promote the introduction of legislation banning abortions on the basis of race, color, national origin, ancestry, sex, or fetal diagnosis or potential diagnosis of disability, a strategy that appeals to antidiscrimination parlance and that has encountered resonance among some of the members in the court (see Box v. Planned Parenthood of Indiana and Kentucky Inc., 139 S. Ct. 1780 [2019] [per curiam], with Justice Thomas holding a concurring opinion that appeals to the racialized critique of abortion and frames abortion as modern eugenics,. Criticizing this approach as strategy to bypass *Roe*, see Melissa Murray, "Race-ing *Roe*: Reproductive Justice, Racial Justice, and the Battle for *Roe v. Wade*," *Harvard Law Review* 134, no. 6 (2021): 2025-02.

the core of *Roe v. Wade* and *Planned Parenthood v. Casey* has been preserved by the Supreme Court.[157] Yet the court's recent shift to the right following the appointment of conservative justices Neil Gorsuch, Brett Kavanaugh, and Amy Coney Barrett in the Trump era has been said to give AUL and other pro-life advocates every reason to have the court continue to restrict abortion rights by further lowering the standard of review or simply abandoning prior precedent.[158]

If US constitutional lawfare around abortion best exemplifies the constitutional erosion strategy, the tactic of constitutional entrenchment to resist the challenge to the traditional family and its supporting gender order is probably best exemplified by some of the dynamics that, especially since the last decade, have taken place in the Arab world. In countries like Egypt or Tunisia, as we discussed in Chapter 3, Islamic forces coming to power, thanks in part to the Arab Spring protests for democratization and social justice, threatened to further curtail rather than expand the rights of women. In particular, electorally won majorities sought ways to constitutionally entrench a vision of gender relations

157 Thus, in *Whole Woman's Health v. Hellerstedt*, 579 U.S. ___ (2016), the Supreme Court struck down a Texan law that became known as HB2, requiring, among other preconditions, that abortion providers obtain admitting privileges at nearby hospitals and that abortion clinics outfit themselves as ambulatory surgical centers – requirements that would have entailed the closing down of all but a few abortion clinics in the state of Texas. In striking down the statute, the Supreme Court rejected the reasoning of the Fifth Circuit Court, which, in interpreting what amounts to an "undue burden" on a woman's right to abortion, had held that barriers to abortion that arose from women's own lack of financial resources were irrelevant to assessing the law's constitutionality. Instead, the court held that women's lived experience of exercising the right to abortion was central to the analysis of the constitutionality of an abortion regulation. It also rejected the invitation to lower the standard of review to that of rational basis and insisted that judges should not simply defer to legislatures but should determine, based on their own assessment of the facts, whether a challenged regulation actually serves an alleged health-related interest. In *June Medical Services, L.L.C. v. Russo*, 591 U.S. ___ (2020), the Supreme Court struck down a Louisiana state law that, in essence, reproduced the regulation of the Texan HB2 law.

158 See Franklin, "The Story of Whole Woman's Health v. Hellerstedt," 242–43. On May 17, 2021, the Supreme Court agreed to hear a challenge to a Mississippi law that would ban most abortions after fifteen weeks of pregnancy – hence before viability – in a case that therefore poses a direct attack on the constitutional right to abortion and the decision resolving it, *Dobbs v. Jackson Women's Health Organization*, according to a draft leaked in May 2022, confirms the serious concerns of it overruling of *Row v Wade*. The United States is not the only country where what seemed to be settled doctrine is coming under challenge. In Germany, too, the debate around abortion has been reignited by criminal convictions of doctors under attack by Evangelical Christians. The first convicted doctor filed a constitutional complaint in February 2021 (BVerfG, 2 BvR 390/21), so we may have a new abortion decision in the foreseeable future.

based on the notion of complementarity, following the dictates of Shari'a law. Yet similar dynamics have also developed in the Christian world, where the constitutional ban or discriminatory treatment of same-sex marriage and unions in Central and Eastern Europe has probably become the most widely shared expression, although the targets of these movements seeking the reaffirmation of the traditional Christian family – often led by autocratic men relying on populist rhetoric and seeking majoritarian support – have also seen the light of day in many African countries and have targeted abortion and other reproductive rights, sex education, and, more recently, trans rights.[159]

To understand the roots of the phenomenon, it must be taken into account that, in postsocialist regimes, the Church has often been identified as one of its victims and that, in some of the countries in the region (such as Poland or Croatia), the Church has been traditionally considered a repository of the national identity. Since the early 1990s, then, it has tried to restore its previous role of moral authority, whether through civil society or directly through governmental collaboration, by means of "a process of re-traditionalization of society."[160] Also, in postsocialist Europe and Russia, the claim is made that gender ideologies represent a new form of totalitarianism equated with neo-Marxism, a form of value imperialism advanced by international and regional organizations and academic elites, antidemocratic in character, which must be

[159] Democratic backsliding has most strongly occurred in Central and Eastern European Union member states such as Hungary and Poland. See Conny Roggeband and Andrea Krizsán, "Reversing Gender Policy Progress: Patterns of Backsliding in Central and Eastern European New Democracies," *European Journal of Politics and Gender* 1, no. 3 (2018): 367–85. In these countries, radical right-wing political parties such as Fidesz and Law and Justice have employed ethnopopulist strategies in defense of "the people" – usually comprised of individuals from a particular ethnicity/race, culture, nation, and religion – as well as majoritarian appeals to win over votes and concentrate power while eroding liberal democracy through attacks against independent institutions and political opponents in both civil society and institutional domains. See Milada Anna Vachudova, "Ethnopopulism and Democratic Backsliding in Central Europe," *East European Politics* 36, no. 3 (2020): 318–40. However, illiberal shifts, with detrimental consequences for gender equality policies, have taken place in South and North European countries too, especially since the 2008 economic crisis and the rise of radical right-wing populism. See Gabriele Dietze and Julia Roth, eds., *Right-Wing Populism and Gender: European Perspectives and Beyond* (Bielefeld: transcript Verlag, 2020); Stefanie Mayer and Birgit Sauer, "Gender Ideology in Austria: Coalitions around an Empty Signifier," in Kuhar and Paternotte, *Anti-gender Campaigns in Europe*, 23–40; Alba Alonso and Emanuela Lombardo, "Gender Equality and De-Democratization Processes: The Case of Spain," *Politics and Governance* 6, no. 3 (2018): 78–89.

[160] Kuhar and Paternotte, *Anti-gender Campaigns in Europe*, 266.

resisted in a context of what is perceived as a rising form of Christianophobia.[161] In terms of constitutional dynamics, we can distinguish countries where the ruling parties are the ones leading the movement by taking advantage of their parliamentary majorities (as in Hungary) or their increasingly government-packed courts (as in Poland) to advance their agendas, and others where the process of constitutional entrenchment follows a bottom-up dynamic.

Constitutional entrenchment has proved particularly useful in Hungary, with the Constitutional Court trying to resist the complete subversion of liberal and egalitarian values that, in a more or less decisive manner, it had defended since the transition. The coming into power of Viktor Orbán's populist movement in 2010 brought about the rejection of a culturally liberal agenda embraced by most of civil society and the reform of school curricula and gave the right-wing Fidesz-KDNO government the two-thirds majority it needed to change the constitution. The new (2011) constitution proclaims human life to be protected from the moment of conception (article II),[162] defines marriage as "the basis of the nation's survival" and a conjugal union between a man and a woman (article L.1),[163] and provides that "Hungary shall encourage the commitment to have children" (article L.2). When, in 2012, partly relying on ECHR case law, the Hungarian Constitutional Court struck down legislation endorsing a very narrow conception of family (defined, for all

161 Ibid., 259.

162 Article II provides that "Human dignity shall be inviolable. Every human being shall have the right to life and human dignity; embryonic and foetal life shall be subject to protection from the moment of conception."

163 In 1995, facing a silent text, the constitutional court recognized that marriage was to be reserved for heterosexual relations, yet acknowledged that excluding same-sex couples from common law civil unions contravened the principle of equal treatment and human dignity. See Alkotmánybíróság (AB) [Constitutional Court], 14/1995. (III. 13), Magyar Közlöny (MK) [Official Gazette of Hungary], 1995/20. In 2008, the Constitutional Court, however, upheld a motion submitted by right-wing parties, striking down Act No. 184/2007 on registered partnerships, because it allowed heterosexual couples to enter into civil unions, and also failed to sufficiently differentiate between marriage and partnership, thus arguably curbing the value of marriage under the constitution. Nevertheless, the court still adjudicated that same-sex partnerships should be recognized by the legislator. See Alkotmánybíróság (AB) [Constitutional Court], 154/2008. [XII. 17.], Alkotmánybíróság Határozatai (AK) [Official Gazette of the Constitutional Court], available at https://hunconcourt.hu/uploads/sites/3/2017/11/en_0154_2008.pdf. In fact, the Hungarian parliament subsequently adopted the act, essentially granting married couples and registered partners the same rights, with the exception of the adoption of each other's children and the passing on of names to partners.

purposes, as marriage between a man and a woman plus direct descendants or adopted children, thus excluding registered partnership-based families) as being insufficiently protective of same-sex unions,[164] the majoritarian forces in power responded in 2013 via a constitutional amendment that entrenched the privileged position of heterosexual and procreative families, also limiting the review powers of the court itself.[165] This move was then followed by an opposition to European norms in support of sexual and reproductive rights and an antihomophobia agenda, as well as by calls on Hungarian women to have more children and the advocacy of family-friendly policies.[166]

If Hungary represents an example of a supermajority in office trying to surpass constitutional limitations on its illiberal policies by way of constitutional entrenchment, Poland offers an example of a country in which restrictive interpretations by the Constitutional Court (whose judicial independence is increasingly called into question) have also been relied on to constitutionally entrench the Catholic identity and tradition of the country against both its communist past and the liberalizing trends taking place in Europe. Although its 1997 constitution was only reformed in 2009 to entrench heterosexual marriage, the Constitutional Court had already interpreted heterosexual marriage in a 2005 decision linked to its EU Treaty of Accession as holding a "distinct constitutional status" whose change could only take place via constitutional reform.[167] Other decisions affirmed the obligation that the Polish state has to "strengthen the ties between the persons making up the family and in particular the ties between parents and children and between spouses,"[168] and yet

[164] See Alkotmánybíróság (AB) [Constitutional Court], 43/2012. (XII. 20.), Magyar Közlöny (MK) [Official Gazette of Hungary], 2012/175.

[165] The newly introduced Article L of the 2011 Hungarian Constitution, as amended in 2013, reads: "1. Hungary shall protect the institution of marriage as the union of a man and a woman established by voluntary decision, and the family as the basis of the nation's survival. Family ties shall be based on marriage and/or the relationship between parents and children. 2. Hungary shall encourage the commitment to have children."

[166] See Adam Bodnar and Anna Sledzinska-Simon, "Between Recognition and Homophobia: Same-Sex Couples in Eastern Europe," in *Same-Sex Couples before National, Supranational and International Jurisdictions*, eds. Daniele Gallo, Luca Paladini, and Pietro Pustorino (Berlin Heidelberg: Springer-Verlag, 2013), 227–30; János Fiala-Butora, András L. Pap, and Anna Śledzińska-Simon, "'Intimate Citizenship' and Illiberalism: Lessons from Hungary, Poland, and Slovakia," *Anti-Discrimination Law Review*, no. 1 (2018): 52–53.

[167] Judgment of the Polish Constitutional Tribunal of May 11, 2005, K 18/04 (the Accession Treaty).

[168] Judgment of the Polish Constitutional Tribunal of May 18, 2005, K 16/04.

another directly stated that "the vision of family adopted by the Constitution is that of a 'lasting union of a man and woman oriented towards motherhood and responsible parenthood.'"[169] And, even though a proposed legislation in 2016 severely curtailing abortion rights – which bishops and lay Catholic groups had pressured the governing Law and Justice ruling party into passing – failed thanks to massive street mobilization, the Constitutional Court handed down a decision in 2020 banning abortions in the case of severe fetal malformations, which are said to account for 98 percent of all terminations carried out in Poland, in a context in which gender ideology was presented as a foreign threat to national identity.

Top-down exercises of constitutional entrenchment, whether through majoritarian dynamics of constitutional reforms or government-packed courts, are not the only ones taking place in the region. Conservative forces in civil society have also accounted for several of the multiple constitutional amendments to resist the constitutional disestablishment of heterosexual marriage[170] and for several of the referendum campaigns

[169] See Judgment of the Polish Constitutional Tribunal of Apr. 12, 2011, SK 62/08. This case law undermined the possibility of providing equal protection to nonconforming familial relationships and contributed to the failure of several proposed bills on registered unions that would have legalized same-sex unions and that were submitted to parliament between 2003 and 2015, the year of the right-wing electoral victory. See Bodnar and Śledzińska-Simon, "Between Recognition and Homophobia," 233–44; Fiala-Butora, Pap, and Śledzińska-Simon, "'Intimate Citizenship' and Illiberalism," 46–48.

[170] Constitutional restrictions of marriage to opposite-sex couples have indeed spread over the last fifteen years in Central and Eastern Europe. See article 46 (1) of the 1992 Constitution of Bulgaria (as amended in 2007); article L.1 of the 2011 Constitution of Hungary; article 110 of the 1922 Constitution of Latvia (as amended in 2006); article 48.2 of the 1994 Constitution of Moldova (as amended in 2006); article 18 of the 1997 Constitution of Poland (as amended in 2009); article 51 of the 1996 Constitution of Ukraine (as amended in 2014); article 71 of the 2007 Constitution of the Republic of Montenegro; article 62 of the 2006 Constitution of Serbia (which, however, states that "Extramarital community shall be equal with marriage, in accordance with the law"); article 61 of the 1991 Croatian Constitution (as amended in 2013); article 40 of the 1991 Republic of North Macedonia (as amended in 2019); and article 41 of the 1992 Constitution of Slovakia (as amended in 2014). The typology of new constitutional clauses ranges from those banning same-sex marriage and those that more commonly define marriage in heterosexual terms to those that allow the legislator to limit marriage to heterosexual couples. Yet the amendments to protect the heterosexual nature of marriage have not been limited to Central and Eastern European countries. Article 112 of the 1982 Constitution of Honduras (modified to this effect in 2004) states: "Marriage and de facto union between persons of the same-sex is prohibited. Marriages or de facto unions between persons of the same sex that are celebrated or recognized under the laws of other countries shall not be valid in

that, with or without success, have accompanied such reform processes, including those in Croatia (2013, successful), Slovakia (2014), and Romania (2018) (the last two unsuccessful owing to low voter turnout). Interestingly, unlike in the United States, where a wave of constitutional amendments of state constitutions naturally came as a backlash against the first legislation and court cases recognizing same-sex marriage,[171] many of the reforms in postsocialist Europe seem to have had a primarily preemptive nature, seeking to resist the Western European trend in favor of same-sex marriage in what could be identified as an "anticipatory countermovement" or a "politics of preemption seeking to protect traditional families from foreign influences,"[172] which at times explicitly called on Christian values, as did the reference inserted in the preamble to the 2014 Latvian Constitution. Ironically, though, speaking of foreign influences, many American organizations of the Christian right, such as ADF International or Liberty Council, clearly assisted in the referendum campaigns.

Narratives of victimization depicting an "oppressed majority" threatened by an alleged totalitarian "gender ideology" have allowed for yet another constitutional strategy to flourish, besides constitutional preemption, erosion, and entrenchment. What could be called *constitutional co-option* results from a combination of the subversion of the constitutional logic of fundamental rights and the supraordination of

Honduras." In fact, many of the newer constitutions drafted in Latin America and Africa over the last decades specify marriage should be between a man and a woman, even though in some exceptional cases, such as in Ecuador, this has not prevented same-sex marriage from being legislatively adopted.

171 Already in 1998, as a reaction to a state court decision (Baehr v. Miike, No. 91-1394, 1996 WL 694235 at 17 [Haw. Cri. Ct. Dec. 3, 1996], *aff'd* 950 P. 2d 1234 [Haw. 1997]), the first state constitutional amendment in Hawaii authorizing the legislature to deny marriage to same-sex couples appeared, mooting the Hawaii case before a final resolution. After the state of Vermont made same-sex civil unions legally equivalent to marriage in 2000 and the Massachusetts Supreme Court ruled that its state constitution guaranteed equal marriage rights for same-sex couples in 2013, President Bush declared in his Jan. 20, 2004, State of the Union address that the nation should defend the sanctity of marriage and called for an amendment to the US Constitution prohibiting same-sex marriage. By the end of 2004, 43 states had passed statutes limiting marriage to a man and a woman, and 11 had enshrined this definition in their constitutions. See Robert J. Hume, *Courthouse Democracy and Minority Rights: Same-Sex Marriage in the States* (Oxford: Oxford University Press, 2013), in particular chapter 7: "Policy Endurance: The Enactment of State Constitutional Amendments Prohibiting Same-sex Marriage."

172 See Martijn Mos, "The Anticipatory Politics of Homophobia: Explaining Constitutional Bans on Same-Sex Marriage in Post-Communist Europe," *East European Politics* 36, no. 3 (2020): 395–416, at 397–98.

religious or ideological freedom, whose outcome is the legitimation or even the de facto hollowing out of other constitutional rights and freedoms previously granted to disempowered groups. In essence, the strategy consists of seeking constitutional accommodation of far-reaching conscience protections through exemptions – whether legally articulated or judicially fought for – which can significantly erode the rights that women and sexual minorities have been conquering over the last decades. In recent years, this tactic is seeing the light of day through legislation seeking the banning of gender and sexuality at school or from academic curricula on the basis of alleged ideological indoctrination, legislation that is being constitutionally contested both in Latin America[173] and Europe.[174] Yet it is probably the spread of conscientious

[173] Municipal legislation against discussions and materials concerning gender and sexuality at school have proliferated in Brazil since 2014, led by a movement ("Escola Sem Partido" – School without Party, in reference to alleged political indoctrination). This triggered a countermovement ("Escola Sem Mordaza" – School without Gag, in reference to alleged censorship). Several actions have been filed at the Supremo Tribunal Federal (Federal Supreme Court). In April 2020, the court declared four municipal laws unconstitutional as a violation against academic freedom, freedom of expression, artistic freedom, and nondiscrimination and equality, as well as other provisions concerning the separation of powers and the secular nature of the state. See Supremo Tribunal Federal (S.T.F.) [Federal Supreme Court], Argüição de Descumprimento de Preceito Fundamental (ADPF) [Argument of Noncompliance of Fundamental Precepts] No. 457, Relator: Min. Alexandre de Moraes, 27.04.2020, Díario da Justiça Eletrônico [D.J.e], 06.05.2020, 13; No. 460, Relator: Min. Luiz Fux, 29.06.2020, Díario da Justiça Eletrônico [D.J.e], 13.07.2020, 181; No. 467, Relator: Min. Guilmar Mendes, 29.05.2020, Díario da Justiça Eletrônico [D.J.e], 08.06.2020, 26; and No. 526, Relator: Min. Cármen Lúcia, 11.05.2020, Díario da Justiça Eletrônico [D.J.e], 03.07.2020, 44. Other arguments of noncompliance are still pending judgment before the court (No. 462, Relator: Min. Edson Fachin; No. 466, Relator: Min. Rosa Weber; and No. 578, Relator: Min. Luiz Fux).

[174] In December 2020, amid much public uproar, the Romanian Constitutional Court rejected the amendment to the law on national education that prohibited the teaching of "activities aimed at spreading the gender identity theory or opinion, understood as the theory or opinion that gender is a different concept from that of biological sex and that the two are not always identical." A petition was submitted to the president against the passing of the law, garnering over 50,000 signatures. In striking down the act, the court understood that a ban on discussing gender in educational settings would unjustifiably limit students' and teachers' rights to free expression and information, as well as the right to health of transgender, nonbinary, and intersex children for whom denying access to information about gender could have deleterious health effects. See Romanian Constitutional Court, press release of Dec. 16, 2020, https://www.ccr.ro/comunicat-de-presa-16-decembrie-2020/. See also Elena Brodeala and Georgina Epure, "Going against the Tide: The Romanian Constitutional Court Rejects a Ban on Gender Studies," *I·CONnect* (blog), Mar. 21, 2021, http://www.iconnectblog.com/2021/03/going-against-the-tide-the-romanian-constitutional-court-rejects-a-ban-on-gender-studies/. It

objection claims that best epitomizes this global phenomenon. What is interesting is that the notion of "religious" or "ideological accommodations," initially crafted to protect minorities, is now being asserted as a way of preserving religious and cultural majority values to the detriment of the equal constitutional status of women and sexual minorities.[175]

In particular, conscientious objections on abortion rights have increasingly sought to exempt, on the basis of complicity-based objections, not only doctors and nurses directly involved in the procedure but also those indirectly and remotely involved (such as nurses offering postprocedure care to patients or doctors referring patients for abortion).[176] These

has been argued that far-right populist actors and authoritarian regimes do not only aim at dismantling existing institutions of knowledge production, illustrated by attacks on academic freedom, but also at promoting a new politics of truth. "Through the construction and diffusion of a frame about 'cultural Marxism,' in which the left would supposedly dominate culture and academia, far-right populists in Europe attack science and engage in a project of deep transformation of knowledge, seeking hegemony over people's minds." See David Paternotte and Mieke Verloo, "De-Democratization and the Politics of Knowledge: Unpacking the Cultural Marxism Narrative," in "De-Democratization and Opposition to Gender Equality Politics in Europe," eds. Emanuela Lombardo, Johanna Kantola, and Ruth Rubio-Marín, special issue, in *Social Politics* 28, no. 3 (2021): 521–31. Note that academic freedom, both at school and university level, is also currently coming under attack with respect to postcolonial studies and critical race theory in countries such as France and the United States, where accusations of indoctrination and divisiveness are challenging attempts to revise curricula to make them more inclusive and fair to the experience of racialized and colonized peoples.

175 See Douglas NeJaime and Reva Siegel, "Conscience Wars in the Americas," *Latin American Law Review*, no. 5 (2020): 1–26.

176 In Europe, various constitutional and supreme courts have been confronted with conscientious objections to abortion. See, for instance, for the United Kingdom, Greater Glasgow & Clyde Health Board v. Doogan and Another, [2014] UKSC 68, [33], [37], addressing the objections of health care professionals and employees to laws that require them to offer postprocedure care to patients. See also Judgment of the Polish Constitutional Tribunal of Oct. 7, 2015, K 12/14, striking down a Law on Medical Professions that failed to include doctors' conscience-based exemptions for situations other than those of life-saving emergencies. Conscientious objections have also been raised in Latin America, sometimes with the explicit goal of limiting the scope of newly conquered rights in the abortion field. In 2017, Chile's Congress legalized abortion and also authorized conscience exemptions for physicians who objected to performing the procedure. See Law No. 21.030, septiembre 27, 2017, Diario Oficial [D.O.]. But soon the Constitutional Tribunal, in response to a challenge posed by conservative politicians who had long opposed abortion, ruled that Congress's limits on conscientious objection were unconstitutional and expanded exemptions from medical professionals performing the procedure to nonprofessionals who "also object, in conscience, to the procedures in which they must intervene" as well as to institutions (Tribunal Constitucional [T.C.], Rol No. 3729-(3751)-17 CPT, Aug. 28, 2017, ¶ 135). For a defense of this wide interpretation of conscientious objection, see also Tribunal Constitucional [T.C.] [Constitutional

claims are also asserted against the selling and insurance coverage of contraception methods, including emergency contraception.[177] Conscientious objections have also become a primary mode of objection to LGBT rights, displayed primarily to object to same-sex marriage and LGBT antidiscrimination legislation.[178] Unlike traditional claims of

Court], 18 de enero 2019, Rol No. 5572-18. A similar strategy was tried in Colombia with less success. In 2006, the Constitutional Court struck down the total abortion ban and declared mandatory a set of exceptions to criminalization (Corte Constitucional [C.C.] [Constitutional Court], mayo 10, 2006, Sentencia C-355/06). When confronted with the conscientious objection of doctors and judges interfering with access to abortion, the Colombian Constitutional Court imposed limits on conscientious objection with attention to the ways in which religious accommodation could impair the rights of groups historically subject to discrimination, expressing particular concern for fundamental constitutional rights "developed out of struggles led by sectors of society that have historically been discriminated against and whose achievements have generally not been well received by a wide array of social sectors that, shielded by the exercise of conscientious objection, attempt to project their private convictions in the public sphere." See Corte Constitucional [C.C.] [Constitutional Court], mayo 28, 2009, Sentencia T-388/09. For another recent decision in the region stating the need that conscientious objection be recognized with clear limits to ensure that it does not become an obstacle to the prompt and safe exercise of abortion rights, see also the decision of the Mexican Supreme Court, Suprema Corte de Justicia de la Nación (Acción de inconstitucionalidad 54/2018), adopted in September of 2021.

177 See Burwell, Secretary of Health and Human Services, et al. v. Hobby Lobby Stores, Inc., et al., 573 U.S. 682 (2014), upholding the claims of for-profit employers challenging a federal health insurance requirement that they cover contraception through health insurance benefits offered to employees and arguing that providing such insurance benefits would make the employers complicit. After *Hobby Lobby*, the US Supreme Court considered the claims of religiously affiliated nonprofit organizations with objections to the government's framework for providing employees with contraceptive insurance. These organizations rejected the government's accommodation mechanism because they claimed that applying for an accommodation (for instance, by completing a form to notify the government) would make them complicit in arrangements that provide their employees with alternative coverage for contraception. See Zubik v. Burwell, 578 U.S. ___ (2016). See also the Spanish Constitutional Court's decision S.T.C., July 7, 2015 (No. 52/2015), upholding a pharmacist's refusal to sell emergency contraception.

178 See, for the United Kingdom, Bull v. Hall, [2013] UKSC 73, [34], in which innkeepers sought an exemption from an antidiscrimination law that included sexual orientation after refusing to rent a double-bed room to a same-sex couple based on their objection "to facilitat[ing] what they regard as sin." See also Masterpiece Cakeshop, Ltd., et al. v. Colorado Civil Rights Commission et al., 584 U.S. ___ (2018), in which the US Supreme Court considered the claim of bakery owner Jack Phillips, who refused to provide wedding cakes for same-sex couples, but did not resolve the question of whether exemptions from antidiscrimination legislation are constitutionally required by the Free Exercise Clause.

religious minorities seeking exemptions from laws of general application to engage in religiously motivated conduct (such as ritual observance or religiously motivated dress or grooming), exemptions that accrue to an enhanced pluralism – a new type of religious conscience claims expressed in conflicts over sexuality, gender, reproduction, and the family – have emerged in the United States, many European countries, and parts of Latin America as a framework for resisting recently enacted laws or case law conferring rights on women and sexual minorities. In so doing, they reinforce norms that the majority has shared and many continue to share, with the consequence that accommodation may result in the infliction of significant harms to citizens who are still socially discriminated against or otherwise disempowered and whose rights are at risk of being severely curtailed and obstructed.[179]

This process, whereby opponents of liberalization react to their losses in terms of decriminalization and constitutionalization by turning to conscience claims in order to resist newly protected rights – a process described by Douglas NeJaime and Reva Siegel as "preservation through transformation"[180] – rests on a narrative shift that allows the majority to speak as a minority and resonates with the narrative that antigender movements denouncing "Christianophobia" have been endorsing. The understanding is, of course, that by invoking "conscience, religious liberty pluralism, and nondiscrimination," rather than religious doctrine, "opponents of reproductive rights and LGBT equality offer more persuasive justification for their positions and partly disable liberals from objecting."[181] And, while there may be ways in which conscientious objection claims are honored but also limited, to avoid "material and dignitary harms" to third parties and the undermining of important governmental interests[182] – for instance, by requiring institutions to anticipate problems and ensure patient access; by limiting complicity claims that can be raised to only some actors and acts; by ensuring alternative access to goods and services; and by limiting conscientious objections to individuals rather than institutions[183] – courts around the

[179] See NeJaime and Siegel, "Conscience Wars in the Americas," 2–3.
[180] Ibid., 11.
[181] Ibid.
[182] NeJaime and Siegel, "Conscience Wars in the Americas," 16.
[183] Ibid., 19–20.

world are often failing to provide a sufficiently narrow reading of the right to conscientious objection. Among other reasons, they may be institutionally ill-suited to take into account the potential cumulative effects of wide assertions of conscience claims when addressing the individual cases brought to them.

Conclusion

At its inception, modern constitutionalism was superimposed on a reproductive family structure, built around marriage, which was both naturalized and romanticized. This family order crafted a specific understanding of women's citizenships centered around the role of mother and caretaker, turning modern family law into the legal source that, de facto, most impacted women's constitutional membership. The degrees and forms in which this family scheme and the gender roles it implied were rendered constitutionally explicit have varied across time and space, as have the ways in which they have affected women, many of whom, for various reasons (including those related to class, ethnicity, race, or sexual orientation), were not able or deemed fit to live up to its idealized standards. Yet the general acceptance of the marital family as "the foundational unit of society" (an expression that is still reproduced in multiple constitutions today) explains why all too often women's attempts to advance toward the affirmation of equal citizenship were first resisted as challenges to the very structure of the constitutional order, rather than simply celebrated as natural steps in the gradual conquest of the vision of coexistence among naturally free human beings that enlightened and liberal theories referred to.

Women's early yet unsuccessful attempts to rely on constitutional texts and interpretations to fight for the right to vote or hold office, to freely choose a profession, or to preserve their nationality regardless of their marital status show that, since the beginning and for the longest time, constitutions, most frequently activated by men, could be useless or even stumbling blocks rather than enabling instruments in the path to emancipation. This situation did not fundamentally change when, overcoming the most distinctive features of exclusionary gender constitutionalism, the female franchise was achieved and sex equality provisions were finally incorporated into constitutional texts. In many cases, the explicitly incorporated sex equality provisions were framed with caveats or came hand in hand with provisions that referred to the protection of motherhood and the family. All these provisions were interpreted as compatible with the separate-spheres tradition and a certain form of family exceptionalism, limiting the scope of the sex equality mandate within the family realm. In essence, when applying them to concrete disputes, courts felt compelled to validate sex-based distinctions between men and women, which they deemed justified not only on the basis of different biological conditions but also to accommodate functional differentiations crafted by traditional gender roles.

Despite the ban on sex discrimination increasingly becoming a defining feature after post–World War II constitutionalism, the basic structure of the gendered political order remained essentially unchallenged until constitutional courts began embracing, from the 1970s onward and in the context of second-wave feminism, an inclusive form of gender constitutionalism, favoring gender neutrality where legal orders had crafted all kinds of distinctions between the sexes and forcing the rejection of the gender stereotypes that had thus far confined women's citizenship. Only then, and only in a few countries at first, was the case for full marital equality ready to be fought constitutionally. This was not a small achievement. Previously, women's marital equality had been resisted through a variety of constitutional means, among them, the argument that, within the family, the notion of family unity (which was also explicitly reflected in some constitutions) had to prevail – with privacy, state neutrality, or state action doctrines supporting minimal interference in "family affairs." Moreover, in jurisdictions where state law coexisted with other sources of religious, customary, or indigenous law, certain forms of multicultural accommodations and federal arrangements also implied that personal law could prevail over constitutional equality mandates, shaping yet another modality of "family exceptionalism" and denying women's equality.

Nevertheless, even when women came to be granted the same rights as men and gender stereotypes gave way to an inclusive form of gender constitutionalism – still the dominant form in many jurisdictions – the legacy of past discrimination and persistent sociocultural expectations around women's role in care and reproduction, as well as their denigrated status, continued to render the goal of women's equal citizenship illusive, limiting women's market equality claims and their broader emancipatory ambitions. Exclusions and limitations of a protectionist nature, but also sex-based compensatory and protective benefits (especially for mothers with family responsibilities and dependent spouses), had been upheld for decades. In fact, the need to preserve some of them prevented the incorporation of a constitutional sex equality provision in some jurisdictions, even though, from the very beginning, many of these protections predominantly benefited only a subset of women considered "deserving" under dominant class and racial prejudices. In due course, constitutional sex equality norms and evolving understandings around gender roles helped expel paternalistic and autonomy-limiting "protections" from the legal order. At the same time, questions about how to respond to other forms of protections linked to motherhood and women's persistent roles as primary caretakers, especially in the employment domain, remained more contentious and ended up giving birth to two different strands of inclusive gender constitutionalism that persist to this day, none of which have shown to be fully satisfactory.

A workerist assimilationist model of constitutional sex equality, better suited for the framework of classic liberal democracies with a negative conception of rights, while not fully opposed to some forms of compensatory benefits for past discrimination, began to regard any form of accommodation of women's caring roles and disproportionate burdens with suspicion. Insisting on the need for a fully egalitarian and gender-neutral treatment of women, this model foregrounded the need to combat gender stereotypes but ignored the fact that, in real life, equality cannot be achieved as long as women continue to devote, under dominant cultural, societal, and religious norms, a disproportionate amount of time and energy to the undervalued and nonpaid tasks of social reproduction.

In turn, a maternalist accommodationist model of constitutional sex equality, better suited for welfarist forms of constitutionalism that traditionally combined sex equality, family, and motherhood protection clauses as well as some form of commitment to substantive rather than purely formal equality, insisted that women's maternal roles must be accommodated and not simply ignored in the marketplace. It thus allowed for and even demanded accommodations that could help (at least some) women to combine paid and unpaid work. It largely ignored, however, that for many women – single mothers, racialized minorities, migrant women, or otherwise poor women – this model would remain for the most part an emancipatory illusion and that even those women whom this model in theory served found their professional options severely limited by institutional cultures, time demands, and career progression norms that had not sufficiently departed from those reflecting the male breadwinner paradigm (with the breadwinner assumed to be free of care obligations, relying on the care provided by others, and permanently available for market demands).

Moreover, despite its undeniable merit in removing sex distinctions and producing gender-neutral legal orders, additional limitations of inclusive gender constitutionalism have become apparent in time. With a narrow focus on striking down formal inequalities or, at best, crafting some pregnancy/maternity protections to render productive and reproductive work minimally compatible with each other (under a narrowly defined logic of asymmetrical or substantive equality), none of the mentioned traditions has so far proved adequate to unveil the gender stereotypes that still plague many of the gender-neutral norms that inhabit our legal orders, including and going beyond the market, and shape legal domains and institutions – i.e., taxation, divorce, custody, alimony, pensions, or migration – where norms crafted around traditional gender roles have proved mostly resistant to constitutional sex equality claims.

Inclusive gender constitutionalism, shaped around men's visions of equality and autonomy, has also failed to sufficiently take into account certain areas in which women could be expected to have distinctive interests and concerns, such as reproduction. In fact, constitutional texts – which, besides the frequent reference to motherhood, have often been silent about reproduction – have sometimes been obstacles to the advancement of women's reproductive autonomy, especially in the maternalist tradition that often naturalized women's motherhood duties, even while rendering the societal responsibility for supporting motherhood somewhat visible. And whereas the traditions foregrounding the struggle against gender stereotypes seemed, in principle, better suited to resist women's normative motherhood, and in fact provided the first examples of constitutions being proactively used to ground a woman's right to an abortion, a constitutional architecture built around privacy rather than equality proved insufficient. Privacy was precisely the constitutional concept that had always given cover to marital abuse and violence; and, even though its display for the sake of a notion of individual rather than family privacy held the valuable promise of harboring a core of individual autonomy regarding sexuality, contraception, and reproduction, the concept proved insufficient to give due visibility to the systemic and discriminatory forms of reproductive abuse experienced by racialized women whose "breeding" was not as cherished. Privacy also offered little emancipatory potential for the many women who could not and cannot access reproductive health and family planning services, among which the poor and racialized tend to be overrepresented everywhere. In general, neither the classic liberal constitutional understanding of sex equality foregrounding negative freedom nor its attenuated form in social democratic constitutionalism, more hegemonic since post–World War II, has provided sufficient basis for a richer set of positive obligations on the part of the state in order for it to be able to significantly "defamilize" and "degender" the care work on which the survival of the species rests and deliver better forms of reproductive justice. Furthermore, even where they exist, socioeconomic rights provisions have often been hard to enforce and have not, for the most part, been focused on care and dependency; instead, they have reproduced assumptions around the male breadwinner scheme, mostly trying to cover up for its failures rather than transforming it in any deep sense.

Finally, neither the "family realm of reproduction" nor the "market realm of production" could exhaust the domains of male hegemony that have, to a smaller or larger extent, been constitutionally protected, limiting women's participatory options. Despite the right to suffrage, women have continued to be hugely underrepresented in public office as well as in corporate and other sites of private governance. Inclusive gender constitutionalism has held little promise to combat this and, once again, has often been a stumbling block. Indeed, in several established constitutional democracies, gender quotas seeking to guarantee women's increased participation and representation in positions of decision-making and authority have encountered constitutional resistance, this time guided in terms of the autonomy of political parties – another surviving bastion of male dominance – formal equality, or simply by referring to the features of hegemonic "general representation" in democratic models. Never mind that the limited success of such models in ensuring women's participation remains precisely an expression of their structural gender bias. Not surprisingly, similar claims around institutional autonomy are currently being raised against attempts to foreground women's equality and parity in and through other sites of governance, including those of corporate, academic, or religious nature.

Originally and structurally rooted in the political exclusion of women, constitutionalism has only become increasingly receptive to women's claims and concerns since the late 1980s and early 1990s, when participatory shifts in both gender equality discourse and constitution-making coincided with a pluralist turn, giving greater visibility to multicultural demands and to the needs of women subordinated by either "local" or "external" forms of subjection and oppression. This participatory gender constitutionalism is epitomized by the phenomenon of women and gender dissidents organizing transnationally and joining both in the creation of international human rights standards and in constitution-making in more than token numbers and various capacities – as litigators, members of constitutional assemblies, constitutional judges, and, more importantly, as civil society. It is also represented by the claims of women who expect constitutional norms to contain elements, such as richer notions of substantive equality or parity mandates, that facilitate their participation within minority cultures or devolved power structures and provide an outlet for their voices. Countries transitioning to democracy after the third democratization wave in the 1990s probably offer the best scenarios to observe this form of participatory constitutionalism, given their ability to constitutionally incorporate evolving human rights standards reflecting, and also benefiting, from processes of regional norm diffusion and contagion. It is thus not surprising that they, too, have been able to better accommodate the gender transformative agendas that women and other minorities have been pushing for since the turn of the century. These agendas advance the constitutional vision of systems of parity democracy built around egalitarian family structures and egalitarian standards, defined not only in regard to equal rights but also equal participation in all relevant domains, including and foregrounding the neglected domain of social reproduction. Older constitutional democracies have not been spared from similar gender participatory and transformative claims, but often their constitutions have been seized by those trying to retain the old system and its hegemonic forms of gender constitutionalism. At the same time, all over the world, constitutional amendments and doctrinal evolutions are sought by those seeking transformation, even in the absence of dramatic ruptures, with women's movements and strategic litigation often being responsible for triggering relevant changes.

Contemporary constitutionalism is full of expressions of this gender transformative agenda that seeks to fully subvert the foundational gender order by rejecting the hetero- and cis-normative procreative family as the foundational unit of society and by pushing for the growing, though still largely insufficient, valorization of reproductive, domestic, and care work as forms of citizenship contribution. The constitutional relevance of the "private sphere" has become more evident than ever. Constitutional engineering in the form of both norm crafting and norm interpretation at the hands of, among others, constitutional and high courts (where, on average, women are also increasingly, though still insufficiently, represented) offers a new horizon of constitutional mechanisms to combat domestic violence and violence against women (often through narrower interpretations of family privacy or due process). Such constitutional mechanisms are also used to speak out against the exclusion of dissident sexualities and gender identities from due recognition and from family, affective, marital, and procreative options (through expanded doctrinal interpretations of dignity, autonomy, personal and family privacy and equality, as well as nondiscrimination clauses, when not outright constitutional amendments, acting as vehicles for change). This new horizon is also populated by expressions of an enriched notion of sexual and reproductive autonomy – respectful of the wish not to procreate and of the needs for procreation in societies that should be enabling reproduction but not imposing it upon anyone – and by expressions of new masculinities and care-centered notions of fatherhood, as well as of the increased valorization of the care contribution of women and the necessary collective assumption of the costs of the social reproduction of the species.

In crucially contributing to this new constitutionalism, and despite their many structural limitations and an understandable measure of skepticism about the lofty promises of constitutionalism, women have engaged in multiple constitutional fights throughout history to turn their emancipatory claims into a constitutional reality, relying both on the constitutional interpretation of silent texts and on attempts to bring about constitutional norms, even before they were politically enfranchised, and most certainly afterward. As could not be otherwise, throughout their various struggles, women have had to face the challenge of speaking when they were not invited or listened to, but also of speaking with one voice. It has been difficult to agree on a substantive vision of emancipation, autonomy, and equality (as the divide between religious and secular women, or women's disagreement around abortion in different jurisdictions, might best exemplify) and to set a priority order between the competing emancipatory causes and the multiple and intersecting axes of oppression that have shaped women's existence across the globe. Throughout this process, women have also been rightly fearful of the costs and pitfalls that the project of gender roles disestablishment could entail. Because the traditional gender order rested on a delicate balance of dignitary and distributive disadvantages for women (in different forms and degrees for different groups of women) but also on compensatory measures for their enforced dependency, many women have feared its dissolution, especially those who had most to lose from it or who were placed in more precarious conditions – hence, the enormous challenges to achieve joint action and the greater success of processes that have had goal-oriented coalitions and sought unity and inclusiveness rather than sisterhood or perfect consistency as a dominant strategy. What is clear, nevertheless, is that, in crafting their constitutional demands, women have not respected the boundaries between the public, as a domain of justice, and the private, as a domain of love and nature. Women have identified coercion, abuse, and exploitation whenever and wherever they encountered it in their own lives, including, and often starting with, the domestic sphere, be it their own or others', and have seized the opportunities they were given to render their interrelations constitutionally relevant. It is the foregrounding of how this "private sphere" has been built at their expense that has animated the gender transformative constitutionalism that today holds the greatest potential.

Gender transformative constitutionalism is calling into question the limits of both an exclusionary and an inclusive type of gender constitutionalism, the latter of which promised equality but could only, at best, deliver the "universalization" of the male paradigm, with more or less nuances, instead of its overall replacement with a competing paradigm, shedding light on the political relevance of the (often coercive and abusive) arrangements around which the "private sphere" was built. Conceptions of personhood founded on notions of autonomy and self-sufficiency are gradually beginning to be replaced with understandings and norms that duly acknowledge the interdependent nature of human beings. Confronted with the growth of several axes of inequality as we are, it becomes clear that living up to these visions requires a more fundamental questioning of the premises of the sociopolitical and economic systems that liberal democratic constitutionalism has sustained so far. We need to radically address the shortcomings of the underlying sexual and racial contracts on which the modern social contract was originally founded, as well as its intrinsic class structure, if this new emancipatory vision seeking to fight against all forms of human exploitation is to see the light of day.

As with every major challenge to dominant norms justifying the legitimacy of existing power structures in the history of political thought – just think of the defeat of monarchical absolutism or the disestablishment of religions – resistance to the disestablishment of patriarchy and its underlying gender order for the sake of a new conception of parity democracy and a care-centered citizenship model is to be expected and has indeed arrived. In recent years, we have been witnessing significant backlash, as well as a true wave of constitutional amendment initiatives (some preemptive, others reactive; some successful, others not so much), in an attempt to retain or restore the "old gender order." As we watch neoconservative and radical religious forces align in various forms to counter the achievement of new milestones in the conquest of women's and sexual minorities' rights, it is important to also have a deep understanding of the causes that explain the popular support for these and similar initiatives – arguably, the human dislocation provoked by globalization; the alienation produced by neoliberal markets seeing no limit to the forms of human commodification – including through the persistent and sexualized objectification of women – and undermining or impeding the development of strong welfare states; a vertiginous digital revolution, inevitably leaving many behind; and existential threats of the magnitude of irreversible environmental degradation and our current pandemic. All of these elements offer scenarios in which foundational social structures, like the "traditional family," might have a certain appeal and serve those who pretend to come to the rescue of "exposed, precarious, and disposable" citizens by offering the protection of national anchoring, demographic survival, and antidotes to the emasculation of the "failed male provider." Around the world, populist governments and sectarian religious forces coalesce in their promise to rescue the heteronormative family, the sexual binary, and the complementarity of the sexes, and, through them, humanity itself. Instead of relying on religious sources, as they once might have, these forces are seizing the constitutional domain as one of their preferred battlefields to fight against the varied forms of subversion of the sexual contract taking place in increasingly secularized societies. With social reproduction concerns often placed at center stage; discourses with racist, homo-, trans-, and xenophobic undertones; diverse constitutional tactics; a whole array of secular arguments around justice and legitimacy (anchored in the "constitutional sphere" and, hence, in the "national higher order sphere"); and a reliance on the straw man of "gender ideology" they purport to fight against, these oppositional forces threaten to undo many of the rights women and sexual minorities have achieved by countering transnational human rights bodies and institutions and their normative agendas – agendas that, in many ways, including through their impact on new constitutionalism, have led the way in the process of gender order disestablishment since the turn of the century.

The underlying reasons for an increasingly generalized feeling of human anxiety must be addressed and societies reinvented in order to provide enough security and hope for people to stop giving up on the reproduction of the species. The pauperization of motherhood, the extractive and colonial dimension of the global care chains, and, more generally, the precarious conditions workers experience around the world must also be addressed if, together with the protection of the environment, we want to place the survival of the human species at the center of our new political and economic organization systems. The time has come to give due visibility to nonhegemonic and care-centered masculinities and to challenge homo- and transphobic prejudices around the need for and the capacity to love and care. What we cannot do, however, is to expect that national retrenchment, a return to patriarchy, the revisitation of old models of hegemonic masculinity (not even in their "generous" paternalistic/protectionist versions), or the persisting exploitation of women's productive and reproductive labor will provide the solution. The solution will neither come from an ever-growing number of men joining the club of those who struggle to survive in precarious jobs or juggle the impossibilities of healthy work and family lives. Institutions, modi operandi, and pre- and redistributive agendas must be more fundamentally called into question if care and social reproduction are to be at the core of our concerns. Constitutionalism may play a modest part in this, including by symbolically conveying the revisitation of our order of priorities, but much more is needed: constitutional means remain limited in power and always distant for the most dispossessed.

As we dance to the rhythm of "A Rapist in Your Path," a Chilean protest song that has become a feminist anthem, and watch that same country, Chile, offer the world the example of the first constituent assembly living up to gender parity ever – a constituent assembly presided by Elisa Loncón, a linguistics scholar, representative of the Mapuche Nation – one thing seems clear: Women will not simply watch as their long-fought emancipatory achievements are increasingly called into question. "Me Too" movements have spread all over the world, breaking long-held and shared silences around different forms of exploitation, violence, and abuse. Women know that they are not alone and are finding the means to fight back, resisting backlash and regression and pushing for further reform. They clearly show no sign of wanting a return to a subordinate form of citizenship they have little reason to glorify. Women will not be silenced again.

In November 2015, in India, women mobilized through a counter-campaign fighting menstrual taboos under the hashtag #HappyToBleed to protest against rules banning women from entering temples and sacred places. Women's voices could be heard all over the Women's March in Washington, DC, in January 2017; in the Madrid feminist strike in March, 2019; in many localities in Poland since October 2020, protesting against abortion rights restrictions; in Chile, once more, chanting slogans like "The revolution will be feminist or none at all," "Never again without us," and "Without women, there is no constitution" while taking to the streets in protest between October 2019 and March 2020, demanding a new constitution; and in Turkey, in April 19, 2021, where women demonstrated against President Erdoğan's decision to withdraw from the Istanbul Convention by an arguably unconstitutional decree. In Mexico, women have legislated new ways to counter violence targeting female politicians and activists, many of which have recently flourished thanks to the country's "parity across the board" constitutional reform of 2014. In Africa, despite the risks and levels of homophobia that do not seem to subside, young gay Africans, including lesbian women, are gaining the courage to stand up for themselves and are organizing through the African Queer Youth Initiative, a network of activists that works across the continent. In the pandemic context, women all over the world are raising their voices to foreground the importance of care infrastructure, as male-led discussions on "building back better" and reactivating the economy proceed as usual. In sum, women are fighting back.

A brand-new constitutional order is on the horizon, one that no longer looks the other way on the rights of women and silenced minorities, one that will place life and the conditions for its thriving in dignity at the heart of the political order, bringing us closer to the kind of world we struggle to live in – one of harmony and respect, love, care, and solidarity. Women have taken center stage, fighting back and pushing forward, trying to prevent the loss of historically gained territory and to finish the job that their female ancestors started – namely, that of conquering citizenship as defined in men's terms but also redefining it in their own terms. In doing so, they seek to perfect democracy.

Just as our beloved and much-missed Justice Ruth Bader Ginsburg taught us all, no country that calls itself a true democracy can do so without ensuring women their "equal citizenship stature." And, as Amanda Gorman reminds us in her beautiful poem "The Hill We Climb," "while democracy can be periodically delayed, it can never be permanently defeated."

INDEX